When Rabbis Abuse:
Power, Gender, and Status in the Dynamics of Sexual Abuse in Jewish Culture

Elana Sztokman

Lioness

Publisher: Lioness Books and Media www.lionessbooks.com
Editor: Jennifer Cappello
Proofreaders: Sybil Sanchez, Rachel Cohen Yeshurun
Cover Designer: Rebeca @Rebecacovers

IN LIBRARY IN-DATA-PUBLICATION
When Rabbis abuse/Dr. Elana Hope Maryles Sztokman
   p. cm.

ISBN: Kindle 978-1-957712-00-0
ISBN: Print 978-1-957712-01-7
ISBN: Audio 978-1-957712-04-8
  1. Social sciences   2. Religion   3. Women's Studies

Praise for When Rabbis Abuse

"Elana Sztokman has done a great service to Jewish life with her meticulous and moving book. She shines a light on communal structures, organizational hierarchies, and Jewish cultural tendencies that too often silence victims and allow offenders to get away with their transgressions. The book should move us to action so that the leaders of our communities, synagogues and institutions will be held accountable to our professed ethics and ideals."

Rabbi Daniel Pressman
Chair, *Va'ad Hakavod* (Ethics Committee), Rabbinical Assembly

"Elana Sztokman's book is an invaluable tool with which to dismantle the structures of Jewish patriarchy and unmask the shame and secrecy that enable sexual abuse and protect offenders. A must-read for anyone who cares about the safety and well-being of every member of the Jewish community."

Letty Cottin Pogrebin
Author of *Shanda: A Memoir of Shame and Secrecy.*

"This is one of the most important books for the Jewish world in years. Sztokman thoughtfully, calmly examines an emotionally charged issue in a way that only a true expert can. Jewish leaders and community members should consider it an essential read."

Elad Nehorai
Writer, activist, and founder of Hevria

"Kudos to Elana Sztokman for this comprehensive study of sexual and gender abuse in the greater Jewish community. This is a timely and important book that will hopefully lead to necessary change, by encouraging victims to report abuse and encouraging communities to hold abusers accountable."

Rabbi Dr. Reverend Haviva Ner-David
Author of *Dreaming Against the Current: A Rabbi's Soul Journey*

"The health of the soul of the Jewish community depends on our willingness and ability to confront the painful truths of clergy abuse - sadly frequent and seldom spoken about publicly. Dr. Elana Sztokman's powerful book gives all of us the opportunity to bear witness to the pain and strength of survivors and the wisdom for how to move forward through a process of reckoning and reenvisioning. Critical reading for all Jewish leaders."

Rabbi Rachel Grant Meyer
Educator, artist, writer, and founder of rabbae jewels

"Dr Sztokman perfectly captures the scope and nature of the problem of sexual harassment in Jewish institutions in all its tragic minutiae. When Rabbis Abuse should be mandatory reading for all institutional leaders."

Asher Lovy
Director of Za'akah

Dedication

In honor of

Barbara Dobkin

For fearlessly powering the engines of change

and

In memory of

Miriam Isserow, z"l

Who always listened with her heart

Contents

I have a name but too often I have been rendered nameless.
Me too.

I have a voice but too often my voice has not been heeded.
Me too.

I have a shape but too often my body has been leered at or made invisible.
Me too.

All these acts.
To make a person.
This person
Disappear.
And yet.
I have a name
And a voice
And a body.

Together, in the midst of the others, I make myself present and available for all survivors and our collective surviving.

Me too.
Me too.
And
Me too.

Devon Spier

Prologue

I have been writing about abuse in Jewish life for a long time. I wrote about it before Harvey Weinstein was exposed as a serial rapist and #MeToo became a movement, before Brett Kavanaugh, the accused sexual predator, became Supreme Court Justice, before Barry Freundel was imprisoned for video voyeurism in the *mikveh*, and before Baruch Lanner was sent to jail for decades of sexually molesting his students

In fact, I have been writing about abuse since I first began engaging with feminist ideas in the mid-1990s. The initial interest that launched my Jewish feminist journey back then began with the *agunah* issue — women denied divorce and stuck in unwanted marriages — and quickly led to the horrifying discovery of how rampant emotional abuse is in Jewish life. Every single *agunah* who sought help from our organization, Mavoi Satum, had been emotionally abused. Often, they were also physically, financially, spiritually, and sexually abused. Estimates of cases of emotional abuse in Jewish life range from one in four relationships to one in seven — bad numbers, no matter how we look at it.

The observation that many types of abuse are interconnected — and alarmingly widespread — led me to investigate this topic more. In my doctoral thesis in anthropology and education, as well as in my books, articles, and online writing, I have explored many of the ways in which Jewish culture is embedded with often troubling norms and hierarchies, and how some people suffer terribly in those systems. I followed many stories, I spoke with people who have experienced very painful episodes, and I wanted to know more about how all this happens. I sought to understand how the Jewish community — a group that prides itself on an ethical tradition and being a "chosen people" or a "light unto the nations" — can also be a place where some of the worst horrors that human beings can impose on each other are also taking place. I needed to know more.

As my writing began to turn more intensely to sexual and emotional abuse, people often asked me if I was sexually abused. For many years my answer was a simple, if hesitant, "No." After all, I was never raped, I thought to myself. I was not sexually molested. But that answer felt unsatisfying. *Nothing happened to me. Why do I care so much?* Why was I so compelled by other people's stories that I chose to write a book about it?

One answer is simply that I go where the evidence leads me. I have been listening with great interest to interviewees for my entire career, following their narratives and stories to see where they take me. And here I am. On the most simplistic level, I arrived here by following the breadcrumbs. I started this book nearly seven years ago, following reactions to an article I had written about how some high-profile sexual abusers had received high-profile support in the community. [1] Although it was a long article that had explored recent events with abusive rabbis and other communal celebrities, it quickly became clear that I had barely scratched the surface. People began contacting me and sharing shocking stories of abuse and the aftermath. Using the tools of my professional and academic training, I began interviewing people. I wrote a few more articles, and then a book proposal. I needed to know more.

As I delved deeper, something began stirring inside of me. Often, as I listened to people's stories, I almost instinctively knew what was coming next. I heard an echo in my head. Over and over, my internal narrator said, "I know. Of course. I've been there."

Of course, I've been there.

I had a few memories of childhood events that are unquestionably abusive, especially by today's terms, but that I rarely thought about. There was the time that my friend Chaya and I were walking to her house on Shabbat afternoon, up Avenue L toward 23rd Street, when a guy from behind us called out, "Girls!", causing us to turn around and see him flash his penis. We quickly ran off, laughing the whole way. We must have been 10 or 11 years old, and for years we thought it was the funniest thing ever. She liked telling people that I have no brothers and had never seen a penis before. That always made people roar with laughter. It didn't leave a strong mark of trauma with me; rather it was just a thing that happened.

Another time, when I was a year or two older, while walking down Avenue J after synagogue one Shabbat with my extended family, a man pranced awkwardly toward us from the opposite direction. As he approached, he swerved into me and grabbed my genitals. I actually thought it was an accident because he seemed drunk and not in control of his actions. But my late Uncle Avi, who was built like a refrigerator, saw this and immediately started chasing the guy. I had never seen Avi run like that! Then the other men and boys from my family joined in. I don't know what happened after that. I barely realized the guy was grabbing at me, and I was entranced by watching Uncle Avi run fast. That's what I remember most from the whole event. The feeling of being protected by a big Maryles gang

---

[1] Elana Sztokman , "On Marc Gafni, the New York Times, and how sexual-predator rabbis get communal support", *Medium*, Jan 7, 2016 https://medium.com/@jewfem/on-marc-gafni-the-new-york-times-and-how-sexual-predator-rabbis-get-communal-support-ada9b97d5479

left a more powerful impression than a two-second grab by a stranger that I barely noticed.

Still, as I listened to interviewees and began revisiting these stories, more explicit — and more troubling — experiences began to flood my memories. The catcalls while walking down the streets of Manhattan or Brooklyn. The guy sitting on the stoop as I passed by, just a few blocks from home, who called out, "I think I'm gonna get me a nice Jewess today." The endless conversations by boys in my Orthodox high school or summer camp rating girls' bodies, including my own. The boyfriend who lay on top of me, completely aroused, and nudged me into actions I was not ready for or interested in. The endless rape jokes and Dolly Parton jokes on television and around the Shabbat table. The science teacher who stood at the front door of our Orthodox day school as we arrived in the morning, glaring at our knees and chests to let us know if we had to change our outfits. The high school social studies teacher who openly commented on girls' breasts and thighs and put the girls with the biggest breasts in front of him, where he giggled and ogled while presumably lecturing about Charlemagne or Henry VIII. The never-ending body commentary from rabbis, teachers, and family members — in public and in private — about whether we look too attractive or not attractive enough, too exposed or too frumpy, a good catch or too wild. The unwanted touch and shoulder massage by an acquaintance at a public event. The mikveh lady who stared at me naked, her eyes too eager and hungry, instead of using a towel to cover the view as custom demands. The time the man I was working for — who was later convicted and imprisoned on multiple charges of rape — ordered me to find him a female massage therapist. The yoga teacher who told me what he thought of my sexuality while I was stuck in an elaborate triangle pose that I quickly fell out of. A different yoga teacher who sat in front of me in butterfly pose, took his shirt off to reveal an obvious erection, and bounced towards me on the floor with a creepy, leering, and sweaty smile. The gynecologist who forced some object and possibly a body part inside of me even though I was screaming, "No." The long stream of employers, leaders, teachers, clergy, and whoever felt they had the knowledge, the right, and the authority to tell us what we, as girls and women, should or shouldn't wear or do or think because of our gender or sexuality, who would emphatically explain how much our bodies caused the men and boys around us to be uncontrollably aroused by our very presence, and what our life purpose as women and girls was. Endless. Just endless.

Years ago, I would unthinkingly say that nothing happened to me, but that is not exactly true. I was not raped in the classic sense — though my experience with the gynecologist was so traumatizing that I didn't go to *any* gynecologist for 17 years — but I no longer say about myself that "nothing happened to me." The more I conducted this research, the more I realized that *lots* of things happened to me. Events that I reflexively dismissed as minor, or even normal actually had a cumulative and often traumatic impact.

Indeed, these events have been formative, shaping a hidden backdrop to my life — and I am sure there are many like me, especially women, for whom that is true as well, people who have a list like this one stowed away deep down in the dark recesses of their souls. We carry around the scars from abuse that is so often normalized. Invasive sexual commentary, body shaming, labels and mockery based on sexual or body presentation, gender-based demands or expectations, or forced behaviors based on sexual or gendered assumptions — these are the things that left me the most indelibly impacted.

As my self-awareness deepened, so, too, did my understanding about what abuse looks like. There are many forms of emotional and sexual abuse that are so ubiquitous that they seem normal, like noise in the background of our lives. As a community, we barely talk about them because we barely hear or see them.

Despite the flood of memories that came forth as I was writing, this book is not about *me* but about *us*. At the heart of this book lies a profile of the process of abuse, along with the many forms that it takes, how it is hidden or supported by culture, and how it impacts both victims and the community. It is also not about specific abusers or an attempt at "outing" anyone. Rather, it is about bringing a megaphone to the voices of the victims who have been too long ignored. It is about collective dynamics and norms and how they take shape as part of Jewish culture. It is a collective story of how people with authority over us use their power to toy with our bodies and minds, using *our* bodies and minds for *their* needs and desires. As a result of these endless uninvited forays into our beings, those abusers leave their victims with a cracked relationship with *our own* bodies and our spirits. We were made to feel that our bodies belong to others, to the Jewish people, to the collective, to the patriarchal order, disconnecting us from our own needs and desires. In some cases, the scars are on the body, but they were also, almost always, on the soul — on our sense of identity, our vision of ourselves in the world, and our self-concept. These are the kinds of scars that can sit in the consciousness of a person for decades, eating away at one's being until there are no foundations left and the whole building comes crashing down. What should have been your self — the part of you where you know who you are because you decided it for yourself, where you know what you want, and where you know how to love — perhaps that part never had a chance to properly form in the first place.

Certainly, this is a fine line for a researcher. I'm in this book even though I don't want to be. And there is a risk of telling one's own story *instead* of those of the interviewees. But I've worked hard to avoid doing that. I have practiced listening and reporting in order to tell other people's stories, and to avoid inserting my own assumptions into other people's narratives. I share small bits of my own life when I think they support the narrative — and in the introduction to the chapter on gender abuse, I wrote a few pages about one of my major life traumas in order to introduce the topic — nevertheless, this book is not *my* story. It is *our* story. It is about Jewish culture and the community that we have been acculturated into.

This book is the product of a long process. I spent years interviewing people who experienced sexual abuse, emotional abuse, non-contact sexual abuse, and gender abuse in the Jewish community. And I collected these into an analysis that taught me a few important lessons.

I learned that abuse can be hard to see at first, and that coming to terms with it is a process within itself.

I learned that abusers do not always look like what we expect. Abuse is rarely done by an ugly stranger in a dark alleyway. Usually it's by a charming, friendly, trusted face in a place that is considered safe and embracing.

I learned that triggers come in many forms, and that the world doesn't always recognize or respect the implications of that reality.

I learned that the scars from abuse can take years — or decades — to heal from, if at all.

I learned that the experience of being disbelieved upon sharing can often be more painful than the abuse itself and can often serve as abuse on top of abuse — what is referred to as "retraumatization" — new wounds on top of healing scars.

I learned that holding space and validating someone's truth can be the most powerful gift we can give victims/survivors.

In addition to these and other lessons that I learned, this book makes some pivotal contributions to our understanding of sexual abuse in general and in the Jewish world in particular. It brings forth the following perspectives:

- **Cross-denominational Jewish culture.** This is the first study to look at sexual abuse from the perspective of Jewish culture as a whole, as opposed to a particular movement, community, or organization. This is important because of how easy it is for people to otherize sexual abuse as a problem "over there", in someone else's domain. This study unpacks those assumptions.
- **Profile of the Jewish abuser.** The book offers a profile of a high-profile abuser in Jewish context, in particular a narcissistic rabbi type, which is something that has never been compiled before — in contrast to, for example, the mountains of information that have been collated about clergy abuse among priests. Similarities between

Jewish clergy and other clergy are also blatantly apt, which is something the Jewish community rarely if ever considers.

- **Jewish-specific dynamics**. The research unearthed many underlying community norms that contribute to traumatization, not only concepts such as *"lashon hara"* — prohibitions against sharing information about other people — but also other Jewish cultural norms that often cut across movements.

- **Connections between sexual, emotional, and non-contact abuse**. It makes connections between physical abuse and non-contact sexual abuse. This is critical because of how easy it is to dismiss what happened if it wasn't rape or physical assault. Physical abuse may be easier to grapple with because it's *clear*. But that doesn't mean that it's *worse*. Many forms of non-contact sexual abuse can be quite traumatizing.

- **Connections between gender discrimination and sexual abuse**. It examines gendered organizational cultures, sexism, patriarchy, and toxicity in order to make connections between the kinds of abuse that women and girls experience. To be sure, people of all genders can be both victims and perpetrators; women can be agents of patriarchy, too. With that, structural sexism is an important part of this story.

- **Impacts on community, not just individuals**. This is the first study, to my knowledge, that explores not only the impacts of abuse on individuals, but also on the community at large.

Acknowledgments

I would like to thank all my interviewees for sharing with me, and for entrusting me to hold their stories. I hope I represented your experiences with loyalty and compassion.

I would like to acknowledge the people working tirelessly on this issue, including: Dr. Shira Berkovits, Asher Lovy, Rabbi Mary Zamore, Shana Aronson, Yehudis Goldsobel, Elana Wein, Rahel Bayar, Julia Tortorello-Allen, Rachel Stomel, Jamie Allen Black, and all of the people involved with the support organizations listed in the Appendix. Kudos also to bloggers Hannah Katsman, Dorron Katsin, and Yerachmiel Lopin for keeping us informed on these issues.

Mountains of respect to all of the brave survivors, writers, and whistleblowers who have turned their experiences into activism and helped move this issue into the public discourse, especially: Dr. Keren McGinity, Debbie Findling, sisters Dassi Ehrlich and Nicole Myers, Sarah Ruth Hoffman, Yehudis Fletcher, Elad Nehorai, Manny Waks, Dr. Sharon Weiss-Greenberg, Genendy Radoff, Rachel Avrunin, Rhonda Abrams, Clare Hedwat, Cheryl Moore, Sheila Katz, Rabbi Rachel Sabath Beit-Halachmi,

Shifra Bronznick, Shayna Sragovicz, and many others, as well as those who bravely shared with investigators for HUC-JIR, URJ, and other institutions. Special thanks to those who participated anonymously in the B'Kavod survey and the Jewish Women Archive survey, both of which are incorporated in this research. Huge kudos to all those who have shared online at #Gamani and at the Jewish Teens for Empowered Consent Instagram page. (Note: I did NOT use ANYTHING from #Gamani in this research as it is private. But I did refer to the anonymous IG posts as they are public.) All of these locations are vital. Every sharing goes towards repairing the culture, empowering others to do the same, and propelling change forward for the entire community.

Journalists on the sexual abuse beat in Jewish media have been at times relentless in their commitment to this issue, especially Hannah Dreyfus, who never backed down in the face of an abuser and uses her platform to promote justice. Also Mark Weiss, Sharon Otterman, Ben Sales, Dan Brown, Sarah Seltzer, Avital Chizik, Gary Rosenblatt, Julie Zauzmer, Arno Rosenfeld, Louis Keen, Nathan Jeffay, Josh Nathan-Katzis, Assaf Shalev, Shira Elk, and Yedidya Gorsetman have fearlessly covered this difficult issue, and their items formed important background to this book.

My special thanks to Susan Weidman Schneider for not only being a visionary on this topic, but also — more personally — for publishing many of my essays in *Lilith* and helping me clarify my voice and my thoughts.

My deepest thanks to the friends, teachers, and colleagues with whom I eagerly consult and chat with on these issues: Prof Rabbi Rachel Adler, Prof Susannah Heschel, Letty Cottin Pogrebin, Rabbi Mary Zamore, Ayallah Adelstein, Jessica Kaz, Erin Girver, Dr. Melanie Landau, Rabbi Dr. Reverend Haviva Ner David, Dr. Sharon Weiss-Greenberg, Elise Rynhold, Ilana Teitelbaum, Devon Spier, Dana Diamond, Lisa Jan Huttner, Loolwa Khazzoom, Wendy Widom, Naomi Eisenberger, Dr. Judith Rosenbaum, Dr. Sara Shapiro-Plevan, Beth Cohen, Rachel Balf, Leah Lax, Heather Stone, Eve Sacks, Judy Golub, Paula Mills, Pamela Becker, Talli Yehuda Rosenbaum, Natalie Krasnostein, Rabbi Shayna Nechama Naveh, Dr. Leah Gniwesch, Rabbi Jane Litman, Rabbi Paula Winnig, Rena Bannet, Rabbi Ruti Regan, and April Baskin.

Dr. Chaya Gorsetman, my dearly missed friend who died during the writing process, was my long-time *chevruta* in studying Jewish communal life, and her spirit is with me everywhere in this book.

Thanks to my advance beta readers and commenters on this book, especially: Sybil Sanchez, Sarah Ruth Hoffman, Sarah Bronzite, Sarah Chandler, Sura Jesselson, Yonina Siegal, Diane Lasken Katz, Elana Gordis, Rabbi Daniel Pressman, Elli Sacks, Leah Rollhaus, and Leah Strigler.

Special thanks to my talented and dedicated editors and proofreaders: Jennifer Cappello, Rachel Cohen Yeshurun, and Sybil Sanchez, for many hours of professionalism and hard work.

Thanks also to my readers, social media followers, and Substack subscribers for their engagement. Every single exchange with each of you gives me energy and hope that change is happening. Despite all its pitfalls, social media has enabled these connections in ways that generations past did not have access to, and this book hopefully represents a positive outcome of those blessed connections.

Deepest gratitude goes to my beautiful family — my spouse, Jacob Sztokman, my children and their partners, and my grandchildren who were born in the midst of all this — for enduring some difficult and dark conversations with me, for offering sources of light, and for sharing the journey with love, even when it's hard. My most heartfelt prayer is that you will never have to know from the stuff I write about.

I owe a huge debt of gratitude to the one and only Barbara Dobkin, who singlehandedly supported my research over the course of a few years, despite many setbacks, and who demonstrated faith in me even when I did not necessarily earn it. Without Barbara, this book would not be here, full stop. This book is dedicated to her.

This book is also dedicated to the memory of the inimitable Miriam Isserow, who tragically died just as it was going to print. Miriam had a critical role in the #GamAni community — literally, "Me Too" in Hebrew. She taught me so much, and we worked together for nearly five years on this issue. She was also an early reader of some of these chapters, and our conversations remain invaluable to me. Her spirit lives on in this work. I miss her.

Finally, I would like to express gratitude to my Creator for bringing me to this moment, for sustaining my life, for making me in Her image, and for making me a vehicle of love and light in Her mission to repair the world.

Dr. Elana Sztokman
Jaffa, Israel
April, 2022

The journey will be longer than you imagined.
Trauma will find you again and again.

Chanel Miller, *Know my Name*

Introduction

Background

When "Leanne"[2] was a teenager, she was a model of an engaged Jewish youth. Leanne was actively involved in her Conservative Jewish community, chanted from the Torah at Shabbat services, participated in Jewish youth groups, and attended a Jewish day school. When she was 19 years old, Leanne continued in her communal activity by working as a counselor in a Jewish summer camp. That's where she encountered an Orthodox rabbi who was the head of the 16-year-old "edah," or age group.

---

[2] All names and identifying details of victims/survivors have been changed to protect their anonymity unless they gave express permission otherwise for the purpose of speaking as an expert in the field. All procedures followed were in accordance with the ethical standards of the responsible committee on human experimentation (institutional and national) and with the Helsinki Declaration of 1975, as revised in 2000. Informed consent was obtained from all participants for being included in the study.

"He was one of those storyteller types," she told me. "With his guitar, always singing songs." Shortly after camp started, the rabbi began coming on to her. "Your whole face lights up when you smile," she said he told her as he relentlessly stalked her. She felt awkward and did not appreciate his advances. "I'm like, he's a divorced guy in his thirties with kids. To me, he's not even someone who I would be thinking about having a relationship with." But he did not let up. He asked her for a date after the Friday night *oneg*, the traditional Shabbat social. She did not want to go but somehow ended up alone with him anyway. He kept up the pursuit — writing her love songs, getting her 10-year-old campers to pressure her to respond to him, and following her around camp — despite her consistent protests. "He shared songs with me that he had written, including one called '[Leanne's] Song: Angel in the Edah.'[3] A line that stands out in my mind is 'We are naked and burning and hurting.'" She tried to dodge him, and when she did, he would ask her why she was doing that. "It was very stressful," she recalled, thirty years later.

At the time, Leanne approached the senior staff to report on this rabbi's behavior — and discovered, to her surprise, that everyone knew about his predilections. One senior rabbi said, "We all know — we don't know what to do. He's out of control." The camp director, she said, was completely dismissive. "You're not a psychologist," he apparently told her. Yet, despite the common knowledge that this rabbi had a pattern of sexually pursuing teenage girls, he was subsequently hired as head of the 16-year-old division. "I was dumbfounded by that decision," she said.

Although Leanne was hoping to go back to camp, she could not bring herself to return with him there. She complained to the new director. "As a rabbi, he has a lot to offer," the new director — also a rabbi — replied, while also appointing the stalker as *Rosh Tefilla* (Head of Prayer). He suggested that she avoid spending time with him, advice he said he was giving other girls as well.

Understandably, Leanne did not find that suggestion helpful. As a result, she quit summer camp, sadly foregoing a formative Jewish experience that had been meaningful and important to her. She felt she had no choice.

The experience of being sexually harassed at her beloved Jewish camp left Leanne bereft and had long-term impacts on her Jewish trajectory. "I was so frustrated and fed up with that experience and with the tolerance for him that when I left camp that day, I essentially left any serious Jewish life. My experience, it seemed, was unimportant. My development as a young Jewish woman was unimportant. *I* was unimportant. What do you think it communicates about the meaning of *tefillah* when the person leading the

---

[3] Style note: Foreign words, such as "*edah*," are italicized the first time they are used in the text, and thereafter they are not. Please refer to the Glossary in the back for definitions of foreign terms.

endeavor has treated you this way? It becomes a sham. That warm feeling that everyone seemed to have during the fabulous Shabbat *mincha* service, for example, was inaccessible to me in that environment."

This is the story of how a person who was theoretically a treasure to the Jewish people—an engaged Jewish youth—was lost to the community. Because of a camp experience in which she was stalked by a rabbi, and in which nobody in charge seemed to care, she walked away. "Were young women not supposed to feel safe at camp?" she asked the director in a letter twenty years later. "Can you see how this might be alienating? How it diminishes one's experience?" Although Leanne eventually received what she called a "heartfelt but misguided reply" the decades of damage had already been done.

Stories of sexual harassment, molestation, abuse, and assault in the Jewish world have started to emerge in the media, on social media, and in communal conversations. The #MeToo movement opened the floodgates and gave permission and legitimacy for victims/survivors to come forward and be heard. In some cases, the legal system, though late to the game, did its job—such as the imprisonment of men like Harvey Weinstein and the late Jeffrey Epstein—while in other cases, abusers are still holding on to their positions. In some places, legislation has responded in ways that assist victims, such as New York State's 2019 Child Victims Act that allows survivors of childhood sexual abuse the opportunity to pursue justice and compensation. The Child Victims Act included a "look-back window" to give victims time to file claims. By the time the window closed in August 2021, over 10,000 claims were filed—including 250 claims involving Jewish institutions, according to Asher Lovy, Director of Za'akah, an advocacy organization on behalf of victims of sexual abuse in the Jewish community that is carefully documenting these claims.[4]

Yet, there is still very little information about the scope of sexual abuse in the Jewish community. There has been no comprehensive, community-wide, quantitative study of the problem. Moreover, while the wider American and worldwide community has been fiercely reckoning with sexual abuse following the #MeToo movement—hundreds of perpetrators have been exposed and have faced consequences ranging from forced resignation to long prison sentences—the response from the Jewish community has been less robust. To wit, Jewish sociologist Steven M. Cohen, despite admitting that his accusers were right and that he sexually harassed women for years, and despite losing at least one of his jobs at Hebrew Union College—Jewish Institute of Religion, continued to be invited to speak as a revered expert in

---

[4] There was a similar window in New Jersey. See, for example, https://njcasa.org/find-help/civil-statue-of-limitations/.

his field.[5] The same was true for other confessed sexual offenders, such as Ari Shavit, who still receives lucrative publishing contracts, is invited as a well-paid expert, and is endorsed by Jewish leaders despite admitting that he sexually assaulted women.[6]

In other cases, discoveries about abuse have had absolutely no impact at all. A scathing report about decades of alleged sexual harassment by philanthropist Michael Steinhardt, for example, resulted in zero consequences.[7] (By contrast, when he was publicly outed as an art thief, at least one petition pressured to remove his name from a building. Tellingly, that call did not come from within the Jewish community.[8])

As with the camp director that Leanne reported to, it appears from a cursory review of recent events that when a testimony of abuse emerges, the accused often receives institutional backing, and the story goes away.[9] There has not yet been a systematic study of those responses to validate this impression.

---

[5] Hannah Dreyfus, "Harassment Allegations Mount Against Leading Jewish Sociologist: Women academics cite long pattern of sexual improprieties at the hands of Steven M. Cohen, who has expressed 'remorse' for his actions," *The Jewish Week*, July 19, 2018, https://jewishweek.timesofIsrael.com/harassment-allegations-mount-against-leading-jewish-sociologist/ .

[6] Jenny Singer, "Ari Shavit, Go Away and Don't Come Back," *Forward*, July 5, 2018, https://forward.com/opinion/404824/ari-shavit-go-away-and-dont-come-back/; Josh Nathan-Kazis, "J Street Comes Under Fire for Quiet Handling of Ari Shavit Sexual Misconduct Claim," *Forward*, November 1, 2016, https://forward.com/news/353099/j-street-comes-under-fire-for-quiet-handling-of-ari-shavit-sexual-misconduc/ .

[7] Sharon Otterman and Hannah Dreyfus, "Michael Steinhardt, a Leader in Jewish Philanthropy, Is Accused of a Pattern of Sexual Harassment," *New York Times*, March 21, 2019, https://www.nytimes.com/2019/03/21/nyregion/michael-steinhardt-sexual-harassment.html .

[8] Asha Ramachandran, "Opinion: NYU should sever all ties with Michael Steinhardt. The board of trustees must change the name of the Steinhardt School of Culture, Education, and Human Development given Steinhardt's proven record as a looter and sexual predator," *Washington Square News*, December 10, 2021, https://nyunews.com/opinion/2021/12/10/nyu-steinhardt-needs-a-name-change/ .

[9] For example, in a 2021 smaller-scale case, where a former Bronfman fellow wrote a testimony about how a male "mentor" persistently crossed boundaries with her into an emotionally, erotically-charged relationship when she was 17 and he was 48, the organization responded by saying that they had conducted an internal investigation and found that the mentor in question did nothing wrong—an investigation committee that did not initially speak to the victim. Later, after some public pressure, the organization changed course and said they would conduct a better investigation. A few months later, they released a second notice affirming that they stand behind the accused and that he did nothing wrong. Shayna Sragovicz, "Tell everyone," *Medium*, October 19 2021, https://medium.com/@shayna99/tell-everyone-38e313990062. ; "A Message from the Board of Directors of The Bronfman Fellowship," October 21, 2021, https://bronfman.org/october-2021-message-from-the-board-of-directors-of-the-bronfman-fellowship/?fbclid=IwAR1HmIONR-Cp-SQhr6J2hIQSvZBpt7sQexiXoc2wowDUwG77d8QoDetLLb0; "A Message to the Bronfman Community from the Board of Directors," March 15, 2022 https://bronfman.org/2022/03/a-message-to-the-bronfman-community-from-the-board-of-directors-march-15-2022/

In October 2017, in response to the #MeToo movement, a group of people led by Jewish philanthropist Naomi Eisenberger and others started a Facebook group called "#GamAni," which is Hebrew for "me too." The goal was to create a communal movement. Full disclosure: I have been one of the moderators of the group since nearly the beginning, led by the late Miriam Isserow as lead administrator who fiercely protected victims, along with other moderators who have come and gone over the years. It's a huge responsibility to manage this group, as people share very personal and traumatizing experiences, sometimes for the first time, and need to know that the group is a safe space. Miriam led that process with determination, often dealing with people in very raw states, and at times mercilessly removing reporters who pressured members to go public before they were ready.

(To be clear, the interviews cited in this book do not come from inside the group. Nevertheless, the conversations and stories that I have witnessed have deeply impacted me and informed my understanding of the topic and communal dynamics.)

The #GamAni group has had some notable moments in the drive for communal accountability. An Israeli politician filed suit against two women in the group who shared stories of allegedly being sexually harassed by him, for example.[10] The group also formed a crucial connecting point for women in the case of Steven M. Cohen, in providing support and collegiality for Dr. Keren McGinity when she went public about how he abused her.[11]

Despite these notable episodes, it's unclear how much the #MeToo movement has had concrete impacts on the Jewish community. A bird's-eye view of social processes suggests that the Jewish community is starting to undergo something of a potential shake-up around this issue, certainly when it comes to grassroots revelations. But how deep does it go? How many other offenders are out there—and what institutions are protecting them? Is there *actually* real change happening or is this just the tip of the iceberg? And what would "real change" look like?

We do not have the answers to these questions yet. Until now, there has not been enough clear research about the prevalence of sexual abuse in the Jewish community in America and around the world. So far, we know very little.

---

[10] Shira Hanau, "Israeli politician sued two women for libel after they accused him of sexual harassment," *Forward*, May 9, 2021, https://forward.com/fast-forward/469246/dov-lipman-sued-two-women-for-libel-after-sexual-harrasment-accusations/ .

[11] Lara Moehlman, "What's the Best Way to Say #MeToo? In the small, insular Jewish professional world, people are often reluctant to come forward with sexual harassment allegations—especially against 'big machers.' That's beginning to change." *Moment*, October 8, 2020, https://momentmag.com/whats-the-best-way-to-say-metoo/ .

How prevalent is sexual abuse in the Jewish community?

We do have bits of data to begin to explore the prevalence of sexual abuse in the Jewish community

In America overall, according to a 2006 report by the Centers for Disease Control looking at the experiences of 17,000 adults, one in four girls and one in six boys were sexually abused before the age of 18.[12] According to Dr. Shira Berkovits, founding CEO of the organization Jewish Sacred Spaces, which conducts sexual abuse trainings in Jewish organizations, "These staggering statistics were initially met with skepticism by the public. Jewish leaders were similarly dismissive, certain that such numbers didn't apply to 'us.' "[13]

The question about how rates of sexual abuse in the Jewish community compare to rates everywhere else — especially the two largest Jewish communities in America and Israel, and also elsewhere — is unclear. While Berkovits points to common assumptions of Jewish exceptionalism, the data available thus far does not bear that out. A 2000 study by Moshe Schein and his colleagues examining the histories of child sexual abuse among 1,005 adults in Israel found that 25 percent of respondents reported experiencing sexual abuse as children. The study also found that women were more likely to have been abused as children than men, and religious males were 3.3 times more likely to experience abuse compared to secular males. Moreover, only 40 percent of respondents ever reported the abuse.[14] It is not entirely clear if all the respondents were Jewish, but the study offered the first strong indication that child sexual abuse is as common in the Jewish state as elsewhere. A 2013 survey of over 10,000 children by Israel's National Council for the Child found that approximately one out of every six Jewish children in Israel are sexually abused.[15] No comparable studies have been done on Jewish populations outside of Israel.

There's more. A 2007 study of 380 married Orthodox American women, led by researcher Rachel Yehuda, found that 26 percent of respondents

---

[12] Centers for Disease Control and Prevention, "Adverse Childhood Experiences (ACE) Study: Major Findings," (2006) www.cdc.gov/violenceprevention/acestudy/about.html .

[13] Shira M. Berkovits, "Institutional Abuse in the Jewish Community," *Tradition: A Journal of Orthodox Jewish Thought* 50, no. 2 (Summer 2017), pp. 11-49, https://www.jstor.org/stable/26879501

[14] M. Schein, A. Biderman, M. Baras, L. Bennett, B. Bisharat, J. Borkan, Y. Fogelman, L. Gordon, D. Steinmetz, & E. Kitai, "The prevalence of a history of child sexual abuse among adults visiting family practitioners in Israel," *Child Abuse & Neglect* 24, no. 5 (2000), pp. 667-675, https://doi.org/10.1016/S0145-2134(00)00128-9 .

[15] The original report, authored by Haifa University professors Zvi Eisikovits and Rachel Lev-Wiesel in 2013, is available in Hebrew at http://society.haifa.ac.il/images/Traina%20findings.pdf.

experienced sexual abuse, with 16 percent of respondents reporting abuse occurring by the age of 13, figures that are similar to the population at large and to the 2000 Schein study.[16] Of the different sub-groups in the study, rates of abuse were highest among women who did not grow up religious but became religious later (*baalot teshuva*), suggesting that perhaps baalot teshuva are vulnerable or targeted. Although the researchers note that the sample size is too small to draw strong generalizations, and married Orthodox women hardly represent the entirety of the Jewish population, this work is noteworthy for a few reasons. It was the first study exclusively about the prevalence of sexual abuse specifically in the religious Jewish community in the United States. Other studies of religious groups included Jews, but this was the first study focusing on religious Jewish victims.[17] This study confirms the fact that this problem exists and is quite possibly widespread— as widespread as it is outside the Jewish community, effectively dispelling any illusion that it does not happen "to us." It also remains one of the few studies focusing on Jewish women. Furthermore, it includes experiences of not only child sexual abuse (CSA) but also abuse among adult Jewish victims.

This finding about the prevalence of sexual abuse in religious Jewish communities is consistent with studies of sexual abuse in other religious groups that have found statistically equivalent levels of abuse between religious and secular groups.[18] A 2018 study of 372 American Jews from across the denominational spectrum, led by David H. Rosmarin, found that the prevalence of CSA in the study group was statistically equivalent to national rates, and was consistent among diverse sub-groups.

Another interesting finding from the Rosmarin study was that sexual abuse, especially rape, was most prevalent among women who left the religion. Former Orthodox Jews were more than four times more likely to report rape than others in the sample.[19] Here, too, the population size is too small for a definitive generalization. But it is startling that the few studies we have all show similar results.

Moreover, the Rosmarin study also looked at the long-term impacts of abuse. The researchers found that sexual abuse was associated with a 34

---

[16] Rachel Yehuda, PhD; Michelle Friedman, MD; Talli Y. Rosenbaum, PT; Ellen Labinsky, PhD; James Schmeidler, PhD, "History of Past Sexual Abuse in Married Observant Jewish Women," *American Journal of Psychiatry* 164, issue 11 (November 2007), pp. 1700-1706, Published Online: 1 Nov. 2007, https://doi.org/10.1176/appi.ajp.2007.06122030 .

[17] See, for example, Cynthia Doxey, Larry Jensen & Janet Jensen, "The Influence of Religion on Victims of Childhood Sexual Abuse," *The International Journal for the Psychology of Religion* 7, no. 3 (1997), pp. 179-186, DOI: 10.1207/s15327582ijpr0703_6.

[18] Doxey, et al.

[19] David H. Rosmarin, Steven Pirutinsky, Moses Appel, Talia Kaplan, David Pelcovitz, "Childhood sexual abuse, mental health, and religion across the Jewish community," *Child Abuse & Neglect* 81 (2018), pp. 21-28, https://doi.org/10.1016/j.chiabu.2018.04.011 .

percent greater likelihood of psychiatric diagnoses such as depression and anxiety, greater mental distress, lower religious observance, lower intrinsic religiosity, and lower overall wellbeing. These impacts of abuse are also comparable with studies of the general population.

What are the dynamics of sexual abuse in the Jewish community?

One of the pivotal questions to arise upon discovery that sexual abuse is probably as prevalent in the Jewish community as it is elsewhere is: *How does this happen?*

A considerable number of anecdotal first-person reports of sexual abuse have come to light since the #MeToo movement began in late 2017, although they were not systematically analyzed. Indeed, a 2020 meta-analysis of studies of sexual abuse in the Orthodox Jewish community by Efrat Lusky-Weisrose and her colleagues found that, overall, there is still a very limited amount of empirical research about the specific dynamics of abuse in the Orthodox population.

Nevertheless, the researchers were able to find 13 articles with qualitative or quantitative research on CSA in the Orthodox community, and they found several key themes in terms of the dynamics of abuse.

One theme that Lusky-Weisrose discovered was about *disclosure*—that is, the first time victims tell another person what happened. The process of disclosure can take months, years, or even decades. In some cases, the first time that victims disclosed was when they told the researcher. The study found that disclosure was difficult for victims across all studies and that responses to disclosure were often very painful, such as not believing the victim, blaming the victim, or insisting on protecting the community rather than the victim.

The disbelieving of victims may also be also connected to what Sybil Sanchez calls "implausibility bias," the tendency not to believe or validate certain people because of their location in the social-cultural hierarchy:

> The historic discounting of women, in particular, as legal entities — either as property owners, judges, witnesses, jury members, or voters — has fostered general disbelief toward women as authoritative, credible sources. This, in turn, has contributed to a culture of impunity around gender abuse by placing the burden of plausibility disproportionately upon the claims of victims, making accountability nearly impossible. In cases of gender abuse, the bias of implausibility has led to innocent victims being retraumatized and treated as the guilty

party, either through embedded cultural assumptions, inadequate human resource structures, inappropriate legal proceedings, or in other, numerous ways.[20]

This pattern of disbelieving women in particular, is perhaps connected to Lusky-Weisrose's finding that most perpetrators were male and most victims were female.

Another finding was about *attitudes* toward CSA in the Orthodox community. The studies showed a frequent lack of awareness and understanding about what constitutes abuse. The researchers also found an easy dismissiveness in which the perpetrators readily downplayed the severity of their actions and would effectively defend the abuse using different kinds of rhetoric, including reliance on Jewish law.

Finally, the researchers examined the *impacts* of abuse and found that victims struggle with Post-Traumatic Stress Disorder (PTSD), religiosity, stigmatization, and sexual behavior.[21]

This analysis was limited to the Orthodox community, under the assumption that this population has unique characteristics. However, that assumption needs to be checked. It is possible that non-Orthodox, non-Jewish, and other faith communities share similar dynamics.

Dr. Amy Neustein's 2009 edited anthology, *Tempest in the Temple: Jewish Communities and Sex Abuse Scandals,* a collection of essays by leaders across denominations on the topic of sexual abuse, describes the challenges of reporting, such as disbelief, gaslighting, and silencing, as well as the impact on victims, including PTSD, distrust, depression, unhealthy sexual boundaries, and struggles with religiosity.[22] The publication of this book marks an important milestone in opening the curtain on child sexual abuse in the Jewish community.

One very important chapter, by Amy Neustein and Michael Lesher, describes some startling dynamics of power in the Orthodox community, in which Orthodox political manipulators can wield significant power to silence victims, all the way through the process of prosecution.[23] This chapter led to the later publication of Michael Lesher's 2014 book, *Sexual Abuse, Shonda and Concealment in Orthodox Jewish Communities,* which documents in further detail cases of long-term Orthodox pedophiles who received the

---

[20] Personal correspondence following interview.

[21] Efrat Lusky-Weisrose, Amitai Marmor, Dafna Tener, "Sexual Abuse in the Orthodox Jewish Community: A Literature Review," *Trauma, Violence, and Abuse,* February 13, 2020, https://doi.org/10.1177/1524838020906548 .

[22] See, for example, Joyanna Silberg and Stephanie Dallam, "Out of the Jewish closet: Facing the hidden secrets of child sexual abuse — and the damage done to victims," in Neustein's *Tempest in the Temple,* pp. 77-104.

[23] Amy Neustein and Michael Lesher, "Justice interrupted: How rabbis can interfere with the prosecution of sex offenders — and strategies to stop them," in Neustein's *Tempest in the Temple,* pp. 197-229.

support of religious leaders and whose backing led to terrifying experiences for victims seeking justice. Some victims have had to leave their communities, move out of the state or the country, and are persecuted and shunned for daring to tell the truth.[24]

Still, the assumption that Orthodox culture is distinct in terms of dynamics of abuse needs to be further examined. Moreover, there are lingering questions about *non-Orthodox* communities, which also have rabbis and power structures that potentially impact the dynamics of abuse. In fact, while there are at least 13 studies that offer some concrete data on sexual abuse in Orthodox communities, there is no comparable study for any of the other Jewish denominations. To wit, the first paper to address sexual abuse in a specific non-Orthodox Jewish community was the investigation of sexual abuse in Hebrew Union College–Jewish Institute of Religion (HUC-JIR) that came out in late 2021. This was not a peer-reviewed study but rather a legal investigation specifically about what happens in some Reform institutions. It did not look at the Reform community as a whole, nor did it ask whether the Reform movement's culture is distinct or shared with other Jewish sub-groups. It is also not a sociological study but a legal evaluation. Nevertheless, the collection of anecdotes of abuse that took place in Reform rabbinical schools affirms that this is happening in those limited settings — and it constitutes the first glimpse into sexual abuse in a denominational culture other than Orthodoxy.[25]

Considering that abuse in Orthodox culture is far ahead of the rest of the Jewish community in terms of being a more frequent subject of research, a lingering question is whether Orthodox culture is, in fact, distinct in terms of sexual abuse. Should we be analyzing Orthodox culture separately from other Jewish denominational cultures, or is there room to talk about an overarching Jewish culture? Studies that focus on CSA in Orthodox communities maintain an assumption that whatever unique characteristics exist in this community somehow illustrate that non-Orthodox communities are protected from these kinds of processes. But we do not actually know if this is true. Those assumptions have never, to my knowledge, been systematically investigated.

Let's take a look at what some of those unique Orthodox features are assumed to be. Psychologist Michael J. Salamon lists some of the religious concepts that are used in the Orthodox community to keep sexual abuse under the rug, such as *lashon hara* (prohibitions against speaking ill of a

---

[24] Michael Lesher, *Sexual Abuse, Shonda and Concealment in Orthodox Jewish Communities* (Jefferson, North Carolina: McFarland and Company, 2014).

[25] Grace E. Speights, Sharon P. Masling, Martha B. Stolley, Jocelyn R. Cuttino, Ira G. Rosenstein, *Report of Investigation into Allegations of Misconduct at Hebrew Union College-Jewish Institute of Religion* (Morgan Lewis, November 3, 2021) http://huc.edu/sites/default/files/About/PDF/HUC%20REPORT%20OF%20INVESTIGATION%20--%2011.04.21.pdf .

fellow Jew), *mesira* (prohibition against turning in another Jew to governmental authorities), and *hillul hashem* (the demand not to do anything that publicly embarrasses the Jewish community).[26] David Katzenstein and Lisa Aronson Fontes examined distinct features of CSA in Orthodox Jewish communities and found five cultural practices they believe to be unique to Orthodoxy, specifically around the frequent failure to disclose: (1) lashon hara; (2) fear and intimidation; (3) stigma and shame; (4) reliance on rabbinical courts; and (5) patriarchal gender roles.[27]

Despite these claims, some researchers maintain that the dynamics of sexual abuse between faith communities share common features, regardless of specific religion or even degree of affiliation. German researcher Nina Spröber and her team conducted a 2014 study of 1,040 CSA victims from Roman Catholic, Protestant, and non-religious institutions and found many similar patterns of abuse across different communities — time of abuse, type of abuse, extent of abuse, the grooming process, age of reporting, emotional impacts, and gender of offenders. They conclude that "child sexual abuse in institutions is attributable to the nature of institutional structures and to societal assumptions about the rights of children more than to the attitudes towards sexuality of a specific religion." In fact, they found that "factors common to all institutions such as group cohesion, hierarchical power structures and dependence, and credibility bias in favor of authority figures are conducive to the occurrence of repeated sexual abuse over long periods of time, regardless of religious affiliation."[28]

In other words, there may be dynamics of abuse that define abuse in the Jewish community overall that are not specifically about denominational affiliation, levels of religiousness, attitudes toward sexuality, or views of Jewish law, but rather something connected to *institutional and communal structures or cultural practices* that are common to faith communities generally. Put differently, it's not necessarily (just) religious ideas that keep abuse going, but societal structures and hierarchies built into faith communities — and behaviors for protecting those power hierarchies — that enable abuse and protect abusers.

Another gap in our current understanding is the predominant emphasis on *child* sexual abuse. Not all victims are children, and yet aside from the Yehuda study, adult victims in Jewish life have barely been systematically

---

[26] Michael J. Salamon, *Abuse in the Jewish Community: Religious and communal factors that undermine the apprehension of offenders and the treatment of victims*, (Urim 2011).

[27] Katzenstein, David and Lisa Aronson Fontes, "Twice Silenced: The Underreporting of Child Sexual Abuse in Orthodox Jewish Communities," *Journal of Child Sexual Abuse* (2017), DOI:10.1080/10538712.2017.1336505.

[28] N. Spröber, T. Schneider, M. Rassenhofer, A. Seitz, H. Liebhardt, L. König, J.M. Fegert, "Child sexual abuse in religiously affiliated and secular institutions: A retrospective descriptive analysis of data provided by victims in a government-sponsored reappraisal program in Germany," *BMC Public Health*, 14, no. 1 (2014), p. 282.

studied at all. That is, almost all of the 13 existing studies of abuse in the Jewish community focus on *child* sexual abuse. Perhaps adults who reveal that they have been abused are less believed, or less believable, because the accused often claim "consensual sex." But, again, these are questions that have not been systematically investigated in the Jewish community at all.

Another issue is what is happening outside of denominational institutions. Thus far, denominational identification has been a core component of defining populations in studies. But an increasing number of Jews do not have any denominational affiliation. We do not know what sexual abuse looks like in Jewish cultures outside of formal groupings or whether they are part of larger cultural dynamics.

The bottom line is, we do not really know how sexual abuse happens across the Jewish world, what causes it to be sustained and supported, what if anything makes Jewish culture and society distinct, whether dynamics differ between denominational communities, whether abusers attack children and adult victims differently, and what are the roots of the dynamics that so often seem to protect abusers instead of victims/survivors.

Discovering rabbis

When I started this research in 2015, I was not expecting rabbis to be the headliners. I was looking at abuse in general in our community. When I began conducting interviews on this topic, I was startled to discover how many of the abusers described by interviewees were rabbis.

Although anthropology does not claim to offer statistical evidence or representative sampling, and although I efforted to maintain listening neutrality and non-judgment, I was nonetheless swept away by hearing so many of these accounts of rabbis who sexually abuse. The title of this book is a result of an incomprehensible number of interviewees in which the abuser was a rabbi. I decided to examine the profile of the rabbi-abuser more carefully to understand what this means for our culture, and to use those insights to analyze *other* cases of high-profile abuse using those paradigms of power in our culture.

Perhaps the dominance of rabbi-abusers in the interviews — nearly half of the interviewees talked about rabbis — should not have been so surprising to me given the plethora of cases that have received attention: Marc Gafni, Moti Elon, Shlomo Carlebach, Baruch Lanner, Ezra Scheinberg, Barry Freundel, Larry Bach, and many more.

Moreover, if we consider that communal cultures in Jewish life may have much in common with those of other faith communities, then the discoveries of how rampant sexual abuse is in other faith communities[29] should be a cautionary tale about Jewish religious leaders as well. Nevertheless, while the Catholic Church sexual abuse scandal has had our increasing attention since the 2002 *Boston Globe* exposé[30], sexual abuse by rabbis and other Jewish leaders is still relatively obscure and is probably vastly underreported.[31] There has, to date, been no systematic, broad analysis of the dynamics of sexual abuse among Jewish clergy.

This obscurity may be connected to the size of the different communities and thus to the breadth of the issue. The Catholic Church, which has 17,600 churches in America alone, has revealed an estimated 16,000 victims of sexual abuse thus far and 3,700 Roman Catholic clergy involved, from among 85 million North American members (out of 1.2 billion worldwide). Protestant Christians have an estimated 314,000 congregations and a membership base of about 60 million, but the community has not yet begun an exploration of alleged child sexual abuse—although there are reports from insurance companies that cover 160,000 Protestant churches, of 7,095 claims of alleged sexual abuse in churches between 1987 and 2007, or an average of 260 claims of alleged sexual abuse per year, which resulted in payments of $87.8 million.[32] By contrast, Jews are few and diffuse: We make up 5.5 million Americans and 15.2 million people worldwide, and we have 3,700 synagogues in America alone that belong to at least five different denominations and have not yet conducted a comprehensive internal study about the scope and dynamics of the issue communally.[33]

It is worth noting, however, that Rabbi Arthur Gross Schaeffer, one of the first rabbis to speak out about this issue, wrote in 1999 that "[w]hile we have no surveys targeting the rabbinic community, most people working in this area believe that an examination of rabbis would reveal similar numbers to those ministers."[34] More recently, Shira Berkovits wrote, "Although its visibility has grown in the Jewish community in recent years, sexual abuse is

---

[29] Reuters, "French Catholic Church had an estimated 3,000 paedophiles since 1950s - commission head," *Reuters*, October 3, 2021,
https://www.reuters.com/world/europe/french-catholic-church-had-estimated-3000-paedophiles-since-1950s-commission-2021-10-03/ .

[30] Michael Rezendes and Matt Carroll, "6 more priests removed on allegations of abuse," in *The Boston Globe Spotlight Investigation: Abuse in the Catholic Church: The Boston Globe* (2002), http://www.bostonglobe.com/arts/movies/spotlight-movie .

[31] Katzenstein and Fontes, "Twice Silenced"

[32] Andrew S. Denney, Kent R. Kerley, and Nickolas G. Gross, "Child sexual abuse in Protestant Christian congregations: a descriptive analysis of offense and offender characteristics," *Religions* 18 (2008), pp. 1-13.

[33] Pew Research Center, *A Portrait of Jewish Americans,* (2013)
https://www.pewforum.org/2013/10/01/chapter-1-population-estimates/

[34] Rabbi Arthur Gross Schaeffer, "Rabbi sexual misconduct: crying out for a communal response," *The Reconstructionist* (1999), pp. 58-62, p. 58.

a human problem, not a uniquely Jewish one."[35] Thus, sexual abuse in the Jewish community may be assumed to contain dynamics that are related to larger trends along with some that are uniquely Jewish.

One of the first sources of information about this topic may be the rabbinic reporting bodies administered by the various Jewish denominations. The report noted above conducted by HUC-JIR is the very first of its kind, as limited as it is. Rabbinical bodies across denominations have come under harsh criticism for being unreliable and possibly even part of the problem.[36] The Conservative movement only in late 2021 revealed the list of rabbis who have been suspended or expelled.[37]

Moreover, it remains unclear whether clergy themselves can or should be trusted as accurate sources for understanding clergy sexual misconduct (CSM). Many argue that rabbinical bodies should not be investigating their own crimes out of a deep conflict of interest. Indeed, the reliance on rabbis for information about abuse may explain some of the black holes in our understanding. Until recently, research on CSM with adults from different religions often relied on clergy self-report surveys, asking religious leaders whether they ever committed CSM. Not surprisingly, these surveys turned out to be rather unreliable, with huge variations in findings, from one percent to 38.5 percent of all clergy, across a wide range of religions and denominations, admitting that they engaged in sexual misconduct.[38]

This data-collection challenge reflects a broader problem that I refer to as the *dubious self-report*. People tend to lie about themselves all the time — we say, "I'm not angry" when we are, or "I didn't eat *so many* cookies," when we finished the tray. We tend to share narratives about ourselves that fit in to the way we *like* to view ourselves rather than how we actually *are*. We tell stories about ourselves that we are even convinced are true rather than face

---

[35] Shira M. Berkovits, "Institutional abuse in the Jewish community," *Tradition* 50, no. 2 (2017), pp. 11-49. https://traditiononline.org/institutional-abuse-in-the-jewish-community-by-shira-m-berkovits/

[36] Hannah Dreyfus, "Can rabbinic ethics committees police their own? Recent cases test rabbinic ethics panels in the age of #MeToo," *The Jewish Week* (2019), https://jewishweek.timesofIsrael.com/recent-cases-test-expertise-of-rabbinic-ethics-panels/.

[37] JTA, "In a shift, Conservative movement publicly lists the rabbis it has expelled and suspended," *JTA*. October 25, 2021, https://jewishjournal.org/2021/10/25/in-a-shift-conservative-movement-publicly-lists-the-rabbis-it-has-expelled-and-suspended/ .

[38] Diana R. Garland and Christen Argueta, "How clergy sexual misconduct happens: A qualitative study of first-hand accounts," *Social Work & Christianity* 37, no. 1 (2010), pp. 1-27.; Perry C. Francis and James Stacks, "The association between spiritual well-being and clergy sexual misconduct," *Journal of Religion and Abuse: Advocacy, Pastoral Care and Prevention* 5 (2003), pp. 79–100.; Katherine R. Meek, Mark R. McMinn, Todd Burnett, Chris Mazarella, and Vitaliy Voytenko, "Sexual Ethics Training in Seminary: Preparing Students to Manage Feelings of Sexual Attractions," *Pastoral Psychology* 53 (2004), pp. 63–79.; John Thoburn and D. Mitchell Whitman, "Clergy affairs: emotional investment, longevity of relationship and affair partners," *Pastoral Psychology* 52 (2004), pp. 491–506.

uncomfortable truths about our own behaviors. Whether this is conscious or subconscious, or a function of cognitive dissonance, shame, guilt or something else, the dubious self-report is a quirky fact of everyday life. But in this case, it is more than a funny quirk; it is a dangerous impediment to our knowledge. If people are reluctant to admit that they ate the last cookie, imagine how reluctant they must be to admit *I am a pedophile*. No wonder data about sexual abuse based on self-report by clergy is entirely unreliable.

The absence of reliability around rabbis' stances vis a vis abuse also explains victims' reluctance to disclose when abusers are rabbis: *How can a victim safely disclose to a rabbi when the abuser himself is a rabbi?*

Another challenge to understanding CSM is in attempts to establish a profile of victims. Perhaps as a result of the Catholic Church revelations, victims of CSM are often perceived as underage boys who are particularly vulnerable. According to a John Jay study of child sexual abuse in religious settings, 80 percent of victims of child sexual abuse are male.[39] However, this does not necessarily reflect all the forms of sexual abuse committed by clergy. According to a study by Mark Chaves and Diana Garland exploring CSM in various religions, over 95 percent of victims of sexual exploitation by clergy are *adult women*.[40] Chaves and Garland, one of the first teams of researchers to conduct broad, comprehensive research on the topic of CSM analyzed the 2008 General Social Survey, a stratified random sample of the US population, and found that 3.1 percent of women who attend religious services at least monthly reported receiving unwanted sexual advances by clergy in their own congregation; 92 percent of these sexual advances had been made in secret, not in open dating relationships; and in half of those cases, the offender was married to someone else at the time. "Thus, one in 33 women has been the object of an unwanted sexual advance by a religious leader; or, more narrowly, one in 40 women who attend a congregation has been the object of an illicit sexual advance by her own married religious leader," they conclude.[41]

These conflicting accounts of the victim profile can be challenging in the effort to understand and uncover CSM. While it is clear that a young child cannot consent to sex with his priest, pastor, or rabbi, adult women on the other hand are theoretically capable of consent, and as such, the abuse is

---

[39] John Jay College of Criminal Justice, "The nature and scope of sexual abuse of minors by Catholic priests and deacons in the United States 1950-2002," *The City University Of New York For The United States Conference Of Catholic Bishops*, February 2004,
http://www.usccb.org/issues-and-action/child-and-youth-protection/upload/the-nature-and-scope-of-sexual-abuse-of-minors-by-catholic-priests-and-deacons-in-the-united-states-1950-2002.pdf .

[40] Mark Chaves and Diane Garland, "The Prevalence of Clergy Sexual Advances toward Adults in Their Congregations," *Journal for the Scientific Study of Religion* 48, no. 4 (2009), pp. 817-824.

[41] Chaves and Garland, p. 3.

often cast by observers as consensual "affairs."[42] However, the perception of adult women as capable of consent ignores the power dynamic involved with being sexually solicited by one's *rabbi*. Many former victims of CSM struggle with this for years after the abuse. "So, what is sexual exploitation as an adult by clergy?" asks researcher, survivor, and advocate Margaret Kennedy. "Sexual exploitation occurs when a person in authority, in role, as Clergy, Minister, Pastor, sexualizes contact with female parishioners who seek his help, for his own gratification. Consent is not the issue, despite being an adult. Consent is compromised. Within a setting where the woman seeks advice, teaching, or spiritual direction of her Pastor/Bishop or her senior/employer... The pastor misuses power and role whenever they sexualize contact. It is sexual exploitation of a woman, or man, to whom they have a duty of care, duty of trust."[43]

There are several key aspects of CSM that potentially distinguish abuse by a religious leader from that in other settings of abuse. Certainly, in some ways, members of the clergy who sexually abuse are just like other offenders. Nils Friberg and Mark Laaser, who studied 25 religious leaders accused of sexual misconduct found that, according to the offenders' self-report, the average number of victims per offender was two, the average career length was 25 years, and the typical offender is highly successful and has a combination of narcissism, sexual compulsion, and need for affirmation.[44] Anson D. Shupe adds that the hierarchical structures of religious institutions, coupled with the moral authority awarded to clergy, create a situation ripe for abuse.[45] Donald Capps offers other significant insights, arguing that religious leaders' unsupervised autonomy, private access to congregation members, and lofty job titles also contribute to the potential for abuse.[46] Patricia L. Liberty describes the use of religious language to groom victims, as well as preying on victims' religious sensibilities. Offenders may use enticing statements such as, "You are an answer to my prayer; I asked God

---

[42] See, for example Ari Feldman, "Reform rabbi was secretly censured for affair with congregant," *Forward*, June 3, 2018, https://forward.com/news/402226/reform-rabbi-was-secretly-censured-for-affair-with-congregant/, an article about a case of rabbinic sexual abuse for which the rabbi eventually lost his pulpit—a second time—even though it took the Ethics Committee nearly twenty years to interpret the many simultaneous "" of this rabbi with congregants as abuse, and even then, the newspaper headline called out one case only as an "affair."

[43] Margaret Kennedy, "Exploitation, not 'affair,'" in *When pastors prey: overcoming clergy sexual abuse of women*, ed. Valli Boobal Batchelor (World Council of Churches Publications, 2013), pp. 26-35.

[44] Nils C. Friberg and Mark R. Laaser, *Before the fall: preventing pastoral sexual abuse*, (Collegeville: The Liturgical Press, 1998).

[45] Anson D. Shupe, *Spoils of the kingdom: Clergy misconduct and religious community*, (Urbana: University of Illinois Press, 2007).

[46] Donald Capps, "Sex in the parish: Social-scientific explanations for why it occurs," *The Journal of Pastoral Care* 47, no. 4 (1993), pp. 350-361.

for someone who can share my deepest thoughts, prayers, and needs and he sent me you."[47]

Clergy also have a unique ability to garner trust at vulnerable moments. As Diana R. Garland and Christen Argueta describe:

> *The clergy's position of power and the trust [the victim] has in him because of that role cause her to doubt her own ability to discern the intent of the action when she would have been clear about its intent if it occurred in a relationship with someone else. Once the behavior becomes overtly sexual, she fears that no one will believe her, or that she will be labeled a seductress. She may be very confused, sometimes enjoying the attention and affection she is receiving from him, making it even more difficult to restore relationship boundaries, even though she is alarmed and frightened. Because the relationship is secret, she cannot reach out to anyone for help, realistically fearing condemnation and destruction of social relationships and, if married, of her family. In fact, the offender is the only one with whom she can discuss her feelings, and such conversations further her isolation and the deepening attachment.[48]*

In addition to clergy privilege described here, there are dynamics in religious settings that work to protect the abuser rather than the victims. Some of the dynamics that keep CSM hidden, according to Garland and Argueta, are: (1) the lack of community response against the clergy; (2) the "culture of niceness" that keeps victims from resisting or standing up to the abuse; (3) technology that keeps communication hidden (e.g., emails and texts); (4) multiple entangled roles with the abuser; and (5) trust in the sanctuary.[49]

Another obstacle to exposing this issue is the prevalence of "non-contact sexual abuse." This can include unwanted sexual commentary, phone sex, sexting, voyeurism, revenge porn, and video voyeurism. The most well-known example of this in the Jewish community is probably the case of Rabbi Barry Freundel, who used hidden cameras to spy on women immersing in the ritual bath. The impact of non-contact sexual abuse is not well researched or defined but there are indications that 20% of the cases of CSM fall into this category, and the traumatic impact is not fully understood.[50]

Another aspect of CSM that may be common across religions is the impact on the victim's spiritual life and identity. Whereas sexual abuse from non-clerical offenders can result in a wide range of devastating impacts, there is

---

[47] Patricia L. Liberty, "It's difficult to explain—The compromise of moral agency for victims of abuse by religious leaders," *Journal of Religion & Abuse* 3 no 3/4 (2001), pp. 81-90.

[48] Garland and Argueta, p. 4.

[49] Garland and Argueta, pp. 10-20.

[50] Denney et al., p. 5.

often an added element of trauma around the destruction of faith and religious connection, as researcher Barbara McLaughlin found in her study on the long-term spiritual impact on victims of CSM.[51] Sura Jesselson, whose synagogue rabbi, Jonathan Rosenblatt, was allegedly sexually abusing teenage boys in her synagogue for years in a non-contact way, said, "It is demoralizing enough when Jewish authority figures misbehave. It is devastating when communities do not support victims despite everyone talking endlessly about *midot* [moral character]."

This information is vital in understanding sexual abuse in Jewish settings, especially those that involve a rabbi. Still, what needs more clarification are the potential similarities and differences between CSM in Jewish communities and in other religious faiths, as well as among Jewish denominational cultures. Perhaps an understanding of the dynamics of sexual abuse in faith communities in general will illuminate our own cultural dynamics in a way that can help bring about change.

The purpose of this research

I set out to fill some gaps in our understanding of sexual abuse in the Jewish culture and to see if I could discover the dynamics that sustain abusive practices across the community. I wanted to know if there are cultural assumptions, behaviors, structures, and language that may be common to Jews in general, crossing specific denominations, institutions, and degrees of affiliation. I wanted to challenge certain working assumptions — such as assumptions that this issue is somehow dominant in Orthodox settings and that children and teens are the main victims — and to see how that plays out. I aimed to know how and why all this abuse is happening in the Jewish community as a whole.

I decided to use my professional tools of qualitative anthropological research to get at the deeper dynamics at work. Since receiving my doctorate in anthropology/sociology, gender studies, and education from Hebrew University in Jerusalem some 15 years ago, I have conducted several anthropological studies related to gender issues in the Jewish community.[52] I am most interested in connections between language, cultural assumptions, and socialization into behaviors that are considered "normative." Those connections enable us to unpack what is really going on around us. To be

---

[51] Barbara R. McLaughlin M.Div., MSW, "Devastated spirituality: The impact of clergy sexual abuse on the survivor's relationship with god and the church," *Sexual Addiction & Compulsivity* 1, vol. 2 (1994), pp. 145-158, DOI: 10.1080/10720169408400039.

[52] See, for example, Elana Sztokman, *The Men's Section: Orthodox Jewish Men in an Egalitarian World* (Brandeis University Press, 2011), and Chaya Rosenfeld Gorsetman, *Educating in the Divine Image: Gender Issues in Jewish Education* (Brandeis University Press, 2013).

sure, this is *not* a quantitative study that offers statistics and numbers. That information is beyond the scope of my work. Rather, this is a *qualitative* study that aims to paint a portrait of how this all happens. My goal is to understand what the abuse looks like, what factors keep it going, how abusers are protected, what the impacts are on survivors, and what this does to communities. Since this is a qualitative study and not a quantitative study, it makes no claims about statistical prevalence. Rather, it weaves together many testimonies of sexual abuse, collected over the course of 3-4 years, in order to gain insight into the particular dynamics of this phenomenon and the ways that the dynamics may reflect particularities of Jewish culture.

This research is about rabbis, but not exclusively. Many, but not all, of the abusers herein are rabbis. I focus on rabbis to a certain extent as a paradigm of a Jewish-centric authority or power figure. All the abusers here were able to manipulate or control their victims, some more than others. They used the tools of power and authority at their disposal to try and have their way with their victims, some more intensively than others. Some of the abuse lasted minutes, and some lasted years. Some victims ran or protected themselves immediately, and some never did. The stories are varied, but they all involve a Jewish abuser and/or Jewish setting, and all involve a person with some form of power over the victim, even if that power is at times subtle.

Understanding the dynamics of rabbis who abuse sheds light on power hierarchies in the community at large, hierarchies that benefit not only rabbis but also organizational leaders, professors, teachers, bosses, thought leaders, counselors, donors, board members, congregants, principals, clients, mentors, scholars, or parents. In each relationship between the abuser and the abused, there are assumed cultural hierarchies. The profile of a rabbi who abuses is informative about how power is wielded elsewhere, and about who is considered too important to be taken down. "Rabbi" is effectively a metaphor for the person with power in the Jewish world.

Methodology

This research[53] is based primarily on a collection of 84 testimonies of abuse in Jewish communal life that I collected from survivors, experts, advocates, and some who are survivors-turned-advocates. My interviews were conducted either in person, via video-call, or via extensive chat or email. They range in length from a brief exchange or text about one incident to several hours of talking— and in several cases across more than one conversation. All interviewees' names and identifying details are kept

---

[53] This research was made possibly thanks to a generous grant from Jewish feminist philanthropist Barbara Dobkin.

private unless they gave express permission to be attributed. Testimonies were also collected through anonymous surveys of the organizations Jewish Women's Archive and B'kavod, as well as from an anonymous Instagram account called "Jewish Teens for Empowered Consent." I also collected a plethora of information from the growing list of public testimonies from survivors and organizational resources. In all, the book includes stories from nearly 300 mostly unnamed respondents across platforms.

Accounts include incidences from synagogues, Jewish schools, Jewish camps, Jewish youth groups, Jewish organizations, volunteering in Jewish settings, Jewish campus experiences, and other Jewish communal settings. I also included several stories about abuse by a parent at home, as parents are arguably the penultimate authority figure in a person's life. Testimonies were collected via in-person interview, online interview, chat, and online study, including sections that were contributed by two Jewish organizations that conducted online studies on this subject. Interviewees range in age from 21 to 78, live across the United States, Israel, and other English-speaking Jewish communities, span the professional and socioeconomic spectrum, and are all Jewish. Most identify as women, several identify as binary or non-conforming, and three identify as men. Incidences of abuse took place in some cases in the 1960s and 1970s, and in other cases in the year of the interview. There is no particular pattern to the stories themselves or to how respondents found me. Some saw my posts online, some heard about my research from friends, and some people are acquaintances whom I told about my research and said replied that they have a story. The sample is not representative of the Jewish community in any systematic way.[54] Yet, the stories here are all connected straightforwardly: They all involve sexual abuse by Jews in a Jewish cultural context.[55]

Note that all names and identifying details of interviewees have been disguised as much as possible without interfering with the content of the story and are described with clearly communicated permission of each interviewee. No names, locations, institutions, or distinct biographical details are revealed, unless the stories were disclosed and vetted by reputable media, in which case I shared the media sources. Interwoven with the respondent testimonies are several published works of victims who came forward publicly, and those are brought in the writers' names.

---

[54] I do not have complete background data on all interviewees' ethnicity, educational level, income, or marital status. Connections between that data and sexual abuse will require a more comprehensive, quantitative study.

[55] There is one exception, which is a case of sexual harassment in a Jewish university in which the harasser was a visiting professor and not Jewish. I kept the story in because there were many people involved in how the case was handled who represented the institution, which is a very high-profile Jewish institution.

Listening to interviewees

To be clear, this research explores the topic of sexual abuse in the Jewish community from the *perspectives of victims*. It is *not* a formal legal investigation or evaluation of processes and procedures. It is a collection of testimonies on the issue exclusively from one point of view. I make no claims on facts or evidence. I am simply bringing here what victims reported they saw, heard, experienced, and felt. This research is *not* evaluation but ethnography. The goal is to paint a portrait of a culture from the perspectives of people dwelling within that culture. I am not fact-checking interviewees. I am not questioning their stories. I am not prodding them to confirm their stories like law enforcement would, or looking for ways to double-check the details of their testimonies. I am recording their memories.

There has been some backlash against believing survivor testimony. This has a lot to do with what Sybil Sanchez dubbed above the "implausibility bias." There are also assertions that memory can at times be unreliable. However, some researchers assert that while victims of trauma may not remember all the details of an event or even the day or year when it happened, the essence of the story remains reliable. As psychologist Dr. Jim Hopper, an expert on sexual abuse and the brain, wrote about Dr. Christine Blasey Ford's testimony of attempted rape by Justice Brett Kavanaugh, "Memories of highly stressful and traumatic experiences, at least their most central details, don't tend to fade over time. And while people may have the superficial abstract narratives that they tell themselves and others about their worst traumas, that's not because the worst details have been lost. It's often because they don't want to remember them, and don't (yet) feel safe to remember them."[56] As sexual abuse and incest survivor Genendy Radoff told me, "My sisters asked me, 'If what you say is true about our grandfather, what were the color of the curtains in his study?' When I tell them that I don't know, they tell me I'm making it up. But the reason I don't know is because I wasn't *focused* on the curtains. I was focused on my grandfather's fingers in my underwear. That detail has never slipped away from my memory."

I'm sharing exactly the details that interviewees wanted to share with me, nothing more and nothing less. It is not my place to drill them on details like the color of the curtains or to instill doubt in the veracity of their statements.

The absence of "the other side of the story" may be viewed as a limitation, but I don't see it that way. The need for "another side" is an adversarial outlook perpetuated in large part by the justice system as well as by media

---

[56] Jim Hopper, "How Reliable Are the Memories of Sexual Assault Victims? The expert testimony excluded from the Kavanaugh hearing," *Scientific American*, September 27, 2018, https://blogs.scientificamerican.com/observations/how-reliable-are-the-memories-of-sexual-assault-victims/ .

cultures that always need a second "angle." The legal system maintains a default position for victims of sexual abuse unlike any other victim of crime: they must prove that they are *not* lying. As Elaine Craig writes in *Putting Trials on Trial: Sexual Assault and the Failure of the Legal Profession*, victims of sexual assault are the *only* crime victims who are systematically disbelieved, and the justice system is designed to cast them as vindictive or delusional liars. Chanel Miller, who was raped by Stanford University student Brock Turner in 2015, intricately describes the torment of this process of being constantly disbelieved in her important memoir, *Know my Name*.[57] That process has become so normalized that our society barely questions it or notices how oppressive it is.[58]

Against that backdrop, taking victims' stories at face value seems like a moral and compassionate thing to do, and an alternative approach to what the justice system offers. The act of simply listening and holding the space for the speaker without questioning and doubting her veracity makes this anthropology. It is not journalistic reporting, nor prosecution, nor criminal justice. It is just listening. It is being human. And it is ultimately a cultural description. This is not a limitation but rather an asset, and perhaps can also serve as a corrective experience.

One last point on my role as researcher: The culture I am opening up is also my own culture. Conducting anthropology in one's own culture can be powerful but also tricky. It is powerful in that I know very well the codes, practices, and language, as I have lived them. The familiarity enables a depth of understanding. But at the same time, there is a risk of inserting my own experiences and biases where they do not belong, as I described in the Prologue. I try to address this by retaining a certain distance from the texts, but there are moments in the telling where I break that distance and share my own experiences because I feel that my stories strengthen or expound on the issues being discussed or enhance to the text. In short, I try to keep my distance from the testimonies, but ultimately, I am telling the story of my own culture, with all that it implies.

Some parameters

What is sexual abuse?

In this book, I use the term "sexual abuse" in its broadest meaning to incorporate all types of sexually motivated behavior that one person does toward another person without the other person's consent. This can be

---

[57] Chanel Miller, *Know my Name* (New York: Penguin, 2019).
[58] Elaine Craig, *Putting Trials on Trial: Sexual Assault and the Failure of the Legal Profession* (McGill-Queen's University Press; Canadian First edition, 2018).

physical assault, such as unwanted touch, groping, grabbing, rape, or attempted rape. It can also be verbal assault that does not involve any contact, such as harassment, catcalling, slut-shaming, sexual solicitation, body commentary, or sexual commentary. It can also be non-verbal assault, such as voyeurism or video voyeurism, suggestive text messaging, online sexual aggression, revenge porn, and sexual bullying. It can involve strangers, friends, co-workers, bosses, volunteers, donors, teachers, counselors, collaborators, clergy, or even family members. The key is that there is no consent.

This can get murky. As Sheila Katz and Rabbi Danya Ruttenberg write:

> [S]exual harassment, sexual misconduct, and sexual assault are not the same things and should not be used interchangeably.... Sexual misconduct is a broad catchall term for unwelcome behavior of a sexual nature that is committed without consent or by force, intimidation, coercion or manipulation – it may be illegal, it may not be. Sexual assault involves sexually touching another person without consent, or the use of coercion or force, and sexual harassment includes a range of actions from verbal transgressions to physical advances and is illegal in most contexts.[59]

I try to use these terms accurately. The term "abuse" is used as an umbrella to include it all—including non-contact sexual abuse, and including gender abuse—which is further expounded on in a chapter dedicated just to that dynamic.

What is "the Jewish community"?

This book defines the Jewish community as spaces where Jews gather. This includes Jewish organizations or NGOs, synagogues, Jewish schools or camps, Jewish programs, Jewish universities, campus Hillels, Israel programs, Jewish businesses, Israeli companies, Jewish governing bodies such as a Jewish Federation, or other similar environments. In essence, this book discusses abuse in Jewish spaces and/or those spaces occupied by Jews. In one case of abuse presented in this book, the perpetrator was not Jewish — an account in which a woman was harassed by a non-Jewish professor at the Jewish university where she worked. I included it because the event caused her to leave that place, which damaged a major artery for her connection to Jewish life—her Jewish workplace. At the same time, I included a testimony about harassment in a Middle Eastern Studies department at a non-Jewish

---

[59] Sheila Katz and Rabbi Danya Ruttenberg, "What to remember when abuse stories break in Jewish communities," *Baltimore Jewish Times*, September 1, 2021, https://www.jewishtimes.com/opinion-what-to-remember-when-abuse-stories-break-in-jewish-communities/ .

university, another potentially gray area, because the department was overwhelmingly Israeli and the atmosphere in the department was to encourage young Jewish academics to work in or for Israel. When confronting these questionable cases, the criteria I used for inclusion was whether the incident occurred in a way or in a setting that impacted the respondent's Jewish identity or connection to Jewish life. If the story was told to me in that way, then I included it under the loose umbrella of "Jewish community."

What is "Jewish culture"?

If we assume that Jews are a group with shared socializations, then Jewish culture is the collection of dynamics of human interaction within the contexts that have been defined as a Jewish communal setting. The assumption here, as with all assumptions about culture, is that there is a commonality to behaviors and norms in gatherings of people who share an ethnic, religious, or social process of acculturation. In other words, we were brought up on similar language, ideas, liturgy, expectations, principles, history, tradition, foods, music, or lore. Obviously, it is quite a big assumption, and perhaps is not always precise. Even just the issue of food, for example, can be easily dismantled. "Jewish food" is more of a reflection of places where Jews lived in different periods than of something intrinsically "Jewish."

Whether Jewish culture is "a" thing or "many" things, I am working on a running assumption that, despite the differences, there are certain underlying commonalities that act as a kind of cultural glue. Even taking into account denominational, geographic, ethnic, and socioeconomic differences, there are aspects to Jewish acculturation that are connected to both social institutions and communal ideas about gender, sexuality, patriarchy, and abuse. Those dynamics are what I am looking to uncover and understand. I revisit these assumptions as I go and reflect on them at the end.

That said, clearly cultural dynamics are not universal. Even if we accept the assumption that there is a such thing as "Jewish culture," and even if I succeed in unveiling the parts of that culture where dynamics of sexual abuse reside, it is not perfectly true. Not all rabbis abuse, not all communal settings are ripe for abuse, not all institutions practice the same behaviors, and so forth. I am absolutely not looking to make any such claim about uniformity or universality. I am just reading cultures.

This is a challenging task, especially as I am looking at some very dark sides of the culture. And nobody wants to think of their own culture as containing something so very unwanted. Nevertheless, that is the task I undertook here.

Language and gender pronouns

The terms I use for the person committing the abuse alternate between "abuser," "predator," "perpetrator," "offender," and in relevant cases, "assailant," "harasser," and "rapist." There are debates in the world of sexual abuse work about whether to use legalistic terms such as "perpetrator." I understand those concerns, and this is certainly not a legal document. Nevertheless, as I do not rely on one correct term to use, I alternate between them all.

I also alternate between "victims," "survivors," and "abused." Here, too, there are debates among people who were acted upon who prefer "survivor" over "victim." However, to use "survivor" across the board that assumes that the person does, in fact, consider herself a survivor, which is not always the case. In an effort to respect the issues, I randomly alternate among terms with no intention of offense.

In terms of gender, I use "they/them" as much as possible when it is does not confuse the text. In general statements, I switch between conventional pronouns mostly randomly. With that, the terms "women/girls" and "men/boys" dominate much of the text to explore the experiences of those who are identified in those ways. I use these terms not to disrespect or exclude those who do not identify within the gender binary but rather as a reflection of how our society creates cultures around those definitions and experiences. There is more work to be done on the specific experiences of sexual abuse of non-binary or trans people. This research is only a stepping stone. Please view my use of gendered terms should be seen as all-inclusive — "women" refers to cis and trans women and non-binary, and "men" refers to cis and trans men and non-binary.

A note about sexual abuse within the family

One category of abuse that receives limited coverage in this volume is incest. Several interviewees reported being sexually abused by close family members, such as a father. These stories are particularly crushing and extremely important. The topic is present in these interviews but is not dominant. I included these accounts in various sections because the topic overlaps in many ways with the issue of abuse by clergy — dynamics of power, authority, grooming, and silencing, as well as the impact on the victims. My overall feeling, however, after conducting this research, is that sexual abuse within the family has many unique issues and deserves its own research study and analysis. A thorough analysis of the topic is a bit beyond the scope of the book and deserves its own study.

How this book is organized

This book is organized into five sections, each with several sub-chapters.[60]

The first section tells the stories, as they are, with minimal analysis. I divided the stories according to the type of role the abuser had in the respondent's life. Although the focus for much of the book is on rabbis, the different kinds of positions in which many tales of abuse took place are also covered. The first chapter is all about rabbis in various settings — synagogues, schools, camps, and more. The second chapter is about bosses who abuse, as well as other workplace-related abusers. The third chapter is about a completely under-reported phenomenon, which is abuse by donors, board members, and congregants.[61]

The second section unpacks the details about how abuse happens in the Jewish community. This begins with grooming — the ways in which abusers "prepare" their victims for the abuse. I then move on to compiling a profile of the abuser in a Jewish cultural setting. Then I examine some of the settings in which abuse occurs, particularly synagogues, schools, youth movement, and camps. The fourth chapter veers a bit and looks at a particular dynamic that enables abuse, what many refer to as "gender abuse," which is a process of systematically weakening, demeaning, and oppressing women, especially in the workplace, so that when sexual abuse takes place, it has a comfortable home. All these chapters taken together tell the story about how abuse happens in Jewish life — who is doing it, how they are doing it, where they are doing it, and how they are supported. This section is, in a certain way, the heart of this book.

The third section is about what happens *after* the abuse takes place. The first chapter is about disclosure — that is, victims coming to terms with what happened. The second chapter in this section is about reporting, which is about accountability and justice. It could mean reporting to supervisors, rabbinic committees, the police, or the media. The third chapter in this section then looks at Jewish language and ideas that are co-opted to support abusers, such as "continuity" or "family," or ideas that abusers use to gain entry, such as anti-Semitism or community, as well as ideas that keep the abuse covered, such as "lashon hara" (not to speak evil).

The fourth section is about the impacts of abuse on both victims and on the community as a whole. This section is divided into two chapters — the

---

[60] I think that my decision to organize this book around the profile of the abuser reflects my adoption of the victim's perspective. The question throughout this research is, what do victims see? If I put the camera in the hands of the victims, so to speak, the first thing that they will see is the abuser in whatever role they have over the victim. I suppose this entire book is an exercise in giving the victims the camera, as it were, so that we can see what they see.

first is about impacts on victims, and the second is about impacts on the community. This is extremely important because this issue—of how the entire Jewish community is affected by all this—is a topic that has never been systematically analyzed. The Jewish community has never had a real conversation about how the presence of so many abusers — especially in leadership positions — impacts the community as a whole.

The fifth section pulls everything together. The discussion chapter summarizes the key findings. And the final chapter looks to the future with ideas for change and healing. It is about what we can glean from this work, and what work might be done in the future to make change.

My goal is to make this work readable and usable for reference, sharing, and teaching. As such, the book is designed in a way to enable most chapters to stand on their own. In the same vein, each chapter opens with its own mini table of contents to make it easy for readers to see the whole picture, and to make choices about skimming and skipping. Each chapter also ends with a list of key take-aways, for the same purposes, especially since the material can be very hard to take in.

Content warning

I cannot overstate the triggering nature of the content found within these pages, which contain very difficult material. I do not hide or gloss over details. If accounts of abuse are painful for you to encounter — which is probably the most human reaction — I suggest skim parts, perhaps skipping parts.

Most importantly, make sure you have outlets for self-care while you are reading, take breaks as needed. I often had to stop writing and take long walks just to separate myself from the material. Please take care, especially if you are a victim.

And if you need immediate assistance, please refer to the Appendix for the list of Resources and reach out for support.

Part I: The Stories

So many years past being raped, I tell myself what happened is 'in the past.' This is only partly true. In too many ways, the past is still with me. The past is written on my body. I carry it every single day. The past sometimes feels like it might kill me. It is a very heavy burden.

Roxane Gay, Hunger

I was too trusting, too naïve. I felt like it was all my fault. It would take me years to accept what now seems obvious: rape is not a punishment for poor judgement.

Chessy Prout, *I Have the Right To: A High School Survivor's Story of Sexual Assault, Justice, and Hope*

Chapter 1: Stories About Rabbis

> **In this chapter**
>
> The Rabbi Teacher
> The Rabbi Scholar
> The Rabbi Pastor
> The Camp Rabbi
> The Rabbi Boss
> The Pulpit Rabbi
> Takeaways about rabbis who abuse

Rabbi Sharon Brous, a popular and high-profile Conservative rabbi based in Los Angeles, delivered a sermon in September 2019, at the height of the #MeToo testimonies, about her experiences with sexual abuse. "I took out a pen and started to list my #MeToo moments…related to my rabbinate," she told her congregation. "In ten minutes, I listed 27 incidents. 27! Some of which could or even should have driven me from the rabbinate altogether. These incidents ranged from gross and insulting to downright terrifying… I put my pen away."[62]

In order to understand what we are talking about when we discuss sexual abuse, we need to start with the stories. As difficult and triggering this may be for some readers, especially those who have experienced abuse, it is essential to get a detailed portrait of what we are dealing with in order to fully understand the issue. Often in media reports of abuse, details are left out for a variety of reasons. Perhaps they are considered too "intimate" or "risqué" for audiences. For example, after Chaim Walder, the popular haredi author, was discovered to have been abusing kids for decades, there were calls in the community to stop talking about it so as not to expose young audiences to that kind of "language." Reports of sexual abuse are sometimes described as "filth" — as if they are stories of adult porn inappropriate for children's ears, rather than descriptions of violent crime — in an effort to

---

[62] Brous, Sharon. 2019. "#WeToo: Discomposing our culture of toxic masculinity: The epidemic of sexual assault and harassment thrives on many layers of cowardice and indifference, all too abundant in our culture of complicity. Now we must attune our ears to the stories told not by those with external power, but those with inner strength." Yom Kippur, 5779, 2019, https://ikar-la.org/wp-content/uploads/YK-Brous-5779-WeToo.pdf.

keep the stories out of the news. Perhaps less cynically, journalists may want to protect the privacy of victims. Still, details are often hidden in order to protect the accused. Reporters often use watered-down language, such as "inappropriate sexual activity," or call rape "sex with a minor," a non sequitur since minors cannot legally consent.[63] These euphemisms end up leaving out the very painful details which would give the general public a better understanding of what "sexual abuse" means. The purpose, then, of this first section, is simply to report the stories, as they were told, in whatever detail the victims wished to share.

This method of opening the analysis with stories I learned from Israeli anthropologist Professor Tamar El-Or, author of several riveting books about religious cultures and who was also my doctoral advisor.[64] My methods follow Professor El-Or's teachings, with a bit of an adjustment. In her research, she had a small number of interviewees and dedicated several pages to each testimony. With over 80 interviews, I did not have that option. Therefore, I condensed and consolidated the texts and organized the narratives according to the profile of the abuser. In this chapter, the abusers are all rabbis, and the stories are further organized according to the type of position that the rabbi held: teacher, rabbinical school rabbi, pastor, camp rabbi, boss, scholar, and finally pulpit rabbi. This structure it reflects the way the abuser appeared in the eyes of the victim — where they stood, what surrounded them, and what power they had.

The Rabbi Teacher

Dozens of stories of sexual abuse in religious schools have emerged over the past decade. In 2021, for example, Israeli rabbi brothers Yitzhak and Moshe Tufik were indicted for sexually abusing students at their Be'er Yehuda yeshivah for boys in Jerusalem; however, the rabbinical court banned discussion of details because they were "too obscene" to be spoken

---

[63] Or as my editor, Jennifer Cappello, reminded me, "sex with an underage woman" is also not a thing. A "woman" is of-age and an "underage female" is a *child*. Jessica Valenti, "When you call a rape anything but rape, you are just making excuses for rapists", *The Guardian*, 24 April 2014,
https://www.theguardian.com/commentisfree/2014/apr/24/rape-game-of-thrones
[64] In her book, *Next Year I Will Know More*, about advanced religious education among religious Zionist women, she opens her analysis with a series of first-person accounts. From there she moves on to a more specific narrative and thematic analysis. Tamar El-Or, *Next Year I will Know More: Literacy and Identity among Young Orthodox Women in Israel.* (Wayne State University Press, 2002.)

out loud.[65] After ten students complained to the police, the rabbinical court advised the religious public not to send students to their yeshiva, but the perpetrators freely walked away.

Reports like this of rabbis and religious teachers who sexually abuse their students in Orthodox settings seem almost rampant and take place around the world. In Melbourne, Australia, Manny Waks exposed the abuse he experienced for years when he was a student at the Chabad yeshivah, and Dassi Ehrlich and her sisters spent years pursuing justice from the sexual abuse at the hands of headmistress Malka Leifer in the ultra-Orthodox Adass community. In the United Kingdom, Yehudis Fletcher testified to being sexually assaulted as a teen by the ultra-Orthodox son of a leading rabbi, Todros Grynhaus, who was then sentenced to 13 years in prison in May 2015.[66] In New York, Rabbi Yoel Malik, the head of a yeshivah in Brooklyn, was arrested in 2013 for taking boys from his school to local hotels and forcing sex acts on them.[67] The list goes on. One nonprofit organization created a "Wall of Shame" to list all the different rabbis who were accused (though it was deemed too controversial and is no longer in operation).

Despite some perceptions, the ultra-Orthodox is not the only community that harbors sexually predatorial rabbis. In 2019, Rabbi Jonathan Skolnick, a principal in SAR Academy in Riverdale, New York — one of the most liberal-leaning modern Orthodox day schools — was arrested by the FBI on charges of possessing and producing child pornography and coercing a 14-year-old boy to send him sexually explicit pictures.[68] Skolnick was reportedly very popular with students and was so manipulative in his methods that he was, according to the FBI, teaching students how to use the internet safely and protect themselves from online predators.[69] SAR reportedly was connected

---

[65] Stuart Winer, "Rabbi brothers suspected of sex abuse at their Jerusalem yeshiva. Rabbinical court rules students should no longer enroll in schools run by Yitzhak and Moshe Tufik, advises victims to file complaints with police". *Times of Israel*, 30 August 2021 https://www.timesofIsrael.com/rabbi-brothers-suspected-of-sex-abuse-at-their-jerusalem-yeshiva/

[66] Karen Glaser, Yehudis Fletcher: speaking out on sex and marriage: Yehudis Fletcher campaigns against ignorance and abuse in her Charedi community - after she courageously gave evidence against a man who assaulted her. *The Jewish Chronicle*, January 06, 2021 https://www.thejc.com/lifestyle/family/yehudis-fletcher-speaking-out-on-sex-and-marriage-1.510427

[67] Mosi Secret, "Brooklyn Rabbi Charged With Sexual Abuse of Boys," *New York Times*, Jan. 31, 2013, https://www.nytimes.com/2013/02/01/nyregion/brooklyn-rabbi-charged-with-sexual-abuse-of-boys.html

[68] Heather J. Smith & Michael Hinman, "Jonathan Skolnick SAR Academy associate principal arrested, fired," *Riverdale Press*, September 16, 2019 https://riverdalepress.com/stories/sar-academy-associate-principal-arrested-fired,70003

[69] Hannah Dreyfus, "Riverdale Again Hit With 'Shocking' Abuse Case. Child porn charges against an SAR principal like an 'earthquake,' parent says. *Jewish Week*, "September 17, 2019, https://jewishweek.timesofIsrael.com/riverdale-again-hit-with-shocking-abuse-case/

with five sexual abusers as staff or VIP speakers, including Skolnick and Rabbi Jonathan Rosenblatt, aka "the sauna rabbi," who would regularly take teenage boys naked to the sauna and is still serving the community in a pulpit role.[70] In fact, former SAR students complained about the school's history with protecting sexual offenders. Three lawsuits were filed against SAR in the Bronx County Supreme Court of New York State under the new Child Victims Act by former SAR students claiming that Stanley Rosenfeld, a former teacher and administrator at the school, sexually abused at least a dozen SAR students during his tenure there in the 1970s and 1980s. They also claim that leadership at the school knew about the abuse and failed to report it to civil authorities.[71]

Other New York Jewish schools have also faced accusations of harboring sexual abusers among their rabbinical teaching staff. Yeshiva University High School for Boys is being sued by 37 former students who reported that Rabbi Macy Gordon and Rabbi George Finkelstein molested them and sodomized them with objects like toothbrushes, and that the school knew and did nothing about it.[72] Similarly, the Yeshivah of Flatbush (my alma mater), is being sued by two former students who accused then-Assistant Principal Robert Paris of molesting them in his office.[73] The Hebrew Academy of Long Beach (HALB) is also facing lawsuits of the alleged sexual abuse of a first-grade student—today a 30-year-old—by their teacher Rabbi Yoseph Ungar. According to the complaint, in 2002, when the victim was in first grade, Ungar actively groomed the boy, included allowing the boy to stay in Ungar's classroom and read during recess, or giving him candy in the closet in exchange for sexual "favors." According to the lawsuit, Ungar

---

[70] Andy Blumenthal," SAR — Safe Haven For Sexual Abusers, Not For Kids," September 20, 2019, https://andyblumenthal.wordpress.com/2019/09/20/sar-safe-haven-for-sexual-abuse-not-for-kids/; Andy Newman and Sharon Otterman, "Debate Over the Rabbi and the Sauna," *New York Times*, May 29, 2015, https://www.nytimes.com/2015/05/31/nyregion/fresh-debate-over-whether-a-rabbi-acted-inappropriately.html

[71] Ben Sales, "SAR Academy Officials Knew of Abuse By Administrator Who Molested 12 Students." *Jewish Week*, October 6, 2018, https://jewishweek.timesofisrael.com/sar-academy-officials-knew-of-abuse-by-administrator-who-molested-12-students/

[72] Emily Davies, 'It is with shame, and it shouldn't be': Dozens sue Yeshiva University High School over alleged sexual abuse, *Washington Post*, August 23, 2019 https://www.washingtonpost.com/nation/2019/08/23/yeshiva-university-high-school-sexual-abuse-lawsuit/

[73] Ben Sales, 'We feel like we failed': How one Jewish school is processing the arrest of a teacher who preyed on children, *JTA*, Sept 19, 2019 https://www.jta.org/2019/09/19/united-states/we-feel-like-we-failed-how-one-jewish-school-is-processing-the-arrest-of-a-teacher-who-preyed-on-children; Amy Klein, A creepy abusive Jewish day school teacher? I'm not surprised. The sickening news that a New York principal was arrested for child porn brought me back to my own junior high experiences — and not in a good way. *Times of Israel Blogs*. Sept 26, 2019, https://blogs.timesofisrael.com/a-creepy-abusive-jewish-day-school-teacher-im-not-surprised/

"fondled Plaintiff's genitals over his clothes, had Plaintiff masturbate Ungar until Ungar ejaculated, had Plaintiff perform oral sex on Ungar until Ungar ejaculated, and kissed the top of Plaintiff's head each time after ejaculating."[74]

Many interviewees either experienced or witnessed abusive rabbis in school settings. Shlomit, an Orthodox Jewish educator in her forties, was witness to several cases of rabbis abusing her classmates and then peers from the time she was young. "A rabbi in my high school molested schoolmates, and he was simply removed from my all-girls school and placed in the boys' school," she explained. "He then went on to become my community rabbi and had sexually inappropriate relationships with congregants. Over a decade ago, he was removed from his post after a shul investigation."

According to interviewees, though, this is hardly limited to Orthodox schools. Abby, who was active in her Reform congregation, recalls:

> The rabbi who was the rabbi of our congregation when I was 11 or so years old, maybe 12, I don't remember exactly, used to sit in his office, with multiple children in a room, with his legs spread, and he wanted us to sit on his lap while we read Hebrew to him. Most children stopped going to Hebrew school because he was there. One time, he said, 'Let's go wash your hands and face' and he would touch me everywhere. After that I made my father come with me. After me, another girl reported that he rubbed her 'front tushy' at her lessons. Another time, he was overheard by the brother of this girl talking about grabbing at a boy, which is when they finally got rid of him.

Leanne, a psychologist and mother of three, was abused by more than one rabbinic figure during her life, all from the Conservative movement that she called home. The first time was when she was in eighth grade on a school retreat, and one of the teachers was "very touchy and grabby. I complained and nobody cared, and I spoke to a few other girls who experienced the same kinds of things, so we helped each other get through it, but it was a fairly traumatic set of experiences dealing with him."

Reut discovered a few years ago that her sixth-grade Hebrew teacher at her modern Orthodox day school "had abused boys in my grade, actually touched them and physically sexually abused them. He had abused boys in my grade and boys a year behind us and boys a year ahead of us." She found this out after the boys went to court and the issue became public. "I got in touch with the people who I have been in touch with for years who I found out were abused by him. We all wanted to show our support."

---

[74]Link to lawsuit affidavit:
https://iapps.courts.state.ny.us/nyscef/ViewDocument?docIndex=r3giqF2bXG97iB2QDmvh
sg==

Note that the rabbis in these stories are from different denominations, not just ultra-Orthodoxy. Also, victims were both boys and girls, and in at least one case the perpetrator was a woman.

The Rabbi Scholar

Many abusive rabbis are able to get away with their behavior because they are revered as scholars. Many rabbinic abusers receive promotions, podiums, and pulpits even when their abuse is known.

In April 2021, in one of the highest-profile revelations thus far about sexual abuse in the Reform movement, the public learned longtime president of the rabbinical school, Rabbi Sheldon Zimmerman, had been using his many powerful pulpits and platforms to groom and abuse women for years if not decades. Some leaders allegedly knew about these issues since 2000, when he was temporarily suspended for what was described at the time as "personal relationships." He had been having a so-called "relationship" with a woman publicly known as "Debbie" since 1970, when she was 15 years old and he was 30. Debbie told Gary Rosenblatt of the *Jewish Week* that Zimmerman became her rabbi and teacher the following year when he was appointed assistant rabbi at Central Synagogue, and he soon began to "relate to her in an inappropriate manner." When she was studying privately with Zimmerman, "he used Martin Buber's 'I and Thou' theology as a framework to explain or justify their intimate contact." Zimmerman also knew how to manipulate religious-spiritual language and ideas to control his victims sexually. HUC-JIR and other Reform institutions are now conducting internal investigations to determine the breadth of this abuse. Twenty years later, the movement is no longer calling this type of episode "personal relationships" but has acknowledged it as "predatory behavior."[75]

These stories demonstrate that women rabbis are also susceptible to abuse, as Rabbi Sharon Brous described, from people who are meant to be peers, teachers, supervisors, and gatekeepers to their careers. Indeed, among

---

[75] Gary Rosenblatt, "A Rabbi's Accuser Wanted Me to Tell Her Story. Here's Why It Took 20 Years. When the Reform movement suspended Sheldon Zimmerman in 2000, a woman wanted the details known but feared retribution". *The Jewish Week*, May 26, 2021, https://jewishweek.timesofisrael.com/a-rabbis-accuser-wanted-me-to-tell-her-story-heres-why-it-took-20-years/; Molly Boigon, "'This was no coverup': Inside the investigation of Rabbi Sheldon Zimmerman," *Forward*. May 17, 2021. https://forward.com/news/469213/sheldon-zimmerman-sexual-relations-rabbis-investigation/; Hannah Dreyfus, "Reform rabbinic giant disciplined for inappropriate relationships now accused of 'sexually predatory behavior," *Forward*, April 27, 2021, https://forward.com/news/468535/reform-cover-up-rabbi-sheldon-zimmerman-sexually-predatory-behavior/

the most startling stories of the abusive rabbi-teacher are from rabbinical school—even ones that consider themselves progressive or feminist and proudly advertise policies of inclusion of women—because of the layers of abusive power and authority in constructing what it means to be a rabbi.

Chloe, a rabbi herself, shared the following story:

> *While in rabbinical school, I was dealing with a semester-long sexual harassment issue from a rabbi-professor who made consistent sexual jokes, flirtations, and once had pornographic images up on his computer that were easily visible to more than just him. At the end of the semester – and what finally caused me to file a formal complaint – was when this guy, who was 50 years my senior, asked what it would take for me to date him. And as I tried to dodge the question, he persisted in asking. While the intention could have been joking, it made me feel intensely uncomfortable.*

Chloe found herself dressing differently and wearing "bulky clothing" so as "not to draw unwanted attention" from her harasser, effectively blaming herself and at the same time making herself less attractive and less noticeable. She discovered that this man was known to have been hitting on female students for thirty years. When a new head of school was hired—a younger woman—she filed a formal complaint. Her complaint was accepted, and as a result he was removed from teaching the core curriculum but not from the school. The head of the school helped her avoid taking any more classes with him. While Chloe was "heartened by the supportive response," she feels the situation is still bad, "especially because this man was widely known for such problematic behavior for decades."

Hannah also shared her story of abuse in rabbinical school:

> *I was a first-year rabbinic student in my first week of class, and I was invited to the apartment of an influential rabbi more than twice my age. Within moments of my arriving, he took his hand and put it on his crotch and said something like, 'See what you do to me.' It was more than 40 years ago, and I still feel ashamed that I let it happen, that it didn't occur to me that it was not just happening to me, and that I never told him how awful he made me feel years later when I could.*

Rabbinical school rabbis can use their position of authority and the victim's vulnerability—he was a senior rabbi, and she was a first-year rabbinical student—to manipulate and exploit their victims.

Many interviewees who are rabbis themselves shared multiple experiences. Daliah said, "I have been sexually harassed and sexually assaulted, attempted date rape, all the things the women experience in their lives." Abby also had a list, just from her life as a rabbi:

> While I was in rabbinical school and for many years after, I would get, 'You're my first female rabbi, can I have a kiss?' or 'I love being able to kiss a rabbi!' or 'I didn't know rabbis could be sexy or good looking,' and other inappropriate comments about women and sexuality. My second year of rabbinical school, a guy who was coming on to me and asking me about adultery or whatever asked if I could get a special dispensation so he could have sex with me. I used to make a joke, 'I spoke to God and God said it was okay if your wife agreed.' It was just pervasive. A guy I worked with, whenever I wanted to ask something controversial, would just say, 'You know you look so good today', like to shut me up. To stop me from talking. There are endless stories like that along the way.

For Abby, like Leanne, Erin, and others, the issues of abuse by a rabbi are not just annoying, painful, and traumatizing but are also obstacles on their path to personal, spiritual, and career fulfillment. This was exacerbated when they reported the cases of abuse and their institutions in turn failed remove the offender and make it a safe environment to continue her studies or training.

I happened to interview Abby very shortly after a famous rabbi had died—one who had abused her and many of her classmates in rabbinical school:

> When he died, people were writing, 'Such a wonderful man,' yada yada, and finally I wrote about how this was making me uncomfortable because he was an abuser and mean and tried to pick up women in class while he was married. He was inappropriate in so many ways. And to men, too. But he was a horrible, horrible man. And a Talmud scholar. And finally, when I wrote a post about this, about 10-15 other women started writing and adding their stories. Including the fact that he was finally censured by the college and relieved of most of his teaching duties because he had a student who brought him up on charges for, among other things, having pornography on his computer when he had her over at his apartment for an appointment with her, and also commenting on her body.

In rabbinical school, both the assailant and the victim are rabbis or would-be rabbis. And men can also be victims, as Daniel, who is also a rabbi, shared:

> As a counselor, as an activist against sexual violence, as a Jewish community leader, as a rabbi – and yes, as a man – I

never thought that I, too, would one day be sexually assaulted by a rabbi. But, as we say in Hebrew, hineni *— here I am. I offered a car ride to a rabbi who is the director of admissions at [my movement's] rabbinical college. He teaches about sex and spirituality, and I was looking forward to making his professional acquaintance. But he wanted sex with me, and he argued back after I declined his multiple sexual advances. Finally, he asked for a hug — I thought it was to say goodbye. The next thing I remember, I was being sexually assaulted by him.*

Our society is not particularly accustomed to hearing about grown men who are victims of sexual assault. But clearly this happens, even among rabbinical colleagues and peers, even among high-profile rabbis, even among people who are physically and emotionally strong and confident, even without any pretense of consent, even when they vocally resist. This is a very important testimony in that it breaks a lot of common stereotypes and assumptions about how sexual assault takes place and about what a victim looks like.

The take-away is this: A victim can be anyone. No matter how smart, strong, wise, or resistant a person is or what gender they are, they can still be assaulted.

Moreover, when predators have positions in rabbinical schools, they also gain authority, reverence, and ample access to potential victims who are reliant on their support and approval.

The phenomenon of sexual abuse in rabbinical institutions is apparently so rampant that today, some denominations are conducting internal investigations about sexual abuse in their rabbinical schools.[76] Today, Rabbi Mary Zamore, head of the Women's Rabbinic Network, helped survivors come forward with their stories. The Reform movement's seminary, rabbinical association, and synagogue network each hired different expert law firms to investigate allegations of cases of harassment and abuse.[77] HUC-JIR as the first to come out publicly with the results of an internal

---

[76] Dreyfus. "Reform rabbinic giant",
https://forward.com/news/468535/reform-cover-up-rabbi-sheldon-zimmerman-sexually-predatory-behavior/
[77] Asasf Shalev, "Reform movement probing itself over history of bungling sex abuse allegations. Denomination's seminary, rabbinical association and synagogue network each hire different law firms to investigate cases of harassment and abuse to better ensure accountability. *Times of Israel*, 12 August 2021, https://www.timesofisrael.com/reform-movement-probing-itself-over-history-of-bungling-sex-abuse-allegations/

investigation in November 2021, and since then, other institutions have followed.[78]

Stories like this beg the questions: *How long this has been going on in rabbinical schools? And how many rabbis are allowed to stay in their positions for years — decades — despite their patterns of abuse?*

Charley, a Jewish professional in her thirties, was raped by a rabbinical student while she was a sophomore in college, a man who later on became a revered young rabbi in a Jewish organization at her college and a staff member of a local Jewish community:

> *Our paths crossed in our youth group and a few other Jewish organizations. I was reintroduced to him [during my sophomore year] by mutual friends who were undergrads who had been on his staff. They idolized him. We were social and chatted on IM, and he had a girlfriend and he invited me to come have a drink during reading week. I went on a really full stomach because there had been a study break where we ate, and I only say that because I actually blacked out from 2-7 a.m., but I don't remember all the details even though there was a lot of blood, and I did a rape kit so I know what happened. I went over at around 10 p.m. and I had four drinks that I didn't watch him pouring me because I trusted him. It was four drinks over the course of four hours, and I had a high tolerance; I was drinking a lot my sophomore year of college and it would not have affected me to the point of blacking out. Not even if I'd had six drinks. It was really surprising to me that I woke up to his alarm clock in the morning. I had been fully dressed. I was wearing a turtleneck, short-sleeve sweater, and jeans that were button-up, not an easy outfit to take off. We had been talking, and there were in retrospect red flags that I thought were just open conversations about sexuality, where he said he liked to get so drunk that he blacked out and didn't remember what happened the next day, and I said, 'I absolutely don't feel that way and I really like sexuality and orgasms are really fun, I don't want to miss them,' and I was really straightforward about it and I remembered it the next day when I was like, 'Fuck, what just happened?' But he set up this scenario where he wanted one thing and I wanted something different, and he ignored me.*

[78] Grace E. Speights, Sharon P. Masling, Martha B. Stolley, Jocelyn R. Cuttino, Ira G. Rosenstein, *Report of Investigation into Allegations of Misconduct at Hebrew Union College-Jewish Institute of Religion*. Morgan Lewis. November 3, 2021, http://huc.edu/about/presidential-task-force-safe-and-respectful-environments/morgan-lewis-investigation-report

In Charley's story, the grooming process was quick, but the attack was severe. There are a few noteworthy elements to this story. Notice that the attacker was able to use his status to gain trust. He ticked many boxes of Jewish involvement and trustworthiness—he was involved in youth movements and was a rabbinical student. Also, this attacker, like many other rabbi attackers, was in a committed relationship at the time of the attack, which made the victim feel "safe." The victim also went into great detail about what she was wearing and how she feels about sex in order to explain or justify—to herself or to the listener—that this was in fact rape and not consensual sex. This is because the setting—friendly drinks, friendly socializing, a quiet night at home with friends and not a potential date—do not fit in to what most people normally think of as rape. That kind of intimacy is part of the process of clergy abuse, in which the abuser gains relaxed, easy access to the victim's everyday life, so it all looks "normal." But that sense of normalcy plays with the victim's mind so she has to remind herself what really happened and why she feels violated.

There is another troubling side to revelations about abuse in rabbinical schools. That is: What are students actually learning about what constitutes acceptable behavior? Does having a rabbinical school president who is a repeat sexual predator influence students' own ideas about cultural norms?

The Rabbi Pastor

Rabbis often play a dominant role in people's lives as a "pastor," or emotional-spiritual carer during times of crisis. Rabbi Professor Rachel Adler, in a 1993 article exploring sexual abuse in the rabbinate, wrote that the pastoral role is particularly murky, as it lacks rules, definitions, and boundaries:

> The boundaries between counselor and client are not as simple and distinct as they are in other types of counseling relationships. Pastoral counseling itself is often a gray area of clerical practice. The ambiguity of pastoral counseling distinguishes it from other treatment modalities. Formal mental health treatment takes place in an office designed for the purpose. Pastoral counseling may occur over coffee at a distraught congregant's kitchen tale, in a hospital lobby, in the woods at a camp. It is often initiated by a rabbi reaching out to a congregant who appears troubled. It may proceed without any formal contract, without requiring any fee, and frequently without any ground-rules about confidentiality, attendance, or termination. Neither are there the same social boundaries as

> *between other therapists and their clients. Counselees may see their rabbi-counselor at dinners and parties. They may be friends with the rabbi's spouse. They may serve on committees that negotiate with the rabbi... They may even vote on the board that reviews the rabbi's contract...*
>
> *One conclusion is inescapable: A setting where boundaries are entangled and counselor and counselee play multiple roles is not one in which deep psychotherapeutic work can ever be safely done.*[79]

Many interviewees confirmed that one of the most vulnerable circumstances for being abused by a rabbi was when they met privately with the rabbi who was acting in a pastoral role. These are often encounters when victims are emotionally fragile and seeking help, guidance, support, and trust. In 2018, for example, Rabbi Ezra Sheinberg—a kabbalist who was considered a rising star in Religious Zionist circles and had a massive following of people coming to him for everything from baby-naming to supernatural healing—was convicted of sexually molesting eight women who came to him for religious counseling. One of his victims, Michal Cohen, an Orthodox 30-year-old mother of two, came forward publicly with her story.

Michal met Sheinberg when she was 21, when her husband studied at Sheinberg's yeshivah Orot Ha'ari in Safed. "The first time he touched me was after a year of meetings with him, in which he started up with me gradually in an intense, emotionally manipulative way. Before the sexual abuse, there was serious emotional abuse." He preyed on her insecurities and vulnerabilities in a calculated way:

> *I thought there was something wrong with me, but everyone around me said he's such a great man. Because it was so gradual, I entered this fragile emotional state where my boundaries were blurred and I couldn't trust all the red lights that were flashing in my mind. As soon as I said 'no,' or dared to ask a question or challenge what he was doing, I heard things like, 'You are not holy enough.' 'You are full of impurities. Maybe I made a mistake trying to help you. I thought you were on a higher level.' With every sentence, I tightened up and believed that the problem was with me, that I'm not pure enough or holy enough for this sacred therapy.*

The rabbi-pastor played with Michal's mind in order to gain her absolute submission and obedience. He also apparently sought out women who were

---

[79] Rachel Adler, "A stumbling block before the blind: Sexual exploitation and pastoral counseling," *CCAR Journal: A Reform Jewish Quarterly*, Spring 1993, 13-54, pp 18-19

already vulnerable, such as those who were orphaned or divorced, or struggling with medical or emotional issues like infertility. "He exploited my issues with infertility," Michal explained. "I was scared of doctors, and I was sure he was going to save me from all this. What he was doing to me felt all wrong, but then I saw Knesset members coming to see him, so I thought to myself, something must be wrong with me."[80]

Although Sheinberg used some tactics that are specific to Orthodox culture—language of "impurity" and "holiness," for example—the dynamic is not exclusive to Orthodox rabbis. As spiritual and pastoral carers, rabbis encounter people in their most vulnerable places, and some know exactly how to manipulate the situation using cultural codes. (I will return to this in the chapter on grooming.)

Many cases described revolve around women seeking rabbis for counseling or guidance. Kayla, for example, was molested by the Conservative rabbi whom she consulted about her plans to get married. Her parents made her see him because they did not approve of her fiancé and was hoping the rabbi would change her mind:

> We met in his office often. [My fiancé] met with him a few times. One day he called and invited me to use his wife's ticket to Mostly Mozart, after which we would talk about going forward. I thought things were promising, that he would be able to bring my parents to accept me and my beloved. We met at the Philharmonic, but soon I sensed that something was different, wrong. He took my hand. He looked at me with nostrils flaring. I sat through the concert thinking, 'I must be imagining this.' But when we got into his car, he tried to kiss me. I pushed him away. He said, 'We'll go back to my apartment to talk. My wife is there.' I assumed that meant it would be safe, so I went. When we got there, I greeted his wife in the kitchen. The rabbi directed me into their living room. I sat on the couch. He came in and stood in front of me, unzipped his pants, took out his penis and wanted me to fellate him. I bolted out of there immediately. For the following weeks he stalked me, calling me at home and at work, trying to convince me that we could be even closer and resolve the situation with my family.

Kayla's abuser took advantage of her emotional vulnerability and his position as the rabbinic carer who was going to fix her life, repair the relationship with her parents, and enable her to get married. Although some

---

[80] Nina Fox, "Early release for sex offender: 'Ezra Sheinberg continues to abuse us, and he will hurt other women'." *Ynet* [Hebrew] 20 August, 2021, https://www.ynet.co.il/judaism/article/bkuoaufet (Translation by Elana Sztokman)

might interpret this as a story in which nothing "happened" in the sense that she ran out before she engaged in an unwanted sex act, the long-term trauma remained. Indeed, attempted rapes can be as traumatizing as rapes, according to some researchers.[81] Not only did this damage her relationship with her parents for years to come and end her engagement—since he was meant to be the catalyst for reconciliation—but it also destroyed her connection to Judaism and religious authority.

Marion was also targeted during a vulnerable time in her life, and she was raped by the rabbi who was supposed to be counseling her in her grief:

> When my mother's mother passed away, we went to a service at her temple. The young rabbi there was very dynamic, very popular, gaining a huge reputation. I didn't know all that. When we were filing out of the service, the rabbi was standing at the door, and I stopped to thank him for his words. He engaged me in conversation and took a great interest in me and my grief. I mean that in the worst way. I met with him in his chambers, and I noticed he wasn't listening. He interrupted me to say that he couldn't listen because I was so beautiful, and he could feel himself being increasingly attracted to me. I was in a state of grief. I was very close to my grandmother. My grandfather had died two years previously, so now my protectors were gone. I was very susceptible to the attention. I needed kindness and was confused. The rabbi took great advantage of me... He [coerced me into having sex with him] in his chambers behind a couch on the floor. I found out later that there were scores of women who had had similar experiences with him.

Here, too, the rabbi was able to gain access because her was supposed to be her carer offering emotional and spiritual support and guidance. What she got instead was rape by a rabbi.

Similarly, Yittel, an ultra-Orthodox young woman from a tightly knit Hassidic community, was sexually abused and repeatedly raped by a rabbi when she was 21, depressed, and in need of counseling. "He used the counseling relationship as well as my vulnerability and naïveté to groom me into a sexual relationship," she said. The rapist used Yittel's dependency on his pastoral care, as well as her innocence and fragility, to prey on her.

---

[81] Becker, J. V, et al. (1982). The effects of sexual assault on rape and attempted rape victims. *Victimology*, 7(1-4), 106–113.

The Camp Rabbi

Meyer Seewald, founder of the now defunct organization Jewish Community Watch, which advocated for victims of sexual assault in the Jewish community, has said that the event that changed his life happened at a Chabad summer camp in 2000 when he was a boy. He reported that Rabbi Mendel Levine touched him in his "private area." He also said that Levine "used to walk around the mikveh with my bunkmates with an erection. Many people claimed it was not molestation, but I can tell you for a fact that in that moment it destroyed my life in many ways until this day." When this story emerged in 2018, another victim came forward. "I heard Seewald's story and I was shocked. It was exactly what had happened to me," he said. "In Michigan, 2001, Levine took me aside, undressed me, and began to rub lotion on my private parts. I wondered what in the world was going on. I'm not looking for revenge, but it did give me issues."[82]

One of the most well-known predatory camp rabbis—who was also a celebrity in youth movements, as well as a school principal and teacher—was Rabbi Baruch Lanner. He was a youth group leader at NCSY for decades and a day school principal in Deal, New Jersey, who was convicted in 2002 of sexually assaulting two girls who were his students. The *Jewish Week* and the Orthodox Union separately collected testimonies from dozens of women who were his campers, members of his youth group, and students. The testimonies described decades of abuse, including "Rabbi Lanner's alleged kissing and fondling scores of teenage girls in the '70s and '80s, repeatedly kicking boys in the groin, and reports of taking a knife to a young man in 1987, and propositioning girls in 1997 at the yeshivah high school where he was principal for 15 years."[83] Judy Klitsner, a leading Jerusalem educator, was 16 years old when Lanner assaulted her. According to her testimony, he tried to caress and kiss her one evening during a Shabbaton in New Jersey. When she rebuffed him, "he began to strangle me with all his strength, and it was only when he saw that I was losing consciousness that he threw me down and walked away."[84]

---

[82] JTA, "Dutch Jews investigate Brooklyn rabbi on molestation charges. Action taken after local newspaper publishes two accusations against Mendel Levine dating back to when he worked as a youth counselor," *JTA*, 8 January 2018, https://www.timesofisrael.com/dutch-jews-investigate-brooklyn-rabbi-on-molestation-charges/

[83] Jacobs, Andrew, "Orthodox Group Details Accusations That New Jersey Rabbi Abused Teenagers," *The New York Times*, December 27, 2000, https://www.nytimes.com/2000/12/27/nyregion/orthodox-group-details-accusations-that-new-jersey-rabbi-abused-teenagers.html

[84] Gary Rosenblatt, "Stolen Innocence: Rabbi Baruch Lanner, the charismatic magnet of NCSY, was revered in the Orthodox Union youth group, despite longtime reports of abuse of teens," *The Jewish Week*, June 23, 2000,

Leanne, who was incessantly harassed and stalked by a rabbi in camp as I described in the Introduction—let's call him Rabbi A—experienced abuse from several different rabbis over the course of her life. Before that experience, Leanne went to a different Jewish summer camp, working as a camp counselor, where a *different* camp rabbi, the director—let's call him Rabbi B—also tried to molest her:

> *The camp director, a rabbi probably in his early 30s, was a little strange, and a couple of things happened that set the stage for a weird relationship with him. Like, during intercession, he came up to me out of the blue, touched my face, and said, 'I love your cheekbones.' This made me freak out. Then I just noticed his behavior, a lot of strange things. Like, we lived in tents in that camp, and I got sick, so he gave me a bed in a room in one of the buildings to rest in. So, I'm in there lying in bed, and there is a knock on the door, and I start to get up but then I hear a key going. And I get out of bed really quickly, and it's him, and he's coming in, and he's coming to check on me. But it was just weird that he didn't wait for me to answer the door. And he starts touching me, touching my hair, and touching my face. It was all weird. And then, he left.*

Again, some might read this story as one in which "nothing happened but his touching was inappropriate and an attempt at assault. Leanne's story also sheds light on the often subtle and confusing process of grooming that can almost seem normal—inviting for a private talk, buying concert tickets, complimenting someone's face, visiting a sick camper. (I elaborate on grooming in Chapter 4.)

The Rabbi Boss

Rabbis also have positions in which they are organizational supervisors, which can create other forms of leverage for abusers. One interviewee, for example, recounted that when she was at a professional conference with the rabbi she worked for, "he climbed into my bed and asked for sex. How he got in, I don't know."

For Cindy, a Jewish professional for whom the synagogue was a workplace, the sexual abuse by her supervising rabbi began with emotional grooming and eventually became physical:

---

https://www.bjpa.org/content/upload/bjpa/stol/Stolen%20Innocence%20-%20Gary%20Rosenblatt%20-%20Jewish%20Week%20-%20Sexual%20Abuse.pdf

I saw the senior rabbi as a powerful authority figure. He had been in the rabbinate for about 25 years and by all measures was successful in building a vibrant congregation. He was almost 25 years older than me. When he first started making suggestive comments, I did not know what to do. When I avoided or denied his advances he would sulk or ignore me.

Eventually, she gave in to his demands, despite how tormenting the situation was for her:

At work I pretended to be a great professional, in his office I pretended to be a girlfriend, at home I pretended to be a wife although I was miserably shackled with shame and guilt. With my precious children I felt inauthentic and pathetic for compromising my values out of what was an irrational fear that I could never work anywhere else unless I had a stellar recommendation from this man who was manipulating and confusing me.

Cindy's account is devastating because she clearly did not want to have sexual contact with the rabbi, yet ended up in a position of being constructed as his "girlfriend." It was clearly coerced sexual abuse, not an "affair" or consensual — yet even Cindy had a difficult time reminding herself of that. She was vulnerable to his pressures in many ways—financially, professionally, and emotionally. He used all of that to get his way with her over a long period of time, an experience that left her bereft, traumatized, confused, and suicidal.

The Pulpit Rabbi

The most prominent position for a rabbi in Jewish culture is arguably the pulpit. It is a visible, high-status, authority-laden, and powerful position, and full of opportunities to mold ideas, groom, and be alone with potential victims.

One of the most famous pulpit rabbis to be accused of sexual abuse is the late Shlomo Carlebach. According to a 1998 exposé in Lilith magazine, Carlebach— who came from a Hasidic background— abandoned the synagogue partition and the Orthodox rules against touch, and instead promoted a hugging culture, which many of his followers quite literally embraced with him. Under that pretense of liberal, loving modernity, he sexually abused women for some forty years. According to the Lilith report:

When he asked her to show him around the camp, Rachel says she felt 'what an honor [it was] to be alone with this great man.' They walked and talked of philosophy and Israel, of stars and poems, and she remembers being 'just enchanted.' He asked her for a hug, and when she agreed, 'he wouldn't let go. I thought the hug was over and I tried to squirm out of it. He started to rub and rock against me.' So unsuspecting was she, she says, 'that at first I thought, "was this some sort of davening?"' She says she tried to push him away, while he 'was dry humping me. Until he came.' And though she does not recall the words that he spoke, she remembers his communicating to her that it was something special in her that had caused this to happen. 'It felt cheap, but he had said thank you.' The next day, he didn't even acknowledge her presence.[85]

Many interviewees described sexual abuse with rabbis, ranging from sexual commentary, to solicitation, to touching, to more. In one of Leanne's experiences of abuse with a rabbi when she was 17 years old, the rabbi of her synagogue — I'll call him Rabbi C — asked to meet her alone after services in the private library:

He was very inappropriate, not physically, but it was a strange conversation, and he started talking about his dilemma. I remember this — it was over 30 years ago but I still remember — he said he had a congregant once whose wife was a paraplegic and couldn't have sexual relations with him, and he wanted to know if it was okay to have an affair. And I was like, 'I'm 17 and you're in your forties. Why are you telling me this?' It was very strange, and I was feeling very uncomfortable. And then he said, 'I'm really glad that we're friends.' I was going to college and my parents were moving away and he said I'm always welcome in his house if I ever need a place to stay. And at that point it was clear.

The rabbi tested all kinds of boundaries — engaging in sexual conversations, calling them "friends," inviting her over when her parents were away, and more. Leanne told me that when she finally told her parents, they quickly put an end to it. The problem was that by distancing the rabbi, they also distanced her from synagogue. She was an avid Torah reader who suddenly stopped receiving assignments from the rabbi. That was retribution for reporting him to her parents, though she did not have a

---

[85] Sarah Blustain, "Rabbi Shlomo Carlebach's Shadow Side", *Lilith*, March 9, 1998 https://lilith.org/articles/rabbi-shlomo-carlebachs-shadow-side/

framework for understanding that. "It left me feeling like, what am I doing wrong here?"

In some cases, junior rabbis are at the mercy of senior rabbis. As one interviewee, who is herself a rabbi, described:

> *Earlier in my career, the senior rabbi I worked with made comments about my physique many times. He commented about how different clothing fitted me. After I gave birth to my first baby, he asked me to twirl around so he could see how my body was bouncing back from birth. I also witnessed him make comments about the physical appearances of congregants — both complimentary and critical.*

She also shared that sexual abuse by the synagogue rabbi happens not only her synagogue but in another one nearby. "A close friend of mine works at another area synagogue. She says that the male rabbi stares and comments at the body of the secretary. He is smitten with her and her physical looks, and he makes it known. The entire office finds this very awkward." In other words, pulpit rabbis have many platforms for interactions that can potentially be abusive.

Women cantors are also quite vulnerable to abuse by their senior rabbis. Cantor Penny Myers reported that she suffered four tumultuous years of sexual harassment, hostility, and inappropriate behavior by the synagogue's then-rabbi Jonathan Freirich. In her formal complaint, she described verbal harassment, such as his describing her as the "beautiful blond cantor" from the *bima* and referring to "Fifty Shades of Cantor."[86]

Zelda, a young academic living in a small town, was actively and aggressively groomed by the rabbi of a congregation she was looking to join. The rabbi ended up abusing her for nearly a year:

> *I was on OK Cupid and get a profile of a 45-year-old guy who lives in my town. I was 29, a student at the local university, so I was surprised that a man that age was writing an eloquent message that opened with, 'I see you are looking for new friends, I think we can really hit it off.' We did this for a few days, and then he said, 'Are you ready to find out who I am?' And when he sent me his link to his rabbi blog, when I found out that he's rabbi, I was so excited, I was in my lab and I stood up in my chair, and I was so excited and feeling lucky and blessed... And he was just so interested in me every way.*

---

[86] Rahel Musleah, "Navigating the Fallout From Sexual Harassment Claims in Synagogues," *Hadassah Magazine*, March 2021, https://www.hadassahmagazine.org/2021/03/02/navigating-fallout-sexual-harassment-claims-synagogues/

> *Wants to know what I'm up to all the time. I was totally*
> *mesmerized. I thought he was a demigod. I thought he was just*
> *so amazing because I always had so much respect for rabbis. In*
> *fact, when he came up that first night [when he raped me the*
> *first time], he asked to come up for hot tea because it was cold,*
> *I actually thought my parents would be ashamed of me if I*
> *don't give the rabbi a cup of tea after a cold walk in the snow –*
> *I should take care of him! Everything in my head was, 'I need*
> *to take care of this man,' from the moment he told me he's a*
> *rabbi, it just flipped a switch in my head that this man needs*
> *to be revered, taken care of, highly respected and regarded. It's*
> *the way I was raised. So, I couldn't comprehend that he didn't*
> *deserve it, because in my mind he inherently deserved that kind*
> *of respect and trust because he's a rabbi.*

Zelda, like Cindy, was lured into a long-term sexual relationship with a much older, married pulpit rabbi whom she felt she could not say "no" to. They were both young and vulnerable in many ways and trapped by their own desires to be good people, to be good Jews. (The detailed grooming tactics of Zelda's abuser begs for more analysis, and I will return to this in the chapter on grooming.) Zelda's description of her respect for the rabbi is crucial in understanding the dynamics of clergy abuse. The very title "rabbi" gives the abuser power and sway over the victims, such that Zelda felt like she could not deny him, and from the first moment he asked to come into her house, she had to oblige.

In Zelda's case, the abuse went on for a long time and was severe:

> *I've never initiated sex with him. He had sex with me like forty*
> *times, always at his demand. A number of times his wife was*
> *part of it because he liked that. He was increasingly weird*
> *sexually and started to ask me to go onto Craigslist with him*
> *and find male strangers who he could do a 'ganging up' on me,*
> *even though I told him I wasn't into it, and I didn't want to.*
> *Like, I thought we're having a friendship, now we're having a*
> *relationship, and now I'm your prostitute. I don't understand.*

This is rape. Even though our cultures often dismiss encounters like this with words like "affair" or "seduction", it is important to name this as rape. There was a power imbalance, the rabbi demanded sex that she did not want, and she unwillingly obliged:

> *That night was rape and still something I am coming to terms*
> *with. The way he did it – invite himself up for tea after inviting*
> *himself over for a walk to discuss a deceased congregant, then*
> *shove his tongue in my mouth, strip me, and give me scary*

looks so that I complied… penetrate without even asking… it was bad, and something I tried to deal with in a million and one ways before I could accept it. It's so hard to live with that level of feeling of powerlessness, that he was able to do that to me.

Like Cindy, Zelda struggled to call this what it was — rape — because it did not look like the kind of experience our culture often associates with rape. It was not a stranger in a dark alleyway forcing himself on her. This was her *rabbi*. He was a charming acquaintance whom she was educated to fully believe and trust who used emotional and verbal coercion instead of brute force. According to the International Coalition Against Sexual Abuse, an estimated 70 precent of rapes take place by an acquaintance in private[87]. This discrepancy between how we are often taught to think about rape and how rape actually happens more often than not can be particularly tormenting for victims. (I expand on these dynamics in a later chapter on impacts.)

Although the stories here are diverse — different settings, different ages of the assailant and the victim, different years, different cities, different denominations — what the stories have in common is the rabbi's use of his status, power, authority, and assumed reverence to get his way with his victims, despite the victim's lack of consent, and the victim's near inability to assert their own power in the situation. The very name *Rabbi* gives the abuser a lot of power.

Takeaways about rabbis who abuse

From a simple reading of accounts of rabbinical sexual abuse, certain aspects of sexual abuse in the Jewish community become clear:

- **Rabbis have a lot of power.** Whether they work in synagogues, schools, camps, universities, organizations, or elsewhere, rabbis — especially male rabbis, who are often viewed as more legitimate, powerful, or worthy than female rabbis[88] — command a certain reverence just with the title, as well as assumptions of virtue and the ability to demand obedience.

---

[87] ICASA, *Acquaintance Rape*, https://icasa.org/uploads/documents/Stats-and-Facts/aquaintancerape.pdf

[88] See, for example, Debra Nussbaum Cohen, "Male Reform Rabbis Earn More than Women", *Forward*, June 24, 2012 https://forward.com/life/158338/male-reform-rabbis-earn-more-than-women/; Julie Zauzmer, "'I not only envisioned it. I fought for it': The first female rabbi isn't done yet," *Washington Post*, May 24, 2016 https://www.washingtonpost.com/news/acts-of-faith/wp/2016/05/24/i-not-only-envisioned-it-i-fought-for-it-the-first-female-rabbi-isnt-done-yet/

- **Rabbis have other sources of power besides the pulpit.** When a rabbi is also an organizational boss or a professor, the aura of power around them multiplies, as the settings give rabbis added layers of authority and reverence.
- **Jews are socialized to listen to their rabbi.** Jews are taught to implicitly trust rabbis and believe what they say, even if it goes against what their inner minds know to be true.
- **Pastoral care can be dangerous.** When rabbis meet privately one-on-one with people, or visit them in their homes, without any supervision or accountability, this can be an ideal setting for a predator.
- **Sometimes abuse happens openly.** Observers may not trust the victims or may simply believe that the rabbi has authority and knows what he is doing.
- **Rabbis have many grooming tactics at their disposal.** They can use spiritual and religious language to lure their victims and get them to do their bidding. Sometimes this process takes a long time, and with some abusers, it can be very calculated. (Recall the rabbi who was luring victims online and was also the one at their school in charge of teaching them about the dangers of online stalkers.)
- **Rabbis also have retaliatory weapons.** They can stop calling on people to lead services or remove lay responsibilities — subtle actions that can deprive victims of things that are important to them.
- **Some victims have experiences of sexual abuse from more than one rabbi.** This is not uncommon; child sex abuse survivors are five times more likely to be the victims of sexual assault later in life.[89] This raises a lot of questions about how predators choose their prey and what abusive rabbis see as a vulnerability in potential victims.
- **These stories raise many questions.** Why do rabbis engage in sexual abuse? Where did they learn that this was normal? And how has it been happening for so long without being stopped?

---

[89] Nina Papalia and James Ogloff, "Child sex abuse survivors are five times more likely to be the victims of sexual assault later in life," *Jakarta Post*, July 29, 2020. https://www.thejakartapost.com/life2020/07/29/child-sex-abuse-survivors-are-five-times-more-likely-to-be-the-victims-of-sexual-assault-later-in-life.html .

Chapter 2: Teachers, Mentors, and Bosses

In this chapter

> **Sexual harassment at work**
> > The Boss
> > The Co-worker
> > The *Macher*
> > And more
> > Is this a Jewish thing?
> **Academia**
> > Mentors
> > Academic supervisors
> > Entire departmental cultures
> > The celebrity
> > Is this a Jewish thing?
> **Takeaways about teachers, bosses, and mentors**

Sexual abuse is, for the most part, about power.[90] The abusers use tactics, methods, and platforms for manipulation in order to sexually impose themselves on their victims, to take power away from their victims, and to make themselves omnipotent controllers of their victims.

One of the first impressions from the immense volume of stories about rabbis who abuse is that the rabbinate offers potential abusers many potent tools to get what they want from their prey. But that is only the beginning.

---

[90] Michal Buchhandler-Raphael, "Sexual Abuse of Power," *University of Florida Journal of Law and Public Policy*, Vol. 21, p. 77, Feb 15, 2010; Lyn Yonac, "Sexual Assault Is About Power. How the #MeToo campaign is restoring power to victims," *Psychology Today*, November 14, 2017. Some people argue that sexual abuse is only about power. See the classic *Against our Will: Men, Women and Rape* by Susan Brownmiller (Ballantine Books 1993, originally printed in 1973) for the origins of this thesis. While these ideas about power are foundational in understanding sexual abuse, I also think that it is wrong to completely dismiss the sexual element of the dynamic. It is not just about power but particularly about the use of *sex* as a form of power and control. Without the sexual element, it would look like something else.

Understanding this begs the question about other locations of power in the Jewish world and the dynamics of abuse in those places as well.

The interviews revealed accounts of abuse in many Jewish settings where perpetrators drew on the tools available to them as a function of their positions, title, and/or money. These include the Jewish workplace, Jewish academia, volunteer boards, and fundraising. Some of these tools of power overlap in several ways: rabbis can be bosses and academics; board members are usually donors; and organizational leaders and senior faculty often network in ways that provide support and protection for one another.

The following two chapters parse out these roles. This chapter examines workplaces — Jewish nonprofits, communal organizations, foundations, and colleges. The next chapter looks at donors, board members, and other superstars.

Sexual harassment at work

Colette Avital, one of the highest-achieving women in Israel's Labor Party, spent much of her political career being the only woman in the room. During the 1980s and 1990s, she was often in the orbit of then-Prime Minister Shimon Peres, and rumors constantly circulated that she was having an affair with him in order to "get ahead" in the men's club. However, in 2021, at the age of 82 and following an illustrious career as Knesset Member and diplomat, she finally revealed that not only were those rumors false, but actually she was sexually assaulted by Peres back then. She told *Ha'aretz* that she was invited to have breakfast with Peres at the hotel where he was staying. When she arrived, however, she was told they would meet in his room for "security reasons." When she entered the hotel room, she said, Peres was "waiting in pajamas" and shoved her toward the bed, but she resisted and left. This story, which sounds very similar to tactics used by convicted rapist Harvey Weinstein to lure his victims by inviting them to his hotel room when he was naked or almost naked,[91] was reportedly just the beginning. She said that in 1984 he assaulted her again, this time more forcefully, in a hotel room in Paris. Meeting him for what she thought was a discussion about potential jobs she could hold in his administration, she said, "he pressed me against the door suddenly and tried to kiss me." Avital said she pushed him away and left the room, "and my legs were shaking when I

---

[91] "Harvey Weinstein scandal: Who has accused him of what?" *BBC*, 10 January 2019 https://www.bbc.com/news/entertainment-arts-41580010

left there. It repulsed me." Although she eventually worked closely with him for years after the incident, she avoided seeing him.[92]

Professional organizations can be dangerous places for women. Indeed, workplaces have been one of the major focal points of #MeToo revelations. In situations in which women want to work, get paid, be creative, and advance in their careers, their lives and futures often depend on the people in charge of them, who are often men, and who ultimately hold all the power and leverage.

It is hardly surprising, then, that one key location of sexual harassment and abuse is in Jewish organizational life. These are places where many gender dynamics coincide and can create traps for potential victims, especially women. In 2019, the Association of Jewish Studies produced a special journal issue called "The Patriarchy," in which I created a two-page infographic pulling together dozens of bits of data about gender inequality in Jewish organizational life. This included facts such as: Only two Jewish Federations were then headed by women; Jewish women executives still make around 60% of what their male counterparts make; women rabbis make on average $43,000 less than male rabbis; men are seven times more likely to have their writings published; and more.[93]

Interestingly, one critique of this infographic that I received was that it was focused so much on Jewish *organizational* patriarchy that it overlooked Jewish *religious* patriarchy. That is, I did not include formal Jewish tradition, law, and customs that feed into the patriarchy, such as the long-standing exclusion of women from the rabbinate, from prayer quorums, and from the courtroom (some of which has been eliminated but only in the past 50 years or less, and not everywhere).

I thought about that critique as I analyzed this research. I wondered about the relationship between rabbinic-centered cultures and communal-centric cultures. Although I chose to initially focus on the outpouring of stories about rabbis, the fact is that stories about sexual abuse in organizational life

---

[92] Gidi Weitz, "Why She Didn't Report That Shimon Peres Sexually Assaulted Her: Colette Avital Tells All. Colette Avital is one of the female pioneers in Israel's foreign service and had a long political career. But she's been tied to one of the ugliest rumors ever spread in Israel\ She's Peres' lover, it was said; that's how she rose up the ladder. Nothing could be further from the truth." *Haaretz*, October 14, 2021, https://www.haaretz.com/Israel-news/.premium.HIGHLIGHT.MAGAZINE-why-she-didn-t-report-that-peres-sexually-assaulted-her-colette-avital-tells-all-1.10295027; TOI Staff, "Ex-Labor MK says Shimon Peres sexually assaulted her in the 1980s. Colette Avital, a former senior diplomat, alleges the late statesman forcibly kissed her during a work meeting while he was PM, assaulted her at Paris hotel several years earlier," *Times of Israel*, 7 October 2021 https://www.timesofIsrael.com/ex-labor-mk-says-shimon-peres-sexually-assaulted-her-in-the-1980s/
[93] Elana Maryles Sztokman, "Dynamics of the Patriarchy in Jewish Communal Life: An Infographic," *AJS Perspectives* Spring 2019, http://perspectives.ajsnet.org/patriarchy-issue/dynamics-of-the-patriarchy-in-jewish-communal-life-an-infographic/

also dominate the testimonies. By the "workplace," I mean not only the literal space for work but work-related settings such as encounters between work colleagues, board members, or organizational volunteers, and off-site meetings, in the staff lounge, at a conference, or at the coffee shop after work. It can even be texting on the weekend. (A later chapter is dedicated exclusively to what is called "gender abuse," that is, patriarchal practices that are not overtly sexual but which contribute to the cultural atmosphere that enables sexual abuse to pervade.)

In the Jewish workplace, then, is an important setting, perhaps as important as synagogues, where different aspects of Jewish culture intersect in ways that at times enable abuse. Here, I share testimonies about sexual abuse that takes place in Jewish workplaces.[94]

The Boss

Many interviewees described ubiquitous sexual commentary from their bosses. These include reports of a "boss who made several references in front of me regarding both his personal sex life and mine"; another boss who would make sexually inappropriate jokes; a supervisor "asking me about my dating life at a staff retreat and pressuring me to look at my tinder profile is extremely common," according to Sarah Chandler a trainer with the organization Ta'amod, who were guided by sexual harassment expert and consultant Fran Sepler. Other bosses did things such as greet employees with "Hi, sexy!" or ask, "Are you pregnant?" or "inappropriate and in-depth personal questions about my dating life," or "make comments that are demeaning and focus on physical attributes rather than relevant work," or "endless body commentary, about my dress or my heels or my overall hotness." Dana, for example, recalled a high-powered director of one of the largest Jewish organizations that she worked with who was known for hitting on women in his organization—during the nearly thirty years when he was its head. "I'm surprised that it's still quiet," she said. "Everyone was always talking about him and his girls who do everything around the office and then go off and do other things. He only hired girls, and only particular types of girls—innocent yeshivah types. There were always stories. I'm surprised that nothing has come out."

Sometimes the abuse involved not just commentary but also unwanted touch. One woman described a boss who "would get too close in my personal space and in others' space, especially while drinking." Another respondent reported that her supervisor "was always standing far too close to me and touching my shoulder/arm/back when it was completely unnecessary. I never felt scared, but certainly uncomfortable." In another

---

[94] These testimonies also include those collected via a research survey conducted by the organization *B'Kavod* that similarly sought to understand dynamics of abuse. These testimonies were included with permission.

account, a respondent described unwanted commentary and touch from a boss who thought he could get away with it because he is gay and supports feminist causes:

> The head boss put his head on my lap in a car on the way to a fundraising meeting after pretending to have a lascivious phone call with another Jewish organizational leader about having three-way sex in a mocking way. He also, at a different time, made a weird joke about going to the bathroom with me. He also had a habit of telling me that he loved me at the end of meetings or intense work conversations. I felt obliged at times to respond emotionally in kind even though it made me uncomfortable. Said expressions and incidences were supposedly platonic and normal because my boss/chair was openly gay and professed to be an ally for women leaders, myself included.

Another interviewee reported that these kinds of comments also sometimes included unwanted touch:

> He would regularly refer to me as his 'favorite' in front of other staff and wink at me while offering me the opportunity to work on an exciting project. I received these invitations far more frequently than other staff though they were as deserving, if not more so, than I. He also touched me often — not explicitly sexual touching, but lots of arm, shoulder, and leg squeezes. I always moved away but never actually asked him to stop.[95]

Sometimes these experiences went beyond touch to actual sexual propositions. One interviewee recalled, "I was regularly propositioned by my supervisor, a man in his early thirties. According to an exposé in the *Jewish Week*, veteran Jewish communal professional Mindy Berkowitz, who spent years working for Len Robinson, said that "he had a reputation for harassing cute blondes. Among the women in the office, everyone knew: You can never be alone with Len. No one wanted to be left alone in the building with him." Shelley Feingold, who also worked for Robinson, said she witnessed him engage in "concerning, inappropriate, and illegal conduct with female minors." Rachel Dawn Davis, who also worked for him when she was a teenager, said that he would hit on two women on staff, both of whom were married. Another woman said that when she went to him for a job interview, he attacked her. She ran to the bathroom and cried until

---

[95] Just to be clear: This kind of action – someone in power is inappropriately touching someone who reports to them – is legally classified as sexual harassment whether or not the person formally or informally refuses or asks them to stop. For more information on this, see Sepler & Associates' *Respect in the Workplace and Leading for Respect*, https://www.linkedin.com/pulse/safe-respectful-workplaces-virtual-edition-fran-sepler /

someone came to get her. Eleven women eventually came forward saying that he sexually assaulted them.[96] The transition from comments to unwanted touch to propositions to attacks seems like an easy slide on the scale of abuse.

These experiences can evolve into something bigger. Anne, who is originally from New York and spent different periods of her adult life in Israel and New York, described a secondhand account of sexual exploitation that was institutionally backed. It took place at her first job in the Jewish world in 1976 at one of the major Jewish organizations in New York, around the time when a new Executive Director was hired:

> *A few weeks after it was announced that [this man] was going to be the new Executive Director, every member of the Board of Directors, every member of the Board of Governors, every editor of every Jewish paper, every Director of every major Jewish organization, including every member of the Conference of Presidents, received a very long and agonizing letter, signed by a woman named Miriam detailing the 'affair' that she was having with her boss. The crux of it was, 'I've kept your secret, you're an Orthodox rabbi, you're head of the synagogue council, but now you're asking me to do something I can't, which is to destroy the child I'm carrying, our child.' It went on like this. A very well-written letter.*

> *What happened with the letter was telling. [He] came to the board and said, 'I'm willing to resign.' All of the women on the Board of Governors and on the staff said, 'Accept his resignation.' All the men – some very powerful men and Jewish celebrities – said, 'No, no, no. Let's make a deal.' The deal would be that he would come on as Executive Director, stay married for a few months, go to the Bahamas or wherever to quietly have a divorce... and it would all be handled quietly.*

> *That story about Miriam – it went to literally every newspaper editor and did not get published. Didn't go anywhere. They all looked at this as an affair instead of as sexual exploitation – even though he was her married boss. They cast her as a ranting, crazy ex-girlfriend, and they tossed her aside. She was*

---

[96] Hannah Dreyfus, "New Allegations Against Robinson Include A Minor. Joanna says she was sexually abused by Len Robinson when she was 17," *Jewish Week*. April 11, 2019 , https://jewishweek.timesofIsrael.com/new-allegations-against-robinson-include-a-minor/ ; Hannah Dreyfus, "After N.J. Camp Exec Sacked, More Women Alleging Sexual Harassment Come Forward. She had always thought of him as a family friend — until he invited her to spend the night with him alone at his private residence in the Poconos," *Jewish Week*, April 18, 2018, https://njjewishnews.timesofIsrael.com/after-n-j-camp-exec-sacked-last-week-more-women-alleging-sexual-harassment-come-forward/

*fired, never worked again in any Jewish organization, and he
went on to have an illustrious career.*

Anne describes an entire culture in which women were used, sexualized, demeaned, mocked, excluded—and also, in the same building, treated for the most part as disposable workers with no voice, power, or decent pay. These dynamics all play into each other and scaffold each other. Miriam was sexually used and impregnated by her boss who then tossed her aside, got her fired, and gained for himself the support of high-profile, powerful men in the community. In this kind of imbalanced power structure, their "affair" could only ever be described as exploitative.

It is also worth noting that women bosses can also be abusive—and, in fact, some of the stories here about unwanted commentary come from female bosses, such as the boss who greeted her employees with "Hi, sexy!" I will add here my own experience with a female board leader at a Jewish organization where I was employed. On one of my first days at work, she invited me for lunch where she spent the entire hour quizzing me about my sex life. She justified it because she works as a sex therapist, but the conversation was entirely uninvited and uncomfortable for me. She later sent me a vibrator as a gift—also uninvited and quite embarrassing. One of my staffers told me that before I came onto that job, she had once walked into the office and announced, "You ALL need vibrators." She thought it was cute and funny, but it felt invasive, completely inappropriate, and crossing sexual boundaries. Had a man done it, the implication would have been obvious.

The Co-Worker

Interestingly, some interviewees also describe sexual abuse by co-workers. This is significant because co-workers ought to be equals, where one does not necessarily have power and sway over the other. But for sexual predators, there are always tools for manipulation and control. One respondent, for example, described how a co-worker "sequentially asked out every female employee under the age of 35 in the office. He had affairs with at least two women that I know of. He asked me out. I said no. He continued to flirt with me and pursue me and I continued to say no. Physically, he grabbed me into a full body hug or body press and wouldn't let go when I tried to squirm away. He was much larger and stronger than I." Unyielding persistence and the unwillingness to accept rejection are sometimes their own form of power.

There are many verbal and physical ways for predators to take over office culture and make it unsafe, even if technically they are not higher up in the organizational ladder, and even if their targets are strong-minded, intelligent adult women who are theoretically equals. One woman described a litany of events from the past five years, all involving older co-workers: "comments about my looks," or "If only I were younger," or calling her "eye candy."

"My response to these comments has been to deflect and ignore, but they have made me feel uncomfortable and have contributed to a sense of unease at work." Some of these comments were from women, which made her just as uncomfortable.

Another interviewee, Risha, described abuse when she was 15 years old and worked at a kosher bakery. Her abuser was a worker who had a small but significant sliver of power: He controlled the freezer. "All the women knew to avoid working alone with one particular man—he'd dragged one woman into the walk-in freezer and tried to rape her. With me, he settled with vulgar comments and coming up behind me while I was on dish duty and telling me how sexy I was." Predators may not actually have official power, but they can use their words and behaviors to take over all kinds of spaces.

Some experiences with co-workers are described as particularly intrusive. As one woman described:

> I went out for dinner and drinks with co-workers. One mentioned that he had friends staying in his apartment and asked if he could stay at mine. I said 'Yes,' and made up the couch for him. In the middle of the night, he climbed into my bed and attempted to initiate contact. I kicked him out of the apartment but had to work with him for the rest of the year.

She added, "This is the first time I've ever told that story."

These experiences can also turn violent. Yael described being assaulted by a work colleague at a Jewish professional conference.

> It was a big event, and there was another person who was staying at the same hotel as me. We were talking late one evening about work-related things, and I was going to my room, and he was going into his, and he ended up pulling me into his hotel room and closing the door. Then he tried to kiss me. I said, 'Don't touch me, I'm religious!' And then he said, 'I'm not asking for sex, I'm just asking for a kiss, it's not a big deal'. And I was like, 'Absolutely not! Don't you dare touch me!' I was screaming, 'I'm shomer negiya.' [I keep prohibitions against touch.] It was a situation of a few minutes, but it was really terrifying. And then I got out. I don't think in the moment I thought he would rape me, but I definitely thought he would force himself on me. He was very adamant. But I was terrified that he might do something that would make me terribly uncomfortable.

Even people who think that they are "safe"—whether because it is a professional setting or because they are visibly "religious"—are not necessarily. In my doctoral research, I found that Orthodox rabbis bombard teenage girls with the message that *tzniut* [body-cover] and being shomer negiya act as "protections" from being sexualized — more specifically, from secular culture that sexualizes women. Apparently, according to Yael, the message gets through to the girls, and can be a shock when they discover that it isn't true. Neither tzniut, nor negiya, nor yichud effectively protect women or girls from being preyed upon.

The *Macher*

Sometimes the abuser is not the top boss but just a supervisor who has a tiny bit of power that he likes to wield — a *"macher."* When Dina, for example, worked for an Israeli organization that she described as a "very uncomfortable and sometimes hostile environment," she experienced one particularly disturbing incident when a major layoff was about to happen. "One colleague, who happened to be a supervisor, told me he was a manager in on the discussions of who should be laid off, and he was calling to tell me that he could guarantee that if I slept with him, I would not be laid off." This is classic "quid pro quo" sexual harassment by a guy who pretended to have power over her. She rejected his offer, kept the job, and later found out that he did *not* have the power over her job that he'd claimed. His whole story was fabricated just to get her to sleep with him. "He was the creepiest guy in the office, who harassed me the whole time."

A person who is the position of "helping" can find power over his victim, as Blima recounted:

> We had a close friend of the family who was like an uncle to me. When I graduated from college, he was helping me find a job and invited me to do some work at the synagogue where he was employed as an administrator. When we were alone in his office one day, he grabbed me up in a 'hug and kiss' and then tried to stick his tongue in my mouth. I was shocked and let him for a few seconds before I pulled away. We never talked about it, and I never told my family, including my father, who was his best friend. I just stopped working with him.

This predator was able to use several platforms of power — he was helping her find a job, he worked for the synagogue, and he was also a friend of the family. Those are many points of power. No wonder his victim never told anyone about what happened, not until this research. This is a dynamic I will return to in the later chapter on disclosure.

And more

There are many other ways that abuse happens in professional or organizational settings. Eliana, for example, who is a community social worker, recalled that when she was still in training, "I did a home visit to my friend's grandfather. He asked me to have wine with him, which I declined. He then pulled me toward him and pushed his tongue in my mouth. I made a joke about it and quickly left." In another incident, Nancy needed to get some papers notarized and found a local Jewish professional in her community:

> *I'm in the guy's office, I show him the papers, explain what I need, and he comes over to point at something, and all of a sudden, he has pushed me backward and stuck his tongue in my mouth. Now what do I do? Do I jump up and run out without the damn papers? I was, like, paralyzed. What I wanted to do was to throw him out the window. What I did instead is, I waited until he signed the papers. Then I took the papers and I left, and I'm thinking to myself, 'Can I smear shit on the windows in his office? Can I try to find out where he lives, and…' You know, I spent a week or two doing that. Plotting revenge. I never did anything. But it was extremely disgusting and disturbing.*

Dawn, an engineer with a managerial position in an Israeli hi-tech company, reported, "This kind of thing happens all the time. The hug that goes on too long. The handshake that goes on too long. The double entendres. It exists. All over."

Is this a Jewish thing?

Certainly, workplace sexual abuse is not unique to the Jewish world. One interviewee, Dina, said she experienced sexual harassment in many places. "My first job as an intern in North Carolina, I had a supervisor who made my life a living hell. I was 19 and he was 50, and I didn't report it, but the general manager found out about it, and they actually fired him. But it's just so pervasive in our culture, no matter what our culture is. It's totally acceptable for men to behave badly and for women to accept it." Another interviewee, Daliah, said that her first of many experiences of sexual harassment in the workplace was when she was a 19-year-old college student working part-time at a paper company. "The regional manager slid his hand across my butt while I was wiping down a shelf, and it was the worst experience. It was horrible. I reported it, and we both ended up being punished. We both had to do a class in sexual harassment." The victim was punished because of what the *abuser* did to *her*.

This is arguably everywhere. Abby, also a communal professional, said that when Clarence Thomas was nominated and Anita Hill described the verbal sexual harassment that she experienced from him, she was in a room full of working mothers and "they *all* said they had comments made like that. They said they didn't know a single woman professional who didn't have that. And the support staff probably had it worse." The lower women were in the hierarchy, the more susceptible they were to abuse.

Perhaps Jewish communal organizations are no better or worse than the rest of the Western organizational world. Or perhaps there are hazy connections between Jewish cultures and broader Western patriarchal cultures. This story from Barbara makes a compelling case for these connections:

> I worked at an art museum as a curator during the late 1970s and 1980s, starting in my twenties. The director, who was an outspoken anti-Semite, repeatedly treated me as a kind of call girl to be assigned to his various trustees, all much older men, some of whom were Jewish. Following the director's prompting, the men surprised me in Europe, while on research trips, at museum opening parties, etc. I did not cooperate. Following that experience, a powerful, much-older Jewish male curator insisted that I come out to New Jersey from New York City and meet with him by his swimming pool to 'discuss' the essay that I was supposed to write about a living male artist whom we both knew. I offered to meet him in the city or speak by phone but that was not what he wanted from me. The curator dropped me from the project when I refused to meet by his swimming pool, where I would have been stranded and vulnerable.

There is something particularly Jewish in this story. A Jewish professional in a senior role used the Jewish "connection" to pretend to "rescue" her from the abuse she was experiencing with non-Jewish men, by manipulating Jewish "codes" like "anti-Semitism" as a pretense for intimate connection. He was actually no different from the other men in expecting her to be his "call girl." But he had an extra "in" with her, his own tool for breaking down her resistance. This story is an illustration of the many vulnerabilities of Jewish women in work settings — anti-Semitism, abuse, the non-Jewish abusive boss, and the Jewish *landsman* who wants special privileges.

In many ways, Jewish organizations seem to be just like non-Jewish organizations in terms of the prevalence of abuse, though there is currently no hard data on that issue. But Jewish predators may prey on particular vulnerabilities, such as fear of anti-Semitism, or a sense of communal allegiance. Moreover, the Jewish world is not insulated from wider problems of abuse. We are not always the pious, virtuous, community of "mensches" that we like to present ourselves to be. Along with the good, communal organizational life *also* has cultures that support dynamics of sexual abuse.

Academia

The Jewish academic world is possibly one of the few areas of Jewish life in which #MeToo has had something of an impact. I am referring in particular to the very swift and public downfall of sociologist Steven M. Cohen, one of the top Jewish sociologists influencing communal policies, whose decades of sexually harassing junior researchers came to an end when Dr. Keren McGinity came forward with her account of the abuse, and then other victims followed suit. Cohen, she wrote (only revealing his identity later), "used his seniority to lure me to dinner with the promise of professional guidance. I suggested we go someplace nearby the venue and invite other people to join us. He vetoed both of those ideas." She was expecting to talk about her career, but he had no intention of doing that:

> He took me to a candlelit Italian restaurant that was entirely unsuitable for an ostensibly professional meeting. He peppered me with personal questions about my love life. He reached across the table and took my hand in his. I could not get out of that restaurant and back to the conference hotel fast enough. But despite my obvious discomfort, he persisted in accompanying me into the elevator and up to my floor. I should have insisted on parting ways in the hotel lobby. But he is a leader in his field and I was afraid to offend him.

> I firmly said 'good night,' told him that he did not have to walk me back to my room, and turned to walk away when he suddenly wrapped his arms around me, pressed his body against mine, and forcefully kissed my neck in a way that only lovers should. I broke free and ran to my room, reeling from what had just happened. I felt violated and betrayed. Adding to my wound, he texted me the next day as if he had not done anything wrong. I continue to feel uncomfortable when I see him at professional events.[97]

After McGinity shared her experience, several other women shared similar experiences about Cohen with reporter Hannah Dreyfus of the *Jewish Week*, who had broken the story. Tara Bognar described her own experience with Cohen when she was 28 years old and beginning her first professional job as his program assistant. Cohen already had a reputation for being "handsy, in that awkward, creepy uncle way," and she was told by his

---

[97] Keren R. McGinity, "American Jewry's #MeToo Problem: A First-Person Encounter," *The Jewish Week.* June 21, 2018,
https://jewishweek.timesofIsrael.com/american-jewrys-metoo-problem-a-first-person-encounter/

colleague that "He's been that way since graduate school," dismissing her experience. Still, Bognar told the *Jewish Week* that Cohen began to "push the limits. In staff meetings, he would place his hand on her knee, shoulder, or back, and keep it there throughout the entire meeting. He would also ask her intimate questions about her love life—questions he would 'never ask' a male colleague, she believed."[98]

As a result of five women coming forward, Cohen lost several of his high-profile jobs, although a year later he was still being invited as a guest lecturer to prestigious panels led by his friends and colleagues. It is also worth pointing out that until that point, Cohen was a member of the Committee on Ethics in Jewish Leadership, an ad hoc committee created in 2016 to respond to issues such as sexual abuse in the community. After his public downfall, his name was removed from that list as well. Had McGinity not started this public process, Cohen may still be in a position not only to sexually harass other academics, but also, alarmingly, hold a position responsible for monitoring abuse in the community.

Mentors

McGinity's story once again illustrates the seriousness of an event in which "nothing happened," as it's blatant in her testimony that Cohen didn't do "nothing". This account also illustrates the power of the professional mentor in helping to build careers, especially in academia, and the pitfalls involved when the mentor is a sexual predator. Women do not grasp what they are walking into when they seek out the help of someone with a predilection for sexual abuse—and how it can stop a career in its tracks.

Rena described an "uncomfortable and awkward" meeting with a potential mentor:

> We went out for a mentoring lunch, and I was trying to figure out what my options were. I was post-PhD, and I was in NY, and he said some really inappropriate things, asking inappropriate questions. When it was time to leave, he offered me all kind of help and gave me this really tight hug and I walked away and said, 'That was a really weird interaction.' At some point we were talking about the job search, and he made some comment that 'finding a job is like relationships and sometimes the sex is good but the relationship isn't, and sometimes the relationship is good but the sex isn't, and you have to find the sex elsewhere.' And I just had this moment, like, 'What just happened in this conversation?' That was a

---

[98] Hannah Dreyfus , "Women academics cite long pattern of sexual improprieties at the hands of Steven M. Cohen, who has expressed 'remorse' for his actions." *The Jewish Week*. July 19, 2018 https://jewishweek.timesofisrael.com/harassment-allegations-mount-against-leading-jewish-sociologist/

weird thing to say in a conversation about academic jobs. And the whole thing made me really uncomfortable. Later on, I was with friends in the New York nonprofit world and they said, 'He's creepy. Stay away from him.' He gave me the creeps and I didn't have any interest in working with him. And I put it aside and I didn't pursue it and I didn't have any more interest in working with someone like that.

For years, Rena did not think of this story as "sexual harassment." After all, by some standards "nothing happened." She wasn't raped or even groped. She wasn't fired from a job. She was not threatened or stalked. She "just" had a professional meeting in which her would-be mentor used sex metaphors and hugged her tightly. That is how she characterized it—despite the fact that it impacted her career. She stayed out of his orbit, which limited her professional choices. It was only after she read McGinity's account that she started to reflect on it and talk to people about it, including McGinity. "I also had a creepy experience, but it didn't go that far," she told her. "And then we had a lot of conversations about it, and then I had a lot of conversations with other people about it, about why did I say that nothing happened, there was nothing to report, it didn't cross a line, whatever that invisible line was. But it got me really thinking about this concept of gatekeeping." The "gatekeeping" is the power to make or break careers and financial lives. People like Cohen have had power and sway over the professional lives of their victims, even when it looks like "nothing happened

Helen's career was also stymied by her abusive gatekeeper. She had been studying for a master's degree in Middle Eastern Studies in the 1982. Although not a Jewish university, the department was extremely Jewish- and Israel-dominated, and many students like her planned on using their studies in order to pursue a life and work in Israel. She shared with me from her diary, prefacing it with the caveat, "there are things I don't remember. Even the most graphic things I didn't write. Like I was embarrassed in front of my own diaries. But the details I remember." Here is what she recalled:

At first, I really liked him. He was a fascinating lecturer – and I thought he was becoming my mentor. In the first diary entry that mentions him – in some Government of the Middle East class, he gave a stern lecture. He came from Israel, and I used that to excuse him at first. It's cultural differences, I told myself. But now that I'm living in Israel, I realize it's not an excuse.

Then he started this thing. I handed in a paper and he called me into his office and he told me it was really bad, and I started crying. Then he held my hand and gave me a tissue and he started building me up, and he said, 'I can help you and get an

A paper out of it,' and he said he would help me through the paper. I thought he would offer to mentor me. And I needed that.

So, I started spending time in his office. And he's asking me all kinds of questions about my background, and chatting me up, and I left his office feeling better, like he's taking an interest in me, how nice. And in the diary, it goes from, 'How nice that he's my friend,' and 'I feel so much more comfortable,' to, 'Wait a minute – is he trying something on me? I don't know what's going on. What have I gotten myself into?' Then it became, 'I want to kill all these grabby men who are trying to grab my body.' And all that. I wrote an entry that I spoke to other classmates and they all have complaints about this professor.

At some point, he started getting more touchy-feely, like, he would come around to my side of the desk. I was spending hours in his office. I was typing a paper on his machine – he actually had me type letters for him, which was also kind of weird. When I think of that now, I think, 'That's what a professor is supposed to get me to do?! Secretarial tasks?!' But the two most blatant things that I remember – besides 'there are things you can do that will get you an A' – once he came around to my side and put his hand on my thigh. I thought, he's from a different culture… then one time he grabbed my breast, like, hand right on the boob! Another time, I'm sitting in a chair and he stands behind me, pressed against me and I could feel his erection on my back. I froze completely. I didn't want these advances but I also didn't want to make him angry, and I didn't want him to stop the mentoring. At some point he also started to withhold my grade. He also started saying weird things to me…

He grabbed my breast, and his erection on my back – those are the things that I didn't write down, but those are the memories that are etched in my memory. Until that moment, I was able to fool myself that maybe he doesn't have bad intentions. Also, I thought, maybe I'm leading him on. Maybe I'm giving him mixed signals. Even though, you know, he was old enough to be my father.

Helen was abused by someone who had a lot of power over her life at a moment of transition when she was vulnerable. He used her, demeaned her, and manipulated her grades—but he was also supposed to be a teacher and a mentor, and his office was a potentially important gateway to getting her advanced degree and planning her future. Instead, he turned her into a secretary and a sex toy, and left her without the academic support that she needed and deserved.

In some cases, the perception that "nothing happened constitutes a major anchor keeping these practices in place. Shayna Sragovicz published an account of a mentorship-turned-sexual-abuse when she was a 17-year-old participant in a Jewish leadership program. She reported struggling with the unexpected emotional invasiveness of the program atmosphere, particularly around was meant to be a mentor-mentee relationship with a professor. She alleged that the relationship escalated and intensified, and that emotional boundaries were crossed:

> For the next several months, from August 2017 to the end of December 2017, Jon and I emailed each other and called on the phone for hours at a time. The official definition of our relationship was 'friend-mentorship' but as time went on, I would call him my mentor and he would call me his friend. Around the High Holidays in September, he texted me via SMS, and we continued to correspond over WhatsApp along with our regular emails and phone calls.

> I was unable to reintegrate into my home environment. I withdrew from every person who I thought would judge me, including two of my siblings and my parents. I went through the motions, but I was completely disengaged. I would go to sleep at 6 p.m. because he probably was not going to email me that day and would wake up uncontrollably every morning at 4 a.m. because I had once received an email from him at that time. I had no control over my body. I vividly remember a conversation expressing my concerns where he responded with, 'If you want to pull out, that's your prerogative, but I'm in this.' I did not even understand what 'this' was. Any time I was distressed, it was because there was something wrong with me that I had to change in order to be right for him. [99]

Had she not been 17 years old and he a 48-year-old married professor being paid to mentor her, this description might describe what could be called an emotional affair. However, in her account, she was a minor, she could not consent, and she was led to believe that this was what normal mentorship looked like.

There is an additional layer to this story that elucidates the power of the academic mentor or adviser who is also an abuser. The mentor, a professor of Jewish education, had published an academic essay just a year earlier in which he argued that the "erotic relationship" between teacher and student

---

[99] Shayna Sragovicz, "Tell Everyone," *Medium*, Oct 19, https://medium.com/@shayna99/tell-everyone-38e313990062

is "inevitable" — though if there is anything defensible in his stance, he claimed that it should not be "acted upon." His paper implies that if there is no *physical* contact, it does not constitute sexual abuse.[100] But that is deeply flawed thinking that enables predators and their supporters to defend actions of non-contact sexual abuse. And as we have seen in so many testimonies, it does not take physical contact to cross that boundary. Significant damage can be inflicted on victims with no touch involved at all.

Academic supervisors

Like mentors, academic supervisors hold power and authority to control or impact the careers of their underlings, which makes them vulnerable to abuse. Julie, a researcher who specializes in Jewish policy, also encountered abuse by a colleague who was supposed to be helping her academic career:

> *I was finishing my PhD and trying to figure out how to position myself professionally and intellectually. I scheduled a series of networking meetings with colleagues and thought leaders in my field. A colleague I had only met once or twice took the time for a long conversation that was helpful and encouraging, full of praise for my work and my political bravery, but then veered sideways into sexual innuendo and offhand comments about extramarital affairs, went back to professional brainstorming and possible jobs and projects, and ended with a hug that was too close and too long for someone I barely knew.*

> *I was grateful for his help but uncomfortable. I knew that if I described our meeting, many people would have told me that I was misinterpreting ordinary behavior. Later, when I mentioned to friends that I had met with him, they confirmed my discomfort, telling me that he had a reputation for being 'creepy' to women, and for verbally bullying female colleagues in public forums. I never really followed up on our conversation, and I didn't pursue the possible collaboration he had mentioned, though it seemed exciting and might have opened professional doors.*

Notice how victims often have to convince themselves that boundaries were crossed — despite their own justified discomfort — because it looks almost "normal" and "nothing happened." Yet, that discomfort can become a block to what should have been career advancement. Similarly, another respondent shared that she was "propositioned by a married man who had

---

[100] Levisohn, Jon A. "Eros and (Religious) Education." (2017) http://hillelofficeofinnovation.org/sites/default/files/ooi_salons_eros_and_religious_educat ion_jon_a_1.pdf

supervised me in an internship while I was in my graduate studies. This one was particularly saddening as I had considered him to be a mentor." She was not only subjected to abuse but also lost a potentially valuable gatekeeper to her next career stage.

Trying to navigate a career in academia while this is the predominant culture means getting past all kinds of unbearable roadblocks. Tali, for example, shared an experience of being incessantly harassed by a supervisor in her science lab in a Jewish university setting:

> I was a post-doc in graduate school working with this pre-tenure professor who is not Jewish, and he's a superstar. The plan was for me to be the lab manager. It's a tenure-track position called a Research Fellow, and the idea would be that I would work for a few months as a post-doc and then transition to that managerial position. My relationship with my boss was that he told me what to do and I tried to please him. He was very exacting. He worked till midnight, his wife would travel nine months a year, and he would work 12 hours a day. All that mattered was work.

> I told my boss that I was getting divorced and needed a day to move apartments. I used to be religious, and I stopped covering my hair immediately. He said, 'Oh, you look beautiful. It's because I can see your hair.' And then over the following few months, he got weirder and more demanding. We were sitting once looking at a scientific paper, and he once said to me, 'Is it just me, or does this graph look like breasts?' Another time, the other woman in our group was doing a presentation on a method with an abbreviation, SAXS, and she calls it 'sax' in her Russian accent, and he starts laughing, 'You said sex, haha,' and it was really weird.

> He asked me to go running with him. At the time, I would run almost every day, and he said, 'I want to go running with you,' even though at the time he wasn't even a runner — I was running half marathons and he couldn't do two kilometers. He started asking me to take him grocery shopping during the middle of the workday. He would say that his wife was out of town. I would try to run away and get out of it and get him to leave me alone, and he insisted that I had to take him grocery shopping once a week. And then he asked me what I was doing for the weekend. He would ask me what's happening with my divorce. He asked to come over so that I wouldn't be alone. He was really creeping me out.

So I at some point, I blocked him on Facebook because I didn't want him to see pictures of me and my family. I avoided him. I didn't want to see him in the hallway. I didn't want him to ask me to go out with him. I didn't want him to make me go grocery shopping instead of doing my work. Then he said he noticed that I'm not his friend anymore and how I blocked him or avoid him, and he said that if we couldn't be friends, then we would have to end our 'collaboration,' and that freaked me out because I'm going to get fired because I blocked him on Facebook?

Tali was being stalked and sexually harassed by her boss, who was also using her as his personal assistant instead of as the science researcher she is. She was working less than she wanted to be and was forced to block out parts of her professional world. In the end, after filing HR complaints and going through formal processes, she was offered a job not in her field with a significant pay cut and no room for advancement. As a result of all this, she eventually left and started her own company, leaving academia altogether.

Entire departmental cultures

A situation that can be even more difficult to navigate is when an entire academic department colludes in these cultural norms. Vivian, a veteran researcher, explained that "Sexual harassment and unwanted sexual advances were events we women lived with, like bad weather. During the years when I was young and vulnerable, if a woman was raped, the first questions asked were: 'What was she wearing?' And 'Did she sleep around?'" Her own experiences with harassment took place across the halls of her academic department, where she had to survive:

Fending off first my director of research and later my doctoral advisor were as integral to surviving graduate school as completing courses, passing exams, and writing my dissertation. Had I gotten a grade in managing unwanted male attention, I suppose it would have been B-. I knew that the most important aspect of saying 'no' was saving the man's pride. Yet my refusals were too often exasperated, even haughty, rather than graceful, at the same time as I can still feel the sting of humiliation that an unwanted advance could bring.

By the time I got my doctorate, I was known as a 'troublemaker'. I had also made a fuss on two occasions when male professors incorporated my research without attribution into their own publications. At the end of my three-hour dissertation defense, the five male professors shook my hand, which meant that I'd earned my degree. But they ignored protocol and did not invite me for the celebratory doctoral drink.

Vivian's story is not about just one perpetrator but an entire organization that comprises sexual abusers. It was scaffolded with other forms of abuse — e.g., not attributing her work, excluding her from meetings, microaggressions aimed at weakening and excluding the victim professionally, and not even bothering to acknowledge her greatest achievement. She was up against an entire wall of sexual abuse — an aspect of sexual abuse that is known as gender abuse. Again, when the abuser is a person who holds powerful sway in the victim's career — or a whole department where sexual abuse is the norm — the victim is left with few pathways to get to where she aspires to be, where she deserves to be.

The celebrity

Part of the power of academic mentors and supervisors is that they are often perceived as celebrities or superstars, especially in the Jewish world. Like rabbis, academic stars and celebrities can hold a lot of communal sway, and as such have a lot of leverage with their victims. This is worth noting in terms of where power lies in the community culture. Author Ari Shavit, for example, who is not an academic but a writer and high-priced speaker frequently sponsored by Jewish organizations especially on college campuses, fully admitted that the accusations of sexual abuse leveled against him were true. He lost his official job at *Ha'aretz* but continued to be an invited speaker, well-paid, and regularly cited for his so-called expertise.[101] Also, even though his actual writing ignores women's scholarship and perspectives, and he sexualizes women's bodies throughout his books, he continues to be celebrated for his ideas.

Similarly, Jeremy Gerber, a Conservative rabbi who was censured by his movement for sexually abusing a congregant, was invited to participate in a popular sex podcast, and even kept his job, despite his abuse.[102]

Another popular Jewish rabbi and author who is making a Netflix series was described by an interviewee as perpetually abusive to women. In the many years she worked with him, she reports that, "He made sexist jokes, he mocked women's bodies, he shamed women — even pregnant women — and was verbally abusive to the women on staff. Everyone knows this about him. It's very frustrating."

The layers of this problem are completely intertwined. As veteran Jewish professional Clare Hedwat wrote, "Chauvinism has distorted those we

---

[101] Jenny Singer, "Ari Shavit: Go away and never come back." *Forward.* July 5, 2018, https://forward.com/opinion/404824/ari-shavit-go-away-and-dont-come-back/
[102] Arno Rosenfeld, "How a rabbi accused of sexual misconduct can stay in his pulpit," *Forward*, Feb 11, 2022, https://forward.com/news/482269/rabbi-suspension-sexual-misconduct-gerber-conservative-rabbincal-assembly/

choose to laud, those we're able to hear, the thinking we're exposed to, and the ideas that shape our community."[103]

Is this a Jewish thing?

Despite the plethora of testimonies collected here, it is hard to know how deep-rooted sexual abuse is in the Jewish academic world. Anecdotally, it feels massive. But that is not solid evidence. Again, we have no quantitative data about this. The fact that no communal resources have been invested in that kind of comprehensive study also speaks volumes.

What we do know from this research is that this pattern of abuse in academia, where sexual harassment and career-controlling abuse are intertwined, clearly takes place in Jewish settings and non-Jewish settings, with both Jewish and non-Jewish abusers. One interviewee told a story about the senior professor in her department at CUNY who "grabbed women's asses in the elevator." Everyone knew about him, she said, and just avoided being on the elevator with him. Another interviewee told a story about a man who would expose himself to women in the library stacks at Columbia University—and when she mentioned it at a department meeting, one of the men said, "I wish a woman would expose herself to me in the stacks," to which everyone else around the table laughed. Another interviewee described how her doctoral supervisor invited her to his house for dinner, where he tried to hit on her in front of her young son.

These stories are certainly not limited to Jewish institutions or even to Jewish perpetrators. Nevertheless, when they are part of Jewish institutional or communal life, they become part of the communal culture. Again, it seems like while we cannot say for sure if Jewish academia is distinct from larger cultures, we can say for sure that it does not seem to be *better*.

Takeaways about teachers, bosses, and mentors

- **Sexual abuse has been going on in Jewish organizations for a while.** Jewish organizational life has a troubling history with sexual abuse, at least since the 1970s, with few signs of improvement.
- **There is a spectrum of abuse.** Sexual abuse at the workplace can be commentary, solicitation, unwanted touch, or even attempted rape. It could even take place over text message, email, or phone.
- **Abuse sometimes hides as "an affair."** What may at first glance look like an "affair" may in fact be abuse—such as if there is an uneven

---

[103] Clare Hedwat, "The Jewish World's #MeToo Crisis is Much Deeper than Ari Shavit and Steven Cohen," *E-Jewish Philanthropy*, August 3, 2018 https://ejewishphilanthropy.com/the-jewish-worlds-metoo-crisis-is-much-deeper-than-ari-shavit-and-steven-cohen/

power hierarchy that precludes real consent or if one person is a minor, which also eliminates the possibility of consent.

- **Power can take many forms.** Sexual abuse is powerful when it is carried out by a boss, but colleagues and co-workers can also perpetuate abusive behaviors using tools at their disposal for gaining power.
- **Power can multiply itself.** There are many overlaps of power available to predators in the Jewish world—a rabbi can also be a boss, a mentor, and/or a Jewish "celebrity." These structures give predators a lot of leverage over their prey.
- **Sometimes it's an entire department.** A lack of transparent mechanisms for reporting and addressing leads to continued abuse. When entire departments, boards, or organizations are infused with cultural norms that allow abuse, it can be a difficult if not impossible trap to navigate.
- **There is a lot of unseen damage to victims.** When abusers are also gatekeepers to women's career advancement—such as academic supervisors, or mentors—the long-term damage can be significant, though in some ways invisible.
- **How does the Jewish community compare? Not well.** While it is not entirely clear how the Jewish community compares to the world, it seems unlikely from the copious testimonies that the Jewish world is *better* on this issue than the rest of the world. There are also some specific Jewish dynamics that offer predators tools, such as using Jewish language and nuances to gain trust.
- **Quantitative data is missing.** The fact that we have no hard data about the prevalence of sexual abuse in the community is a gaping hole in our understanding—and very telling about communal priorities.

Chapter 3: Donors and Other Superstars

One of the industries in which sexual abuse seems to be rampant—and generally far from the headlines—is fundraising. A 2018 study conducted by the Harris Poll on behalf of the AFP Foundation for Philanthropy and the Chronicle of Philanthropy found that half of all female fundraisers experience sexual harassment either as victims or witnesses. The overwhelming majority of harassers are donors. (Some seven percent of male fundraisers also experienced harassment.) The study found that in nearly all cases, the perpetrator was a male. The most common types of sexual harassment, according to the study, were inappropriate sexual comments (80 percent) and unwanted touching or physical contact (55 percent). Moreover, of those experiencing abuse, almost three-quarters (74 percent) reported having had at least two harassment experiences, and 51 percent reported having three or more experiences.[104]

---

[104] AFP, "One-Quarter of All Female Fundraisers Report Sexual Harassment: Donors Account for Nearly Two-Thirds of Harassers," *AFP*. August 22, 2018 https://afpglobal.org/one-quarter-all-female-fundraisers-report-sexual-harassment?fbclid=IwAR15drXFmHnHTyrcmLuxoH2eHpnNcumDTMHFbhMnz841MT0_H05tfAQH2x8

Despite these jarring statistics, sexual abuse and harassment by donors seems to be one of the least-discussed areas of abuse. Volunteer boards, lay leaders, and funders often hold an inordinate amount of power in organizations.

This may sound counterintuitive. After all, being a donor is not an "official" position anywhere. It does not require a degree, or a particular education, or even a contract or long-term commitment. Some organizations have thousands of donors, some of whom may make a donation of ten dollars a year. How much power can a donor actually have if they are not even "officially" in an organization? How do donors compare to rabbis, directors, and professors in terms of power and authority?

The copious stories of sexual harassment that emerged in this research elucidate this dynamic.

The Steinhardt allegations

One of the most telling public revelations about dynamics of sexual abuse in Jewish organizational culture came from the investigative disclosures about Jewish megadonor Michael Steinhardt.

In 2019, the topic of sexual abuse by donors emerged in the public arena when the *New York Times* and *ProPublica* ran a detailed investigative report about decades of abuse by Steinhardt. Reporters Hannah Dreyfus and Sharon Otterman collected direct testimonies from seven women and 16 bystanders about how Steinhardt "asked them to have sex with him, made sexual requests of them while they were relying on or seeking his support, [or] regularly made comments to women about their bodies and their fertility." Below are a few of the testimonies:

> Sheila Katz was a young executive at Hillel International, the Jewish college outreach organization, when she was sent to visit the philanthropist Michael H. Steinhardt, a New York billionaire. He had once been a major donor, and her goal was to persuade him to increase his support. But in their first encounter, he asked her repeatedly if she wanted to have sex with him.... [H]e repeatedly asked if she would have sex with the 'king of Israel,' which he had told her was his preferred title....
>
> [H]e brought in two male employees and offered a million dollars if she were to marry one of them, she said. After the filming ended, Mr. Steinhardt told her it was an 'abomination' that a woman who looked like her was not married and said he

would not fund her projects until she returned with a husband and child....

Deborah Mohile Goldberg worked for Birthright Israel a nonprofit co-founded by Mr. Steinhardt, when he asked her if she and a female colleague would like to join him in a threesome, she said. Two women who worked at a small Jewish nonprofit recalled Mr. Steinhardt using similar language in 2008. They both said that during a meeting at his office to make a pitch for funding, Mr. Steinhardt suggested that they all take a bath together, in what he called a 'ménage à trois.' One of the women, the Executive Director of the organization, asked that her identity be withheld because she feared that people on her board would pull their donations if she spoke publicly. Her former colleague asked that her identity be withheld to protect the Executive Director....

Natalie Goldfein, who was an officer at a small nonprofit that Mr. Steinhardt had helped establish, said he suggested in a meeting that they have babies together....

Rabbi Rachel Sabath Beit-Halachmi, a Jewish scholar.... said Mr. Steinhardt suggested that she become his concubine while he was funding her first rabbinical position in the mid-1990s...

Rabbi Irving Greenberg, who was the president of the Steinhardt Foundation for Jewish Life for a decade, said he repeatedly rebuked Mr. Steinhardt for.... his comments to women focused on their appearance and fertility. [105]

Steinhardt was engaging in this behavior for decades, according to this report, and people around him knew it and for the most part dismissed it.

Unlike Steven M. Cohen, Steinhardt did not face any consequences following these public disclosures. Donors cannot be "fired" the way employees can. But even if they could, it is apparently unlikely that most organizations would reject the millions of dollars of funding that donors supply. Mostly, according to the *New York Times* report, Steinhardt's behavior "went largely unchecked for years because of his status and wealth."

---

[105] Sharon Otterman and Hannah Dreyfus, "Michael Steinhardt, a Leader in Jewish Philanthropy, Is Accused of a Pattern of Sexual Harassment. Several women said Mr. Steinhardt made sexual requests of them while they were relying on or seeking his support. He denies many of the actions attributed to him," *New York Times*, March 21, 2019 https://www.nytimes.com/2019/03/21/nyregion/michael-steinhardt-sexual-harassment.html?action=click&module=Top%20Stories&pgtype=Homepage

To wit, Shifra Bronznick, one of the few Jewish professionals to publicly challenge Steinhardt for his behavior, described to me how much resistance that experience engendered. At a large Jewish conference, Michael Steinhardt got up to the podium to thank the conference organizer:

> He said, 'I want everyone to vote on whether [the Executive Director] should have a baby.'
>
> Nobody said anything. So, at the end, I took the microphone, and I said, 'Michael crossed the line with what he said.' You could hear a pin drop. For months after, I was getting calls about this. They were all angry at me. They said that I would never work in the Jewish community again. [The woman I defended] was angry at me. She said he's her biggest donor. Because he's a billionaire, you become the crazy one.

Donors, then, are not only potential abusers: they are also possibly the ones who most easily get away with it. They are powerful, they face no mechanism for accountability, there are no protections for victims, there are no consequences for their behavior, and they are perhaps the most feared in organizational life.

Donors

Many informants shared stories of abuse with donors. Anne reported that when she was hired as a fundraiser for a major Israeli organization in the late 1980s, someone in the office said, "She's never going to be able to raise any money." Anne was surprised. "He never met me. How would he know? And then I took a look at what was going on." She witnessed women around her participating in the sexualized expectations of them. "He was right. I was never going to be that person who was going to fundraise that way. It wasn't going to happen." Anne believes that times have changed and that today this would be less likely to happen in the open. But that assumption is not confirmed by my research.

Since #MeToo, several women have come forth publicly with testimonies about sexual abuse from donors in the Jewish community. Rhonda Abrams, for example, a veteran Jewish professional and fundraiser professional, wrote an op-ed for the *Jewish Telegraphic Agency* detailing years of sexual abuse by donors and lay leaders:

> I received an email from a prominent donor in our community asking to meet for breakfast. I have felt uneasy around him before, as he has suggested the type of clothing I should wear for professional events, but like many women in my position, I

have become an expert at laughing off inappropriate comments. And meeting with donors to sustain our program is, after all, my job.

When I arrived at our breakfast, we met each other with a hug, which is a common greeting in our tight-knit Jewish community. But this time, the donor reached down and grabbed my butt before putting his arm around my shoulders and walking me to our table. I called him out immediately.

'Did you just grab my butt?' I exclaimed.

'No, I didn't,' he said with a wink.

[Later in the evening] the donor told me that my bra strap was showing and asked if I wanted to cover up or show him more. As we left the restaurant, he pulled me in close to his face in what felt like an attempt to kiss me on the mouth, our noses nearly touching, then placed his hands near my breasts and made a squeezing gesture, saying he needed 'to grab a thing or two.'[106]

These experiences slide from body commentary to jokes to grabs to physical assault. Once the boundaries are crossed with a small violation, the bigger violations easily follow.

In 2018, Cheryl Moore, a long-time Jewish volunteer who has held lay leadership positions in various major Jewish organizations on local, national, and international levels, chronicled a litany of experiences in *e-Jewish Philanthropy* about some of her many experiences of sexual harassment by donors:

I was about to reel in a big donor to a national organization, and one of its top staffers told me, in front of a group of other staffers and volunteers, that if I closed the potential donor, he could get me alone in a room and 'on the lap of' an Israeli leader I admired.

A staffer of the same organization asked me, in a packed bar filled with conference attendees, why we were not 'f*cking each other's brains out.'

A powerful lay leader of a national organization told me that he had saved a chair for me next to an important United States

---

[106] Rhonda Abrams, "One of my donors harassed me. I couldn't afford to stay silent," *JTA*, Dec 21, 2017, https://www.jta.org/2017/12/21/opinion/one-of-my-donors-harassed-me-i-couldnt-afford-to-stay-silent

> Senator, because he knew that senator 'would just love some special attention from me.'
>
> There was the mega-donor who, as we sat in the crowded lobby of the David Citadel Hotel in Jerusalem reached over and squeezed my breast. When I gasped, he said, 'I thought you'd be flattered.'

Moore was a volunteer lay leader, and the assailants were donors whose behavior ranged from sexual commentary to sexual solicitation to ultimately physical assault. The situation, though, made it very difficult for Moore to continue doing her job. As one interviewee explained, "If I am an Executive Director and a staffer reports this kind of thing, of course I'm not going to report them because I don't want to be seen as complaining. I want to be 'in' with this potential donor, so I won't risk that." Similarly, Moore felt there was no recourse for her:

> I am almost never at a loss for words , but when these things happened, I just smiled and awkwardly laughed. What could I say? 'I'm not remotely interested in having sex with you.' 'Why are you pimping me out?' Those are not in my repertoire of responses when I am in public and actively trying to achieve something for a cause in which I believe. I also had the strong impression that if I had protested in a serious way, I would have been met with a condescending comment about how I was overreacting. Each of those interactions left me feeling ashamed and wondering what it was about me that projected that I would go along.[107]

This essay includes several important observations. One is that a professional woman in public, trying to maintain a professional persona and also do her job, has very little recourse. Another is that even if the victim has done nothing wrong, she may feel "ashamed." The lack of available responses intersects with fears of being accused of "overreacting," a larger silencing tactic that professional women face. Finally, even among volunteers, these experiences have a deep negative impact on the victim. Ultimately, when the assailant is a donor, the victim is powerless because the assailant has all the power, and there are no mechanisms for accountability. So much so, in fact, that Moore decided to leave Jewish communal work behind altogether because of this rampant culture of sexual abuse — and her powerlessness in the face of it.

---

[107] Cheryl Moore, "#metoo in the Jewish Community," e-Jewish Philanthropy, September 17, 2018
https://ejewishphilanthropy.com/metoo-in-the-jewish-community/

The easy slide from words to actions

The stories of sexual abuse by donors and volunteers who face zero accountability and no frameworks for being censured show a very important aspect of sexual abuse in general, which is the slide from words to assault.

In 2018, a project called B'Kavod collected survey reports about workplace respect and safety in the Jewish community. The responses from 165 interviewees offer a trove of testimonies focusing on abuse by donors, a majority of them from the past 5-10 years. I organized the responses into a kind of taxonomy of abuse that demonstrates how these different forms of abuse feed into each other.

Body commentary and sexual innuendo

The simplest form of sexual abuse to get away with is body commentary. Words quickly disappear into the ether, they can be swept away with a wave or a chuckle if the comment is not well-received, and there is no touch involved. It is like the first knock on the boundary wall to see how easily it will come down. Here are a few examples from respondents:

> The CEO of a major Federation, in his late 40s, whom I was trying to solicit funding from, was overly familiar, commenting on my appearance, asking about my dating life, sitting too closely, using flirtatious language, and showing a clear preference that I not bring my male colleague to our meetings. I also saw the same person, in a situation at a bar with about five young people, mostly women, clearly cross a line into sexually inappropriate and explicit language with a young woman who works in the Jewish world. He had more positional power than all of us, and no one spoke up...

> A donor/communal thought leader often makes sexual comments either as 'jokes' with innuendo that relate to me and colleagues (and him) or just generally vulgar comments alluding to/injecting sex into conversations that clearly have NO place for it...

> I was leading a roundtable discussion. One donor in particular seemed really interested in our organization's work. One by one people left, but he remained, asking questions and expressing interest. He moved chairs so that he could sit closer to me. As we spoke, he told me that he would support our work. A moment later he said, 'You know I felt so attracted to you from the moment you walked in the room and started speaking.' I ended the conversation. Later that night I received

an email from him at 2:30 a.m. stating that he had been thinking about me and our conversation, and he was so 'inspired by my light'...

When I was working as a program manager in my first job out of college, jokes were often made – 'You're pretty, so you should be in this meeting with a potential donor' – jokes about my dating life or inappropriate questions. It made me feel as though my worth was dependent in a way on looking good. As an intern I told my boss what had occurred and she laughed and said, 'Well he gave 25K today so you must have done something right.' That made me feel really unsafe and unprotected and I soon left the position.

Body commentary, sex jokes, and sexual innuendo are easily dismissed but in fact have lingering impacts of breaking boundaries, creating awkwardness and shame, pressuring employees to use their sexuality to get donations, and ultimately leaving workers unprotected from all kinds of abuse or assault. This lack of protection opens the door to the next "level" — touching.

Unwanted sexual touch

Many respondents described unwanted touch, such as groping and grabbing, as well as leering, which is also a form of physical invasiveness. Sometimes these behaviors are hard to describe as abuse, such as what several respondents described as a donor who will "hug too close," or "smell my hair," or "linger just a little too long," or "have his hands on my leg." These "little" invasions are about testing sexual boundaries. Moreover, these behaviors are often intertwined — as one respondent described a "donor touching me while asking about my sex life" — thereby violating boundaries using words and hands at the same time. Here are a few more testimonies from various respondents:

Last year a donor placed his hand on my thigh/knee as we were on a train to Washington for a White House event. The same donor has commented in the past that I'm 'hot' or 'looking good' ...

Recently, I was treated inappropriately by the director of a foundation who made several advances on me – calling me late at night, touching my leg, sending me jewelry and other gifts, asking me out for drinks, inappropriate comments about my looks on Facebook photos ...

Donor touching me, conversation about my sex life, spent the evening ostentatiously looking down the front of my fairly modest dress. No steps taken — I felt like I'd jeopardize our funding…

This past year, at a major philanthropic event, during the cocktail portion, one of the biggest philanthropists present whom I had met only a few moments earlier, called me over to join his group and introduced me and my organization to the group. As he was speaking and praising my work, his hand began massaging my neck. I froze, and looked around the circle, but though his hand was clearly visible, no one seemed to be reacting — they just kept laughing at his jokes. I ducked out from under his hand and stood on the other side of the circle. He followed me there and began massaging the nape of my neck again. This time, his hand crept down my shirt. Again, not one of the other donors said a word. I excused myself. Half an hour later, the man again encountered me at the food table, and again his hand was massaging my neck.

All of these events happened within a year prior to the 2018 survey collection, not in the 1970s. Most of them include both sexual commentary and unwanted touch, and the victims felt like they were stuck in the situation because they felt talking back to a donor would have consequences for the organization and for themselves.

Sexual advances and propositions

The next phase of knocking down the wall of sexual boundaries is direct sexual propositions. With donors, this is often done openly. Below are several testimonies on this issue:

I was standing with three older men at a conference. One asked another if he knew me and he responded, 'I was trying to pick her up at the bar earlier.' The one who made that comment was in a position to support my organization…

I was working as an intern at a Jewish nonprofit while I was in college. A potential donor made an aggressive unwanted sexual advance at me, and I had to physically push him off me while we were alone in a taxi…

I was hit on, sexually assaulted, and propositioned by colleagues, lay leaders, and donors ranging in age from peers to men in their 80s…

As Executive Director, I was directly propositioned by a married donor I was professionally soliciting for a donation from his company's philanthropic giving program that he ran…

This kind of sexual abuse in fundraising put victims in a terrible position. In addition to all the impacts of sexual abuse generally — shame, awkwardness, inability to function and move around safely — this kind of sexual propositioning also put victims under pressure to go with it in order to get the donation, effectively risking the functioning of their organizations by putting funding on the line. That is a lot of pressure.

One interviewee, Ruth, a fundraising professional with a major Jewish organization in New York, shared with me an egregious story of being pressured to enter a sexual relationship with a potential donor in order to secure the donation. At a fundraising cocktail party for the organization where she was working, the major donor, "David," walked in with another man named "Alan," and the situation quickly escalated from unwelcome commentary to touch to direct sexual solicitation:

> I knew Alan from the Upper West Side. I was standing around talking to David, when Alan and this other guy started joking around, asking me if I'm single, telling me that I need to get married. David says to me, 'You and Alan should go out. Go outside, take your big red lips, and go kiss him.'

> It was very inappropriate, but I laughed it off. I didn't feel threatened. I wasn't afraid of losing my job. It was just uncomfortable. We were standing around laughing.

> Alan wasn't saying, 'No, no, no.' He was looking around to see where this was going.

> Then it was time to leave, I was working the door saying goodbye, Alan and David came by and David said again, 'You should really kiss him.' He said, 'I will kiss him if you kiss him,' and the two of them laid into each other. I grabbed my cell phone, and I said, 'I'm going to take a picture.' I said it as a joke; I did not take a picture of the two of them kissing. And they laughed and walked out. I should have taken the picture.

> The next day, Alan called and asked me out. Alan knew I wasn't interested because I ran into him over the years. He was the kind of guy who would walk up to me at parties, but I blew him off and walked away. I was not interested, and he knew that. But he was taking advantage of what David did. It was very uncomfortable, and I didn't know what to do. Because suddenly now he's the guy who came with David — the guy who'd just donated $1 million — and he himself is a potential donor.

> I went into my boss's office and said, 'I have a problem. Alan called and asked me out.'

She said, 'Are you interested?'

I said, 'No.'

And she said, 'Oh, well, that's a shame because Sara [the director] really wants him as a donor.'

At the time I felt like she might be saying, 'Don't feel like you have to,' but I think what she as actually trying to say to me was, 'Well, Sara really wants him as a donor so try to make him happy.' She couldn't actually say that. But she started talking to other people and then the whole office started talking about it. So, I had her, I had the Executive Director, I had his secretary, there were people weighing in on whether it's like prostitution for me to go sleep with him.

At the end of the day, it was like, 'Well, if you're not interested, certainly you shouldn't go out with him, but it's a shame to lose a donor.'

I was basically between a rock and hard place. And I didn't go out with him. I said, 'I'm not a whore. I'm not going to sleep with a guy because Sara wants him to be a donor.'

She replied, 'It's a shame to lose a donor.'

This story, which is reminiscent of the infamous *Mad Men* storyline in which a secretary was encouraged to sleep with a potential client in order to get his business, is one of the most shocking to emerge from this research. It illustrates the enormous sway that donors have not only with a potential victim but also with the structure surrounding her. Donors apparently are justified in assumptions that they can expect sexual "favors." The entire organization here rallied around whatever the donor wanted, no matter how outrageous or abusive. Even when she said, "I'm not a whore," she was still encouraged to go through with it. The women around her and above her who potentially should have been more sympathetic to her situation were encouraging her to provide sexual favors in order to secure the donation. As Jewish educator and social policy researcher Sarah Bronzite commented, "This is not just a donor abusing the power they hold as a donor. This is a line manager explicitly acknowledging that sexual approaches are known about and that they—and senior management further up the line—are comfortable with the idea that sexual favors are just another weapon in a fundraisers' armory. There are managers and bosses within our community who are effectively pimping for the donors and therefore directly enabling their behavior."

This is another example of how all these different behaviors are connected—the "jokes," the touch, and the solicitation. It also illustrates how, in situations in which a donor sexually assaults a staffer, the donor has all the power and the leverage, and the victim often has none.

Board members

Harassment by donors shares many of the same dynamics as harassment by board members, as the violator is not paid staff or in any kind of supervised position that requires formal accountability — and yet holds enormous power and leverage in the organization. Board members are also often major donors, compounding the pressure.

Interviewees and respondents shared stories about abusive board members that include sexual commentary, unwanted touch, and sexual propositioning. One woman said she was "hit on regularly by a lay leader." Another reported that she experienced a "range" of abuse from board members, "from being called 'honey' or 'sweetie' to flirting and unwanted compliments about my body and sexuality, to speculation about my romantic life." Other testimonies include, "inappropriate comments from donors or lay leaders about my body, relationship status, dating life, or marriage," "being asked out by donors in work settings," and "overhearing demeaning commentary about women's appearances and sexuality in the workplace." One respondent commented that "It persisted despite my firm rejection and indication of fidelity to my marriage." One respondent shared the following incident of physical sexual assault:

> The board chair of an important partner organization asked me to have a lunch meeting. After lunch, he asked me to walk and continue to talk. We sat on a bench, and he tried to kiss me. I turned my head, said goodbye, and ran back to my office in tears. The next day, he sent me a vaguely threatening email.

Sexual abuse in organizational life easily slides from behaviors that can be construed as innocuous — a lunch, a joke, a compliment — to boundary violations, sexual solicitation, and attack.

Moreover, there seem to be no real impediments to abuse by a lay leader, who cannot be censured or fired and is considered too valuable to the organization to threaten. Nothing gets in the way — not persistent rejection, not "fidelity to my marriage," not "modest dress," and not being religious. Klara, an Orthodox woman who was the Executive Director of a prestigious Jewish communal umbrella organization, reported that, "My board chair repeatedly would comment on my clothing that I didn't dress 'like I was Orthodox' and my skirts were too short to be Orthodox. When I requested regularly scheduled meetings with the board chair (rather than him just showing up in my office, which he did) he told me 'I spend as much time with you as your husband, at least he gets benefits.'"

Abusers in organizational life have many protections — power, leverage, authority, platforms, and their security in being invaluable, especially if they are lay leaders.

Significantly, it is not only staffers who get abused by board leaders, as Cheryl Moore's accounts painfully illustrate. Sometimes board members harass other board members, which also causes pain to the victims and creates dysfunction in the organizational operations. Zena describes how she was asked to join the board of governors of one of the largest Jewish organizations in the world:

> *It was an incredible opportunity and I agreed to join. I was the only board member from my community, from my state, and with only one other person from my region. During one of our quarterly meetings, we had a retreat at the Dead Sea. After several morning sessions I was sitting outside with an older male member of the Board of Governors and following some polite chit-chat. He asked me if I would go to bed with him that night. He knew I was married. He knew my husband. I knew his wife. I was speechless and took several moments to find my voice. He asked if he had offended me and offered an apology if he had. I replied with the story of the feathers.... that they could never be stuffed back into the pillow once they were all let out. That night I shoved a chair under the doorknob of my hotel room. I was frightened. I was violated. I was alone.*

Even as an aggressively recruited board member, she had no protections — literally, viscerally, no protection — from sexual predators on her own board.

Congregants versus women rabbis

One more place in Jewish communal life where predators resemble donors in their freedom and lack of oversight is in synagogue, where the predators can be congregants. In fact, for the women for whom synagogues are a place of work — rabbis, cantors, educators, and staffers — congregants *are*, in many cases, both donors and board members, and are often treated with the same freedom to do and say what they want to staff. For women rabbis, this can make synagogues — their communities and workplaces — dangerous settings.

One respondent reported that, "A congregant repeatedly referred to me as 'sexy,'" undermining her ability to function and be perceived as a scholarly, serious rabbi. Emily, who is a cantor, described the abuse by a congregant, who "starting hitting on me really inappropriately, almost sexually bullying. And he was someone who gave a lot of money to the synagogue and was in the rabbi's social circle." Here, too, Emily had no protection because he was both a congregant and a donor. "It became a terrible situation. And I ended up leaving that synagogue, completely devastated."

Women rabbis seem to have it coming at them from all directions. One pulpit rabbi reported that a congregant "consistently referred to my body and clothing and made public remarks about my physical appearance." Another respondent, also a pulpit rabbi, described a "wide range" of experiences:

> From being dismissed for being a woman to a congregant once emailing me to tell me I had been bad and should be spanked. Yup, spanked! I once had a rabbi mentor when I was a student make unwanted sexual advances towards me via email. I had a long talk with a congregant once about sexually harassing another congregant and at the end of the conversation he asked me out and told me I was flirting with him. There are a few men in the congregation who hug too long or too hard or stand too close, who tell me I am attractive and comment on my appearance in ways that are uncomfortable. Once, a colleague I worked with started commenting about my appearance and openly flirting. It was so uncomfortable that I had to speak to my supervisor who then had to call him in for a talk about appropriate workplace behavior. The co-worker then retaliated and sabotaged much of the work I was doing. There are more.

Another rabbi reported a similarly wide range of assaults from congregants.

> A kiss on the mouth and tight embrace that went on too long and was overly intimate; inappropriate comments – calling me 'baby,' 'honey,' telling me when I had a husky voice from a cold that I 'sound sexy' – recently, maybe two years ago; overly intimate touching – scratching from the base of my back upward. I actually didn't know who it was at first, and I thought it was my husband because of the nature of the touch – and was shocked when it turned out to be a congregant.

Odelia, who is staff clergy in a synagogue, described the creeping abuse from a man who wasn't even a regular but an occasional visitor and Torah reader:

*He would wink at me. He stood too close to me. He continued
leering at me and winking. At lunch, he came over to me and
got too close once again, saying 'You should wear your hair up
more often. It looks good, you have good bone structure.' I was
taken aback and said weakly, 'Have a good trip home. Take
care,' without looking at him.*

Like donors, congregants cannot exactly be fired, censured, or removed
from their proximity to their victims, often leaving women rabbis in a trap.

Abby added that some women rabbis are even more vulnerable than
others. "Once I got divorced it was like I was an available specimen, not just
a female specimen." Similarly, a respondent who is a pulpit rabbi described
harassment by the board president at a job interview. "The president of the
congregation patted my butt while I was on the bima during a job interview."
She reported it, he denied it, she was not offered the job, and she probably
would not have taken it even if she had been.

The "protected" class of abusers

All of the forms of abuse mentioned in this chapter—by donors, board
members, lay leaders, and congregants—reflect positions in the community
that are in many ways untouchable. Logistically, there is no oversight or
mechanism for checking behaviors of people in unpaid, informal positions.
They cannot be "fired." But more than that, they are all considered
irreplaceable and invaluable, often more so than their victims. One
respondent explained, "There's a problematic dynamic between board and
staff—where I think that there is a tolerance for lay leaders and donors to
engage in inappropriate behavior or comments that are tolerated for the
benefit of the organization—that often leave staff feeling unprotected."

Cheryl Moore summarized the issue as a function of the entire toxic
culture:

*What do all of [these] interactions have in common? Very
public, outrageous and/or crude comments and behavior,
observed by others, but questioned by no one. I think that each
of these men enjoyed being able to 'get away with' the behavior.
It was machismo at its core. Knowing that they would not be
called out was part of the thrill. After all, they could have made
their comments and gestures in private. Instead, they chose
public places, often packed with people. They knew that no one
would criticize or stop them, that they would not be asked to
step down, or divorced. It was as if they were directly
challenging those around them to step in. I wasn't the first*

person that they had treated this way and I wouldn't be the last. What occurred had nothing to do with something that I projected. It happened when I was single and when I was married, when I was very young and more mature, when I was new to the volunteer world and known as an effective leader.

Many interviewees and respondents shared similar sentiments. As Avital explained about her own experiences with Steinhardt, "He is a very wealthy man who is known as a predator, but everyone keeps taking his money. Nothing about his life suggests that there are repercussions. So, saying 'He's the bad guy' without looking at the bigger system is not helpful. It's not just about him, it's about who has enabled him. To name him does not solve the problem. Who are the other enablers? Board members, staff, other donors."

Indeed, many interviewees shared a lack of protection from the people around them, and in some cases—like the boss "Sara" who effectively encouraged pimping out her employee to secure a donation—even supported it. For example, Klara whose abusive Board Chair regularly made himself at home in her office, had no outlet, no ally, and no protection in her space. "I reached out to other Executive Committee members and was told I should be careful and to let this go."

Avital described a meeting in which Steinhardt publicly harassed a woman who then went into fundraising meeting with him and accepted his donation. "If a young staffer said he did this, would we still take the money despite the behavior?" she asked. "She could have said, I'm really offended by your behavior and we don't want to do business with you. But that's not what happens." Other would-be protectors and allies responded with a shrugging off, or advice such as "be careful around him" or "avoid him" or "bring someone else into the room when you meet with him," or "figure out how to stay two-three steps ahead of him." One reported that she "learned to box out my space" when I'm around him." In many cases, nothing resulted of the victims' complaints. "I've just come to live with it." Victims had to change their own behavior—several reported dressing differently, and several left their jobs. Cheryl Moore left Jewish communal life altogether, as did Leanne.

Perhaps this dynamic is not entirely unique to Jewish settings. As Leah told me, "My sister is on Wall Street, and she has been saying for years that Steinhardt's behavior does not stand out on Wall Street. It's the real bro-culture." On the other hand, she says, in Jewish settings, it has a whole other justification. "Only here it's for a 'good cause,'" she explained. "We're just marrying off Jews, what's your objection?" Leah called it a "big alibi."

Takeaways about abuse by donors and other celebrities

There are several characteristics of these accounts that are worth noting.

- **Abuse does not always look violent.** At first, abuse can look like awkward commentary. It is often hard to explain why a "too-long hug" or a public sexual proposition is hurtful and damaging.
- **It comes down to consent.** The absence of consent is the deciding factor in determining whether an event was abusive. Unwanted invasion of sexual boundaries is abuse, period, even if some people laugh about it or dismiss it as "nothing."
- **The culture easily dismisses abuse by donors and other superstars.** For so long, sexual innuendo and propositions have been laughed off by men in power, and the rest of the world played along—or pretended to play along. Many of us have been socialized to dismiss all this as "nothing". It is not "nothing." In fact, Sarah Chandler said that her organization trains all levels of staff to report and respond to even "small" complaints because "this is a key proven method of preventing more serious abuse."
- **There is an easy slide from body commentary to sex jokes to unwanted touch to solicitation to attack.** Often the violations start gradually, with a laugh or a rub, to test how easily the boundaries are broken.
- **Donors, lay leaders, and board members are often deemed unassailable.** Going up against them means jeopardizing an entire organization. Reporting it, or demanding action, is perceived as biting the hand that feeds you. The effective message is that donors are untouchable and irreplaceable, but victims are not.
- **Women can also be abusers**, and certainly can be enablers, even when they may profess support of women. There is a deliberate, consistent, and regularly used slide from gender socialization and control to supporting and even carrying out forms of sexual abuse, even among women.[108]

---

[108] In my doctoral dissertation about gender socialization in Orthodox girls' high schools in Israel, I found a cultural pattern in which women acted as megaphones for patriarchal norms, and encouraged girls to obey the rules of body as constructed by the rabbis around them. This was especially true in school settings in which women dominated the teaching staff but all religious rules and authority were referred to the school rabbi, one of the few men in the building. I called this practice "indoctrination with a pretty face", as many of the women engaged in these practices were young, sweet, perky, friendly, and even loving. This cultural practice seems deeply connected to findings in this study. Just as abusers who are charming and engaging have a dangerous ability to mold their victims' minds and convince them to follow and obey, to, too, women who charmingly transmit patriarchal norms in the guise of

- **Female board members can also be preyed upon.** This can be by other board members, and this is no less damaging to the victims and to the organizations than when staffers are the victims.
- **Female rabbis have it coming from all sides**. They may be subjected to abuse by superiors, lay leaders, and congregants alike, in situations in which they are often powerless. At the same time they are often in positions to support abusers or even in some cases abuse people themselves.
- **"Good guys" can also be abusers.** Men who advocate publicly for progressive causes or women's rights, or hide behind their own sexual orientation as a protection against accusations, can also be abusers in private.
- **Power structures can be messy.** This entire dynamic — of donors or congregants as abusers and women rabbis as victims — challenges perceptions about power and hierarchy in the Jewish community. If an abusive congregant who is also a donor/board member is able to sexually abuse a female rabbi or cantor and get away with it because of their perceived value, then the question is, who are the people who have the real power in the Jewish community?
- **Money speaks loudest.** The most powerful takeaway from this chapter is about the role of money in the community. As the Talmud says, *baal hameah baal hadeah* — whoever holds the hundred-dollar bill, so to speak, gets to have the last word.
- **Unless the victim is a woman.** In that case, as Brenda's case illustrates, a female donor/board member is *still* deemed less reliable and less valuable to the organization and community than the rabbi, even an abusive rabbi.
- **There is often a third party of bystanders.** That is often the institution in which these abuses occur. The abuse is accepted because people put the reputation of the institution itself above victims. In protecting the synagogues, nonprofits, and schools instead of exposing and ridding the institutions of abuse, there is an insidious undermining of the values of these institutions.
- **There are layers of damage to this dynamic**. The damaging impacts from these cultures of sexual abuse are personal, organizational, and communal. The institutions lose talent and progress while remaining tied to the whims and behaviors of abusive personalities. The victims experience blocked job opportunities, work, and career

---

loving, beautiful, engaging, and beautifully spiritual practices have a dangerous ability to mold girls' behaviors; Elana Maryles Sztokman, *Gender, Ethnicity, and Class in State Religious Education for Girls in Israel: The Story of the Levy Junior High School, 1999-2002,* Thesis for the degree of Doctor of Philosophy, Submitted to the Senate of the Hebrew University of Jerusalem February 2005.

advancement. And the community suffers from the dominance of abusive cultures. I explore these ideas more in the coming chapters.

Part II: The Abuse Process

I've always thought that under rape in the dictionary it should tell the truth. It is not just forcible intercourse; rape means to inhabit and destroy everything.

Alice Sebold, *Lucky*

In order to escape accountability for his crimes, the perpetrator does everything in his power to promote forgetting. If secrecy fails, the perpetrator attacks the credibility of his victim. If he cannot silence her absolutely, he tries to make sure no one listens.

Judith Lewis Herman, *Trauma and Recovery: The Aftermath of Violence—From Domestic Abuse to Political Terror*

Chapter 4: Grooming Tactics

Sexual abuse rarely happens out of the blue. As Patricia Evans, an expert in emotional abuse, writes in her book, *Controlling People*, sexual abusers generally engage in a process of controlling people by manipulating situations and cultivating an environment over time in order to get what they want out of their victims. This does not take place over one event but is a series of micro-events that have a gradual, snowballing effect on the victim. These can take many different forms and at times can even be disguised as fun, caring, or even loving gestures. But in the context of abuse, it becomes clear that these are driven by narcissistic desires and are part of a calculated, purposeful process to control someone else.[109] In a sense, while sexual assault is so often imagined as an act of sudden violence by a stranger in a darkened alley, the reality is generally quite different. Sexual abuse is usually a spread-out dynamic aimed at ultimate control, in which the abuser works to get another person to agree to something that they don't want to do, something that is a desire of the perpetrator but not of the victim.

This process of preparing the victim for abuse is often referred to as "grooming." According to the Rape, Abuse and Incest National Network (RAINN), grooming is a series of "manipulative behaviors that the abuser uses to gain access to a potential victim — as well as, in some cases — the victim's parents — to coerce them to agree to the abuse, and reduce the risk of being caught."[110] It is a system of gaining trust and breaking down resistance from the victim in order to have their way. These are processes that can potentially work on children, teens, and adults of all genders, and can take place in person or online.

All long-term abusers use grooming tactics, whether they are teachers, coaches, counselors, co-workers, or donors. Although much has been written about grooming processes among priests and coaches, to my knowledge there has been no comprehensive research study exploring the grooming process among Jewish clergy or Jewish leaders. That leaves us with a gaping hole in our understanding of sexual abuse in the Jewish community. This chapter aims to fill that void and to find out how grooming processes in Jewish settings compare to grooming tactics in other settings.

---

[109] Patricia Evans, *Controlling People: How to Recognize, Understand, and Deal with People Who Try to Control You*, Adams Media, 2003

[110] "Sexual assault: Grooming: Know the Warning Signs," RAINN, https://www.rainn.org/news/grooming-know-warning-signs

Stages of grooming

In 2018, researchers Jason Spraitz and his colleagues constructed a behavioral taxonomy of priest sexual grooming based on 147 testimonies of abuse. They came up with eight specific activities in the grooming process.[111]

(1) Use of drugs, cigarettes, or alcohol
(2) Overnight stays or trips
(3) Developing positive relationships with parents
(4) The guise of friendship
(5) Playing favorites (making the victim feel "special")
(6) Physical play (e.g., roughhousing)
(7) Gifts and "cool stuff"
(8) Misuse of "respect" (i.e., commanding absolute respect and loyalty)

The taxonomy can be applied to other settings of child sexual abuse (CSA), such as abusive coaches or teachers. A 2019 study checked this taxonomy against cases of CSA by monks and found that the taxonomy, for the most part, worked in that clergy population as well.[112]

Psychiatrist Dr. Michael Welner encapsulates mountains of research on the grooming process for CSA into six broad stages:

Stage 1: Targeting the victim. Sizing up the victim's vulnerabilities (e.g., children who have experienced divorce, loss, or other trauma).

Stage 2: Gaining the victim's trust. Being present, caring, and inserting himself into the child's life.

Stage 3: Filling a need. Providing exactly what the child needs, whether extra attention or gifts.

Stage 4: Isolating the child. Creating situations in which they are alone, such as tutoring or coaching, making it a "special" relationship.

Stage 5: Sexualizing the relationship. Talking, pictures, opportunities for removing clothes (e.g., swimming).

Stage 6: Maintaining control. Protecting silence and isolation.

---

[111] Spraitz, Jason & Bowen, Kendra & Strange, Louisa. (2018). "Proposing a Behavioral Taxonomy of Priest Sexual Grooming," *International Journal for Crime, Justice and Social Democracy.* 7. 30. 10.5204/ijcjsd.v7i1.387
[112] Spraitz JD, Bowen KN. "Examination of a Nascent Taxonomy of Priest Sexual Grooming," *Sexual Abuse.* 2019;31(6):707-728. doi:10.1177/1079063218809095

By this point, Welner says, the children are entangled and often face threats and blame. They fear ending the relationship, which would also end "the emotional and material needs that are fulfilled by the relationship, whether it be the dirt bikes the child gets to ride, the coaching one receives, special outings, or other gifts. The child may feel that the loss of the relationship and the consequences of exposing it will humiliate and render them even more unwanted."[113]

In seeking to understand the grooming processes used by abusers in the Jewish community, these kinds of taxonomies are a very helpful start. There is reason to believe that CSA by clergy across different religions shares characteristics. A comprehensive 2021 report about clergy abuse in the UK, for example, includes Jewish testimony alongside testimony from the Anglican Church and the Roman Catholic communities, under the assumption that the dynamics are comparable.[114] Clergy have an assumed status in the community, people are taught to trust them and not to question their authority, they use "God language" and know the spiritual-religious codes and language that their victims like to hear, and they know how to use religious ideas and dicta to break down their victims' resistance. In addition, there are some universal characteristics of childhood—i.e., love of play, friendship, and gifts—that feed into dynamics of grooming, possibly across many different settings and relationships.

However, rabbis who abuse children are only one piece of the broader cultural dynamics of sexual abuse in the Jewish community that demand our attention. While there is quite a bit of research on sexual abuse committed by clergy on *children*, there seems to be a lot less research on clergy abuse committed on *adults*, especially women. The Survivors Network of those Abused by Priests (SNAP) argues that clergy abuse committed on female victims tends to receive less attention than abuse committed on male victims.[115] In the Jewish world, where research on CSM is already so limited,

---

[113] Dr. Michael Welner, "Child Sexual Abuse: 6 Stages of Grooming," *Oprah*, October 18, 2010, https://www.oprah.com/oprahshow/child-sexual-abuse-6-stages-of-grooming/.(I know what you're thinking: *Oprah? Really? That's your source?* I hear you! But really this little piece is very good in my opinion. It is perfectly relevant here and neatly encapsulates quite a bit of research.)

[114] Professor Alexis Jay, Professor Sir Malcolm Evans, Ivor Frank Drusilla Sharpling, *Child protection in religious organisations and settings Investigation Report September 2021 A report of the Inquiry Panel*, https://www.iicsa.org.uk/key-documents/26895/view/child-protection-religious-organisations-settings-investigation-report-september-2021.pdf

[115] Marjie Lundstrom, "Female Victims of Clergy Abuse: Female victims often overlooked in horror stories of clergy abuse," *Sacramento Bee*, Thursday, March 21, 2002 https://www.snapnetwork.org/female_victims/females_often_overlooked.htm In my many searches for academic literature on this topic, I found hundreds of articles about CSA among clergy, but very few on adult victims, especially women. I have a few theories about this, which relate to larger cultural attitudes towards women who are sexually abused. As I

our understanding of how adults are groomed is almost nonexistent. While predators are believed to use similar strategies everywhere, these strategies look different depending on the setting and the tools at their disposal. The "cool stuff" and "befriending parents" may not apply or have different expressions, for example, for adult victims as opposed to children.[116] Catholic priests, for example, use their positions as trusted members of the clergy, their proximity to schools, and religious language, customs, and ideals of their faith, in order to lure their victims. What are the tools available to Jewish clergy, how are these strategies applied in Jewish settings, and how are they adapted to adult victims, especially women — these are crucial questions that have not yet been systematically studied, and urgently demand attention.

In addition, there is also a gap in our understanding of grooming tactics used by other abuser categories in the Jewish world, such as bosses, teachers, academics, donors, board members, and congregants. My assumption here is that, just as there are likely similarities between tactics used by rabbis and priests, there are also likely similarities between tactics used by rabbis and Jewish academics or donors or board chairs. I posit that there are underlying communal and cultural cues that also provide tools for manipulation and control.

The most comprehensive and compelling taxonomy of grooming tactics by rabbis that I found was constructed in an extensive blog by Sarah Ruth Hoffman, an academic researcher who was also a victim of a severe case of sexual assault by a rabbi over an eleven-month period. Her analysis, which is based in part on her own personal experiences as well as comprehensive research about clergy abuse and narcissistic abuse,[117] is a formidable description of the minutiae of grooming by rabbis. Hoffman goes back and forth between her considerable scholarship and the very intense and

---

mentioned in the introduction, the skepticism that women face when they come forward about sexual abuse is uniquely distinct from all other victims of violence and crimes. I posit that it is not just the justice system that oppresses and torments women who were sexually abused but also the wider culture. I think that the contrast between how child victims are treated versus how adult female victims are treated is a reflection of those cultural attitudes and biases that regularly blame women for their own traumas. But proving that theory in this context of Jewish culture would require a comprehensive research study that is beyond the scope of this paper. I therefore leave these thoughts here as a hypothesis and suggestion for further research.

[116] Significantly, while 95 percent of abusers are male and victims of child sexual abuse are split roughly in half among boys and girls, victims of adult sexual abuse are predominantly women (one in three women versus one in six men are victims of sexual abuse). "The Silent Majority: Adult Victims of Sexual Exploitation by Clergy," http://www.adultsabusedbyclergy.org/ .

[117] Nancy Werking Poling, *Victim to Survivor: Women Recovering from Clergy Sexual Abuse*, Wipf and Stoc, 2009

Stage/Category	Grooming Tactic	Examples
Targeting to gain trust by filling a need (victim is entranced)	Targeting the victim	Finding the victim's vulnerability, such as a recent death, divorce, illness, or loneliness.
	Charming generosity – becoming the "savior"	Flirting, flattery, attention, and taking a strong interest in the victim, often using the guise of generous "savior
	False intimacy	Language such as feeling "special", "bonded", "alike", or "soulmates."
Breaking down resistance (victim can't say "no")	Constant unsolicited communication	Endless texts, messages, follows, and/or calls
	Relentless repetition	Non-stop pursuit despite protest
	Prizes and "candy"	Giving the victim the things that they crave the most, such as candy (kids) or a raise (adults)
	Love-bombing	Showering the victim with over-the top gifts, notes, or surprises.
	Flattery and ingratiation	Excessive, extreme compliments, such as, "You are going to win the Nobel Prize" or "You have the best cheekbones"
Gaining loyalty and obedience (victim can't leave)	Feigning vulnerability/Sympathy-seeking	Crying to the victim about feeling weak, lonely, or "misunderstood."
	Imposing	Placing themselves in the victim's life without asking, or forcing the victim to hear excessive detail about their personal life.
	Isolation, secrecy and the double bind	Forcing the victim to lie in order to protect the abuser from being exposed.

Stage/Category	Grooming Tactic	Examples
Destabilizing the victim (victim is confused and weakened)	Intermittent reinforcement	Alternate between giving a lot of attention and completely ignoring the victim in order to play with their mind.
	The synthetic intimacy trance	Hypnotic attention of being watched under a microscope.
	Mocking and sexual jokes	"How about a threesome? Just joking."
Mind games (victim questions their sanity)	Gaslighting	When the victim protests, the abuser says, "I'm worried about you. You are not seeing things clearly."
	Spiritual bypass	Coopting spiritual ideas to justify abuse, such as, "The Kabbalah has such beautiful things to say about women's breasts. Let me show you."
	Lying and lying by omission	Creating fake online profiles, making up stories to gain attention.
	Dangling a third party	"That other woman has a better body than you."
Controlling the external narrative (victim's story is unreliable)	Blame-shifting and scapegoating	Right before getting caught, the abuser goes to the board and says, "That person is abusing ME!"
	The "good guy" defense	"How could you say I would do such a thing? I'm such a good person!"
	"It's just an affair"	The abuser, in a position of power, claims that the abuse was "consensual."
	The "vindictive woman" spin	"She is just trying to get back at me for ending the affair."

Table 1: Stages of grooming by abusive rabbis and other abusers.

painful process she went through herself. As a result, she produced a list of 26 common grooming tactics that offer a detailed portrait about how rabbis are able to manipulate their victims. It is not a list of stages but rather a staggering of concurrent tactics. Hoffman writes:

> The problem is not in a single instance of any one of these tactics; it is the combination of these tactics over a period of time that renders them so overpowering. For instance, I can recall that at least 10 of these tactics were used on me during the same 14-day period, in rapid rotation, sometimes simultaneously. That is why it is so difficult to see it when you are in it; it is all happening all at once — and fast.[118]

Using Hoffman's comprehensive analysis as the primary basis in combination with taxonomies cited above, among others, I analyzed the testimonies of my interviewees and emerged with the following framework of the process of grooming in Jewish culture:

Stage 1: Targeting to gain trust by filling a need (victim is entranced)

Stage 2: Breaking down resistance (victim can't say "no")

Stage 3: Gaining loyalty and obedience (victim can't leave)

Stage 4: Destabilizing the victim (victim is confused and weakened)

Stage 5: Mind games (victim doubts their own sanity)

Stage 6: Controlling the external narrative (victim's story is not believed)

These stages are not perfectly linear and will often overlap. There is a certain logical, calculated order, but it is not absolute or fixed. Also, most abusers do not use all the tactics all at once but seem to have favorites, as each testimony describes its particular dynamics. There are also many other tactics of grooming and emotional abuse that have not been included, such as "moving the goalposts," "bait and switch," "projection," and more. Many books, videos, and blogs list tactics of abuse. I am sure victims reading this will be able to add their own experiences into this framework.

In addition, often one tactic plants the seeds for a later tactic. Abusers often find ways to prepare the groundwork for the next stage — creating instability and self-doubt in the victim, for example, in order to pave the way for lying and gaslighting. In that sense, the stages are all deeply intertwined.

---

[118] Sarah Ruth Hoffman, "Rabbinic abuse: 26 power & control tactics," *Times of Israel Blog* https://blogs.timesofIsrael.com/rabbinic-abuse-26-power-control-tactics/

This framework covers many and most of the common aspects of sexual abuse in a Jewish context as they emerged from this research — especially but not exclusively that involving rabbis — and paints a detailed portrait of what grooming looks like in Jewish cultural and communal settings.

Stage 1: Targeting to gain trust by filling a need

The stage before the actual abuse starts when the predator seeks out his prey. This involves specific tactics aimed at finding the perfect victim, one who is potentially vulnerable and pliable in the eyes of a predator. The result of this tactic is that the victim is hooked — entranced by the charm, flattered, and convinced that this "relationship" is a wonderful thing.

Targeting the victim

This is the very first step of all grooming tactics, whether victims were aware of it or not. According to CSA advocacy group Darkness to Light,[119] the target is often helpless, poor, lonely, and/or broke, or simply has a deep desire for something their parents cannot or will not provide — from illegal substances to travel opportunities to a need to feel loved. The groomer first fills that need or desire by focusing intensely on the unique needs and desires of the particular target and then giving them exactly those things while simultaneously escalating or intensifying the relationship. Then, because the victim is receiving something they cannot get from their parents, they feel that they are in collusion with their abuser, which creates a deep, dark entanglement.

With adult targets, this tactic similarly involves finding the victim's points of vulnerability — such as a death in the family or what Hoffman calls "the thing that is aching in her soul." This can be a person experiencing loss, divorce, loneliness, addiction, or any other personal crisis in which they are looking for some care. "Every single story that I've come across begins with a woman who is highly trusting of clergy and going through a special time in her life. Every. Single. One," Hoffman writes. While abusers of children provide what parents cannot, an abuser of married adult women frequently provides what the victim's spouse "cannot or can no longer provide, be it Jewish partnership (many victims I know were married to non-Jews) or identity (many victims were converts) or just love and attention." In an interview with me, Hoffman described victims whose spouses were going through addiction and mental health issues and were emotionally

---

[119] Darkness to Light, "Grooming and Red Flag Behaviors," https://www.d2l.org/child-groomingsigns-behavior-awareness/ .

unavailable, and the clergy member "swooped in" to give her that thing she craved most.

Although there are many ways to target a victim, there is a particular type of grooming that is available to rabbinic figures and other clergy, which comes in the form of pastoral care. Many stories involve glaring examples of this—funeral, bat mitzvah class, depression, or other moments of emotional vulnerability. Often the rabbi-abuser will target people who are going through a divorce—or even worse, recovering from sexual abuse.

Marion, for example, who was a victim of abuse at home and whose grandparents ended up raising her, was targeted at her grandmother's funeral, where the rabbi spent hours alone with her, as if to counsel her. At the end of that "session," he raped her behind the couch in the funeral home. "I was in a state of grief," she said, and "very susceptible to the attention. I needed kindness and was confused. The rabbi took great advantage of me without my really knowing."

Other victims described their own vulnerability and susceptibility. Brenda, for example, says that the rabbi targeted her when she was at a very stressful time in her life and having what she described as "emotional issues":

> I was making my son's bar mitzvah, and it was a lot of work. I was having some emotional issues because I'm more observant than my family and most of my family is pretty secular and it's always challenging to get my family to be engaged, and I was feeling stressed and hurt because a lot of my relatives had decided not to come.

Notice that Brenda's vulnerabilities were very Jewish-centric. It had to do with a bar mitzvah, religiousness, and tensions in family over religious observance. This opened the door to the "help" of her rabbi. Reut, whose rabbi was found to have been abusing teenagers for decades, said that the rabbi would target kids who were "having a hard time." He would "invite them into his private study and say, come pour out your heart to me. You can talk to me about your problems with your family and things like that."

Cindy, who was abused by her rabbi-boss, was vulnerable because she was isolated and financially insecure, as well as a past victim of abuse:

> As the sole income earner of my family, living several states away from any relatives other than my husband and child, thinking the responsibility of my immediate family was entirely on me, believing him because of his gender and experience and authority, plus having had a lifetime of being sexually objectified – I was the perfect target for him to 'love.'

Cindy was dependent on her abuser financially, professionally, and communally, all of which made her vulnerable.

Nicole, who was "two weeks into a difficult breakup and starving for company," shared that she was, "thrilled to be on the receiving end of these text messages at 10 p.m., having just walked into the house alone. I was hungry for a distraction. The timing couldn't have been more perfect…. He would help me pass the time when I was lonely." She invited him over, and then he forcefully tried to rape her.

Other people in positions of power use this tactic, not just rabbis. Drori, who was raped by the director of a Jewish organization on her college campus, said, "I had recently told the rabbi about my father's death, and then suddenly the director wanted to speak to me in private." She believes that the director exploited the vulnerability she expressed to the office rabbi, using his position as caretaker of Jewish students to gain her trust.

One of the most vulnerable populations are people with disabilities. According to the US Justice Department, people with certain disabilities "are the victims of sexual assaults at rates more than seven times those for people without disabilities."[120]

Dina, a high-profile Jewish professional who is confined to a wheelchair, described the experiences of being vulnerable and targeted:

> *Probably my worst experience was when I was living in Israel and one Saturday night I was coming back to Jerusalem from Tel Aviv by train because the inner-city buses are not accessible. I had to take the last train, and by the time I got to Jerusalem, I had to get the last bus, which was inaccessible. The battery to my wheelchair was also low, so I didn't think I would get home whatsoever. I called some friends, but finding an accessible vehicle was also hard. So, I just started rolling my way home. It was dark and empty, and as I was rolling on the roadway, a haredi man was driving this utility truck — it looked like a bread truck — and he slowed up next to me and asked if I needed help. I didn't speak much Hebrew but I explained that the bus wasn't accessible, and he offered to take me home. I politely thanked him and said, 'No because you need a ramp,' and he said, 'Oh, I have a ramp.' And because it*

---

[120] Joseph Shapiro, "The Sexual Assault Epidemic No One Talks About," *NPR*, January 8, 2018, https://www.npr.org/2018/01/08/570224090/the-sexual-assault-epidemic-no-one-talks-about; Amylee Mailhot Amborski, Eve-Line Bussieres, Marie-Pier Vaillancourt-Morel, and Christian C. Joyal, "Sexual Violence Against Persons with Disabilities: A Meta-Analysis," *Trauma and Abuse*, March 4 2021, https://journals.sagepub.com/doi/10.1177/1524838021995975.

looked like a food truck, it looked possible. And because he was religious and had a beard and tzitzit I trusted him.

He said, 'Just pull around over here,' which was near the stadium. It was weird, I didn't know why he wanted to go there, but I thought, maybe to get away from traffic. We got to this side alley, and he started walking toward me. And then he started rubbing my back and I knew something was wrong. And then he took my things away from me and started to molest me and put his hand up my skirt. I kept saying no, and my Hebrew is not good so I couldn't say much more, and I was scared and he ignored all of it and it continued to get worse and worse. At one point he reached under me to pick me up like a baby and I was able to turn my chair to swivel fast so he lost balance. I kept saying my friends were coming, even though I wasn't convinced that they would actually come. A car started to approach, and I said, that's my friend, and he ran off in the van. He actually circled back, and when he did, an ambulance came — it was my friends and they saw me — and I was shaking, and they knew.

This account highlights the distinct vulnerabilities of people with disabilities. It is also a crucial reminder that there are many types of vulnerabilities, and abusers know how to exploit all of them.

Dina's story also demonstrates that Jewish culture has codes for people who are trustworthy — the rabbi, the religious-looking man, the man doing a favor, the "modestly dressed" one, and a sense perhaps of "one of our own." And yet, those very codes can be used by abusers to lure unsuspecting victims, which can take the entire grooming process of gaining trust and condense it into a matter of minutes.

Charming generosity — becoming the "savior"

Once the abuser is able to target the vulnerable victim, they can move on to the next tactic of charming generosity, in which he exploits that vulnerability to gain trust. This tactic involves flirting, flattery, flowery language, attention, intelligent conversation, taking a strong interest in the victim, and being a "nice guy" — like the guy with the truck stopping for a woman in a wheelchair.

The rabbi abuser often combines these two tactics — targeting the victim's vulnerability and using the guise of generous "savior" to gain trust and break down walls. The fact that a person has the title of "rabbi" is in itself a tool for breaking boundaries, because victims often have a deep-seated reverence for the rabbi. They may not fathom, during this process of generous targeting, that the rabbi is also the person who is setting them up for sexual abuse.

Andy Blumenthal, an outspoken critic of Rabbi Jonathan Rosenblatt — the aforementioned so-called "sauna rabbi" — described this kind of "generosity" he received from one of Rosenblatt's staunchest supporters:

> Dr. Donald Liss was significantly older than me and my friends growing up and frequently invited us to his house in Riverdale to 'learn' Torah and for Shabbat meals, although the learning frequently turned into talk and banter and 'wrestling.' Dr. Liss, a doctor of rehabilitative and sports medicine, claimed great interest in my physical fitness as a youth and my practice of martial arts. He started to run and work out with me and my best friend, and this, at times, led to more 'wrestling' matches.
>
> Later, Dr. Liss provided me a summer job in his and his brother's practice at Englewood Hospital. Dr Liss was quite well off and took advantage of the fact that my family was less so and I needed a job. He provided me the opportunity to work out there in their gym during lunch and then when I would change in the locker room, he would invariably show up to talk with me.
>
> Other times, he invited me to go on vacation with his family to the Poconos to babysit his kids. I remember one particular time, I went running on the trail there, and he came. When we got back to the house we were staying in, he dropped all his clothes in the kitchen area in front of me and his wife and, totally nude, just started talking.[121]

This story is a classic example of an abuser giving the potential victim what they crave most — in this case, a job, an opportunity, and a gym — which also emphasizes the victim's dependence on the abuser, and perhaps expectations of gratitude.

Similarly, Nicole described how her abuser gave her exactly the attention she craved when she was feeling vulnerable. He would send her text messages checking in on her, "Hope you had nice seders," or "Haven't heard from you." She became enamored by his care.

Reut explained how the "savior" tactic is connected to preying on people's vulnerabilities. The rabbi of her synagogue — who did not abuser her personally but many of her child's friends — did this masterfully:

---

[121] Andy (Avraham) Blumenthal, "Leadership, Technology, Life And Faith," August 19, 2015 http://www.andyblumenthal.com/2015/08/birds-of-feather.html

> *He chose to make that one of his areas of expertise – dealing with people at their most vulnerable moments. He comes into their life at their most vulnerable moments when somebody is ill, when somebody is dying, and you are there to nurture, to take care of, to comfort, to be the receptacle of anybody's memories or anything that they want to share with you. He wrote beautiful eulogies for people, for people's funerals. Beautiful ones. People adored him for this.*

Esther similarly explained how these two tactics – targeting her vulnerability and becoming her "savior" – worked hand in hand. "I confided many things to him in our counseling sessions," she said, including "troubles in my marriage," which he later used to abuse her. Cindy, who worked in a synagogue office and was sexually abused over an extended period by the rabbi who was both her boss and the pulpit rabbi, similarly described how the rabbi turned himself into her "savior "He would carefully criticize my husband and my parents, point out all the flaws in my marriage, swoop in as my 'knight in shining armor' whenever I had a personal problem, and generally mess with my head." He also gave her a huge pay raise while he was grooming and soliciting her. The abuser set up the entire relationship with his victim so that she would see him as the "savior," which is ultimately just a projection of the overinflated ego that demands constant adoration.

This can be hard to identify as grooming because, as Reut said, this was "the usual rabbi thing, to want to spend time with the bar mitzvah boy or offer to work on learning something with a kid before the parents had to make the speech," or to counsel women after a loss. Moreover, people admired this about the rabbi. "He made people feel like they were important. You know if the rabbi pays attention to you, and he is supposedly so highfalutin, you may be ecstatic about all this extra attention when you need it most." As you may recall, Zelda was so entranced by the fact a rabbi from her new community had been taking such an interest in her that she jumped up from her chair in her lab, "so excited and feeling lucky and blessed."

False intimacy

During this process, the abuser knows how to make the victim feel like a special object of love, often by telling her exactly the things that she wants or needs to hear, based on his careful scouting of her ideas and interests. He may also use language of love to talk about being "alike", or "bonded," "special," "*bashert*", or "soulmates."

Brenda recalls how the rabbi connected with her around things that he knew were important to her – "about AIPAC, or about LGBT issues because he has a brother and I have a brother who are gay." Zelda described how her abuser would call her his "spiritual *chevruta*" – study partner – and talk about their "special divine connection." He also using the things that she loved to gain her adoration. "He quoted Rumi, he played guitar for me, sent me eloquent messages," while they were chatting anonymously on a dating app. She didn't know that he had stalked her Facebook page to find out specific details about her. "We talked about books that I read, Holocaust survivor books, mysticism, and families." He knew exactly what she wanted to hear, and he used this to gain her loyalty, allegiance, and adulation.

Interestingly, this is a tactic that also invites Jewish cultural codes. Words like "chevruta" or "bashert" conjure up Jewish imagery around divinely guided relationships, and this language can be used to trap victims. Note also that some of these codes can be used for children or adult victims — such as being "bonded" — whereas others are most effective on adults, such as "bashert".

These tactics also set the groundwork for the next stage of grooming, which is breaking down resistance.

Stage 2: Breaking down resistance

Once the predator enters the life of their victim, the next stage involves breaking down her resistance so that she finds it difficult to say "no" to him. They do this with a variety of calculated tactics that may be mistaken for overwhelming love. They aim to completely overtake the victim so that she is too guilt-ridden or simply too exhausted to resist their encroachment.

Constant unsolicited communication

This grooming tactic involves sending messages at all hours and from all directions. Brenda described this:

> A lot of things he did were really weird, borderline boundary-crossing and inappropriate. Like, for example he followed me on Facebook, like every day. We would text and email and use Messenger, and he would comment on or acknowledge pretty much every single thing I posted. And it gave me the sense of, 'Oh, he cares about my life, he's following me, he's interested in me.' But I also knew that it was a little — just, I don't know. Like, he once sent me a random text that said, 'Thinking of you today.' Which is not a normal rabbinic kind of text. It felt like he was sending me coded messages.

Zelda recalls a similar process:

> *He started writing me three times a day on Facebook. I thought, 'This is weird, I'm young, I don't have a family, I haven't launched my career yet, and why is this guy — he's got a wife and three kids and all these congregants who look up to him — writing me three times a day, what is this?' He was just so interested in me every way. Wants to know what I'm up to all the time. Later on, I realized that he was trying to figure out where I am and where I go, but this was his control scheme.*

Nicole says, "I told him I wasn't interested, but he kept texting me anyway. I engaged on and off out of boredom. I craved a distraction." Again, the victim's vulnerability — in Nicole's case, her loneliness following a broken relationship — keeps the tactic working. Moreover, despite her strong resistance, the abuser may keep pressing until she stops resisting.

Relentless repetition

Nonstop repetition — much like constant communication — is a calculated way to dominate and weaken resistance. The abuser keeps at it until the victim is too tired or annoyed to say "no", like an attack from all entry points.

Hoffman describes this kind of repetition: "We are so lucky to have found one another. We are so much alike. I am wrapped around your finger. We work so well together. You are the only one who understands me. We are definitely soulmates." She says it came in the form of messages on her phone throughout the day as well as in-person conversations. "I did not detect that I was feeling worn down, as I was busy keeping up with all of the other tactics," she adds. "My own feelings and intuition became buried — drowned out by constant communication."

Leanne describes how her abuser "pursued me nonstop despite my protest." She said that "He just persisted... even after I clarified my lack of interest in a romantic relationship with him. He seemed unwilling to stop his pursuit. He was [in a leadership position] and he would interfere with my getting food for my campers." Tali also faced that kind of relentless pursuit by her workplace harasser in the form of nonstop requests for her to do things with him outside their office. She was a daily runner, and he would constantly ask her to take him running. He would ask her to go grocery shopping for him, even though that had nothing to do with her job, and she eventually relented. He would ask to come over to her house and would not desist. "He was creeping me out," she said, but she eventually relented anyway.

Relentless pursuit can also come in the form of seemingly joking or pressing boundaries. One of Lanner's victims, Marcie Lenk, who was his student at Frisch and part of his NCSY youth group, said that she endured constant remarks from him about her body often in front of her friends. Or he would purposely squeeze through a classroom doorway at the moment she was walking through, rubbing against her, and say, "Ooh, that felt good." He would also "invite kids to his house for Shabbos, and say to me, 'So, are you going to sleep with me this Shabbos?' I'd say, 'I'm sleeping at your house this Shabbos.' It was a game of manipulation to him, a test to see how far he could go. He'd look at me innocently and say, 'right.' That kind of behavior was constant." [122] The abuser pushes and pushes and pushes until they get their way.

Prizes and candy

This tactic, of giving the victim things that they deeply crave, is one of the hallmarks of abuse, and comes in many forms. Since it usually follows after the abuser has inserted themselves into the victim's life, the abuser knows how to custom-design the specific prize according to what they know their victim wants.

The case of abuse by a first-grade teacher at HALB, for example, offers a vivid portrait of the use of candy to lure a young child. According to the complaint filed in New York[123] about Rabbi Yoseph Ungar, when the victim was in first grade, Ungar let him stay in the classroom and read during recess, allowed him to take board games and books from the classroom, and told him to go into a "special closet" where there was candy for him. When Ungar allowed the boy to have candy, Ungar said "You have to do something to get the candy." That is when Ungar closed the door behind them and sodomized him.[124] According to this report, the predator knew exactly what would lure the child — literally a secret closet of candy — in order to have his way with the child.

[122] Gary Rosenblatt, "Stolen Innocence, Jewish Week Rabbi Baruch Lanner, the charismatic magnet of NCSY, was revered in the Orthodox Union youth group, despite longtime reports of abuse of teens," *Jewish Week*, June 23, 2000, https://www.bjpa.org/content/upload/bjpa/stol/Stolen%20Innocence%20-%20Gary%20Rosenblatt%20-%20Jewish%20Week%20-%20Sexual%20Abuse.pdf
[123] Ben Sales, "'We feel like we failed': How one Jewish school is processing the arrest of a teacher who preyed on children," *JTA*, Sept 19, 2019, https://www.jta.org/2019/09/19/united-states/we-feel-like-we-failed-how-one-jewish-school-is-processing-the-arrest-of-a-teacher-who-preyed-on-children; Amy Klein, "A creepy abusive Jewish day school teacher? I'm not surprised. The sickening news that a New York principal was arrested for child porn brought me back to my own junior high experiences — and not in a good way," *Times of Israel Blogs*. Sept 26, 2019, https://blogs.timesofisrael.com/a-creepy-abusive-jewish-day-school-teacher-im-not-surprised/
[124] Supreme Court Of The State Of New York County Of Nassau Daniel Weiss Plaintiff, -Against- Nassau County Hebrew Academy Of Long Beach School, John And Jane Doe 1-30, Members Of The Defendants' Place Of Board Of Trustees Of Hebrew Academy Of Business. Https://Iapps.Courts.State.Ny.Us/Nyscef/Viewdocument?Docindex=R3giqf2bxg97ib2qdmvhsg==

Malka Leifer, the Australian ultra-Orthodox headmistress who allegedly abused her students for years, also used forms of "prizes" — that is, offering her victims exactly what they wanted or needed. One of her victims, who described coming from an abusive home, said, "I was craving attention and she set herself up to give me that attention. She built up this whole relationship with me and I thought, 'Wow, I love this person and she loves me and finally I'm worthy.'" [125]

Adults have their own versions of prizes, which may take the form of a spiritual teaching, mentorship, special attention, or even a home-cooked meal. These acts of fawning preempt victims' resistance and makes it difficult for the victim to complain about the abuse. When the victim is receiving gifts that she wants, it makes it very hard to say "no" to the giver. The ingratiation and guilt take over.

Everyone has weak spots and desires, and predators know how to exploit them. For women who are struggling financially, money can be a "prize." Cindy, for example, recalls how, when she finally started giving in to her abuser's sexual demands, he gave her a significant pay raise, which only added to her shame and guilt. Marion, who was an amateur musician, was promised by her harasser that he would connect her with his friends in the music business. That never happened — though under that pretense, he invited her to share his hotel room with him. For women who crave care, the prizes can be praise and adoration. Liat recalled, "He praised my contributions to the synagogue."

Predators know exactly how to find the deepest desires of their prey and are able to use that to gain loyalty and obedience. Leanne's abuser, for example, bought two concert tickets and invited her to go to the concert with him. Even though she refused the offer, he continued to follow her and then asked for a hug. Kayla's rapist also bought her concert tickets to a group she loved. "I thought things were promising… that he would be able to bring my parents to accept me and my beloved." It was after the concert that he first assaulted her.

Love-bombing

Prizes and gifts combined with relentless repetition add up to a particularly potent tactic: "love-bombing". This is when demonstrations of faux-attention for the sake of control and manipulation intensify to the extreme. This can be an overwhelming tactic that involves showering the newbie with gifts, handwritten notes, or other "surprises," and is actually

---

[125] Ori Golan, "Washing away the trauma of abuse: Dassi Erlich, who says she suffered sexual abuse in an Australian ultra-Orthodox community, tells of her long journey, accuses former community of not taking steps to protect the next victim," *Jerusalem Post*, July 6 2017, https://www.jpost.com/magazine/a-new-life-498946

favored by religious cults because it draws people in.[126] Love-bombing, like other tactics, breaks down resistance by overwhelming the victim while disguising itself as care. It also often uses religious codes and God language. As Hoffman describes her own experience:

> *Within weeks of meeting me, my abuser showered me with beautiful personalized gifts, handwritten cards, and offered me a surrogate 'family.' He sent songs, poems, and things that discussed Jewish mysticism and romance and sexuality. One handwritten card professed love after knowing me for less than a month! The first half of the relationship was colored by fun and interesting trips, special family events (that I felt weird being invited to), surprises, and declarations and professions of 'love' and 'soulmate' status. After knowing me for only a few months, he professed, 'I could not see myself falling out of love with you in 100 lifetimes!' It was overwhelming and extremely effective, as I was extremely vulnerable at that time in my life and just 'couldn't afford' to not accept love from such a seemingly innocuous rabbi, no matter how fabricated.*

Love-bombing is also connected to tactics of feeding into the victim's specific points of vulnerability and offering "prizes" exactly in the place that she wanted them—in this case, a feeling of belonging. This tactic is so easily disguised as exuberant love until it turns on its head.

Interestingly, "love-bombing" gained headlines in 2021 when singer-songwriter FKA twigs filed a civil lawsuit against former partner Shia LaBeouf for long-term physical, emotional, and sexual abuse. Her accounts referred to details of "love-bombing" in which he "showered her with affection and attention soon after they met, jumping over the fence of her London home to leave love notes and sending her up to twenty bunches of flowers a day." But that quickly evolved into demands for return. "Soon he set up impossible tests for her to prove her affection for him, like a hugs and kisses quota, and berated and cut her down when she inevitably failed."[127]

---

[126] Katie O'Malley, "What's 'Love Bombing' And How To Tell If You've Been A Victim Of It. From showering you with gifts to messaging you non-stop throughout the day, we delve into the worrying behaviours of a 'love bomber', who might have convinced you they're 'the one'," *Elle*, August 2, 2017, https://www.elle.com/uk/life-and-culture/culture/news/a37470/what-is-love-bombing

[127] Katie Bishop, "'Love Bombing' Is the Scary Control Tactic Narcissists Don't Want You to Know About FKA twigs has accused Shia LaBeouf of this form of manipulation — here's why it can be so hard to spot," *In-Style*. Feb 23, 2021, https://www.instyle.com/lifestyle/love-bombing For a more scholarly analysis of love-bombing, see: Strutzenberg, C. C., Wiersma-Mosley, J. D., Jozkowski, K. N., & Becnel, J. N. (2017). "Love-bombing: A Narcissistic Approach to Relationship Formation," *Discovery, The Student Journal of Dale Bumpers College of*

The love-bombing tactic tends to heat up when the victim tries to pull away. "Whenever I started to pull away or express discontent, he would remind me that I was his 'chevruta,' a 'friend for a higher purpose,' that his children 'idolized' me or needed me somehow, that our connection was so special, so mystical, and 'where the erotic manifests.'"

With this tactic, as with so many others, rabbis have extra tools at their disposal, using the excuse of sharing Jewish learning as an opportunity to overwhelm the victim. Hoffman was swept up by the abuser's constant deliveries of Jewish-themed love declarations because it fed into not only her desire to be loved and cared for but also her deep desire for Jewish connection.

Note that even at this stage, many victims start to doubt themselves. They say shaky or uncertain things like, "It was weird, but I can't say exactly why." Each stage of grooming plants seeds for the following stages.

Flattery and ingratiation

This grooming tactic involves over-the-top expressions of love — connected to love-bombing — as well as awestruck compliments that the victim wants to hear, such as "You're going to win the Nobel Prize!" Just as love-bombing is a setup for demands of approval, flattery is quickly followed by demands for victim's attention. For example, when Leanne's abuser "came up to me out of the blue, touched my face, and said, 'I love your cheekbones,'" this could have easily been mistaken for a compliment. But the action not only involved unwanted touch and unrequested body commentary, it was also extreme, invasive, and over the top. The outlandishness of it was a purposeful attempt to test her boundaries and break down her resistance. Later on, he could enter unannounced into the room where she was lying in bed — and she would feel the challenge of resisting.

Zelda shared a very similar process. From two weeks after meeting, "he told me that I'm so beautiful and I'm so smart and every other woman in the world including his wife pales in comparison to me." The flattery and passionate declarations of love and how "special" the victim is are used to create a sense of entitlement or ingratiation to get the victim to let down her guard and cave to his demands.

Flattery can be particularly enticing. Brenda described the impact of the flattery:

> There was another part of me where I was also flattered. Because, you know, I am in my late forties, I have four kids,

Agricultural, Food and Life Sciences, 18(1), 81-89.
https://scholarworks.uark.edu/discoverymag/vol18/iss1/14

I'm not like someone out on the scene, I met my husband when I was 21. You feel middle aged, you feel like that part of your life is over, so part of me was flattered. But I also knew that it wasn't right. So, I kept it to myself.

Daliah says that it is easy for a rabbi to violate people in vulnerable moments in their lives using tactics of flattery. "If someone comes in and says they are grateful, you can use that as an opening to victimize and power abuse."

Indeed, all of these tactics break down resistance through a combination of flattery, fear, and guilt. *How can you say "no" to someone who has done so much for you? How can you walk away from someone who thinks you are that special? Will anyone else love you the same way?* These thoughts can be very disarming.

Stage 3: Gaining loyalty and obedience

Once abusers break down resistance, the next stage is to gain complete loyalty and obedience from their victims. It is like creating a single-person cult, in which the victim feels they owe their absolute loyalty to the abuser, which makes the victim even more vulnerable and dependent. This strategy is key in order to enable a long-term abusive relationship in which the abuser gets exactly what they want, regardless of what the victim wants.

Feigning vulnerability/Sympathy-seeking

That sense of entitlement, in which the abuser convinces the victim to do things that they do not want to do, is also often connected to this tactic of feigning vulnerability or seeking sympathy. This is when the predator works to garner sympathy from their prey by pretending to be the weak one or the victim who needs help or who is "misunderstood." This manipulation makes the victim responsible by preying on her own tendency to be empathetic. It also lowers boundaries and deflates resistance, such as Cindy's abuser confiding about his "marital woes" and "loneliness."

While Brenda's abuser was tormenting her, she nevertheless fell for his sympathy-seeking. She thought to herself, "He's a young single rabbi. This is why he's hurting me, because he has feelings for me and doesn't know how to handle it. I'm going to have compassion for him." Victims may also feel like their job is to help the rabbi.

Zelda's abuser, for example, promoted his narrative of "poor lonely rabbi":

> *He wanted to show me how much stress he has and how lonely he is in his pulpit, even though he also has a lot of power. He made himself out to be sad because he has a hard time finding people who he can confide in. He used that kind of vulnerability to get me to invite him into my home, even though I didn't want to. He talked me into letting him come over just to take a walk, to process his hardship…. Everything in my head was, 'I need to take care of this man.'*

This subconscious pull, that rabbis need to be revered and cared for, can be very powerful and also make it hard to walk away. In fact, despite how desperately Zelda tried to break it off, it took her months, in large part because her abuser kept invoking this poor, sympathy-seeking rabbi trope in order to get her to do his bidding. For a long time, it worked. As Cindy explains, "I gave up innumerable hours outside of the congregation to be there for him, [while I] cried from guilt, shame, and plummeting self-worth."

Imposing

This grooming tactic involves placing burdens on the victim, to "hold his secrets," leaving pieces of himself behind for her to watch, or boldly advancing the relationship without consent. Or, as Reut said, the abusive rabbi "insinuates himself into things." This places responsibility on the victim for caring about the abuser, which victims called "overwhelming."

Hoffman describes how "he just started calling me his 'girlfriend' without a dialogue about it first," so she then became burdened with that title without asking for it. "Or how he left a newly purchased toothbrush and toothpaste in my home in the first weeks of knowing me, without asking me. Who did he think he was? The rabbi. Rabbis can get away with quite a lot." Hoffman explains the tactic as follows:

> *A predatory rabbi might impose secrets, which helps to create the illusion of a 'special bond.' Suddenly the victim is burdened with a huge secret – she is now suddenly in an unexpected sexual relationship with the rabbi. I felt confused, intimidated, and shocked. 'Should I feel lucky? Flattered? Annoyed? Scared? Angry? What does one feel in a situation like this? Does his wife know? Do I tell her? Should I report him somewhere? But where?'*

Cindy similarly described how her abuser imposed on her by "confiding in me about his personal loneliness, telling me about his marital woes, telling me about the previous affairs he had with other women I had come to know in the community, told me about how commonplace such behavior was in the rabbinate." He forced her to hold his story, his emotions, his secrets, even though she did not ask for that and the burden of the abusive relationship was now on her.

Leanne also described how the rabbi imposed on her when she was 17 years old, needing to talk to her about his "dilemma." When he discussed with her—a minor—about the congregant with the paraplegic wife and whether the wife's condition was an excuse for the congregant to have an affair, the rabbi was using the tactic of imposing— but Leanne did not have the language to recognize that. All she could say was that it was "very strange" and made her feel "very uncomfortable." He also incorporated other tactics like isolating her and trying to make her feel "special." Tellingly, at the end of the conversation, he said, "I'm really glad that we're friends," as if to say he'd succeeded in his goal of breaking down her boundaries, of grooming her for the next thing.

Esther explained what imposing looked like for her:

> It became my responsibility to protect his relationships... It would be my fault if he lost these people. He appealed to the very best parts of me – my love, my empathy, my sense of my responsibility, and my desire for no one to be harmed.

Similarly, Zelda recalled, "he said he feels younger because of me, and he is having sensations and sexual abilities that he hasn't had in thirty years" and suddenly that became her responsibility to maintain. As a result, he was able to completely break all sexual boundaries with her that she did not want, such as having unprotected anal and vaginal sex, because he convinced her that it was her responsibility to maintain his sexual virility. He completely imposed on her the responsibility to keep him youthful and satisfied, and she did not know how to resist that.

Isolation, secrecy, and the double bind

Every case of long-term sexual abuse involves secrecy. It is a centerpiece of the abuser's tactic for getting away with it. It often involves imposing two a demand that conflicts with disclosure, trapping victims in a double bind between protecting the abuser and protecting oneself. This grooming tactic thus keeps the victim in the position of feeling that they must stay silent.

Baruch Lanner used this tactic with his victims:

> With girls, he allegedly tended to focus his attentions on attractive, well-developed teens from nonobservant and often troubled families, showering them with praise but demanding complete devotion and secrecy. He would constantly tease them about their bodies, make lewd and suggestive comments,

and sometimes try to kiss and fondle them when they were alone with him, warning them never to tell anyone. [128]

Brenda described the double bind of needing to be able to work with her abuser on synagogue committees that the senior rabbi assigned to her:

I created and started the chesed [charity] committee at my kids' schools ten years ago; it was my vision and a lot of people helped me with it and it's an integral part of the school now. The senior rabbi of the synagogue approached me to implement a program like that in the synagogue and said that the other rabbi [who was abusing me] was going to be my liaison. He didn't know that I had these issues with the rabbi. I kept it to myself. The whole thing got me so nervous and on eggshells, how am I going to do this?

When an abuser is also part of the victim's synagogue and community life, and also holds the key to the victim's ambitions — even if those are voluntary, communal, or religious ambitions, as opposed to paid-career ambitions — it puts the victim in a complex double bind.

The secrecy also often involves social isolation. This is particularly tormenting for people abused by their community rabbi. Zelda reported not being able to go to synagogue or have any friends because the rabbi was afraid of being caught. Her abuser controlled all of that. "I couldn't have Jewish friends in the community. If I got close to anyone Jewish, he would freak out because he was afraid that they would find out about [the abuse] and destroy his career." Another respondent similarly described the loneliness of being abused by her community rabbi and having nowhere to turn. After the abuse ended, that isolation remained, and she eventually chose to move across the country, marry a non-Jewish man and leave Jewish life altogether.

Stage 4: Destabilizing the victim

The secrecy, isolation, guilt, and self-doubt all feed in to a deep injury that the abuser causes, which is destabilization. In order to maintain the abuse, the assailant has to keep the victim sunk in self-doubt, uncertainty, and powerlessness so they won't walk away or exit the abusive relationship.

---

[128] Rosenblatt, "Stolen Innocence"
https://www.bjpa.org/content/upload/bjpa/stol/Stolen%20Innocence%20-%20Gary%20Rosenblatt%20-%20Jewish%20Week%20-%20Sexual%20Abuse.pdf

Intermittent reinforcement

This tactic, a tormenting reward system that is unpredictable and random, makes the victim incessantly desperate for the abuser's reward. Lori, for example, described how the rabbi would warmly invite her for a counseling session, and then alternate between being nice to her and being angry at her. She did not know what to expect, so she constantly walked on eggshells.

Brenda described how the rabbi would often publicly ignore her, literally turn his back to her, "all this time he was pretending I don't exist." She recalls that "he wouldn't speak to me in public. At all. Ever." He would also actively ignore her if she was in the room, while he was being "nice and charming to everyone around me." For example, "when he was coming around with the Torah, he would kiss the women on either side of me and behind me, and just completely skip me as if I didn't exist. It was like a psychological game. Meanwhile, at other times, he would do the exact opposite. "He was doing this weird, hot/cold thing with me all the time and it was really upsetting me." Sometimes, she recalled, "he would look at me from afar in a non-rabbinic way, like I am a girl in the bar, staring at me in a way that he was conveying he was sexually attracted to me. It's hard to explain what that is, but you know it when you see it." And then at other times, he would ignore her completely or ghost her. "He would do it all in public but in a way that nobody else would know. Everything he did was covert and manipulative and kind of secret, but secret in public."

This tactic alternates between positive and negative reinforcement, between intimacy and silent treatments, and relies on maintaining secrecy and control. It involves punishments of silence or withholding things that the victim cherishes or desires, and it plays with victims' self-concept. She did not tell anyone for a long time because she "thought nobody would believe me" and also because, "it just seemed like it must be something that I did." It is a very elaborate and destabilizing tactic that causes victims to doubt themselves:

> So many mind games. I was always on edge. Like, is he going to talk to me today? Like, we would have a private meeting, we would meet for coffee, and it would be lovely, and the next day we would have a board meeting and he wouldn't speak to me. Even to say hello. It was so weird. I was so confused.

Incredibly, this behavior worked to get Brenda even more loyal to him and dependent on him. "I was really upset about it, but at the same time I was compassionate toward him, which I probably shouldn't have been."

For some victims—such as Cindy—this tactic felt like "the most damaging of all." It can enter the victim into a constant state of insecurity, instability, and emotional dependence on the abuser.

The synthetic intimacy trance

This grooming tactic, which involves a kind of hypnotic attention of being watched under a microscope, was named by Hoffman based on a tactic described by Adelyn Birch called "Trance and hypnosis":

> *Psychopaths naturally focus intensely on their targets, just as a predator focuses intensely on its prey. They are very 'present' when they're 'interested' in someone, and that intense presence — communicated through unwavering eye contact and focused, heightened attention — can induce a similar reaction in the person who is the object of their focus... Many people say the 'psychopathic stare' causes chills and a feeling of aversion... but if someone you're interested in [such as your rabbi or teacher] does it, then it will come across as flattering interest and attention. You will likely feel captivated.*[129]

Several women described this feeling of having been under some kind of spell. Michal Cohen, one of Ezra Sheinberg's victims, described how her abuser would stare intently at her as if reading what was in her head. He apparently did that so much with his victims that it became what he was known for: the person who could "read into people's souls."[130]

Zelda said, "I was just stupid enough when I was under his spell, with him, and that is something I'm just figuring out how to repair now."

Mocking and sexual jokes

This tactic involves using jokes to put the other person down or demeaning her with laughter in front of other people in a way that diminishes the victim's dignity and sense of self. This was Steinhardt's primary tactic, in which he "joked" about threesomes or about women's sexuality, even from the podium of major conferences in which audiences laughed. His defenders, like Charles Bronfman, dismissed all this as "kibbitzing", saying that this was how he had been for decades, as if that made it okay. The culture was at times reflected in programs he supported,

---

[129] Adelyn Birch, *30 Covert Emotional Manipulation Tactics: How manipulators take control in personal relationships.* (Createspace 2015)
[130] Nina Fox, "Early release for sex offender: 'Ezra Sheinberg continues to abuse us, and he will hurt other women'," *Ynet* [Hebrew] 20 August, 2021, https://www.ynet.co.il/judaism/article/bkuoaufet (Translation by Elana Sztokman)

where one former participant said, "We would joke that the only reason our camp was funded was so that we could find nice Jewish boys to marry."

Sexual jokes were a primary complaint from many interviewees, especially those working in organizational settings, as we saw in the compilations of stories in work settings. Recall that Avital's abuser would walk in on her regularly and harass her. When she tried to get him to stop, he said, "I spend as much time with you as your husband, at least he gets benefits." She didn't find the "joke" amusing.

Baruch Lanner used jokes along with violence to gain control and destabilize his targets:

> Dealing with boys, Rabbi Lanner reportedly would use four-letter words and tell crude jokes freely in his private conversations with them, disparage those not in his inner circle, and often greet them with a swift, hard kick in the groin. When they sometimes would crumple to the ground in pain, he would laugh, insisting he was just showing he was one of the guys. [131]

Jokes can be used as pressure tactics as well, such as the case in which Ruth was pressured by a big donor to kiss another potential donor—as if it were funny. They all laughed about it for a bit—until the pressure continued, the man called her to ask her out, and her boss gently encouraged her to do it for the sake of securing the donation.

Jokes, especially those that mock the victim, are part of the grooming process. Hoffman has many examples in which her abuser used this tactic, such as when she was giving an oral presentation for her dissertation and he responded by making a sexualized joke about the word "oral." Or when she was having surgery and he quipped about his interest in her body parts.

Jokes like this degrade a victim's sense of self, are belittling and objectifying, and are part of how abusers maintain their sense of power and control. This can be especially true during the process of trying to exit the abusive relationship. Cindy, for example, said, "When I confronted him with the ethics code of his rabbinical organization, he laughed at me and told me I was naïve." Mocking jokes disempower the victims and give the "joker" power.

Mostly, jokes are one of the tactics that destabilize victims by making them doubt themselves. *Is he serious? Is he joking? Does he like me? I am not sure. I can't tell. I don't know anything anymore.* This sets the groundwork for one of the most traumatic aspects of emotional abuse: mind games.

---

[131] Rosenblatt,"Stolen Innocence,"
https://www.bjpa.org/content/upload/bjpa/stol/Stolen%20Innocence%20-%20Gary%20Rosenblatt%20-%20Jewish%20Week%20-%20Sexual%20Abuse.pdf

Stage 5: Mind games

Like all abuse, sexual abuse ultimately involves mind games by the abuser, who is often skilled at manipulating their victims and making them completely doubt themselves and even their own sanity. Victims lose touch with their own ability to trust themselves, which opens them up to all kinds of trauma.

Gaslighting

Gaslighting is possibly the most common form of mind games, a tactic of denying reality in order to make the victim question their own sanity and give the abuser power and control over the victim's mind, even telling her directly that she is crazy. Recall the example in which Rhonda Abrams called out immediately when the donor groped her behind, and he replied, "No I didn't," with a wink — a tactic that combines gaslighting and mocking. The experience made her momentarily question her own handle on reality. For many victims, it sounds like a voice in their head: *Did that happen? Am I making it up? Maybe. I'm not sure.* And that self-doubt in the victim is one of the greatest powers that abusers have.

Many victims experience this in the course of their trauma, and gaslighting is considered one of the mainstays of narcissistic abuse. Hoffman, for example, described how she found herself crying about the abuse when her abuser "gently rubbed my back [and] called me 'unstable,'" as if to say it was all in her mind. "His tone of voice sounded sweet ('You are very unstable right now, I am worried about you'), but what he was actually doing was denying my sense of reality and undermining my self-reliance."

Gaslighting can also take place on a larger scale and is especially dominant in the process of reporting and disclosure. When a major article was published about the hookup culture on Birthright Israel trips[132] — which included testimonies from dozens of participants and staffers — some Birthright providers insisted the allegations were untrue. "In training sessions... no one ever said that the purpose was to encourage romantic

---

[132] Birthright Israel is a fully-paid trip to Israel for young adults who have never been to Israel, a program that was created by Steinhardt and others in order to foster Jewish connection to Israel – and also, it seems, to get Jews to marry other Jews and keep the nation going. Sarah M. Seltzer, Birthright Israel and #MeToo. Jewish Currents spoke with more than 50 Birthright Israel participants and staffers about their experiences with the often-fraught sexual and gender dynamics on the famous free trip to Israel. Here is what we found. *Jewish Currents*, April 18, 2018 https://jewishcurrents.org/birthright-Israel-and-metoo

connections."[133] The use of "no one" effectively silences the entire discussion and makes the victims out to be either lying or divorced from reality. (I will return to this point in the chapter on disclosure.)

Spiritual bypass

This is a tactic in which the abuser relies on his own interpretations of religious rules and ideas, bypassing the "normal" rules, in order to convince the victim to do what he wants. This may entail misapplying spiritual ideas in order to render himself less accountable — such as using terms like "chevruta," "bashert," or "teshuva" in skewed ways to avoid responsibility.

Carlebach was a master of invoking Jewish spiritual language in order to abuse women and girls. According to the Lilith report on his abuse:

> *Robin Goldberg, today a teacher of women's studies and a research psychoanalyst on women's issues in California, was 12 years old when Shlomo visited her Orthodox Harrisburg, Pennsylvania, community to lead a singing and dancing concert. He invited all the young people for a preconcert preparation. And it was during the dancing that he started touching her. He kept coming back to her, she reports, whispering in her ear, saying 'holy maidele,' and fondling her breast.[134]*

Carlebach used the pretense of religious dancing, along with words like "holy" to confuse and destabilize his victim.

Cindy recalls, for example, that her abuser said "what he was doing was normal, that the rabbinical ethics code was there because it had to be, but basically he was 'above the law' in this matter — because his unhappy marriage and my unique qualities all made this okay and justifiable." She added, "I did not grow up in a synagogue or around rabbis, and I believed his claims." He was able to prey on her insecurity about religious knowledge and assumptions about his rabbinical authority and superiority.

For Zelda as well, the use of spiritual and religious codes to get around his behavior was vivid:

> *It was so twisted by how he would use scripture. He would appropriate religion and Torah and spirituality to get me to*

---

[133] Jason Harris, "Hookup Culture? Not On The Birthright Trips I've Led," *Times of Israel Blog.* April 30, 2019,. https://jewishweek.timesofIsrael.com/hookup-culture-not-on-the-birthright-trips-ive-led/

[134] Boigon, Molly, "'This was no coverup': Inside the investigation of Rabbi Sheldon Zimmerman," *Forward*, May 17, 2021, https://forward.com/news/469213/sheldon-zimmerman-sexual-relations-rabbis-investigation/

have sex with him. I believed him when he said it was a special spiritual connection. He talked about how we had a special chevruta relationship, a special relationship where the 'erotic' manifests, and there were just no boundaries.

That's a hard thing for me to admit, for someone who is very educated. I have two graduate degrees, I'm working on my third, and I don't like to think I'm easily fooled. And I don't like to think I'm so ignorant of my own religion that I would fall for this, 'Oh, Kabbalah! I'm touching your boobs' shit. But I did. I was totally mesmerized; I thought he was a demigod. I thought he was just so amazing because I always had so much respect for rabbis.

Similarly, Esther describes how her abuser used spirituality to sexually control her:

Looking back, I can see that the problem was far more than the breach of a sexual boundary. It was also the betrayal of a spiritual one. The rabbi knew I was looking for a spiritual purpose, a way to act in God's love for the world. He took the profound spiritual experience I was having and channeled it toward himself, for his own purposes. He interposed himself between me and my experience of God.

This is a very important point because it is a set of tactics that is possibly unique to the dynamic of rabbis abusing women who want to be closer to Judaism or Jewish life. When people come to rabbis for pastoral care, spiritual guidance, or even conversion, the rabbi is in a powerful position of ownership of her process. He is the gatekeeper and the source of all knowledge about her religious life. That is a lot of power.

Perhaps the most blatant example of the rabbi as holder of the victim's spiritual connection is in the case of Barry Freundel, the so-called "mikveh rabbi" who went to prison for video-stalking women in the mikveh. His victims were in his synagogue's ritual bath because he told them they had to be. They had come to him to convert to Judaism, and as such their spiritual journeys were entirely based on his approval, and instructions. So, when he told them to go to the baths at a certain time and stand in a certain place — which, as it turned out, was in perfect view of his hidden cameras — they listened. Their entire connection to Judaism went through him. He was able to bypass all Jewish spiritual norms and get his victims to do his bidding because he held all the power and authority for their conversion to Judaism.

Lying and lying by omission

This grooming tactic may be denial, exaggeration, or saying whatever they need to say in order to continue the manipulation and gain control.

Zelda said that her abuser found her on OK Cupid via a profile that was "totally made up." She believes it was completely adapted to manipulate her, showing obscure interests that she had, like a particular music group she liked, the small town she was brought up in, and so forth. "None of it was actually true," she said. He had fabricated an entire identity just for the purpose of grooming her into submission.

This process of "lots of lying" was very difficult and confusing for Brenda because synagogue and religious practice were always a matter of integrity and authenticity for her. At the time, she did not have the language or framework to understand what she was experiencing. She found explanations only after the abuse ended:

> I read this book by Shannon Thomas called Healing from Hidden Abuse.[135] I didn't read it until way after all this. When I finally read it, what resonated was that rarely was each individual thing he did so individually terrible. It was all excusable. Everything you can have an excuse for. Like, 'That wasn't so nice, but...' People like this keep piling it on and piling on till it gets to be unbearable. There were so many secret things. Hurtful things. Lots of lies.

Dangling a third party (or triangulation)

This grooming tactic is a form of sadism that involves introducing another party to torment the victim and further pressure the victim into submission. This has many variations and versions. For example, Hoffman writes that she experienced this frequently with her abuser, where he would invite two victims for one trip without telling either of them about the other. "He had each woman under the impression that she was the only one. He watches them as they figure it out over dinner. Then he enjoys the chaos that follows." Another example is an abuser who comments on other women and compares them. Nicole described how her abuser "was sure to tell me repeatedly that 'she's got a tight, hot body,'" ensuring that Nicole knew she was being compared to his wife. Here is how Zelda described it:

> He had his phone with him, and he would say, 'Oh, look, on Wednesday I'm going to coffee with Irene,' and I said, 'Oh, who's Irene?' He said, 'Oh, I just met her, here's a picture.' And he pulls up a picture on his phone and it's a dating app

---

[135] Shannon Thomas, Healing from Hidden Abuse, Thomas 2016

profile of a woman named Irene. And I said, 'Oh, you told me that you shut down your profile when you met me because I was your whole heart and soul,' and he said, 'No, no, I reopened it a few weeks ago, I've been seeing four other women.' Four! Not one. Four! And he named them all and showed me their profiles, so excited, no guilt, no remorse, no sense of shame. Like, I'm just supposed to be like, this is normal. And I was like, oh, and I couldn't even be angry, because it was so, huh? Because this behavior was all so out of the realm of what I consider normal human behavior. I was stupefied. I was speechless. And then I was like, how do I deal with this? I wanted to be nice.

Ironically, this tactic may cause the victim to be even more loyal to the abuser. Victims may feel so invested in the relationship that leaving feels unthinkable, and they will stay despite the detrimental effects to their self-respect.

Moreover, this is a glaring example of the interplay between grooming tactics on women and broader constructs of gender socialization. Women everywhere are socialized into being caring and considerate of others while not being taught to care for themselves. This socialization ultimately helps abusers by reducing women's ability to break away from damaging relationships and is thus used by perpetrators as a means both to groom and then to maintain engagement. It's the *"I should be nice"* socialization that keeps so many women trapped.

Stage 6: Controlling the external narrative

This last stage of grooming is slightly different from the rest in that this is where the abuser turns his attention to the "audience", so to speak, to the people who are discovering the abuse and are about to pass judgment. This tactic is primarily aimed at families, communities, board members, and/or the media. The abuser uses all the tactics of emotional manipulation, spin, and charm to shape how the audience will react. The abuser does this when the abuse is likely coming to an end. He will often tactically plan out his exit strategy with key manipulations to get away with it, and these tactics so often work to keep him from being caught — or if he is caught, to help him keep his followers, his reputation, and his job. These tactics are intricately connected to gaslighting and other mind games in that they make the victims doubt themselves — while it can feel like the whole world is lining up against them, too. This stage is also part of the disclosure and reporting processes, and the tactics listed here are revisited in those chapters as well.

Blame-shifting and Scapegoating

This tactic is where the abuser deflects blame from their own actions onto the victim. For Brenda, when she tried to end the abuse, she discovered to her horror that the rabbi preempted her by going to the synagogue board and telling them that *she* had been abusing *him*. When Brenda told him that she needed to break the whole thing off with him, he quickly turned on her:

> He got really angry and defensive about it. Like, he told me that this is all due to my mental problems. He also said, with like an evil face, I swear, with a sneer of disgust and a laugh, he said, 'Oh my God, I would never like you.' I said to myself, even if that was true, a kind person would never say that. It was just a mean, nasty, 'Ew, I would never like you.' And he said, 'We have no special relationship, you're just a congregant,' and I was like, really?! After all this time, after lunches and coffees, and I've had you in my house for holidays and I helped your career, I'm just a congregant?

It is terribly easy for abusers to cast their victims as mentally ill. In fact, research shows that this dynamic is used regularly and with great efficiency in cases of divorce. When a woman reports abuse by her husband, she is *more* likely to be cast as mentally ill and to lose custody of her children than if she does not complain and the court discovers this on its own. For example, a 2004 study funded by the National Institute of Justice found that mothers were more likely to receive primary custody if they had *not* made allegations of domestic abuse, while fathers were equally likely to get custody whether there were allegations against them or not—meaning "women who were open about being abused received less protection for themselves and their children than those who were not" because the women were "hyper-vigilant, agitated, guarded, volatile"—characteristics that "can make mothers look unstable or unfit, but are also commonplace reactions to trauma or even symptoms of PTSD." Joan Meier, a George Washington University law school scholar, explained that "An angry woman might be vengeful and fabricating. But angry fathers? We have no problem with them. It's so thick with gender stereotypes, you can cut it with a knife."[136] Similarly, victims of sexual abuse—who may at times display the same PTSD behaviors—are readily cast as unreliable. The US military, for example, had a regular policy of dismissing women who reported sexual assault and labeling them with a psychiatric diagnosis as mentally unstable. "Each received the psychiatric

---

[136] Kathryn Joyce, "She Said Her Husband Hit Her. She Lost Custody of Their Kids," *Longreads*, July 2020, https://longreads.com/2020/07/08/domestic-violence-custody-family-court-disputes/amp/?fbclid=IwAR2ss7VxPVBMxxfiPr-JSD4QfKFdU7si3pa0ljPAc5bCuect3_KF-nCZrUQ

diagnosis and military discharge after reporting a sexual assault. Stephanie Schroeder, one of the women who experienced that after being raped in the military, told reporters, "I'm not crazy...I am actually relatively normal." Jenny McClendon, who also reported sexual assault, had a similar reaction. "I remember thinking this is absurd. This is ridiculous. How could I be emotionally unstable? I'm very clear of mind, especially considering what had happened. It was a ludicrous diagnosis." Yet, a 2012 investigation found that women across all branches of the armed forces who experienced a sexual assault received a command dismissive of the allegations and a psychiatric discharge. The narrative that they were crazy stuck—and with consistent ease.[137]

Daliah describes how this happened to her. "The whole dismissal of the woman as crazy was easy." Similarly, when Brenda went to the senior rabbi for help in dealing with the junior rabbi who had abused her, he had already internalized the blame-shifting:

> I said to the senior rabbi, 'He's so awful to me, please help me. So he said, 'Why didn't you come to me sooner?' I tried to explain it, and I said among other things that the abuser is power hungry. The senior rabbi said, 'Him? Power hungry? What are you talking about? You're the one who has power in the community. You are the one who is a leader in the community, you have a beautiful family. You are the one who has stature and respect. You're wealthy. He's just a poor little single rabbi.' Which isn't true. I mean, he's an adult. In his mid-to-late-30s. He's an adult and an ordained rabbi. And then every conversation after that was about me, and about healing and moving on. I was a total wreck at this point. But every time I would speak to this rabbi, I would hear, 'He was trying to help you heal.'

The complete distortion of her experience was a combination of gaslighting, blame-shifting, and spinning the narrative. Interestingly, workplace trainer Sarah Chandler said that "Why didn't you come sooner?" is an extremely common blame-shifting tactic in response to reporting. I also interviewed Fran Sepler, a consultant, investigator, and trainer who works on building respectful workplaces and preventing all forms of misconduct in Jewish organizations, who Sarah studied with. She also took issue with the senior rabbi's response, with how she saw him "slicing the power structures":

---

[137] David S. Martin, "Rape victims say military labels them 'crazy'," *CNN*, April 14, 2012, http://edition.cnn.com/2012/04/14/health/military-sexual-assaults-personality-disorder/index.html

The slicing of power structures is very selective in that matter. He says you have all the power, completely ignoring, of course, gender dynamics, completely ignoring that the junior rabbi is a rabbi, and being either willfully or genuinely unaware of the wide swath of bullying that isn't yelling and screaming at people but is relational aggression. And so, if he had really listened to what she had to say before jumping to conclusions and trying to analyze and slice the power structure according to his mind frame, he might have been deeply affected by understanding that this was harming somebody who was valuable to his congregation, and would have then said, 'Well, we've got to do something about this.'

All of this left Brenda bereft, and on some level questioning her own sanity.

I would like to point out how disturbing Brenda's story is in light of the testimonies in a previous chapter of women rabbis who described being abused by male congregants — and who were left powerless in that dynamic because donors, congregants, and board members are deemed untouchable. Brenda was all three, but that principle did not apply to her. In fact, she was quickly turned into the aggressor. It is striking that this senior rabbi had no qualms about blaming a female congregant — even a wealthy, heavily involved congregant who had dedicated 20 years of volunteer service to the synagogue and had sat on many boards and gave massive donations — and accusing her of abusing the rabbi. At the same time, women rabbis are told that it is impossible to censure male congregants for sexual abuse. The gender aspect of this dynamic is striking.

The "good guy" defense

This grooming tactic, which will likely begin when the victim starts to take back the reins of her life, involves pointing out that the abuser is a "good guy." Think of it as the Bill Cosby effect, in which the endearing father-type, kid-lover of Jell-O commercials who even played a loving obstetrician on his wholesome family show, is at the same time committing sexual abuse and rape using roofies on dozens of women. When these stories eventually emerged — over 60 stories so far — it was hard for the public to wrap their heads around the contrast between his public persona and his secret private life.

Many abusers present themselves under guises of being the "good guy." Marc Gafni, for example, who has been accused of abuse for decades, presents himself as a spiritual guide. Congregational rabbi Larry Bach, who was censured by the Central Conference of Reform Rabbis for abuse, describes himself as a hero, writing music and speaking about social justice.

This can also be an overt tactic to position themselves as the exact opposite of what they are — to be seen as hero instead of predator. Jonathan Skolnick, for example, took on the role of teaching students how to use the internet safely and protect themselves from online predators, to make himself not only the cool and popular social-media-savvy teacher but also to position himself as the "good guy," as well as the potential "savior, " as described above.[138]

The good guy defense is used to disarm victims. Hoffman gives a few examples of this from her experiences. Her abuser, who has been abusing women for years and allegedly trafficking women,[139] would say, "I'm a good guy. Really. I never beat my wife. I hold a decent job. I spend time with my kids." Or, "Well, it's not like I hit you. It was just one small push. It could be worse." Or, "It's not like I gave you an STD or anything serious happened."

Many interviewees reported feeling trapped in their abusive situations because their abusers were considered "good guys," whether this means being the beloved rabbi, the beloved donor, the beloved scholar, or just an overall "good guy" beloved by all.

The good guy defense can be very confusing. In the Jewish world, this may look like the person who runs a charity for the environment or human rights, or who embraces loving, progressive causes. Or it may look like the rabbinical school rabbi who verbally champions women's equality on the pulpit while soliciting women for sex in his office. It can be a mind-numbing split-personality. Recall that one interviewee experienced ongoing abuses by her boss that "were supposedly platonic and normal because he was openly gay and professed to be an ally for women leaders, myself included." This account, which includes verbal sexual abuse and physical boundary crossing — although it stops short at solicitation — is a classic example of the good guy defense. It is the abuser's sense that he is one of the "good guys" who defends women publicly and has no use for them sexually, and therefore his behavior cannot possibly be construed as abusive or problematic.[140] She also felt that there was no way for her to explain that he was abusing her — getting too close to her, putting his head on her lap, making sexual jokes about her in the office — if, among other things, he was

---

[138] Hannah Dreyfus, "Riverdale Again Hit With 'Shocking' Abuse Case. Child porn charges against an SAR principal like an 'earthquake,' parent says," *Jewish Week*, September 17, 2019 https://jewishweek.timesofIsrael.com/riverdale-again-hit-with-shocking-abuse-case/

[139] Sarah Ruth Hoffman, "Recognizing Human Trafficking: Difficult Up Close," *Times of Israel*, Jan 3, 2022, https://blogs.timesofIsrael.com/recognizing-human-trafficking-difficult-up-close/

[140] Christine Ristaino, "When nice guys behave like monsters," *Washington Post*. April 11, 2014 https://www.washingtonpost.com/blogs/she-the-people/wp/2014/04/11/when-nice-guys-behave-like-monsters/

gay. But more than that, she was reluctant to go up against the "good guy" who was fighting for women.

There are many examples of "good guys" who were abusing women, such as former New York State Attorney General Eric Schneiderman (also Jewish), a champion of women's rights who used his office to support victims of Harvey Weinstein—and who had a history of choking his victims nearly to death. As Jill Filipovic writes about Schneiderman in the *New York Times*:

> *It hurts the most when it's one of the 'good' ones…. At home, it seems, Mr. Schneiderman was a sexual sadist and manipulative misogynist. At work, he was a champion of women's rights… even writing a bill specifically to punish the same kind of strangulation he is said to have forced on some of his partners. How do we reconcile these two versions of a single man?…*
>
> *The reality may be darker: that the power he derived from his role in progressive politics was intertwined with his abuse. He seems to have used his feminist-minded political work to advance his own career, to ingratiate himself with the women he would go on to harm, and to cover up his cruelties.*
>
> *Even the men we thought we could trust — especially, perhaps, the ostentatiously good ones — may not be quite what they seem.*
>
> *Maybe, if the abuse allegations are true, Mr. Schneiderman had two separate lives, totally alienating his abusive self from his feminist one, and maybe he lives every day with the shame of that cognitive dissonance. Or maybe his feminist self is part of the bigger power play and he simply enjoys getting one over on all of us…. He rode the women's movements' coattails, into much more fame than a state attorney general typically enjoys.*
>
> *Mr. Schneiderman also seems to have used his feminist reputation as a tool to access the exact kind of women he apparently enjoyed breaking down, while his liberal bona fides made the women who say he mistreated them second-guess themselves, and stay quiet.*
>
> *According to one woman quoted in the* New Yorker *piece, Mr. Schneiderman told her that high-powered professional women want to be sexually dominated, and said: 'Yeah, you act a certain way and look a certain way, but I know that at heart you are a dirty little slut. You want to be my whore.' Then, she*

*says, he slapped her across the face, twice. She didn't report it
because 'He's a good attorney general, he's doing good things.
I didn't want to jeopardize that.'*[141]

The realization that men who are publicly seen as "good guys" or even feminist defenders of women are privately abusing women can be tormenting, as Filipovic describes. To wit, there are even photographs of Harvey Weinstein accompanying Hillary Clinton to a Planned Parenthood gala. That should tell us everything we need to know about the good guy defense.

Indeed, many abusers get away with years of abuse, even after they are discovered, because of how powerful this defense is. The good guy defense challenges deep-rooted notions about what a sexual predator ought to look like. This image, combined with many other grooming tactics, the charm, adoration, faux-caring, and sometimes public celebrity do not match one's first thought of "rapist." This is often a big hurdle for victims, as it makes it difficult to identify their experience as assault. (More on the profile of an abuser in the next chapter.)

"It's just an affair"

Clergy abuse is also easily brushed off and dismissed as consensual "affairs." But "affair" is inaccurate when one person—the rabbi—has many powers over the other. Rabbi Yonasan Abraham, for example, a top member of the London rabbinical court that determines who is considered Jewish as well as the personal status of Jews in the community, was dismissed in 2019 for "having an affair" with a married woman, a case in which the power differential was enormous.[142] He was not only a (married and supposedly very religious) judge but also head of the synagogue where she was a congregant and where she had sought his spiritual guidance. "This was definitely abuse," said one interviewee who knows the victim. "The whole world is telling her it was 'an affair.' This is terrible gaslighting."

Daliah, a Reconstructionist rabbi whose father was a Reform rabbi, said that, growing up, "I knew that my father's friends were having affairs with congregants. I knew about all this stuff." But it is not clear that an "affair" with a rabbi who has power, authority, status, stature, and sway over his

---

[141] Jill Filipovic, "The Problem With 'Feminist' Men," *New York Times*, May 8, 2018 https://www.nytimes.com/2018/05/08/opinion/schneiderman-abuse-feminist**Error! Bookmark not defined.**-men.html

[142] Jerusalem Post Staff, "Senior London rabbi removed from position after having affair. The rabbi was faced with harsh criticism, many of which claimed that in his rank and position, he is held to a higher moral standard," *Jerusalem Post*, April 14, 2019, https://www.jpost.com/diaspora/senior-london-rabbi-removed-from-position-after-having-affair-586751

congregants can ever be truly consensual. A rabbi who sexually propositions a congregant, even if in other contexts this would look and sound like flirting, is coming from a place of power and authority and is by definition an uneven power relationship in which consent is dubious at best.

Daliah had an encounter with a sexual predator who was hired as the Director of Education at her synagogue. An article written by one of his victims titled, "The Rabbi's Mistress" about the abuse she suffered and how she was dismissed as simply having an "affair" alerted Daliah to this rabbi's history. Daliah posted about this on social media and began getting calls from around the country from women whom he abused.

"Another female rabbi said that he roofied her at a movement convention! And then, after Torah study one day, a woman in the community met him and he basically preyed on her and he tried to force her to give him a blow job [and] did this whole thing about 'I'm your rabbi.'" This rabbi, who had a history and clear tactics of sexual abuse, was dismissed as someone having an "affair," even though he specifically used his position as rabbi as an instrument of force and coercion. This is a tricky situation to explain because it does not always *look* like a power hierarchy—as opposed to, say, a boss, a professor, or a rabbi grooming a child.

Meanwhile, this rabbi excused his offenses as consensual affairs—even when the women did not consent—and was expelled from the movement, not because they did an ethics investigation but because he refused to sit down with the overriding body to discuss it, which is grounds for immediate expulsion. But he kept teaching in the community anyway, eventually found a different synagogue to work at, and also taught at the school and worked at the local Federation as well.

The term "affair" erases all sense that the relationship involved pressure and that the rabbi was predatorial. Esther talked about the impact of the congregation calling her abusive relationship with the married rabbi of her congregation an "affair:"

> I was fully entrapped [and] absolutely terrified. I knew that something was very wrong, but my sense of my soul's purpose revolved around the belief that we were called by God to do holy work together. If I stopped believing that we had a sacred purpose together, then I had lost everything to no purpose.

Again, the rabbi's successful co-opting of religious language kept Esther attached to him, even if it felt all wrong. When the board found out, they asked her to keep it a secret. "They were afraid that if it came to light, the synagogue's reputation would suffer, the rabbi would have to resign, and they would lose him."

Reut is baffled by her community's perceptions of women as complicit instead of coerced. She said that the abuser in her community is still advertised as providing counseling services years after he was outed, even though that is how he preys on his victims. "An extremely religious-looking rabbi somehow convinced these women that having sex with them was part of what they need... How can people not understand that this is abuse?"

I would like to also point out that the rabbis abusing congregants and calling it an "affair" are from different denominations.[143] And labeling abuse "an affair" is a dynamic that continues to cut across denominations and communities.

The "vindictive woman" spin

A further extension of the "affair" narrative is the add-on of the vindictive woman who wanted the "affair" until she spitefully changed her mind. When the woman called "Debbie" who was abused as a teen by Sheldon Zimmerman in the 1970s wanted to come forward, she was afraid of being cast as a "vindictive woman." The culture of the time, according to reporter Gary Rosenblatt who broke the story, "put the burden on accusers like Debbie to convince the public that abuse had taken place. They also had a reasonable expectation that their accounts and character would be questioned. Meanwhile, Zimmerman was not only a leader of the Reform movement but a beloved spiritual leader and educator of great charm and charisma with a large and loyal following. 'I was single, I was very involved in my work and it seemed too risky to challenge him [the rabbi] publicly,' Debbie told me."[144]

This "vindictive woman" spin is a common narrative that makes the abuse look like something that the victim wanted and makes the victim look not only mentally off-balance but also mean-spirited. As Hoffman writes, "This tactic is the final cut, the kicking her when she is already down just as she is starting to get up and find her strength and her value. And when the victim sees this, it is the gory finale, the most vile and deepest possible

---

[143] The Conservative movement's Code of Conduct states clearly, "If sexual boundaries are violated by the rabbi, it is understood that that relationship is not regarded as consensual," A Code of Professional Conduct for Members of the Rabbinical Assembly (Section V.2.(3)) https://www.rabbinicalassembly.org/sites/default/files/public/ethical_guidelines/code-of-conduct-2018-members.pdf. The code of conduct is the *theory* while the actions experienced by the interviewees are the *practice*.

[144] Gary Rosenblatt, "A Rabbi's Accuser Wanted Me to Tell Her Story. Here's Why It Took 20 Years. When the Reform movement suspended Sheldon Zimmerman in 2000, a woman wanted the details known but feared retribution." *The Jewish Week*. May 26, 2021, https://jewishweek.timesofisrael.com/a-rabbis-accuser-wanted-me-to-tell-her-story-heres-why-it-took-20-years/

objectification of her humanity." Just as the world easily accepts that rape victims are crazy, it is also easy to see them as angry and spiteful.

How "Jewish" is all this?

This chapter aimed to create a portrait of the grooming process for sexual abuse in the Jewish world. I encountered three main challenges to this objective.

One main challenge is that not all abusers are alike—they have different settings to operate in, different positions, different genders, and different types of victims. A camp counselor grooming a child may not necessarily use the same tactics as a rabbi grooming an adult woman, for example. Despite that challenge, many clear common denominators emerged in this research that paint a fairly comprehensive portrait. Certainly not every abuser ticks all the boxes, but the connections and overlaps among tactics are clear. Other tactics invariably do not appear on this list, but the descriptions here — which are the ones that emerged as dominant among my interviewees — offer powerful insights into the many insidious ways in which predators play with their victims' minds before they ever touch their bodies.

A second major challenge is that, so often, a tactic viewed in isolation does not look like grooming. It may look like care, or just look rabbinic or pastoral. That reality, in itself, can be crazy-making. As Hoffman writes, "Just because you do not see these tactics in action does not mean that the clergy person in question is not an abuser. Around other people, the rabbi may appear completely normal. The abuse that victims face is covert and difficult to articulate, and leaves the victim feeling crazy.[145] This is a challenge across many cultures. But in faith settings, where leaders are expected to be trustworthy, authentic, and caring, it can be very hard at first to distinguish an act of care from an act of grooming. This is why the detailed portrait is so critical. One item on the list may not, in itself, necessarily amount to grooming. But taken together in context, it becomes clear.

Finally, the third and perhaps biggest challenge is isolating what aspects of this grooming process are particularly "Jewish." The answer may in fact be that, for the most part, strategies of abuse are similar if not identical across faith cultures. The predator seeks out their victim's vulnerabilities then works hard to gain trust, break down boundaries, weaken their prey, and control both the victim and the outside narratives through a host of serious

---

[145] Hoffman, "Rabbinic abuse,: 26 power & control tactics," *Times of Israel Blog* https://blogs.timesofisrael.com/rabbinic-abuse-26-power-control-tactics/

mind games. This is certainly the pattern across communities, cultures, and countries.

However, predators use the tools at their disposal, and in that sense, there are some distinctly Jewish language and cultural patterns, as well as societal expectations that Jewish abusers use. For example, while grooming generally relies on victim vulnerabilities, rabbis often have privileged access to those— such as officiating during moments of loss, illness, or personal spiritual crisis. Similarly, Jewish culture is often built around codes that identify "insiders," whether that is Hebrew language, references to Bible or Jewish prayer, or even Jewish ideas such as "teshuva" (penance) or holiness. One abuser used references to Buber's "I and Thou," another used Kabbalah, and another used the fight against anti-Semitism. These are examples of cultural codes that create a sense of insider-intimacy in a uniquely Jewish way.

Takeaways about grooming

Several key insights about grooming in specifically Jewish cultural contexts emerged from these interviews:

- **Prowling religious and communal events and virtual spaces such as social media.** In many stories, victims were being watched at Jewish events, from camp "oneg" to synagogue kiddush to Jewish fundraisers to Jewish dating apps. It may be worthwhile to consider what counts as acceptable touching or boundary breaking at places like this where people are so focused on socializing that predatory behaviors go unchecked.

- **Use of Jewish ideas and spiritual concepts to lure and trap victims.** Many victims were drawn to their predator's use of Jewish ideas that they considered valuable or even sacred—such as chevruta, holiness, divine purpose, fighting anti-Semitism, supporting Israel, or even sketchy kabbalistic ideas about unity and women's bodies. Jews in powerful positions are able to tap into deep desires among their victims for Jewish meaning, and that can be dangerous.

- **Exploiting the desire for communal connectivity.** Similarly, one of the points of vulnerability for many victims is the desire for belonging and connection. This desire may be particularly strong among people who are isolated in some way — who have a non-Jewish parent or partner, who are physically or emotionally challenged or "different", who are lonely, or who are new to the community .[146] Predators can both exploit and exacerbate that vulnerability, especially when the abuse happens in the context or a location of that cherished Jewish connectedness.

- **The "poor lonely rabbi" defense.** Interestingly, while many predators use the tactic of victimizing themselves to gain sympathy, many interviewees reported a more specific tactic of the rabbi describing himself as a poor, lonely soul. That is a red flag.

- **Relying on a rabbinic "aura."** The way people are socialized into giving absolute respect to the rabbi, no matter what, interfered with their ability to see what was really going on. Perhaps it is worth reconsidering how the community bestows that kind of infallibility on some of its leaders.

- **Using pastoral care as a lure.** Across all faith communities, predators can use their position of being a pastoral carer to detect vulnerability and zoom in for the attack. In the Jewish community, it is not only rabbis who have that role; camp directors, professors, and teachers can have that power as well. Where people in certain positions are allowed to sit privately with those less powerful than themselves, and where one person has the cultural authority to give "counsel," these are points of danger. The overreliance on rabbis in all spheres of Jewish life also gives potential predators disproportionate power over their victims.

- **Exploiting communal power structures.** Communal institutions with all their hierarchies can embolden abusers. Victims shared stories about the synagogue board that supported the abusive rabbi, the rabbinical school that kept the predator on for decades, the organizaitonal director head who was an abuser but also considered a skillful fundraiser, the rapist who was beloved in the synagogue and in camp because he played the guitar, the serial harasser who nobody said a word about because he donated millions dollars a year to Jewish causes—these structures can be used to support abusers and keep them preying on victims.

- **Exposing grassroots social hierarchies.** Similarly, it is not just the formal hierarchies that support abuse but also informal cultural-social hierarchies. People who are treated as "less than" in the community—converts, "baalei teshuva", newly religious, newly Jewish, non-Caucasian, disabled, single women, divorcees, or who belong to a whole host of groups that are often discriminated against and made to feel inferior due to their gender, physical appearance, skin color, ethnicity, sexuality, or life choices —often become easy

---

[146] Sarah Ruth Hoffman, "Rabbinic Sexual Abuse and Patrilineal Descent,". *Times of Israel Blog.* Dec 12, 2108, https://blogs.timesofIsrael.com/rabbinic-sexual-abuse-and-patrilineal-descent

prey. And overall men are generally higher up the social hierarchy due to Jewish history, traditions, custom or law, and for male predators, that patriarchy offers tools for enabling abuse. The community should seriously consider the impact of these implied hierarchies on the prevalence of sexual abuse.

- **Cultural criteria for Jewish power.** Abusers in Jewish life receive power through their status, whether that's based on being a rabbi, having advanced degrees, writing books, having access, or holding money. While deference to those with money is arguably common in many cultures, it is worth pointing out how dominant it seems to be in Jewish communal settings. Moreover, people with the title "rabbi" are assumed to be more knowledgeable, holier, or more pious — and thus more trustworthy and even untouchable. The criteria that the community uses for determining a person's worth demands reexamination in how status works to enable and hide abuse.

Chapter 5: Profile of the Abuser

The revelation that our Jewish culture provides rabbis with tools that enable abuse can be jarring. Rabbis are entrusted to be conduits of piety, protectors of a holy tradition, and spiritual guides. Yet, in reality, sometimes they are, and sometimes they are not. That raises a tormenting question: How does a person who pursues a path of piety *also* engage in some of the ugliest, darkest acts that human beings can inflict upon others?

That is not necessarily a Jewish question alone. It is also a question for priests, monks, imams, yoga gurus, and anyone who twists their pious pulpit for sinister goals. And it isn't just about rabbis and clergy. As we have seen, abuse can be enabled by just about any power structure.

But abuse is not simply a function of a perpetrator's *position*. It is also a function of the perpetrator's *personality*. Certainly, positions of absolute authority and reverence give abusers the tools for abuse. But not everyone in those positions engages in abuse. The abuser also has to *want* to engage in abuse, and predilection needs to be seen and understood.

This chapter aims to unpack the characteristics of the high-profile Jewish abusers based on testimonies not only about rabbis but also about donors, bosses, academics, celebrities, and other abusers that emerged in this research.

Profile of the intimate-partner abuser

One useful tool for analysis is a *profile of the abuser* that is used by professionals in the field to assist victims of intimate-partner violence. Items on profile checklists vary slightly between activists, advocates, researchers, and survivors. However, there are generally 25-30 characteristics that are recognized as a powerful and accurate profile standard that can be used to identify an abusive partner.

Below is a compilation of checklists that I put together compiled from lists used by three organizations for training domestic violence victim advocates:

1. **Charismatic**. Charming, fun, romantic, funny, adoring, intensely emotional, engaging.
2. **Wants to be the "knight in shining armor."** Comes in like a hero or "savior" wanting to rescue his partner.
3. **Has a "split personality."** Dr. Jekyll and Mr. Hyde; sweet, kind, and thoughtful one moment; angry, moody, and violent the next.
4. **Hyper-focused on the other.** Always looking at the victim, staring intently at her, not letting her out of their sight.
5. **Big ego.** Acts entitled and self-important and above the law; always bragging.
6. **Needs constant praise.** Requires validation and admiration from others in order to boost their ego.
7. **Defensive.** Does not like criticism; takes everything personally; is easily ignited.
8. **Stereotypical gender roles.** Demands that women be submissive, inferior, and servile.
9. **Demanding.** Demands loyalty, and worship; wants all of the victim's attention all the time; demands that the victim attend to all the abuser's needs—emotional, psychological, physical, and domestic.
10. **Controlling** Hungry for power and control; always needs to know where the victim is and with whom; controls all decision-making over finances, movement, friends, time.
11. **Jealous.** Displays extreme examples of jealousy and control over whom the victim speaks to or spends time with.

12. **Isolating.** Bars victim from seeing friends and family, accuses friends and family of trying to destroy the relationship.
13. **Sexually controlling.** Makes demands and has expectations for their own needs, not the needs of others; demands sex regardless of the victim's wishes or desires — even if the victim is ill; prefers primarily submissive sex that may involve acts that restrain or make the victim helpless.
14. **Verbally abusive.** Judging, criticizing, humiliating, or degrading his victim.
15. **Manipulates through criticism.** "You are fat, ugly, stupid. You should be grateful I am with you."
16. **Push and pull.** Drives victim away; offers to do anything to get victim back — and repeats the abusive behavior.
17. **Blaming.** Blames everyone else for their problems and reactions; "Look what you made me do."
18. **Pleads the victim.** "You're hurting me by not listening to me."
19. **Mocking.** Makes fun of the victim or embarrasses her in front of others.
20. **Explosive temper.** Flies into rage with little or no provocation.
21. **Threats of violence.** "I'll hit you"; "I'll kill you"; "I'll break your neck"; "I can destroy your life."
22. **Actual violence.** May have fits of violence, throw things, or break the wall with their fist. Also believes in violence, saying, "Women want to be controlled and dominated."
23. **In denial.** Either denies that the physical violence occurred or says that it was not that serious or severe, and that the victim is overreacting.
24. **Social problems.** Gets in trouble at work, in the community, and even with the law.
25. **Addicted.** Has addictions such as to drugs, alcohol, gambling, and/or porn.
26. **Cruelty to animals.** Enjoys hurting or torturing animals.
27. **Callous and lacking empathy.** Uncomfortable with feelings and will never apologize or express vulnerability.
28. **Gets worse with change.** Major life changes, such as a new baby or job, often lead them to become even more violent and cruel.[147]

---

[147] Genesis Women's Shelter and Support, *The profile of an abuser*, https://www.genesisshelter.org/the-profile-of-an-abuser/; Patrick Wanis, *The Profile: 25 traits of an abuser* https://www.patrickwanis.com/the-profile-25-traits-of-an-abuser/; Shalva Cares, *Profile of an Abuser*, https://shalvacares.org/about-domestic-abuse/profile-of-an-abuser/ Many organizations use similar checklists, especially when teaching people how to identify whether they are in an abusive relationship.

From what we know about the grooming process based on the previous chapter, we can already see that there is a lot of overlap between the items in this list and the dominant behaviors in sexual abuse. Some items that jump out are issues such as control, hyper-focus on the victim, lack of empathy, and the use of verbal tools of abuse, like mocking — all of which are common in many of the victim stories. This includes sexually controlling behavior, which is a *sine qua non* of sexual abuse.

Profile of the narcissist

Another helpful profile is that of the narcissist. According to definitions of narcissistic personality disorder (NPD), narcissists are controlling and hyper-focused on their own needs, desires, and impulses. The profile of a narcissist is comprised of roughly 9-12 traits, depending on different sources. *The Diagnostic and Statistical Manual of Mental Disorders*, (DSM-5)[148] describes NPD as possessing at least five of these criteria:

1. **Has an inflated sense of self-importance.** Feels like they are the best, most successful/competent/intelligent in any situation.
2. **Believes they are special.** Expects special treatment, believes they deserve favors, apologies, or whatever they want.
3. **Has feeling of entitlement.** Insists on having the best everything — the best car, office, or designer clothes; monopolizes conversations; looks down on people perceived as "inferior."
4. **Preoccupied with fantasies about power, success, and beauty.** Tends to create and believe exaggerated, unrealistic narratives around their own success, relationships.
5. **Needs constant admiration.** Requires a steady stream of attention, approval, and recognition to keep ego inflated.
6. **Arrogant.** Shows haughty behaviors or attitudes.
7. **Exaggerates achievements and talents.** Has no problem embellishing the facts — or even outright lying — about their life, résumé, and experiences.
8. **Reacts negatively to criticism.** Quick to blame others whenever a situation doesn't go as planned, does not accept criticism or admit to mistakes because it's always someone else's fault.
9. **Jealous.** Wants people to feel envious of them and is extremely envious of those who have what they want.

[148] *American Psychiatric Association, Diagnostic and Statistical Manual of Mental Disorders, 5th Edition: DSM-5 5th Edition* https://psychiatry.org/psychiatrists/practice/dsm

10. **Exploits others.** Doesn't think twice about using or taking advantage of other people to achieve their ends, cares about other people on a superficial level, and doesn't really think of others' needs.

11. **Lacks empathy.** Has an inability or unwillingness to recognize the needs and feelings of others, hyper-sensitive to how people treat them yet are unable to put themselves in other people's shoes and empathize with their experiences. Doesn't "go deep" in any of their relationships and doesn't care. [149]

Here, too, it is possible to identify some of these traits in the abusers from the testimonies we already examined. Certainly, issues such as "exploits others," "lacks empathy," "lies," and "has feelings of entitlement" are core components of the sexual abuser's profile.

Significantly, one of the subtypes of narcissists is the "spiritual narcissist," in which the narcissist uses religious and spiritual language—such as, "I am holier than you" or "I am chosen by God"—to maintain his control dynamics. The primary abuse tactic of the spiritual narcissist is intimidation, though that is not their only tool. They can also use charm and intelligence to overpower their victims. [150]

Following the suicide of Orthodox celebrity children's author Chaim Walder after revelations that he abused dozens of children as well as some adult women over the course of decades, Orthodox Jewish psychologist Michael J. Salamon summarized the abusive profile as follows:

> *Sexual abusers are, in the popular jargon, psychopaths. They display many of the following behaviors: A disregard for right and wrong, lying to exploit and deceive, expressions of cynicism and callousness, using others for personal gain or personal pleasure, having excessive arrogance and being highly opinionated, repeatedly violating the rights of others through intimidation and dishonesty, impulsivity, aggression, and a lack of empathy, no remorse, no consideration for negative consequences of their behavior and risk taking. If caught they attempt to lie or bully their way out of it. If they can't, they project blame on to their victims. If they still can't and are feeling trapped, they are likely to commit suicide, as one recent review study found. In fact, those accused of child sexual abuse are anywhere from three to 50 times more likely to die by suicide than the general population. This is in line with the general understanding of a psychopath's behavior.*

---

[149] Christina Gregory, and Krista Soriano "Tell Me All I Need to Know About Narcissistic Personality Disorder," *Psycom,* https://www.psycom.net/personality-disorders/narcissistic/
[150] Gregory and Soriano, "Tell Me All I Need to Know," https://www.psycom.net/personality-disorders/narcissistic/

The attitudes that they can never be wrong coupled with the 'You will miss me when I am gone' manipulation fit the framework of the pathology.[151]

Using these various descriptions as guides, I set out to analyze the testimonies and produce a profile of a sexual abuser in Jewish culture based on my interviews. As with the DSM criteria, not every abuser reflects every listed quality. Nevertheless, the traits listed below are those that dominated the research and seem to be most common to the abusive persona within Jewish spheres. It is an incomplete profile, and victims may find that there are elements from the lists I cited above that are not included and yet perfectly applicable to the people who abused them. The ones that I brought here are the ones that stood out in the interviews, and that have interesting insights about Jewish culture as a context for how these personality traits find expression. This is a framework that can and should be further adjusted, expanded, and honed.

A personality of the Jewish abuser

There are certain recurring themes in the descriptions of the abuser in Jewish culture , which are often very similar to those of abusive personalities and narcissists but often with a synagogue-centric twist or another Jewish cultural hue.

Charisma and eloquence

One key aspect of the abuser's personality is charisma. For interviewees, this can be defined as a charming personality, a good public speaker, an attractive appearance, sense of humor, or the perceived ability to command attention. Baruch Lanner was often described as "charismatic" with his students. Lanner was kept on in his role at NCSY because he was thought to have "such a magnificent impact" on young people, as Rabbi Pinchas Stolper, his supervisor, explained.[152] The charismatic person is also often referred to as a "leader." As Nancy, who saw abuse by a camp counselor, explained, "You're thinking to yourself, 'This handsome hunk is interested in me? He's a leader of the group. The other boys respected him. He's such a leader, he's so intelligent, he's so charismatic.'" Many victims pursued by rabbis,

---

[151] Michael J. Salamon, "Walder Shamed Himself," *Times of Israel blog*, Dec 29, 2021, https://blogs.timesofisrael.com/walder-shamed-himself/?fbclid=iwar0jhb-2l8xdbqoor8l7bxqfmpjyxtvn3ygjtclwey4wb4o9qxzclsn8x54
[152] Rosenblatt, "Stolen Innocence," https://www.bjpa.org/content/upload/bjpa/stol/Stolen%20Innocence%20-%20Gary%20Rosenblatt%20-%20Jewish%20Week%20-%20Sexual%20Abuse.pdf

counselors, or celebrity-types see themselves as "lucky" to be "chosen" by the charismatic "leader."

Indeed, many abusers are adept at leading groups, camps, programs, or services. Carlebach , for example, was a classic "charismatic" leader in this sense, famous for being able to move and control people with his music — so much so that even 25 years after his death, when his abuse has been widely acknowledged, his music is still used by communities everywhere. Synagogues are nicknamed for him, conferences are held in his memory, and there is even an Israeli town that is entirely devoted to him.[153]

Charley described her rabbinical student, prayer-leading rapist as someone great with music and words. "He can lead a room in prayer and song, in speaking. He is very relatable, talking to people at their level and making them feel connected." Zelda also described her rabbi-abuser as someone who regularly charmed congregations with words and song. He played the guitar and delivered uplifting sermons that were broadcast around the world. The "charismatic leader" abuser is often the person who can lead services emotionally, who can give an inspiring sermon, who can play guitar, and who commands an audience.

This is significant because it points to a very Jewish-specific definition of charisma. In other cultures and religions, the ability to play the guitar and hold a nice *kumsitz* may not count for much. But in Jewish cultures, it is a powerful draw, and often casts an aura of status.

Interviewees also describe their abusers' "charm," how he exudes "warmth" and makes people feel good, especially at or after services or during pastoral care. He knows how to compliment, joke around, flirt, make the potential victim feel like they are being seen and heard, and to uplift the conversation in a spiritual or emotional way. As Brenda said about her abuser, "He was very charismatic, and everyone loved him and he was sweet and kind. He makes people feel like they are the most important people in the world. He has a large following. He makes people feel that they are special and great." Similarly, Esther says her abuser is "a very charismatic leader — charming, socially adept, gregarious":

> *He was the sort of person who made you feel that he knew you in a way that no one else did. Looking back, I can see the manipulation involved — the way in which he consistently reflected to everyone exactly what they wanted to see in themselves. But at the time, I had no cause for suspicion. Everyone, it seemed — in the Jewish community, in the interfaith community, in the secular community — loved him*

---

[153] Blustain, Sarah, "Rabbi Shlomo Carlebach's Shadow Side", *Lilith*, March 9, 1998 https://lilith.org/articles/rabbi-shlomo-carlebachs-shadow-side/

and wanted to know him. A constant refrain in all three communities was 'Who doesn't love the rabbi?'

Jewish versions of "charisma," then, involve the ability to command a Jewish setting through services, music, humor, and/or socializing.

The charisma is also about performance. "He's a kind of a dramatic person also and a little bit of an actor and likes putting on funny voices," Reut said of the rabbi who had been abusing boys in her synagogue for decades. She added that he liked having big crowds at his house. "He's like a big entertainer, and he likes to make big buffets in their kitchen and he's a good cook." In short, the abuser knows how to work the room. Reut said, "People just love him."

This "warmth" is easily interpreted positively, and can be a tool for breaking boundaries. Brenda continued that "what was a little weird, he would kiss women on the cheek. He was very flirtatious. He became like Mr. Uber-popular very quickly." Similarly, Reut said that the rabbi was able to get away with being obnoxious because he was "entertaining." "When he entertains, he makes fun of people, or gossips about people in the synagogue. It's all a little strange." Even though his charisma made her uncomfortable, people dismissed it because he had the makings of a "popular" rabbi .

Charisma also involves being able to manipulate people using their own cultural codes and language. One of Malka Leifer's victims describes this kind of charisma:

> *She'd say, 'I am like a mother to you,' 'I can love you and be there for you.' The preferential treatment included one-on-one lessons in Jewish values and morals. I was very proud of being the favorite, very proud… [I]t was quite a status in the school. Mrs. Leifer was the most important person in the school. Everyone idolized her.*[154]

Charismatic abusers may exude charm in different ways in different settings, but what they have in common is that they know how to behave in a way that will make people around them feel good — loved, amused, entertained, tended to. The abuser uses a combination of laughter, emotional cajoling, playfulness, performance, and charm to woo both potential victims and the surrounding crowds.

These qualities are so valued in Jewish culture that even when people discover that their charismatic prayer leader is also an abuser, they may look the other way — because of how much his charismatic leadership is valued. To wit, when Leanne complained about her abuse, the camp director said

---

[154] Ori Golan, "Washing away the trauma of abuse: Dassi Erlich, who says she suffered sexual abuse in an Australian ultra-Orthodox community, tells of her long journey, accuses former community of not taking steps to protect the next victim," *Jerusalem Post*, July 6 2017. https://www.jpost.com/magazine/a-new-life-498946

that they knew about his abusive behaviors but decided to hire him back again the next year as "Head of Prayer" because "He runs a very nice service." Similarly, when the Reut's rabbi was outed as an abuser and testimonies were reported in a national newspaper, people in the community continued to support the abuser. Here is how she explained their attitude:

> People are like, 'He was there for my family. So how could I be against him? How could I believe any of these things? Look how wonderful he is. He was so wonderful. My family, he sat by my mother's bedside. He came into our house in the middle of the night after my father died, and he sat there. He sat with me and talked to my children and explained to them what death is and how they can perpetuate the memory of the person that we just lost.' Even when everyone knew the stories about him, he was invited all over the place to speak as a scholar-in-residence. He spoke to high schools, spoke to day schools.

Reut's description of the abuser who is loved for being "warm" and "charismatic" encapsulates what many interviewees described. But she adds, significantly that even *after* the abuse is known, people still prefer to focus on his "charisma" and ignore the abuse. That is extremely telling.

Ultimately, abusers are skilled in how to charm, wield power, and manipulate Jewish values in order to be alone with their victims without scrutiny. And in Jewish culture, those abilities are often top priority — even more important than *not being a sexual predator*. That hierarchy of cultural norms and values provides abusers the ultimate protection. If they can lead a service, they can do whatever else they want.

Split personality, Dr. Jekyll/Mr. Hyde

The fact that the abusers are described as charismatic one minute and sexually abusive the next suggests that they are also split personalities, the "Dr. Jekyll/Mr. Hyde" characteristic. This is considered one of the most telling signs of someone who engages in domestic violence, and it is clearly part of the sexual predator as well.

Many of the abused described rabbis who went from giving a soaring sermon one minute to inviting victims into their studies to be molested the next. Zelda described a severely split personality, where the "beloved communal rabbi" would be talking about mysticism and love from the pulpit while he had several concurrent mistresses behind the curtain.

Baruch Lanner was also described by his victims as having a split personality. Rabbi Etan Tokayer, who was abused by Lanner throughout junior high and high school, recalled:

> He was a very important role model to me during my formative years... But while Baruch was so deep and spiritual in his

> *public performances, he was cruel and crude in his private*
> *encounters. There seemed to be two Lanners, the destructive*
> *and the good, and that caused great tension in me. I wanted*
> *and needed his friendship and approval, yet he inspired great*
> *fear as well.*[155]

The pulpit provides a perfect cover for the split personality. It enables the abuser to create a public veneer of sanctity and superiority alongside a private practice of doing what he wants with his victims.

Obsessive need for control

The previous chapter on grooming described many ways in which abusers displayed their obsessive needs for control over their victims. These involved controlling the victims' behaviors and beliefs and controlling the entire narrative of the abuse. In fact, the abuser requires absolute control in order to continue the abuse. Rabbi Tokayer described Baruch Lanner as someone who "preyed on the insecurities of young people and fostered a cult of personality, using his power to manipulate and control us when we were vulnerable." AS Gary Rosenblatt reported, "The emotional power Rabbi Lanner had over these impressionable youngsters was formidable. 'He was like a god to us,' several men and women said. They basked in his praise, but if he turned on them, and he could do so easily, they were bereft. The price he demanded was loyalty. 'I was not allowed to criticize or question him. I had to trade in my dignity and honesty for the feeling of power he gave me. And I had to give up control of my life to him.'"

This control aspect, which is key to the abusive profile, is often intertwined with other behaviors and grooming patterns, such as charisma and hyper-focus on the victim. It can also be disguised as an intense, unwavering interest.

Often, these qualities can be interconnected — that is, charisma and charm can intertwine with a hyper-focus on the victim. Marion, for example, who was raped by the rabbi after her mother's funeral, said that the rabbi "took a great interest in me and my grief. I mean that in the worst way." The combination of his charisma, his hyper-focus, and her emotional vulnerability created a situation that ended up being devastating for her. Tanya described the "intricate and terrifying hold this man had on my mind." Similarly, Zelda described her abuser as controlling her from the minute he introduced himself.

In some ways, this was classic abuse, but it also was Jewishly manipulated. "It was twisted by how he would use scripture. He would

---

[155] Rosenblatt, "Stolen Innocence,"
https://www.bjpa.org/content/upload/bjpa/stol/Stolen%20Innocence%20-%20Gary%20Rosenblatt%20-%20Jewish%20Week%20-%20Sexual%20Abuse.pdf

appropriate religion and Torah and spirituality to get me to have sex with him." That is a very Jewish twist on this trait — using Torah to take control.

Need for ego-stoking

Baruch Lanner also demanded control and absolute loyalty in concert with adoration. As the *Jewish Week* reported:

> *Rabbi Lanner's need for control was a dominant theme in numerous interviews and conversations. What emerges is a pattern of an extremely bright, talented and troubled man who created his own universe of adoring teens — a universe in which loyalty to him was paramount.*
>
> *'Do you love me?' Rabbi Lanner would repeatedly ask teen officers of NCSY during required daily phone calls to him, either early in the morning or late at night. 'Tell me you love me,' he would demand. 'Tell me you love me.' And they did.*[156]

This trait — the need for adoration mixed with the need for control — is on the checklist for abusive intimate partners as well as narcissism, and describes many rabbi offenders. Marc Gafni, for example, calls himself a "visionary philosopher."[157] Eliezer , who went to prison for sexual assault and came back to run his Shavu Banim yeshiva, calls himself "Rabbi Berland, *Shlita*," a religious term for someone exalted and holy, like Moses himself, and tells people he is the messiah.[158] Charley says about her rabbinical student-rapist, "People really worshiped the ground he walked on, especially those younger than him. That fed his own ego."

Baruch Lanner was a classic case of using his victims for his ego needs:

> *The emotional power Rabbi Lanner had over these impressionable youngsters was formidable. 'He was like a god to us,' several men and women said. They basked in his praise, but if he turned on them, and he could easily, they were bereft. The price he demanded was loyalty. 'I was not allowed to criticize or question him,' recalled one former NCSYer, now a rabbi. 'I had to trade in my dignity and honesty for the feeling*

---

156 Rosenblatt, "Stolen Innocence,"
https://www.bjpa.org/content/upload/bjpa/stol/Stolen%20Innocence%20-%20Gary%20Rosenblatt%20-%20Jewish%20Week%20-%20Sexual%20Abuse.pdf
157 Marc Gafni website. https://www.marcgafni.com/prophets-for-profit/
158 Marissa Newman, "The ex-aides of a messianic, sex-convict rabbi fight from within to cast him out. Bratslav hasidic leaders have issued a rare ban on Eliezer Berland, a cult leader seen as a modern 'Sabbatai Tzvi'; the rest of the Haredi world is proving reluctant to follow suit," *Times of Israel*, 5 September 2018, https://www.timesofisrael.com/the-ex-aides-of-a-messianic-sex-convict-rabbi-fight-from-within-to-cast-him-out/

> *of power he gave me. And I had to give up control of my life to him.'*
>
> *Some of the teens called Rabbi Lanner 'Charlie' among themselves, referring to convicted cultist killer Charles Manson, and spoke of the female teens the rabbi favored as 'Baruch's girls.'[159]*

The obsessive demand for adoration, especially as combined with a range of grooming tactics, also enforces control over the victim's ideas and behaviors to break down resistance, as we saw in the analysis of the grooming process.

God complex: Believes they are "special"

Many abusers who considered themselves "special," boldly shared with their victims how they believed that they were special, whether this was bragging about being on exclusive lists or invited to elite events, or having unparalleled knowledge or intelligence, better than anyone else's. Carlebach was described as "larger than life", which enabled him to get away with his exploits.[160]

Some abusers tell the victims that *they* must be "special," too, in order to have this "special connection" with the rabbi or the leader.

This "God complex" describes many of the interviewees' offenders. Esther says about her abuser, "People venerated, even deified him. They called him a 'holy man' with a 'calling.' When he went to visit the ill father of a congregant, the man's son called out to his father, 'Dad, God's here.' It was as though he could do no wrong."

As with narcissists and intimate partner abusers, this sense of "specialness" often finds expression in feeling "above the law." This may involve flouting laws that "normal" people are bound by and believing that they deserve to get away with it, whether "it" was addictions, embezzlements, or multiple "affairs." Former Chief Rabbi of Israel Yona Metzger, for example, was accused of sexual abuse but went to prison for embezzlement. Rabbi Eliezer Berland was jailed for several years on counts of sexual abuse and is now facing counts of tax evasion and fraud, though he

---

[159] Rosenblatt, "Stolen Innocence,"
https://www.bjpa.org/content/upload/bjpa/stol/Stolen%20Innocence%20-%20Gary%20Rosenblatt%20-%20Jewish%20Week%20-%20Sexual%20Abuse.pdf
[160] Sarah Blustain, "Rabbi Shlomo Carlebach's Shadow Side", *Lilith*, March 9, 1998
https://lilith.org/articles/rabbi-shlomo-carlebachs-shadow-side/

is currently out and running his empire.[161] Berland is also tied to murder.[162] Most recently, Michael Steinhardt—who has decades of allegations of sexual abuse—was forced to return $70 million of stolen art.[163] These are examples of the narcissistic abuser considering himself above the law and profoundly entitled to what he sees and wants, whether that is stolen artwork or another person's body. As Rabbi Daniel Pressman, head of the Rabbinic Assembly's Va'ad Hakavod (Ethics Committee), told me, "We have seen more than one case where a rabbi who had crossed sexual boundaries was also misusing his discretionary fund."

Leah, who spent many years working at a sexual abuse hotline, confirmed this:

> *Having had this experience with the hotline, there was always a point where we would discover [the accused] was corrupt in general. That he was embezzling or something. A man who felt he was entitled. Men for whom regular rules did not apply. Sometimes people ask how these guys get away with it, and it's because they are 'special.' A man who felt he was entitled and thinks he can get away with it. And sadly, often they are right.*

Some abusers seem to get off on sharing their secret excessive exploits with their victims. Cindy said that her abuser enjoyed confiding in her about his other "affairs" and how he was basically "above the law." Zelda confirmed this as well and described her rabbi-abuser as someone who bragged to her about doing drugs on the synagogue grounds on Friday night after services, who beat his wife, and more. "We're talking about a rabbi and his wife who are going to sex clubs. Can you imagine going to a sex club and running into your rabbi?"

---

[161] TOI Staff, "Convicted sex offender rabbi released to house arrest in ongoing fraud case. Court places severe restrictions on Eliezer Berland, including ban on contacting any of his followers, posting NIS 1.2 million bail, and having 2 wardens with him at all times," *Times of Israel*, 15 February 2021, https://www.timesofIsrael.com/convicted-sex-offender-rabbi-released-to-house-arrest-in-ongoing-fraud-case/

[162] Jerusalem Post Staff, "Berland murder case: Benny Ze'evi revealed as second man accused. Ze'evi is the second man indicted for the 1986 murder of Nissim Sheetrit that was connected to the 'Modesty Guard' of the 'Shuvu Banim' sect," *Jerusalem Post*, December 5, 2021 https://www.jpost.com/breaking-news/benny-zeevi-son-of-rehavam-zeevi-is-the-accused-murderer-in-berland-case-687884

[163] "D.A. Vance: Michael Steinhardt Surrenders 180 Stolen Antiquities Valued at $70 Million. Seized Artifacts will be Repatriated to 11 Countries. Steinhardt Agrees to Unprecedented Lifetime Ban on Acquiring Antiquities," *Manhattan DA*, Dec 6, 2021 https://www.manhattanda.org/d-a-vance-michael-steinhardt-surrenders-180-stolen-antiquities-valued-at-70-million/?fbclid=IwAR20PvO1Dh5A0H28P9b_8kI3dxq8qasyiYG8iwMThoYAjs6raUSeUbxdesQ

Lack of empathy

Another aspect of the rabbinic abuser's personality is often lack of empathy, an item that manifests in profiles of both the intimate-partner abuser and the narcissistic personality. Still, the lack of empathy in a spiritual leader can be jarring, considering it is one of the main functions of a rabbi, pastor, or counselor. Brenda said that her abuser "had zero empathy":

> Zero. I told him that I had a bout of depression so he said that it was all apparently about my depression that had misguided me. Not once has he ever apologized for anything. He's a con artist. On every level. But people don't see it.

She also remarked that the lack of empathy could be seen in his inability to apologize—not even when he failed to come to synagogue for her father's *yahrzeit* (anniversary of death), which she needed and counted on him for.

The lack of empathy in a rabbi, combined with the personality of public charm, often translates as a kind of false performance of care. Many women fall for this trap, in which the rabbi uses his charm and status to make his victims feel that he is caring for them when he is just planning a route for abuse. As Esther said, "His silence, his lack of affect, his lack of empathy, and his lack of accountability were devastating."

Marion explained how damaging this dynamic is for someone who is seeking spiritual care. "A rabbi is in a unique position for a sexual predator to be a source of support and spiritual strength when women's souls are in need. This would not have happened if he hadn't been in the position that he was in. And, of course, the sexual predation is even more egregious for a rabbi who is there for the opposite of predation."

The lack of empathy, combined with the public performance of care, can be extremely confusing — and make people who need rabbinic care quite vulnerable. In public, the abusive rabbi looks exactly like the thing that the target desperately needs or desires, while behind closed doors he is exactly the opposite. The confusion destabilizes the victim through a cruel combination of suspicion and hope.

Fits of anger and threats

Another telling aspect of the rabbi-abuser is often being prone to angry rages. Debbie Findling, for example, who wrote about how former head of Jewish camping Len Robinson sexually harassed her, said that when she was about to report him, he began "leaving me increasingly agitated voicemail messages, threatening me and telling me I was ruining his life by reporting his misdeeds." Similarly, Baruch Lanner, who was abusing girls and boys for decades, was notorious for his rash violence—kicking boys in the groin, punching a girl in the mouth, and yelling abusive slurs at those he deemed disloyal. When Brenda tried to break off the abusive relationship, her rabbi-abuser "got really angry and defensive... mean, nasty."

This quality, too, resembles that of the intimate-partner abuser. As one interviewee told me, when she started sharing her experiences with people around her, the abuser sent a threatening letter to her supervisor and ultimately got her fired. Other interviewees described their abusers' use of law suits. Abusers often use litigation and other threats as instruments of rage to further hurt and silence their victims, such as the case of the former Knesset Member who sued two women for sharing (in a closed online group) their stories of how he sexually harassed them. I have had some personal experience with this, too. A close friend of mine was molested by her rabbi when we were teenagers, and when she talked to a reporter about it, the newspaper was threatened with being sued and they killed the story.

Other victims have had to take drastic measures to avoid the wrath of their abusers. More than one moved to a different city to get far away from their abusers — not only for their own healing but also out of fear of retribution. One woman moved several times and believes that her abuser is part of a larger trafficking ring. Another moved across the country and completely changed her name so as not to be found by her abuser. Another interviewee told me not to share her story in this book — not even with pseudonyms and changing details — because she is terrified about the abuser finding her. Michael Lesher documents many terrifying accounts of these kinds of threats by abusers and their protectors, particularly in the Orthodox world.[164]

Blames others

As with Brenda's abuser, angry reactions — especially upon rejection or ending the abuse — often include a stinging element of blame. The habit of blaming others is a cornerstone of emotional abuse and is also part of the profile of a narcissistic abuser.

For victims of abuse by a rabbi or Jewish leader, that blame may take the form of using Jewish texts. Tanya, who was molested by a soon-to-be rabbi when he visited her family home, wrote:

> Each morning after being molested, I would wake up and walk into the living room, and see him wildly shuckling, rocking back and forth while beating his chest. He said he was doing teshuvah, repenting for what he had done the night before, and he told me that I should join him in doing teshuvah, too. I didn't pray or do teshuvah but just stared at him in disbelief. He really believed that I was a partner in sin. And then it would happen again: After every fervent bout of repentance, he

---

[164] Michael Lesher, *Sexual Abuse.*

would wake me up in the middle of the night the following week.

When the blame tactic takes on the God-language, it can be particularly potent. Esther had a similar experience:

I took on the fiction that identified the rabbi with all things good, and myself with all things evil. In the eyes of everyone who knew him — and then, in my eyes — the rabbi could do no wrong, and I could do no right. He was gentle, kind, generous, and always right; I was impatient, judgmental, selfish, and always wrong. He was never responsible for anything. I was always to blame for everything.

A rabbi-abuser may also blame the victim for congregational dynamics he experienced, or other experiences.

For rabbi-abusers, the failure to accept responsibility and the tendency to blame are tools that play with the victim's mind, gain control, and at times use particularly perverse Jewish dynamics.

Spiritual narcissism in Jewish culture

The testimonies of interviewees reveal that many if not most of the characteristics of narcissistic personality disorder and intimate partner abuse manifest in the dynamic of sexual abuse by rabbis. Charisma, the split personality, control, hyper-focus on the victim, big ego, need for adoration, belief in his own "specialness," lack of empathy, and tendency to blame are all characteristics described by interviewees about their rabbi-abusers. There are more, but these are the ones that stood out most in my research.

Three salient points emerge about connections between sexual abuse and Jewish culture, especially rabbi-centric cultures: the spiritual bypass, spiritual narcissism, and Jewish constructs of charisma.

Spiritual bypass

One major takeaway from the process of constructing a profile of the Jewish abuser is the way in which rabbi-abusers use spiritual concepts to get away with their exploits — the "spiritual bypass." It is what Zelda eloquently called, "The 'Oh, Kabbalah! I'm touching your boobs!' shit." The rabbi-abuser knows how to underpin and twist Jewish religious and spiritual material in order to get the victim to surrender. It preys on people's desire to engage spiritually and emotionally with someone they can trust. Rabbinic predators know how to use this for their own ends. The appropriation of spiritual themes works in concert with the God language and the charisma in the synagogue setting.

Leah Silber, one of Baruch Lanner's victims, describes a similar dynamic. "I was very drawn to religion and the Torah, and he would use his learning, citing rabbinic sources as a technique to work on me," she said. But when he asked her to marry him and she rebuffed him, "he smacked me in the face" and nearly broke her jaw. "Baruch is repulsive, and yet he has so much charisma, so much brilliance," she said. "I can't even explain it to myself." The predator, with his split personality and tendency to alternate between rewards and punishment, was able to prey on his victim's love of Judaism to get his way with her. She is still enchanted with him, decades later, despite all the real pain he caused her.

These testimonies about how Jewish texts and ideas were used to manipulate vulnerable people — adults and kids — got me thinking about my own experiences of 13 years in yeshivah day school, two years in summer camp, and countless seminars, shabbatons, and informal activities in which I heard rabbis promote all kinds of ideas in the name of Judaism. We heard incessant preaching about our sexuality, our dress, our bodies, our gestures, our purposes as females in the world according to God's will, and more. I began to understand that way before physical-sexual abuse takes place, religious teachers, rabbis, and counselors are given permission to use Jewish texts to tell people what we should be doing with our bodies. Personally, I have come to believe that this issue of spiritual bypass goes way deeper than what the interviewees described and is in some ways at the core of Jewish culture across communities and denominations.

Spiritual narcissism

When the Jewish religious figure uses Jewish spiritual material to lure victims for abuse, this is a distinct form abuse that falls into the category of "spiritual narcissism." It's a kind of interplay between the God complex, Jewish scholarship, and the particularly Jewish form of charisma in which the one who speaks well and sounds eloquent and smart is given unquestioned reverence. It is a dynamic in which Jewish spiritual ideas and texts are used by the narcissist to maintain power and control over his victims.

Spiritual narcissism is a social ill that may precede sexual abuse. "Spiritual narcissism creates the pretense of holiness as an ego strategy to mask insecurity, receive approval, or avoid struggle and growth," writes Rabbi Alan Lurie. "I'm a spiritual person' it proclaims proudly. 'I travel to alternate realities, see auras, heal chakras, predict the future, talk to spirits... harness the powers of the Universe to attract success... The truth is that I'm more evolved than you!'"[165] In Lurie's analysis, the spiritual narcissist sees themselves as more religious, observant, divine, holy, educated, knowledgeable about Judaism, or closer to God than their victim and therefore deserving of unyielding attention, respect, and ultimately submission.

In a 2021 *Scientific American* story about spiritual narcissism, Scott Barry Kaufman reviewed a series of studies that demonstrate that intense spiritual practices that claim to quiet the ego often actually inflate it. Participants emerged with a heightening of ideas that are cornerstones of narcissistic belief systems: *I am aware of things that others are not aware of, I am more in touch with my senses than most others. I am more aware of what is between heaven and earth than most people, The world would be a better place if others too had the insights that I have now*, and the like. He concludes that the correlation between American versions of spirituality and narcissism are probably "bidirectional":

> *It's likely that spiritual practices can be used as a tool to bolster the narcissistic self, enhancing one's feeling that one is special and entitled to special privileges. But it's also likely that some spiritual training programs attract people with strong personal development goals that are related to Western narcissistic culture. As the researchers note, the idea of exploring one's own personal thoughts and feelings and becoming an 'enlightened being' may be particularly attractive to people with high levels of both overt and covert narcissism.*[166]

In other words, the position of being a rabbi and engaging in religious-spiritual activities and texts arguably invites a kind of narcissistic attitude. However, it is entirely possible that the process is reverse — that the rabbinate calls people who have narcissistic tendencies. Perhaps those with abusive tendencies are drawn to positions of power within structural hierarchies that will provide them with the sphere of influence and protection needed to carry out their abusive desires. To be clear, I am not suggesting that *all* rabbis are narcissists. Rather, I am saying that perhaps the qualities associated with

---

[165] Rabbi Alan Lurie, "The Allure of Narcissistic Spirituality. The desire to control others in order to create a 'perfect' environment that nurtures our sensitivities is a calling card of spiritual narcissism. True spirituality takes place in the holy messiness of the world," *Huffington Post Blog*, Jan 6,2011, https://www.huffpost.com/entry/the-allure-of-spiritual-n_b_803415

[166] Scott Barry Kaufman, "The Science of Spiritual Narcissism. Self-enhancement through spiritual practices can fool some of us into thinking we're evolving and growing when all we're growing is our ego," *Scientific American*. January 11, 2021, https://www.scientificamerican.com/article/the-science-of-spiritual-narcissism/

"rabbi" appeal to narcissists and provide an attractive home where they can comfortably do their thing.

The question can also be asked about other high-profile positions in the Jewish world. Do these positions construct narcissism, or perhaps they attract people with narcissistic tendencies?

Unfortunately, to complicate matters, in his attempt to unpack the dangers of spiritual narcissism, Kaufman relies heavily on the philosophies of the spiritual-yoga guru Chögyam Trungpa Rinpoche as a thought leader on this topic. Trungpa, a self-appointed philosopher-king/Buddhist saint of the "Shambhala" school, was also, according to a comprehensive investigative report in *The Walrus*, a cult leader, polygamist, and violent abuser who subjected his wives to "sexual demands, pinches, punches and kicks" and "drunken hallucinated conversations with the long-dead sages of medieval Tibet." His saintly aura was designed to "hide a legacy of deception, exploitation, behavioral control, and systemic abuse" and "every type of mistreatment imaginable, from emotional manipulation and extreme neglect to molestation and rape—stories that turn Shambhala's brand narrative, with its promises of utopia, upside down." His son, Mipham Rinpoche, and his successor, Thomas Rich, were no better.[167]

This discovery came at a pivotal moment in my search for an understanding of spiritual abuse. Kaufman, the rabbi explaining spiritual abuse, was relying on the ideologies of a cult leader who is both a charismatic demigod and one of the worst spiritual abusers in the world. My search for a safe space in the world of background literature epitomizes the quagmire of seeking out safe Jewish spaces — finding rabbinic figures who are not sullied by cultures of spiritual narcissism. Even in searching for an understanding of these dynamics, it is hard to find scholars and thinkers to trust and rely on who are not themselves tainted by the seemingly common intermingling of spiritual leadership and abuse.

So many people are vulnerable to abuse because they, too, seek out rabbis in order to grapple with other hurts and violations experienced elsewhere. Victims who went searching for spiritual guidance and understanding, or for wisdom and clarity, found themselves in the hands of someone who instead used and exploited people for their own narcissistic aims. I couldn't even get through a search for information *about* spiritual narcissism without falling into that trap.[168]

One is left to wonder how deeply connected these dynamics truly are.

---

[167] Matthew Remski, "Survivors of an International Buddhist Cult Share Their Stories. An investigation into decades of abuse at Shambhala International," *The Walrus*, November/December 2020, https://thewalrus.ca/survivors-of-an-international-buddhist-cult-share-their-stories/

[168] To be fair, Kaufman's article in *Scientific American* was published about a month or two after *The Walrus* exposé came out. Maybe they hadn't seen it yet.

Charisma as Jewish performance

The third item that casts a particularly Jewish aura on the profile of the abuser is definitions of "charisma."

I would like to preface this analysis by saying that I recognize how jarring a conversation about rabbinic charisma might be in the context of sexual abuse. After all, in Jewish culture, charisma is considered a gold standard for leadership. It is perhaps shocking that "charisma" is considered one of the main red flags of abuse. It turns our culture on its head. When I shared some early texts of this research, I received some very angry pushback about the notion that charisma in rabbis may be the opposite of what we tend to think it is.

Nevertheless, the connection between charisma and abuse was amply verified way before I began this research. Almost every book, blog, and listicle about emotional abuse examines the role of charisma and charm in the abusive personality. The only real question is: What does "charisma" actually look like in Jewish settings?

What emerges from these testimonies is that Jewish charisma is often focused on synagogue, prayer, music, and speaking Torah. The "charismatic" leader is one who can sing or play guitar in a way that makes everyone want to sing, who can lead prayer services in a way that makes people feel "warm" or uplifted, or who knows the right words to say to make people feel tended to or inspired. This charisma extends out of the sanctuary to places like the kiddush, where a rabbi who smiles and charms is considered worthy, or to high schools where earnest seekers look for guidance, or to summer camp where counselors break down barriers and woo their way into campers' bodies and minds, or to weddings, hospital beds, and funerals where unknowing targets lean on them with full trust.

How can it be that the very same characteristics that are considered the most highly prized in the culture are the ones that belong to narcissistic sexual abusers?

That is a critical question that this research opens. It is a social-communal-cultural question about *which* people are considered of highest value and why. The question goes beyond rabbis. If the most prized rabbis are the ones who display a characteristic called "charisma," which often masks a narcissistic personality, then perhaps that same quality is prized in other locations where abusers seem to dwell — as celebrity-scholars, board members, donors, and people considered Jewish leaders in general.

Takeaways about the profile of the abuser

This chapter, which analyzed the profile of the abuser in a Jewish context, has elicited some disturbing understandings.

- **Abusers tend to be narcissists.** While this may sound like an obvious point, it is worth elucidating in order to recognize the signs and to teach Jewish communities and congregations to recognize the signs.

- **Charisma has a particular look in Jewish culture.** The Jewish leader is often revered for what is called "charisma," a trait closely associated in the culture with "leadership." It signifies verbal eloquence, a powerful voice, an attractive smile, an ability to woo people in private or in public, perhaps a jovial flirtatiousness, the ability to lead in song and/or prayer, and the loyal adoration of followers. A person with charisma in this culture also enjoys all those traits—leading a crowd, controlling people's reactions, and having adoring followers.

- **Narcissism may be woven into the cultural expectations of the rabbi.** If perhaps rabbis were once seen as frail, powerless, and gentle, today that is no longer the case. Today, rabbis are expected to have the kind of outward charisma described above—that is, strong command of language, forceful speaking abilities, a powerful presence, and an ability to charm audiences—qualities that unfortunately share overlaps with narcissistic personalities. As Brenda said, "People in clergy who have this kind of narcissistic personality disorder, it drives them to become rabbis—it automatically gives them what they crave—status, power, respect."

- **Many abusers have a Dr. Jekyll/Mr Hyde persona.** All abusers have redeeming qualities, and many are deeply revered for their charismatic traits such as being able to lead a service, being able to comfort mourners, being great entertainers, or being charming and sweet. But the abuser splits between two personas: the charmer and the manipulative controller. This can be very confusing for those being privately abused by the charming leader, and perplexing for outside observers who never see the abuser's dark side.

- **Rabbis are quite possibly being trained this way.** Rabbis may in fact be trained to be charismatic performers. As Daliah said, in rabbinical school she learned that "People are going to be constantly putting you on a pedestal.... constantly giving you *kavod* [honor] when you've done nothing to earn it but have this title. You can start thinking that you have earned this kavod, but you have not. There are bad people out there who see those cracks and step in. It's just terrible. So awful." This gets to the core of Jewish culture. "We have a culture of celebrity," Charley said. "And I think that that leaves a lot of room especially in unchecked power." Or as Zelda said, "It's a power trip."

- **Signs of spiritual narcissism can be disguised as a passion for pastoral care.** The moments when a person invites a rabbi into their private sanctuary can be the most dangerous. Brenda, who is now on her synague search committee, is very wary of this trap. "You ask a rabbi how they feel about the pastoral role of funerals or visiting the sick, etc., and some of them use the words, 'It's the favorite part of my job.' I feel like it can easily be the favorite because it makes them feel powerful because you get to enter the most private and deepest parts of their life, and it's a privilege. I am listening for a rabbi to talk about it in language of humility, how truly difficult it is to separate yourself and be there for someone when something horrible is going on."

- **People are socialized into adoring charismatic rabbis.** People are socialized to prostrate themselves, metaphorically, in front of rabbis. As Daliah said, "We are taught to be grateful to our rabbis and that creates hierarchy, which makes some people vulnerable."

- **People love the charismatic leaders, even when they are abusive.** One of the most disturbing insights was that even after people discover that their charming rabbis are also abusers, they often still support them. Sometimes, board members or supervisors know that the rabbi is a narcissistic abuser but choose to look away and/or retain the rabbi for other reasons: he leads a pretty service, he knows how to play the guitar, or he is beloved among donors. Rabbinic charisma is so revered in the culture that it is at times more important than all else — including being a person who does not sexually abuse others. That should give the community some pause.

Chapter 6: Settings Ripe for Abuse

In the year following the discovery that Harvey Weinstein was a serial rapist, over 200 powerful men lost their jobs as a result of accusations against them, according to an accounting by *The New York Times*. The list includes many Jewish men, such as former Democratic senator Al Franken; then-CBS chief Les Moonves; actors Dustin Hoffman, Jeffrey Tambor, and Jeremy Piven; directors Woody Allen, James Toback, and Brett Ratner; playwright Israel Horowitz; journalists Mark Halperin and Michael Oreskes; conductor James Levine; radio show hosts Leonard Lopate and Jonathan Schwartz; the *New Republic*'s former literary editor Leon Wieseltier; former NBC anchor Matt Lauer; *Paris Review* editor Lorin Stein; and others.[169] That is disturbing.

But that is only part of the story because, of all those Jewish men listed by *The New York Times*, none of them actually worked in the Jewish world. Some are Jewish in name only and operate far from Jewish cultural and communal centers. The list of Jewish men whose abuse takes place *within a Jewish milieu* is still not fully known. This has a lot to do with the fact that, judging just by the testimonies collected for this research, almost none of them have been held accountable for their actions.

Take, for example, Michael Steinhardt, one of the most high-profile and powerful men within the Jewish communal and organizational world to be publicly accused. The milieu in which he operates is extraordinarily Jewish. His whole identity and persona are wrapped up in acting on behalf of the Jewish people. The reported incidents took place in Jewish cultural settings and were often sprinkled with Jewish language and codes, such as the need to propagate the Jewish people.

Yet, tellingly, the exposé about his abuse did not lead to any communal action. Unlike the Jewish men on *The New York Times*'s list of 200 men who lost their jobs, Steinhardt's positions remained completely safe following the allegation.[170]

This begs a deeper question about sexual abuse and Jewish men who commit it. If Jewish men are disproportionately among the accused, and if those in Jewish environments are least likely to face consequences, what does that tell us about how Jewish cultures support sexual abuse?

Moreover, Steinhardt's actions were justified by so many of his enablers based on his Jewish record and on the importance of his "generosity" for the Jewish people. The culture of supporting abusers instead of victims because of the perceived needs of the Jewish collective is a quintessential Jewish story. This should be a red flag, suggesting that not only are abusive Jewish men in Jewish settings unlikely to be ousted for their behavior, they are also likely to retain communal support.

---

[169] Audrey Carlsen, Maya Salam, Claire Cain Miller, Denise Lu, Ash Ngu, Jugal K. Patel And Zach Wichter, "#MeToo Brought Down 201 Powerful Men. Nearly Half of Their Replacements Are Women," *New York Times*, Oct. 29, 2018 https://www.nytimes.com/interactive/2018/10/23/us/metoo-replacements.html; Allison Kaplan Sommer, "Not Just Weinstein: The Year #MeToo Rocked and Shocked the Jewish World," Over the past year, a high number of powerful Jewish men have been accused of sexual misconduct. While it has provided fodder for anti-Semites, activists say addressing the problem is vital, *Ha'aretz*, Sept 18, 2018, https://www.haaretz.com/israel-news/.premium-not-just-weinstein-the-year-metoo-rocked-and-shocked-the-jewish-world-1.6480994

[170] That may have changed after revelations that he is also an art thief. Following those reports, at least one university faces a petition to change the name of the school named after him. This also reflects a damning reality in which property theft is considered more serious than sexual abuse.

Thus far in this section of the research on unpacking how abuse happens, I've examined steps in the grooming process and the profile of the abuser: the "*what*" and the "*who*." The next component of context is the "*where*." The question I am looking to understand in this chapter is: What are the characteristics of Jewish societal or organizational *settings* that allow abuse to happen?

This chapter is not a comprehensive review of every potential setting for abuse. Rather, I've selected several locations that dominated the interviewees' stories, and I looked for indications about what factors open up each of the settings to abuse. The primary physical settings that emerged that I explore in this chapter are synagogues, Jewish schools, and informal settings like camps, youth movements, and Israel programs. The next chapter takes a close-up look at the specific setting of the Jewish workplace, which deserves its own analysis.

Synagogues

Many of the stories described here take place in and around synagogues, both the physical structure and the social structure. Brenda's entire life revolved around the synagogue, which was not just her spiritual home but also her social network and her professional (though unpaid) setting. Many stories of abuse took place in the rabbi's inner sanctum, such as the library or the rabbi's study or office. But many other instances of everyday harassment and abuse take place in synagogue-connected settings, not just by male rabbis but also by congregants and rabbis toward women clergy.

Jewish connectivity

One aspect of synagogue life that is both a feature and a risk is its emphasis on connection. The synagogue setting is a voluntary communal space that people attend for the express purpose of letting down their guard, inviting Jewish connectivity, and breaking boundaries. But this boundary breaking also makes it easy for abusers to reach their victims.

In the chapter about congregants who abuse female clergy, I included many testimonies about congregants who interpreted this loose atmosphere as an opportunity to reach out and touch the female rabbi, literally. Emily, for example, who is a cantor, described how her Temple president's husband "would always try to put his arm around me, even in front of my husband. My husband and I called him 'CLB' (creepy little bastard) amongst ourselves." Once, he "leaned over and whispered, 'I finally have you alone, all to myself.'" Odelia, who works as an assistant rabbi in a Conservative synagogue, described her discomfort with a congregant who would often compliment her excessively, stand too close to her, wink at her, and leer at her. This kind of flirtatious joviality is often dismissed as an innocuous part of community culture and Jewish relationship-building where "everyone is hugging everyone." Rena calls it the "Jewish hugging" problem. Her Jewish professionals conference "is the one conference where everyone hugs each other all the time. I go to these other professional conferences, nobody hugs each other." The "closeness" may have some cultural and social benefits, but it can also open the door for unwanted sexual advances.

This is especially risky for female clergy, who seem to be targets for predators in the synagogue setting.

Another aspect of this boundary-breaking culture is that women often end up dismissing their own discomfort and unwillingly allowing others to act in ways that they do not want to consent to. Yona, for example, described how a Jewish colleague would regularly comment about her body, or "try to bond with me about our Judaism. I'm totally convinced that he felt he had particular license to treat me this way—that he was in some way being 'helpful' or 'protective'—because we were both Jewish." Or, as Rena explained, "You're asking yourself, 'If everyone is hugging each other, why did this one feel uncomfortable?' So, you don't say anything. Because you're not sure what's going on."

Rena says that girls and women in particular are receiving mixed messages. "On the one hand, we got a feminist egalitarian message but also that we were there to put up with whatever the boys initiated—that boys were initiators and we were the recipients." Yona concurs that the warm, huggy message lacks attention to risks of abuse. "I think it's particularly important that Jews acknowledge the ways that Jewish men's sexuality is as twisted by patriarchy as anyone else's." In other words, just because a culture is huggy, that doesn't mean that it is safe from predators.

Synagogues sometimes are eager to bring anyone in — even abusers — that they fail to protect women from real danger. Gloria described how she ended up dating someone who was a "regular" at the synagogue, attending daily morning and evening services, even though others in the community knew that "he was abusive to women in relationships... The rabbis knew there was an active restraining order on him." She ended up in a relationship with him that became severely abusive and left her physically impaired. He eventually landed in prison as a result, but she is angry that nobody in the synagogue warned her about him, even though they knew he was problematic.

The social and cultural norms that promote excessive closeness mean that women, often female clergy, find themselves living with behaviors they do not want — or else finding the door. That may mean leaving a job or a community, otherwise simply allowing abuse to happen. As Carmela, a Reform rabbi, explained, the culture in which women are expected to allow others to break their boundaries is the "background static" of working in a synagogue:

> It anesthetizes you to the point that you don't know you're living in this world. When it's embedded into the place, the de jure, like the law of the land, you acclimate. It's like the lobster in the pot. You don't know the water is starting to boil. So, you just accept it. And that's why the static is dangerous.

Emotional and spiritual manipulation

The synagogue can also be a place where rabbis are allowed to use their pulpit as a tool for emotional manipulation — where they can showcase their charm, charisma, and rhetorical gifts to recruit the entire congregation as their supporters and enablers. Zelda experienced this while she was trying to break away from the abuse:

> The first sermon he gave after I left was about forgiveness, how he made it like, 'It's okay if I enslave you because it's really only part of God's plan.' And there was nothing in there about needing to feel bad. It was about, 'You'll thank me one day.' It was unbelievable.

Zelda's experience demonstrates the use of the pulpit as a manipulative tool, almost preparing the setting for the moment when he will be accused and needs to recruit communal support. It also illustrates another crucial aspect of the synagogue setting that enables abuse, which is the God-language, part of the spiritual bypass. He sets himself up as an agent of God, as a tool of "God's plan," and he becomes the sole arbiter of "God's will," which is whatever he wants it to be. This is particularly effective in synagogues because many women seek synagogue experiences in order to fulfill spiritual longing, where people are craving someone to give them answers that they seek—and sexual predators can take advantage of that.

The synagogue setting, then, is a place where the rabbi has ultimate power, as if he is an arm of God. Remember how Zelda jumped out of her chair in excitement when she found out that the rabbi of the synagogue was interested in her. That is the impact of the synagogue setting on the rabbi's status. The rabbi is like an angel of God with a halo around him, tasked with saving the people. This makes him untouchable — and it makes potential victims extremely vulnerable. As Marion explained, "A Rabbi is in a unique position for a sexual predator to be a source of support and spiritual strength when women's souls are in need." She said that she would not have been raped by a rabbi "if he weren't in the position that he was in."

Patriarchy

Another key aspect of many synagogue settings that enables abuse is patriarchal culture. This refers to the ease with which women are excluded, ignored, or counted out — even in liberal denominations. Leanne, for example, who is not Orthodox, says, "Judaism is an example of a patriarchy. In what other institution do we say, 'Well, women have this role and men have this role and that's just the way it is because God wants it this way'? That makes no sense to me at all. So, we have people who in the rest of their lives are completely egalitarian who are suddenly completely content with a total two-class system based on gender."

Brenda, who is not Orthodox, had her complaints about the younger rabbi's behavior completely dismissed by the senior rabbis. She says that that the senior rabbi's often sexist rulings — such as refusing to accommodate the needs of mothers — contributed to an overall atmosphere that supported rabbis, men, and abusers over victims and women.

Shlomit, who is Orthodox, had many similar experiences. "I've lived in a community where a rabbi of a large and thriving congregation feels free to call the left names, mock feminists, express extreme anti-Arab rhetoric, and basically engage in right-wing politics from the pulpit, after dressing it up as Torah. No one has stopped him. A board member of his shul told a friend of mine he thinks the rabbi 'gets off' talking about rape." This attitude is often taken for granted as part of Orthodox norms, but Shlomit says, "It took me a lot of years to realize that this relationship was unhealthy and that there was abuse going on, not just to me, also to other people." That is, using the pulpit to put down people and mock their sexuality or gender is a form of abuse. "How is it okay to do this to another person, to crush their soul, to talk about other people in a certain way, publicly?... If you don't conform to my notion of feed my masculinity and my sense of power, I'm going to crush you." Shlomit eventually left the synagogue and the community.

For women like Shlomit, Brenda, and Leanne, who live in very different communities and belong to different denominations, the synagogue experience is swathed in a patriarchal culture in which women are cast as outsiders and as others, making them vulnerable to abuse. Not being counted for a prayer quorum, not being asked to lead services, not having one's kaddish need met, and other ways in which women are often not seen in synagogue, these are what Rena calls "subtle things" that create a setting and culture that can be unsafe for women.

Although I have included patriarchal culture as an aspect of synagogues culture that supports abuse, it isn't just synagogues. Pretty much all other Jewish settings also constitute arms of the patriarchy that enable abuse. I will return to this point.

Jewish Schools

Another setting in which a lot of incidents of abuse take place is Jewish schools, which raises many questions about what it is about school settings that enable this dynamic.

Teacher authority, autonomy, and trust

One aspect of school life that supports abuse is the unsupervised authority that is given to teachers, especially rabbis. Teachers are trusted to be alone with students, even one-on-one, and to say whatever they want to students. I have many memories of being alone with teachers in which they said inappropriate things to me, commented on my body, joked about my sexuality, or even touched me. I was never "molested" in the classic sense, but I have very clear memories of being verbally and physically imposed on by my teachers in the sense that they were completely free to insert themselves into my personal, internal discourse about myself and relationship with my body, and I had no recourse or escape, or even the basic knowledge that I could say "no" to the entire process. Moreover, since they were in positions of authority, I took their words to be true, and struggled with certain dubious assertions about me for years to come.

The case of abuse at the Hebrew Academy of Long Beach (HALB) by first-grade teacher Rabbi Yoseph Ungar is a vivid illustration about how the norms of teacher authority can trap victims. According to a complaint filed in New York State's 2019 Child Victims Act, Ungar arranged times to be alone with the student during recess and for special privileges. During an estimated 20 "visits," he raped the first grader, and then had the boy clean up the ejaculate.[171] The boy kept returning to the place where he was raped because the rapist was his teacher, a person he was socialized to believe is trustworthy and an authority who must be obeyed. When the teacher said, "Report to me," the child did so time and again, despite the torture he was going through. Such is that power of the teacher's authority.

In the case of Malka Leifer, the school headmistress who is accused of sexually abusing her students for years, was so trusted in her community that her victims had no idea of how to escape her abuse, or even that they were allowed to:

> *The fact the abuse occurred under the guise of Jewish education*
> *by the headmistress made the breach of trust monstrous. He*

---

[171] Supreme Court Of The State Of New York County Of Nassau Daniel Weiss Plaintiff, - Against- Nassau County Hebrew Academy Of Long Beach School, John And Jane Doe 1-30, Members Of The Defendants' Place Of Board Of Trustees Of Hebrew Academy Of Business, https://Iapps.Courts.State.Ny.Us/Nyscef/Viewdocument?Docindex=R3giqf2bxg97ib2qdmvh sg==

> *said Leifer's conduct as headmistress went unchecked by the school. 'She would single out girls and take them off for private chats, they would be pulled out of lessons,' Justice Rush found. 'She would take children from time to time to her own house, which a senior teacher at the school knew was occurring and seemingly never questioned the conduct because of Leifer's standing in the Adass community. On school camps, she could effectively disappear with students for hours at a time.'[172]*

Jewish educators are often given complete freedom to have private time with students without any supervision or accountability. The students, in turn, are taught to trust them. Even when the community knows what is happening, the educator may remain in their position, with no attention to the abuse or the children's need for protection.

The "Pied Piper" syndrome

In some cases, a teacher is even idolized by students (see "Charisma"), which often proffers untouchable status on the teacher.

Veteran Jewish educator Paul Shaviv wrote about a phenomenon he calls "the Pied Piper" syndrome in Jewish schools, referring to the teacher who has charisma, a disdain for rules, anti-establishment ideas and behaviors, an abhorrence of authority over him, and a tendency and to leave a "trail of wreckage" behind him:

> *'Pied Pipers' — charismatic teachers who misuse their charisma — tend to break boundaries and in doing so become very attractive to their students, especially if their home situations are less than ideal. The Pied Piper becomes substitute a father figure and certain adolescents willfully follow them in an almost abnormal way. Often, very often, these Pied Pipers turn out to have a sexually abusive dimension.*
>
> *They can be brilliant in inspiring students to go beyond their wildest expectations, and are often regarded (by their following of students, by parents, and by the Board or the community) as the 'most important' or 'best' members of staff. There is always, however, a price to be paid. The teacher's personality becomes the center of the classroom rather than the course content. A 'Pied Piper' will deeply affect and influence some*

---

[172] "Malka Leifer: Melbourne woman awarded $1.27m in damages over ultra-Orthodox Jewish school abuse," *ABC News*, 16 Sep 2015 , https://www.abc.net.au/news/2015-09-16/malka-leifer-abuse-allegations-melbourne-woman-awarded-1.27-mill/6780040

students — but will almost always leave a trail of emotional wreckage in his/her wake.[173]

Baruch Lanner, who abused students for years, is a classic example of the Pied Piper, the one who has "special" status because he seems to have a constant following among kids—no matter what he is actually doing to them. One of his self-described defenders, Dr. John Krug, a psychologist who was hired by Lanner when he was principal of the Hillel Yeshivah High School in Deal, NJ, and worked with him there for more than a dozen years, said, "He's a combination genius and *talmid chochem* [scholar]. He's very charismatic, flamboyant, given to histrionics. He's the master of the double entendre and he marches to a different drummer."[174] One of Lanner's victims, Dena Greenspan Lehrman, recalled how he was able to overstep all other forms of authority. "He said, 'Listen to me before you listen to your father,' and when I think back on that, it blows me away."[175]

Another classic Pied Piper-type of Jewish educator is Rabbi Avram Bina of the post-high school Netiv Aryeh yeshivah in Jerusalem. In 2012, Yedidya Gorsetman and Gary Rosenblatt wrote a comprehensive investigative report about the verbal, emotional, and physical abuse that he reportedly imposes on his students — name-calling, yelling, ghosting, food deprivation, slaps across the face, and other physical assaults. Some of these descriptions are reminiscent of the intermittent reinforcement and punishments I brought in the chapter on grooming. He also reportedly gave his students misogynistic advice on how to be sexually exploitative. In my book, *The Men's Section: Orthodox Jewish Men in an Egalitarian World,* one of my interviewees, a former student of Bina, said that he would tell them, "*shiksas* are for practice" — meaning, they should have sex with non-Jewish women (using a derogatory term) before they get married, just for "practice."[176]A blog called Bina Abuse asks in its tagline, "If one of Rabbi Bina's student commits suicide, will the Jewish community say they didn't know what was going on at Netiv Aryeh?" Everyone seems to know that Bina abuses his students. And yet, his

---

[173] Paul J. Shaviv, *The Jewish High School: A complete management guide: Leadership, Policy and Operations for Principals, Administrators, and Lay Leaders*, CreateSpace Independent Publishing Platform 2009; See also, Elli Fischer, "On 'hard' and 'soft' charisma in Jewish education: Toward a taxonomy of risk," *TOI Blog*, June 23, 2016, https://blogs.timesofisrael.com/on-hard-and-soft-charisma-in-jewish-education-toward-a-taxonomy-of-risk/?fbclid=IwAR0lrENThMr6GrQrJs8IUtZbgh6TkouX5JLMUxiKI0wjImVq6hCqPLoLti0

[174] Rosenblatt, "Stolen Innocence," https://www.bjpa.org/content/upload/bjpa/stol/Stolen%20Innocence%20-%20Gary%20Rosenblatt%20-%20Jewish%20Week%20-%20Sexual%20Abuse.pdf

[175] Rosenblatt, "Stolen Innocence," https://www.bjpa.org/content/upload/bjpa/stol/Stolen%20Innocence%20-%20Gary%20Rosenblatt%20-%20Jewish%20Week%20-%20Sexual%20Abuse.pdf

[176] Elana Sztokman, *The Men's Section: Orthodox Jewish Men in an Egalitarian World* (Brandeis University Press, 2011).

defenders cite his "warmth" and "charisma," much like other rabbis and teachers who have a following despite the open secret about their toxicity. Gorsetman and Rosenblatt reported that people "defend him as a warm, remarkably caring man who has had a very positive impact on the overwhelming majority of the thousands of students he has taught." He is a classic Pied Piper — he can get away with whatever he wants because he has so many followers. [177]

The problem with schools is that, on some level, school cultures create spaces that are very comfortable for Pied Pipers. First of all, schools are designed for situations in which teachers are alone in the classroom with no other adults supervising them or checking what they say or do in there. Second of all, many school cultures value "popularity" above all else. In many places, being a "popular" teacher is a coveted title, and much of school life revolves around that dynamic. This gives charismatic teachers a lot of status, leeway, and support. Administrators, boards, and parents often want that personality around because it seems to add value to the school — and they do not recognize the abusive and dangerous dynamic for what it is.

Oddly, one person who challenged Shaviv's analysis and defended a "Pied Piper approach" to education is Professor Jon Levisohn, a leading Jewish education philosopher who was accused by Shayna Sragovicz of psycho-sexual abuse on a leadership training program (and which the program's investigation later cleared him of). In an essay in e-*Jewish Philanthropy* called, "Passion in religious education", Levisohn asked, "When a teacher demonstrates passion, when a class seems to get drawn into a focus on the teacher's persona, does that inevitably threaten the boundaries between teacher and student?" He claims that viewing the Pied Piper personality as "dangerous" is wrong. He says that this outlook eliminates a kind of teaching that he advocates for in which, "some shared object of inquiry that holds the attention — and attracts the desire — of both teacher and student." He adds that this "is a model of pedagogy that can channel passion in productive ways for religious education." [178] It is hard for me to comprehend why an educator would go to such lengths to push back against the work of protecting kids from abusive educators. With everything we know about the Baruch Lanners of the world, this essay seems to be defending the very behaviors that enable abuse to take place in schools.

---

[177] Yedidya Gorsetman and Gary Rosenblatt, "Has The 'Tough Love' Rebbe Gone Too Far?" *Jewish Week*, January 24, 2012, https://www.jta.org/2012/01/24/ny/has-the-tough-love-rebbe-gone-too-far; Bina Abuse, "If one of Rabbi Bina's student commits suicide, will the Jewish community say they didn't know what was going on at Netiv Aryeh?" https://binaabuse.wordpress.com/

[178] Jon A. Levisohn, "Passion in Religious Education," *e-Jewish Philanthropy* February 20, 2017 https://ejewishphilanthropy.com/passion-in-religious-education/

Brushing it off

This prizing of the charismatic Pied Piper may be one reason why, in so many cases of abuse in school, the problem is poorly dealt with or ignored.

Many schools deal with revelations of abuse by sending the accused teachers away — instead of, say, outing them or reporting them. The Australian Chabad school where CSA advocate Manny Waks was molested sent one of the perpetrators to another school in America, making it someone else's problem. The late Yeshiva University Chancellor Rabbi Norman Lamm admitted that he dealt with the rampant abuse by George Finkelstein by sending him to Florida — where he continued to abuse boys.[179] Shlomit recalled that "a rabbi in my high school molested schoolmates and was simply removed from my all-girls' school and placed in the boys' school. He then went on to become my community rabbi and had sexually inappropriate relationships with congregants."

In some cases, schools do not bother dealing with it at all and leave students to their own devices. Leanne recalled that in her school, "there was a teacher who was very inappropriate, very touchy and grabby, and I complained and nobody cared. I spoke to a few other girls who experienced the same kinds of things, so we helped each other get through it, but it was a fairly traumatic set of experiences dealing with him." She told people about it, and nobody in a position of authority did anything.

The same thing happened in the Yeshivah of Flatbush when I studied there in the seventies and eighties. One history teacher was known to verbally harass girls about our bodies, openly discussing the size of girls' breasts and bragging about putting the big-chested girls in front of him. He would snicker, the boys would snicker, and the girls would be mortified. He taught there for decades — everyone knew, and nobody ever did anything about it.

Student culture

In some cases, there is almost a sense that high school teachers can get away with being "sexual" with students because it is somehow "playful," or "fun," and part of what teenagers do, so if teachers participate, it's all part of the game.

This brings up the question of how student culture factors into all this. When teachers are allowed to say and do whatever they want without

---

[179] Forward Staff, "Yeshiva U.'s Rabbi George Finkelstein Acted Inappropriately Even After Ouster After he was forced out of the high school in 1995 because of inappropriate wrestling with boys," *Ha'aretz* March 1, 2013
https://www.haaretz.com/jewish/yeshiva-u-s-rabbi-george-finkelstein-acted-inappropriately-even-after-ouster-1.5232101

consequence, it should hardly come as a surprise that students pick up the same message.

Around the world, stories are emerging about Jewish schools and cultures of sexual abuse, not only from rabbis but also from other staff and peers. For example, in April 2021, two London-based Jewish schools were outed by former pupils for maintaining cultures in which sexual abuse is rampant.[180] According to the many complaints anonymously shared about sexual abuse in London's Jewish schools, at least one incident involved a teacher, but the most were about abuse taking place among students on an everyday basis. The 18 claims against Britain's two most prestigious and largest Jewish schools—JFS and the Jewish Community Secondary School—include rape, assault, harassment, groping, spreading sexually explicit photos with hundreds of students, public discussion about bodies, and comparison of female students' bodies with those of porn stars. As one student said, "Sexual assault was completely normalized" at the school. Here are a few examples:

> I was in the lunch queue and he put his hand up my skirt and groped me… No one said anything…

> [It was] normal for boys of any age to grope girls…

> What I remember most is once bending over to pick something up and a boy came up behind me and began grinding against me. [One bystander responded], 'I think he likes you" …

> [A male student broke into a girls' bathroom and began shouting], 'Tell me your name, tell me your name, come out now,' as he threatened to open a stall that a girl was in…[181]

Peer-on-peer abuse in Jewish schools is not limited to the UK. Gail recalled being abused in eighth grade by another student in her American school:

> I remember exactly who assaulted me in the back of Mrs. Regna's science room during homeroom in 8th grade. I remember what they did, what they said, and what they said after. I don't remember the date, the time of year, who else was or was not around, what I wore, what I ate that day.

---

[180] Jacob Judah, "Prestigious Jewish schools in London reel over allegations of sexual abuse. Dozens of users on the British website Everyone's Invited share stories of rape, assault, and harassment, but some former students say fear of anti-Semitism are holding more back," *Times of Israel*, 30 April 2021 https://www.timesofIsrael.com/prestigious-jewish-schools-in-london-reel-over-allegations-of-sexual-abuse/

[181] Judah, "Prestigious Jewish schools," https://www.timesofIsrael.com/prestigious-jewish-schools-in-london-reel-over-allegations-of-sexual-abuse/

These incidents raise many difficult questions about how a school culture evolved into a place in which sexual abuse is normalized. It also raises questions about the relationships between students and teachers—both religious and non-religious teachers, rabbis, or otherwise—in such a way that teachers are somehow unwilling or unable to educate students that sexual abuse is wrong. One cannot help but wonder how deep or normalized the culture of sexual abuse is in Jewish educational environments.

Moreover, these issues bring out a kind of chicken and egg question. Are schools attractive to sexual predators because blurred sexual boundaries are tolerated among teenagers and create a perfect environment for them, or are boundaries undefined among teenagers because sometimes the people meant to protecting students' boundaries are sexual predators themselves? Put differently, are students actually learning how to be abusers from the adults around them? And is a common cultural attitude of "teenagers have raging hormones" actually an invitation for abuse both by peers and adults around them?

Informal education

Camps and youth groups

In the first chapter where I introduced stories with abusive rabbis, I brought the testimony of Meyer Seewald who described a summer camp experience in which Rabbi Mendel Levine allegedly touched him in his "private area" and walked around the bunk with an erection.[182] In another story about Jewish summer camps that came public since #MeToo, United Synagogue Youth (USY)—the USA-based youth group of the Conservative movement—cut ties with its former longtime director Jules Gutin after former youth group members accused him of inviting USY participants to sleep in his bed and, in at least one instance, included sexually touching one of the young men. Gutin is at least the second USY official to be accused of sexual abuse against teenage participants. Robert Fisher, former director of the group's Pacific Southwest Region, admitted in 2002 to inviting three boys to sleep in his bed, touching one of them sexually, and pressuring another to undress for him.[183] Similarly, Len Robinson, the former director of NJY

---

[182] JTA, "Dutch Jews investigate Brooklyn rabbi on molestation charges. Action taken after local newspaper publishes two accusations against Mendel Levine dating back to when he worked as a youth counselor," *JTA*, January 8, 2018, https://www.timesofisrael.com/dutch-jews-investigate-brooklyn-rabbi-on-molestation-charges/

[183] Ben Sales, "Conservative youth group cuts ties with ex-head accused of sexual misconduct. Jules Gutin denies allegations, which the CEO of the United Synagogue of Conservative Judaism says 'were wide ranging and all inappropriate'," *Times of Israel*, 18 December 2017

Camps and previously a star in the JCC network, resigned in 2018 after it came to light that he sexually abused many girls at his camps over the years.[184] Debbie Findling described in an essay in the *Jewish Week* how Robinson in the course of a single conversation asked if he could hold her hand, tried to kiss her, and propositioned her to have sex with him and his wife. She later discovered that he had allegedly been doing this kind of thing for years. [185]

The camp setting, as in any informal educational setting, can be ripe for abuse. It is a place where boundaries are blurred, where there are few formal control settings, where teenagers often experiment with their sexuality, and where charismatic leaders are revered. "My time as a summer camp counselor at a Jewish camp was filled with inappropriate behavior from older male staff members," one respondent recalled.

In February 2022, the Union for Reform Judaism (URJ) released a study that looked almost exclusively at sexual abuse that took place in the movement's informal youth settings. The report found dozens of incidences of abuse of children and adults across their many programs. They also reported what they referred to as "boundary-crossing"—uncomfortable behaviors that they do not count as "abuse,"—such as unwanted and uncomfortable touching, rubbing, and massaging.[186]

Therein lies a crucial dynamic of sexual abuse, especially in informal youth settings: the gradual breaking down of boundaries, may not "count" as abuse but allows predators to swoop in and do their thing.

Breaking rules and boundaries

One obvious aspect of informal settings is that many rules are relaxed. There are no tests or homework, dress codes are looser, and the overall goal

---

https://www.timesofisrael.com/conservative-youth-group-cuts-ties-with-ex-head-accused-of-sexual-misconduct/

[184] Hannah Dreyfus, "More Women Come Forward Against N.J. Camp Exec Alleging Sexual Harassment. She had always thought of him as a family friend — until he invited her to spend the night with him alone at his private residence in the Poconos," *Jewish Week*, April 18, 2018, https://jewishweek.timesofisrael.com/after-n-j-camp-exec-sacked-last-week-more-women-alleging-sexual-harassment-come-forward/

[185] Debbie Findling, "Is The Jewish Community Perpetuating Sexual Harassment?" *Jewish Week*. March 20, 2018 https://jewishweek.timesofisrael.com/is-the-jewish-community-perpetuating-sexual-harassment/; Hannah Dreyfus, "New Allegations Against Robinson Include A Minor. Joanna says she was sexually abused by Len Robinson when she was 17," *Jewish Week*. April 11, 2019,https://jewishweek.timesofisrael.com/new-allegations-against-robinson-include-a-minor/; Hannah Dreyfus, "After N.J. Camp Exec Sacked, More Women Alleging Sexual Harassment Come Forward," *Jewish Week*, April 18, 2018, https://njjewishnews.timesofisrael.com/after-n-j-camp-exec-sacked-last-week-more-women-alleging-sexual-harassment-come-forward/

[186] Mary Beth Hogan, Tricia Sherno, *The Report of the Independent Investigation*, Feb 17, 2022 https://urj.org/sites/default/files/2022-02/URJ_Investigation_Report.pdf

is to have fun. For kids, this is a major draw. But for predators, this opens the door to many opportunities for breaking boundaries. Shelley Feingold, for example, recalls that Robinson would invite young female counselors to "unwind" with him in a local sports bar after-hours. He would "buy pitchers of beer for underage female counselors" and drink and joke with them late into the night. "I thought it was interesting that counselors could be fired for being found with alcohol on campgrounds, but Len felt perfectly comfortable buying drinks for 17-, 18- and 19-year-old girls," she said. As the "adult in the room," he was able to break the rules, which he used to ingratiate himself with his prey. The easy breaking of boundaries is also how Leanne's abuser entered her space in camp. He was free to approach her, to chat with her, to ask her to go on walks with him—and ultimately walk into her bunk while she was in bed and start touching her.

Predators at camp may try to act like teenagers, to appear "cool," and to hang out with teenagers. Hildy Somerville, who had spent her entire childhood at Robinson's camps and considered him a family friend, was harassed by him when she was 25 and went to meet him for a job interview. After taking "shot after shot" of vodka and insisting that she have a "vodka on the rocks," Robinson, whom she described as "totally wasted," began asking her intimate questions about her sex life. "He said I was the 'perfect height' to give my old camp boyfriend oral sex," she recalled. All the while, he continued to move his chair "closer and closer to me" until he reached out to place a hand on her arm. In other words, he moved into her space by first drinking with her, then talking about her teenage sex life, as if he were a peer, a replacement for her boyfriend, and finally touching her as if he had already been invited to.

Similarly, Gail shared that, "My temple youth group director invited his friend to a youth group event. The two of them — men in their early thirties — invited me and two of my friends to a hot tub with them. They had us sit on their laps. We were twelve." There is a mixing of adult and children's spaces and an attempt by predators to get into the kids' lives and then bring them into their own sexualized fantasy worlds.

It is one thing for kids to stretch boundaries among themselves, though that also can end badly (which I describe in detail below, under "Hookup culture). But it is quite another for adults to break boundaries vis-à-vis children, especially ones they are supposed to be caring for, educating, and protecting.

For predators, an absence of boundaries can make them feel invincible. Baruch Lanner, for example, who was brought to the OU Beit Din in 1989 because of his abuse and was supposedly banned from direct contact with young people, "continued to take an active part in Shabbatons around the country at least a few times a year, delivering *divrei Torah*, or sermons, as well as mingling with individual teens… where he was 'lauded and lionized.'"

One observer, a musician for the organization who attended many events, said "he was never monitored. He had contact with the kids all along." One time, the musician sat with Lanner when he began "speaking to a girl who was a senior in high school [and] making sexual references to her in a lighthearted way, 'getting into that sexual stuff.' [The musician] interrupted, warning the rabbi about his behavior, and Rabbi Lanner responded, 'I know, I've got to be careful.'" He was not afraid of anything. Not his victims, not his community, and not his supervisors who were meant to be protecting kids from people like him. Even after he was caught, he still roamed free.

Hookup culture

Jewish summer camps and youth groups have another problem, which is the "hookup" culture, which leaves kids vulnerable not only to adult predators but also to abuse by teenage peers. Nancy described what is probably a very typical encounter in camp, where one of the kids becomes predatorial and there are no boundaries or protections for the rest:

> When I was in youth movements, boys did try. And there were boys who might be a little more aggressive. Consent wasn't a thing. It was more like, let's see what we can get away with. Most of the boys were very nice. But they're boys, and they tried. Like, they might put their hand further than they should in a movie house. How much noise are you going to make in a movie house to get the guy's hand off, you know what I mean? The girls would talk about it. And they would decide, either I'll go to the movie with you only if you promise not to, or whatever. Everyone handled it their own way. We never had a discussion about it.

Although this may be dismissed as a kind of "boys will be boys" scenario, it is very risky. There is a lot of sexual pressure, one person feels entitled, and there is very little adult direction, guidance, or supervision. As Rena said, "Everyone is flirting, your kids, and you don't know when the flirting is appropriate and when it's inappropriate."

Although Nancy and Rena are both over the age of 50, sexual pressure in Jewish camp is not merely a remnant of yesteryear. In fact, it has perhaps gotten worse. A 2021 investigative story in *New Voices* by Shira Wolkenfeld delved deeper into the sexualized cultures in Jewish camps and found a shocking culture of sexual assault packaged as "hooking up." Wolkenfeld interviewed dozens of former campers and staff to find out what this hookup culture looks like. She shared a story, for example, about a teenage girl who walked into a Friday night service, sat down at a table with her friends and a few new faces, and within a few minutes, "as Shabbat services began, his hands were on her thighs, between her legs, and groping her breasts. She asked him to stop; he did not. When she was able to extricate herself from the table, one friend asked if she knew the boy. She said no. 'That's just what happens,' her friend replied. 'We shouldn't have sat with strangers.'"[187] Wolkenfeld concludes that the expectation of girls to be readily available for sexual activity permeates Jewish youth groups. The stories "aren't isolated or uncommon experiences in American Jewish youth groups. Rather, this sort of situation is a natural progression of a culture where teens report feeling oversexualized, under pressure to hook up with one another, and lacking education around consent."

Worse, adults in charge often know that this is happening and at times seem to *encourage* it. "With Jewish camps, you have really very specific cultures," Daniel Brenner, the chief of education and programming at Moving Traditions told the *Washington Post* in a story about sex cultures in Jewish camp. "They value this ideal that you meet your bashert, your intended life partner, at summer camp. They will put the names of couples who met at camp in their dining hall up on the wall on a plaque—that's a very real part of traditional religious community that does have certain ideas about coupling."

But clearly, it's more than just wholesome coupling towards a "life partner." There is often pressure to "partner up" and engage in sexual activity—even with counselors in their twenties. In a study by Moving Traditions on issues relating to romance and sexuality at 25 Jewish camps, they found that these lines are often blurred. "How do you be positive toward romance or sexuality, and at the same time not create a situation where it's not clear where the boundaries are?" the researchers asked. Les Skolnick, who leads trainings for Jewish camps on LGBT inclusion and other topics, told the *Post*, "I very clearly remember getting to… camp and being told there's no sex at camp—and then later on that evening, being told that anything else was fair game." Another former camper said that the pressure to have sex "would begin before we even stepped foot at our various camps for the summer and felt prevalent from the first day of the session." Another said, "many people at their camps would succumb to the pressure without understanding their own limits because no one had talked to them about consent, establishing boundaries and expressing their feelings to a partner."[188]

---

[187] Shira Wolkenfeld, "Investigation: How Jewish Youth Groups Are Breeding A Toxic Sexual Culture For Teens," *New Voices*. July 13, 2021, https://newvoices.org/2021/07/13/investigation-how-jewish-youth-groups-are-breeding-a-toxic-sexual-culture-for-teens/?fbclid=IwAR1nKU0b_vZ1Wj96eaBla4_EE-LVPlqVeYvbXogVDTlThlhqle2nl9RYKzo

[188] Zauzmer, Julie, "#MeToo goes to Jewish summer camp, a traditional place for teenage romance", *Washington Post*, July 14, 2018. https://www.washingtonpost.com/local/social-issues/metoo-goes-to-jewish-summer-camp-a-traditional-place-for-teenage-

A sexually charged environment, where there are no parents present and where kids are unclear about sexual boundaries or even encouraged to find partners, and where sexual activity is also fodder for mocking and shaming, is ripe for painful experiences.

This is not about teenagers happily and jointly fooling around. Something more sinister is happening. An Instagram account called "Jewish Teens for Empowered Consent" has been collecting testimonies about sexual abuse in Jewish youth movements. The accounts reflect a deeply embedded culture of sexual assault under the guise of "normal" activity.[189] Here is an example of a post:

> Even as young as 6th grade, hookup culture was engraved into every...event. Older staff and even people's parents would advertise it to kids as 'meeting young Jewish people.'... Every event I have ever been to, there are always guys making lists of girls who are the 'hottest.' You always hear guys, especially older ones, talking about who they're going to 'go after.' You feel left out and pressured into hooking up with guys. Even girls will discuss with each other who their 'target' is for that event. It's pressuring and suffocating to not be able to enjoy yourself in a mostly positive Jewish environment when everyone is pressuring each other into hookups just to prove to other people that they can 'get' someone. I've been pressured into hookups I didn't want to do multiple times at events. These hookups never involve genuine interest or feelings. Just pressure from other teens.

According to this anonymous poster, the pressure to engage in unwanted sexual activity comes from teens as well as adults—even parents. The pressure also incorporates Jewish social-cultural aspects of "meeting other Jews," and it starts with the onset of puberty. Teenagers feel that they have no choice but to engage in unwanted sex acts, and what should be a fun social experience is ruined for them. Another Instagram poster shared this story:

> I was assaulted at the dance [at the International Convention]. A boy came up to me from behind, at least a foot taller than I was, and held me by the waist so hard while he invaded and manipulated my body that I was left with bruising. He never even so much as saw my face. At 14, in the middle of a sea of thousands of people, I was completely and utterly alone. I had never felt so objectified and helpless.

---

romance/2018/07/14/05c1fb28-86b8-11e8-8f6c-46cb43e3f306_story.html?utm_term=.9fe2b8c11aa6
[189] https://www.instagram.com/jews4empoweredconsent/?hl=en

Again, violent sexual assault is reportedly happening in the midst of everyday Jewish youth social gatherings. And the victims are often left to tend to their wounds alone.

The damage from this culture cuts deep, and can be lasting:

> *I don't think I would've felt as self-conscious about not having kissed someone had it not been for the hookup culture rampant at camp. I don't think I would've felt so unattractive had I not worried so much about 'catching up' to everyone else... It's affected my sexual and romantic relationships to this day...*

The impact of this culture damages participants, especially girls, who are being watched, judged, measured, labeled, targeted, and pursued. Melissa gave an illustration of this dynamic:

> *One friend of mine was fooling around with a guy — not sex, but making out, cuddling — and my bunkmate started making fun of her in a nasty, gendered way. And my counselor, instead of saying, 'I'm not condoning the behavior but you can't just sit here and make fun of her,' instead she was like, 'Haha, so funny, blabedy blah . . .' and later, they'd be like, 'I'm allowed to not like her and I don't care that Laura's friends with her, she was making out.' So when experiences like that would happen, counselors or other authority figures wouldn't step in and say, 'Hey, we need to talk about this in a way that is healthy.' Instead, they were like, 'Haha,' which didn't make me feel like they were people I could go to when there was a real problem.*

The environment of sexual pressure, combined with an absence of clear guidelines or understandings, is ripe for abuse. The culture also enables elements of grooming and abuse: mockery, sexual pressure, and putting kids in a double bind about participating Melissa, who was one of the senior staff members of her camp—at the age of 26—confirmed that there is a lot of sexual abuse happening at camp that it is supported by social-cultural pressures and lack of education and awareness, and that the staff often were over their heads:

> *I think it's crazy to think about the summer camps. There were a lot of kids assaulting other kids... We weren't ever taught the concept of consent. They were very, like, 'You have to go make Jewish babies,' and if you were talking to boys, it was like, 'You might be talking to your future husband.' So, if someone was having a sexual experience and they went bad, you didn't feel like you had anyone you could talk to.*

There is also a gendered, patriarchal component to this dynamic as well. While the absence of awareness about consent can affect people of all genders, that gap combined with the "pressure to make babies" is uniquely aimed at girls. It also promotes an idea about sex as something that boys demanded from girls and that girls were expected to give to them. As Rena explained, "There's this undertone, a very mixed message that girls were getting; on the one hand a feminist egalitarian message but also that we were there to put up with whatever the boys wanted, and that boys were initiators and we were the recipients."

What's worse, girls are not only pressured to engage in unwanted sex acts with male *peers*; they are also pressured to submit to the pursuit of male *counselors*. In one youth group, sex between counselors and campers was even prized in a "points" system for hooking up. According to an expose by Josh Nathan-Kazis at the *Forward*, in this game — which has been going on for twenty years — point values are assigned to each member, ages 14 to 18, based on what role the member plays within the group hierarchy:

> *A hookup with a regular member is worth one point, according to one version of the rules posted years ago on Facebook and confirmed by a current… student leader. A hookup with a local chapter president is worth three points. A hookup with a member of the international student board is worth eight points. That version of the rules awards nine points for hookups with the youth movement's adult staff members.*

The "points system" explicitly links sex to power and status within the youth organization.[190] The rule awarding nine points for hooking up with adult staff members directly enables staff to take advantage of younger members — as young as 14-years-old — by allowing them the potential to reframe abuse or even rape as a consensual hookup under the guise of helping them to win the most points.

The points game can end very badly, as another anonymous poster wrote on the Instagram account:

> *The organization's traditions and culture perpetuate a norm of hyper-sexualization that ultimately coerces participants to engage in acts they may not be ready for. At my first [youth group] convention, the older members in my chapter told my thirteen-year-old self to 'pick any Aleph' so that they could 'set*

---

[190] Josh Nathan-Katzis, "'Super Creepy' Game Hands Out Points For Hooking Up At Youth Group," *Forward*, November 30, 2017 https://forward.com/news/388645/underground-hookup-game-at-jewish-youth-group-awards-points-for-making-out/?fbclid=IwAR3LGsv918uaGzgr7Eg5hePjXqitWOXYFAx4osQ3tkcW8fXRM5R1KDg8Zu8

*it up.' That is exactly the message [the youth group] broadcasts
to its members from the get-go: no one is off limits.*

An "Aleph" in this culture is an older camper or counselor. This person
says that her thirteen-year-old camper self was encouraged by the older staff
to "pick one out."

When young girls are encouraged or even pressured to engage in sexual
activity with boys or men pursuing them for their own social status — and
where the other adults either look away or even encourage it — the setting is
ripe for predators to swoop in. Someone who acts youthful and fun and
offers campers "prizes" like alcohol or special attention, can probably find
an easy way to trap their "targets."

Indeed, Lucy described sexual assault at camp by a 16-year-old staffer
when she was 12 years old:

> *When I was 12, I was at a Jewish camp in the Berkshires.
> Second summer. Happiest place on earth. I ended up being
> 'boyfriend/girlfriend' with an older 16-year-old CIT
> [counselor-in-training] and I thought I was the coolest thing
> ever. On the second to last night of camp he asked me to take a
> walk while everyone was watching a movie. We went toward
> the forest, and he stopped near a bush. He asked if I wanted to
> kiss, and I said yes. We did for a while. Before I knew what was
> happening, he had taken off his pants and underpants. He
> asked me if I wanted to put my mouth on his penis. I said no.
> He cajoled me and said, 'Just a little bit, don't worry, just for
> a second.' Feeling the pressure, and being 12 years old, I did it.
> And then before I knew what was happening again, I was on
> the ground. He had my arms pinned down and he was inside
> of me. I stayed silent. I didn't move. I went limp. He finished
> and kissed me on the forehead. I got up and went back to the
> movie with him.*

At the age of 12, Lucy was violently raped at her Jewish summer camp,
the "happiest place on earth," by a 16-year-old counselor in training.

An added layer of the trauma here is that the abuse is taking place where
education for sexuality is meant to be taking place. Melissa gave an example
of what happened when she tried to intervene in a situation in which she
suspected that a girl was being abused by her boyfriend. She contacted an
adviser named Miriam, whose official job was "adviser," and who handed
out fliers that read, "Reach out to Miriam if you are being abused." Melissa
shared her suspicions with Miriam. "The response I got was, 'That doesn't
happen here, they're good kids, blah blah blah.' And I was like, 'Maybe you
should keep an eye on this.' I don't think anyone ever talked about this."

As one anonymous poster on the Instagram account wrote:

> *Not only is this extremely dangerous in the sense that it's a direct pipeline which spews out sexual predators, but it indoctrinates young and impressionable kids with the false notion that hooking up is a constant and universal desire. This places pressure on members from a young age to feel as though they won't be making the most of an event if they aren't engaging in this culture, and thus leaves room for, at the very least, implicit coercion and regret.[191]*

In this culture — in which the adults at camp are permitted or even expected to act like the kids, and to have the same feelings and behaviors as the kids — predation becomes the definition of sexuality.

Perhaps not surprisingly, as campers become young adults, the problem intensifies. The summer program evolves into young adult programs, especially with travel far from home, and the abuse arguably gets worse. In 2018, Sarah Seltzer wrote an investigative report about sexual cultures on the Birthright Israel tours — that is, the free Israel trips for Jewish young adults — based on 50 testimonies spanning 14 years of the program. She found that "a pervasive environment of sexual pressure that encourages Jews to meet, marry, and, someday, procreate with other Jews while being awed by the beauty and culture of Israel. This expectation is communicated before the trip even begins via social media, and on the trips is expressed most directly around encounters between American women and Israeli soldiers."[192] Like Jewish summer camps, young adult programs are often charged with sexual pressure and unclear sexual boundaries, with supervising adults and clear guidelines about sexuality far from view. As Melissa said, all her friends know that Israel trips are "all about hooking up." Some providers "jokingly" call the programs "hormonal *mifgashim*" (encounters), as if sexual abuse is just a natural response to get-togethers between Jewish young adults.

Charley said that her rabbinical-student rapist was formerly a staffer on an Israel trip, and she said that when her friends found out who raped her, they weren't surprised because he "had a reputation" from his years as a counselor on Jewish programs. "He was dating one of the participants, which was considered unacceptable and in later years people got fired for the exact same thing." Charley's rapist did not face any consequences for any of his assaults, even though many people knew about them.

It is worth pointing out that Birthright has been largely funded by megadonor Michael Steinhardt, who has been allegedly sexually harassing

---

[191] https://www.instagram.com/p/CL2MMWfLX-Y /
[192] Sarah M. Seltzer, "Birthright Israel and #MeToo. *Jewish Currents* spoke with more than 50 Birthright Israel participants and staffers about their experiences with the often-fraught sexual and gender dynamics on the famous free trip to Israel Here is what we found," *Jewish Currents*, April 18, 2018 https://jewishcurrents.org/birthright-Israel-and-metoo

women for decades. It makes one wonder about the connection between the cultures of programs and the cultures of their funders.

Nevertheless, not all is gloom and doom. A group of Jewish college students came together during the pandemic to fight back against hookup cultures in Jewish camps and other settings. Madeline Canfield, Lila Goldstein, Ellanora Lerner, Lilah Peck, Maddy Pollack, and Dahlia Soussan wrote an essay in *e-Jewish Philanthropy* in which they take issue with the ways in which the adults in the room have allowed this to happen:

> *Jews are not fully grasping the consequences of imposing blatant components of rape culture onto teens... Youth groups were developed with the explicit purpose of getting more Jews under chuppahs with each other. Hypersexualization, despite its issues, is upheld as a means to that end. ...The efficacy of this strategy is dubious at best. Some long-term relationships do grow out of youth groups, but at a lofty cost: the shallowness of hookup culture impedes the formation of genuine, complex relationships and identity. It reinforces heteronormativity, misogyny, and acceptance of sexual harassment. Membership growth is prioritized to the point that many potential members are alienated by the sexualization youth groups employ to pump up recruitment. As for those who do cross the threshold, it's challenging to negotiate a space intended to build confidence while being degraded as a sex object by peers and experiencing commodification as just another number by organizations singularly focused on their stats...[H]ookup culture's dominance is incredibly isolating for teens who aren't comfortable participating in it. Identity building spaces cannot be predicated on objectification.*[193]

In addition to powerfully speaking out, young Jewish adults are also coming together to change the hookup culture. The Instagram account where former campers shared stories of abuse has evolved into an educational program called, "Jewish teens for empowered consent". Their work includes "'consent education programming' that unpacks hookup culture comprehensive surveying of youth group members, alumni, and prospective members who chose not to attend youth groups to understand the pervasiveness of hookup culture and hypersexualization; and eradication of

---

[193] Madeline Canfield, Lila Goldstein, Ellanora Lerner, Lilah Peck, Maddy Pollack, and Dahlia Soussan, "For Continuity's Sake? Addressing Hookup Culture in Jewish Youth Groups," *e-Jewish Philanthropy*, September 3, 2020 https://ejewishphilanthropy.com/for-continuitys-sake-addressing-hookup-culture-in-jewish-youth-groups/

sexualized cheers and point systems, as well as other hookup games and awards." [194] Where there's life there's hope.

Home

I would like to take a moment to step away from analyzing public or communal settings and touch on a particularly hard topic. One of the most tragic revelations from interviewees was that, for some victims, home itself was the setting for abuse. For these interviewees, the place that was meant to be a person's safest space was the most dangerous. Although most of this research focuses on abuse that happens out of the home, a number of interviewees described incestuous abuse, and I am bringing their accounts here as examples of what it looks like when children are violated in their safest places. Ultimately, the Jewish community comprises these families, even when there is abuse within a family unit— and continuously reinforces and permeates their home culture, beliefs, and practices.

Genendy Radoff's memoir, *The Price of Truth,* is a powerful starting point for understanding the dynamics of incest, especially in her ultra-Orthodox community where secrecy abounds and men have all the power to speak, act, and be seen. Genendy was raped and molested by her father, her grandfather, and the men in the yeshivah that her grandfather ran, until she was seven years old. The men were apparently taught that until the age of seven, children are "allowed" because they do not feel or remember things. According to her account, the abuse happened both at home and at the yeshiva, sometimes in her bedroom, sometimes in her grandfather's study, and sometimes in the men's dorm rooms. The abuse was able to be kept secret for many reasons. Her mother did not want to know, her family did not believe her, and the abusers supported each other. She even recounts an incident with a doctor who instructed her father on how to abuse her without leaving any "blood" or marks that might sound an alarm. These experiences contribute to the suspicion that the men know about each other's activities and support each other. [195]

Several of my interviewees were sexually abused by their fathers, such as Fay, whose ultra-Orthodox mother would not let her talk about it. Hinda, too, was sexually abused by her father from ages three through eight, "at which point I fought back." Although he stopped sexually abusing her, he continued to be violent with her. "My father was a raging alcoholic and spent

---

[194] Jewish Teens for Empowered Consent
https://www.jewishteensforempoweredconsent.org/
[195] Genendy Radoff, *The Price Of Truth: A True Story Of Child Sexual Abuse In The Orthodox Jewish World And One Girl's Courage To Survive And Heal,* (Lioness Books 2019)

much of his time screaming at me and threatening me." Marion, who was raped by her rabbi at her grandmother's funeral, said that the experience was particularly devastating because her grandmother had protected her from her abusive father. Alyssa was also attacked repeatedly by her father. The abuse was kept secret by a series of violent threats:

> My father threatened me from the very beginning, when I was still a toddler, that the police would come and put him and my mom in jail and I would have nowhere to live, or that they'd come take me away and put me in a children's home and my parents would be gone forever, then he'd say he'd murder my mom if I told anyone and since he was a monster and I was beyond terrified of him, I believed him. He said he'd kill my cat, too, which was the only living thing that I'd loved and that loved me. Eventually, he threatened to kill me. I believed every word he said.

Several interviewees described sexual abuse that they experienced in a home environment by non-family members, which is also an invasion of deep trust. Risha was raped at home by her brother's friend who she said, "saw me as a fuck object and felt he was entitled to attack me and rape me." Eliana was attacked by her friend's grandfather at his home while she was visiting him. "He asked me to have wine with him, which I declined. He then pulled me toward him and pushed his tongue in my mouth. I made a joke about it and quickly left."

Lara was also molested at the home of her mother's best friend when she was 12 or 13:

> We went to her house, and she was having a social, and some of my parents' friends, one was a man, I remember he was very tall and he was a butcher, he had a butcher shop. I knew him from these meetings, on occasion, we would get together. I remember leaving the living area and going into the next room where there was a television, and I was sitting there. He sat down next to me, and I wasn't scared. He said, 'So Laraleh, how are you?' and within five minutes he had me, pulled me by the shoulders and tried to French kiss me. At the time I didn't even know what that really was, but I understood later. I went into shock. Because he was familiar, a friend of the family... I pushed myself as best I could and ran into the bathroom and locked the door. And was really in shock. But I didn't run out or get my father. My father would have probably beaten the crap out of him had he known. But I didn't tell him or tell anyone. I pulled inside myself and repressed it.

Homes are meant to be safe spaces, and yet at times they hold the darkest secrets of pain and abuse. In a culture in which the "Jewish home" is meant to be sacred, these stories are powerful illustrations that the culture does not always live up to what it claims to be. That constitutes a violation of trust for all of us.

I suspect that many of my interviewees experienced abuse at home. Many offered quick and vague references to childhood sexual trauma that influenced their vulnerability to abuse later on. Even for people openly sharing trauma, the particular experiences of incest can be too overbearing to share. The accounts may also be too long and intricate to explain in a 2-3 hour interview. Many victims of incest, when they choose to tell their stories, require volumes to get their stories out, such as survivor-authors Genendy Radoff or Manny Waks. The topic is both incredibly germane and too vast for this book.

Frankly, a comprehensive analysis of the dynamics of incest in the Jewish community, which is desperately needed, deserves its own book. This section provides a glimpse into the issue, but only a brief one. It is not nearly sufficient. But incest is an intricate part of the cultural story I am unraveling here, even if it still remains only partially seen. I have included it briefly because first of all, incest is clearly part of the spectrum of sexual abuse in Jewish culture. Parents and other abusive relatives share many if not all of the same character traits and grooming tactics of abuse — narcissism, the need to control, emotional manipulation, spiritual bypass, and more. Quite a lot of the analysis I offer here is perfectly applicable to victims of incest. The topic needs more attention, but this is a start.

Second of all, an important take-away is that abuse by a parent at home is possibly the most dangerous, because there is no way out. The victim often has no safe space in the entire world. All the issues and impacts that are described here are multiplied manifold when the abuser is a family member.

Finally, the primary take-away from hearing accounts of incest goes to a core point of my research. That is: As long as sexual abuse is happening in places that purport to be nice, fun, caring, protective, holy, or sacred, nothing in the culture can be trusted to be what it says it is. And no place is truly safe. This should alarm not only people who have been abused but, frankly, the entire community.

Takeaways about settings that enable abuse

This chapter, which explored several of the main Jewish social-cultural settings in which sexual abuse takes place, compiles several significant characteristics of these environments:

- **Charisma, charisma, charisma.** Over and again, we see how "charismatic" people in positions of authority can use their power to prey on students, campers, subordinates, and/or congregants.
- **Protecting the "Pied Piper."** The reverence for the charismatic abuser does not only come from potential victims but also from supervisors, parents, directors, and organizational leaders. They often fail in their safeguarding duties and fail to act on information they have that could prevent additional acts of abuse because they benefit from having a "Pied Piper" on staff. As Sarah Bronzite said succinctly, "It's not the kids who are starstruck; it's the adults. That's a terrible indictment of our leadership."
- **Lack of clear rules and boundaries**. Educators, rabbis, and counselors are given a lot of autonomy and opportunity to be alone with kids, often with parents far from view. Many environments lack clear rules and boundaries for kids, and many girls are left not knowing that they are allowed to say "no" even to a "creepy hug." This leaves a lot of leeway for predators — especially those in the guise of counselors, teachers, or even adult administrators — to have their way. It continues to adulthood where synagogues and professional conferences also become places where women may feel that they cannot say "no" to a "creepy hug."
- **Where Jewishness is equated with boundariless sexual abuse**. When camps, youth groups, and summer camps use ideas of "Jewish family," "Jewish future," or "Jewish continuity" in a way that encourages sexual abuse or assault, the impact is that victims associate Jewishness with assault. As one of the Instagram posters wrote, "Most dangerously, I conditioned myself to believe that those feelings weren't valid because this was merely what I had signed up for... Meaningful Jewish experiences cannot be separated from hyper-sexualized spaces."
- **Orthodox settings, too.** Just because Orthodox schools encourage "*negiya*" — no contact between boys and girls — separation of the sexes does not make them immune from these dynamics. Furthermore, since Orthodox rules of *yichud* — the prohibition against men and women being alone — do not apply between immediate family members, and rules of negiya do not apply to people of the same sex, the risk of CSA is not completely eliminated even if those rules are strictly followed. Thus, Orthodox schools also have problems of sexual abuse between kids, and between teachers and kids or counselors and kids.
- **Patriarchy.** Assumptions about gender — e.g., assumptions of women as assistants rather than as leaders; ideas about women/girls as "baby machines" or valued for their "hotness"; or pressures on

female servitude and performance of sexual favors—these form the underpinning of abuse in a wide range of settings. Whether in workplaces or camps, whether the victims are adults or children, one of the primary components of settings that allow for abuse is an underlying patriarchal culture. Patriarchy supports abusers and leaves victims and potential victims vulnerable in a multitude of ways.

- **Interplay between kids' cultures and adults' cultures**. Where adults want to prey on kids, educational settings in which there is sexual pressure and a lack of boundaries keep the door open to them. But it's a chicken–egg situation. Are the adults taking advantage of the culture, or do adults create, support, and even encourage the culture?

- **Hypersexualization, hookup culture, and sexual pressure with a Jewish "wink-wink"**. Many summer camps and other environments actually expect participants to engage in sexual activity and use the Jewish language of "finding a Jewish partner" to promote it. The pervasiveness of these cultures is nothing short of alarming — although young women are using social media as a tool to start pushing back against the culture.

- **It starts at the top.** Patriarchal cultures that objectify women and promote gender hierarchies help promote cultures that support sexual abuse. If the people creating and running the programs and institutions are themselves guilty of this, the culture trickles down. Much of the policy research on intermarriage was conducted by a serial sexual harasser, and many of the programs where the hookup culture is rampant are funded by an accused sexually harassing megadonor. The discovery of cultures of abuse in so many seeming disparate locations— among senior policy-makers, among funders of educational programs, among teachers and counselors, and in places where youth hang out— raises massive questions about how these things are connected. The dynamics seems conspicuously and dangerously intertwined.

Chapter 7: Gender Abuse

In this chapter

Understanding gender abuse
Tactics of gender abuse
    Exclusion and erasure of women
    Making women small or invisible
    Verbal and emotional microaggressions
    Sexist commentary
    Economic inequality
    Disrespecting women's real lives
The political context: The Trump Effect
Interplay between sexual abuse and gender abuse
Takeaways about gender abuse

In September 1998, I started my very first job in the Jewish communal world after completing my master's degree in Jewish education — and I was excited. I was a 28-year-old mother of three finally getting out into the world and eager to embark on work as a research assistant at this prominent Jewish foundation, the beginning of my journey to serve the Jewish community in which I was born and bred. On my first day, I opened the door to the office, walked in, and said to the receptionist, "Good morning!"

"SHHHHH!" the receptionist replied in a panic.

I was stunned. I looked around, wondering what was going on. All the secretaries were sitting at their desks staring at me.

I didn't understand. The receptionist turned to one of the women in the foyer and said, "Didn't anyone give her the talk?"

What talk? I wondered, getting nervous.

"The talk," it turned out, was a list of instructions for how the women of the organization were expected to behave when the CEO was in the house. The CEO, a 70-something professor emeritus and one of only three men in the building, had expectations. That included quiet at all times, every piece of paper in its place, and the women around serving his every need. The kitchen cabinets were stocked with the brand of juice he drank, the supply closet was neatly piled with the specific folders that he liked, and we all walked around without shoes when he was around. Secretaries were fired for sticking the wrong Scotch tape on the divider tabs in the binders used for board meetings. *The wrong Scotch tape.*

While everyone frantically complied — including me, a so-called "research assistant" with my shiny new master's degree, fretting over the correct alignment of binder dividers — we would regularly hear him yelling from two floors up. His second-in-command, whom I'll call Marjorie, a very well-educated and well-regarded Jewish professional who both got the brunt of his fury and also acted as his great defender to the world, would come downstairs and give us orders and instructions as per his demands. That was how the office worked.

When VIPs arrived — academics, scholars, rabbis, donors, or the foundation's founder — none of this was apparent. We all scuttled around serving not only the CEO — who was always charming and gracious when outsiders were watching — but also the VIPs. It was exciting to have people around who were considered "important," even if I personally had never heard of some of them, but it was also nerve-wracking. At any moment, a misstep could cost you your job. I once screwed up by answering a request of one of the VIP guests honestly. She had asked if her hotel had a pool, and I said that it did not, which was the truth. Marjorie found out and ripped into me for not finding a way to move her to another location where she would have pool access. She didn't want *honesty* from me but *servitude.* My position survived that error, but I was on thin ice. The whole time. Me and my fancy degree.

I kept at it, in this demeaning, scary, go-nowhere, all-fluff position in a highbrow foundation named for the guy whose name is on buildings all around the Jewish world. This was my first "real" job in Jewish communal life, the first one since I became a mother and finished my degree, and I didn't have what to compare it to. Plus, I both wanted and needed this work. Mostly, I had no framework in which to understand how wrong this all was. Even though it was awful from literally the second I walked in there, I could not imagine quitting a job on the first day. So, I stayed — for four years.

This was not a case of sexual abuse or even harassment. It was just everyday, run-of-the-mill, toxic workplace culture. And the entire place was infected with it. The foundation head, who visited maybe once a year, was worse. When he arrived, even the CEO came downstairs with the staff and walked on eggshells himself.

But the toxicity was often gendered. The entire administrative staff was female. The entire top floor, except for Marjorie, was male. Even though I shared a job title with two other men, I was the only one expected to be running around doing mindless admin work. The other two had offices next to the CEO, where they stayed all day long, writing their books and getting handsome speaking gigs.

One of those guys, whom I'll call George, ended up being my supervisor for two years as he ran one of the international training programs — and in some ways, he was the worst. He was younger and more charming than the CEO, and he did not yell from the top floor. In fact, many people would call him a "nice guy" for his ability to smile, engage, and give a good speech. His methods for humiliating women were subtler and harder to see coming, but they turned out to be much more damaging to the women around him. Beneath that "nice" veneer lay an arsenal of verbal and emotional tactics of abuse that could completely unglue you. He would mock women's bodies, find your insecurities and undermine you with them, and play mind-twisting games to make you feel like you were nothing. "Look at you," he once said to me as I was sitting across from his desk trying to figure out what I had done wrong this time. "Look at your demeanor." I had no idea what he was talking about, but I stayed still and silent. "Who would want to be in the same room as you?" Things like that. For years after that, I was extremely self-conscious about my "demeanor," even though I had no idea what that even meant.

When the CEO died, he was lionized as a visionary educator, although many of us who knew the truth felt like the kid in "The Emperor's New Clothes". When the head of the foundation died a few years later, nobody dared whisper a bad word about him. He was, after all, a man who donated tens of millions of dollars to Jewish causes, despite simultaneously being someone who left behind a culture of gendered toxicity that infected every VIP visitor, and cohort of program participants that walked through the door.

This kind of abuse is not necessarily about sex. It isn't about a boss or a donor offering a sexual quid pro quo. It isn't even necessarily about body commentary, though that was a big part of my experience. This is about this intense and insidious workplace culture that systematically demeans, dehumanizes, shames, torments, and weakens staff members, especially women, leaving us without power or defenses.

This is gender abuse. It is a form of toxic masculinity. Or sometimes it is just toxicity, as sometimes people of all backgrounds and genders can promote, participate, and perpetuate it — and can also be the victims of it. But, more often than not, it is a cultural dynamic rooted in patriarchal power structures that keep women and vulnerable people small. It is a combination of words, microaggressions, and systemic structures that maintain gender hierarchies and other hurtful practices. And it exists in many Jewish settings: workplaces, synagogues, schools, and more.

I decided to include in this book a chapter on gender abuse because it is impossible to fully understand how sexual abuse happens in Jewish communal structures without taking a look at this cultural backdrop.

That may be a controversial decision. After all, gender abuse is not intuitively about sexual abuse. People of all genders can abuse and be abused. And not all toxicity ends in sexual abuse. That is true. But it's not the whole story.

One person whom I spoke to about this said bluntly, "Just because some guys are assholes, it doesn't mean they are all sexual predators." But if toxicity is normalized — especially gendered toxicity — that opens the floodgates to all other forms of toxicity. That attitude establishes norms that suggest that it is okay for people to suffer in the workplace whether because of their gender or their place in the hierarchy — or both. That is exactly how sexual abuse gets normalized.

The harmful impacts of bullying at work are indisputable. According to a meta-analysis by Sandy Hershcovis of the University of Manitoba and Julian Barling of Queen's University, who reviewed 110 research papers on nonviolent forms of workplace aggression, both bullying and sexual harassment can create negative work environments and unhealthy consequences for employees, but workplace aggression has more severe consequences. They examined what they called "bullying," which means persistently criticizing employees' work, yelling, spreading gossip or lies, ignoring or excluding workers, or insulting employees' habits, attitudes, or private life. They found that these practices have a devastating impact on workers' job stress, anxiety levels, mental and physical health, as well as job turnover and emotional ties to the job.[196]

Some people have been arguing that these issues — gender abuse and sexual abuse in the Jewish workplace — are intricately connected. Fran Sepler, said to me, "If you're being abused on the basis of your sex or your gender, that is sexual abuse. Even if it's not sexual in nature." Sybil Sanchez, who calls herself a "recuperating Jewish professional," as well as Jewish communal leaders Cheryl Moore and Clare Hedwat, have all written about these connections. And many of my interviewees talked about these connections as well. tellingly, the HUC-JIR investigation into sexual abuse in their campuses dedicated the first section of their report to gender discrimination. With those validations, I decided to dedicate a chapter in this book to the patriarchal backdrop to Jewish communal life that sets the stage for many other kinds of abuse.

---

[196] Hershcovis, Sandy & Barling, Julian. (2010), "Comparing Victim Attributions and Outcomes for Workplace Aggression and Sexual Harassment, *The Journal of Applied Psychology*. 95. 874-88.

Understanding gender abuse

As I said, the assumption that gender abuse is part of the broader spectrum of sexual abuse was verified by the HUC-JIR report on sexual abuse. The report dedicated a significant portion of the research to gender abuse as part of the continuum of what is considered sexual "misconduct." The report calls it "gender discrimination" and includes situations such as:

- **Overt discrimination.** Comparing women rabbis to "sacred prostitutes," accusing women rabbis of ruining men's careers, punishing women for being pregnant, dismissing feminist or female scholarship, having only men's bathrooms on campus, applying double standards to women faculty, or mocking women.

- **Microaggressions.** Men interrupting women and/or failing to acknowledge women's contributions, omitting women's professional titles, or calling a female professor a "sweet girl," bringing "token women" to appear, or berating women for not being quiet and submissive enough.

- **Body commentary.** Women being berated for "looking masculine," women being told to "look cuter" or dress more "feminine," women being told to smile more, women being told to lose weight or to get gastric bypass surgery for better job prospects, or by contrast being told to "fatten up" in order to be taken seriously.[197]

The assumption of the evaluators was that these behaviors and dynamics are part of the broad spectrum of sexual abuse. Similarly, as the #MeToo movement was unfolding in 2018, Sybil Sanchez wrote an article for *e-Jewish Philanthropy* in which she chronicled the litany of gender abuses that she experienced during her career. She makes the point that sexual abuse is not just about harassment but also about underlying cultures of sexism and patriarchy. "I can't engage in organized Jewish life without flashing back to what it was like to work amidst the subtle yet constant drum of sexism," she wrote, explaining that she left her rising career in the Jewish world because of it. "Women are groomed for harassment in Jewish communal life because male dominance remains implicitly normative. The flipside of male dominance is female insignificance," she wrote. When she first entered the field, she said, "I learned to act as if I didn't know as much as others and to

---

[197] Grace E. Speights, Sharon P. Masling, Martha B. Stolley, Jocelyn R. Cuttino, Ira G. Rosenstein, *Report of Investigation into Allegations of Misconduct at Hebrew Union College-Jewish Institute of Religion*. November 3, 2021
http://huc.edu/sites/default/files/About/PDF/HUC%20REPORT%20OF%20INVESTIGATION%20--%2011.04.21.pdf

let men, and other lay leaders, speak first. The consequences otherwise were belittlement, off-putting jokes, or general social awkwardness. Likewise, I was taught to never disagree with lay leaders. A 'kiss up, kick down' mentality prevailed." She learned how to play this game; when she was allowed to speak, and when she had to silently abide by the pecking order:

> The message 'don't be too smart' persisted, but its implementation changed… I had little control over my budget and other resources. If I requested more attention than deemed appropriate, I risked criticism for being alarmist or demanding… In fact, 'The Boys,' was a catch phrase within a particular circle of women colleagues. We would successfully navigate complex politics until an issue reached a threshold of attention, at which point 'The Boys' arrived. Swooping into the midst of our nuance, they would publicize their opinions before we were ready, creating unnecessary controversy and organizational friction along the way. They were the headliners, and we were the worker bees.

What Sanchez describes here is gender abuse. These are behaviors — sometimes subtle and sometimes overt — that demean, shame, and generally hold women in their place. They keep women from thriving and advancing professionally, financially, socially, culturally, and intellectually. These behaviors include women's exclusion, verbal and emotional shaming, economic inequalities, and many ways to keep women small. They at times set the stage for sexual abuse. But even when sexual abuse does not take place, these practices make work cultures difficult, if not impossible, for women. As Rabbi Mary Zamore, Executive Director of the Women's Rabbinic Network, explained to me, "Sexual harassment is one manifestation of gender abuse and misogyny. Sexual abuse is, among other things, is a physical manifestation, an objectification, but it is not the only way the women are objectified and held back in Jewish communal life."

Shlomit who is the head of a Jewish school that she created after two decades of working in schools where she faced incessant gender abuse, explained how this works, especially in her Orthodox world:

> In thinking about my story, I see a story where men have power. Sometimes they have power by engaging in sexual abuse. Sometimes they have power by engaging in abuse of power. And it is often at the expense of women who, in the Orthodox world, they KNOW they can override. They don't have to advance women.

In a convening of Orthodox Jewish women who head co-ed schools, Shlomit said that "all our experiences were the same. The men had the speaking engagements. The men had a pathway forward in career advancement because men are promoted." She said it is all "systemic sexism."

Although Shlomit is referring to her Orthodox experience, my interviewees come from different backgrounds and denominations, and their descriptions are similar. As Penelope said, "We are marinating in a culture that doesn't respect women. We're soaking in it! Because you're soaking in it, you don't realize that it permeates everything."

Tactics of gender abuse

Many tactics are used to keep women down. The ones that I focus on here that dominated in the interviews are: exclusion and erasure of women, making women small or invisible, verbal and emotional microaggressions, sexist commentary, economic inequality, and disrespecting women's real lives.

Exclusion and erasure of women

In my first post-schooling workplace that I described above, in which the men on the second floor verbally abused secretaries on the ground floor, many gender structures collided to make the setting difficult for women. One was that while all the administrative staff was composed of women, the entire academic faculty was composed of men. For many years, their leadership training program was almost entirely men as well. When the four women on the program (out of 25) complained about this, they were told, "There are not enough qualified women to teach." The four women sat down and within an hour compiled a list of 100 women whom they would have been eager to learn from. It had no effect.

This line — that it is impossible to find women who are as qualified as men — is heard in other workplaces as well. One Jewish educational institution where I was working (*after* I had completed my doctorate and worked around the world in Jewish education) published an entire book of essays on Jewish education without including a single female writer. The editor came into the director's office as I was sitting there to brag about his book, and handed me a copy. I flipped through it and then asked him why there were no women writers. He said that the contributors were all speakers at a conference — ergo, there were no women writers *or* women speakers. The director looked me straight in the eye and said, "There are no women of that caliber to speak about Jewish education." I sat there speechless. Me and my fancy degrees.

The exclusion of women from locations of decision-making, leadership, authority, and power is a pervasive problem in the Jewish world. As I explained earlier, only two women head major Jewish Federations, only one Jewish newspaper has a woman editor-in-chief, fewer than 17 percent of top executives in Jewish organizations are women—who make on average 60 percent of what men make—fewer than one-third of board members in Jewish organizations are women, and on and on. Men dominate in high-paid speaking gigs, in op-eds, in book contracts, on panels, and on pulpits.[198] These issues cut across denominations and cities, and form what Mindy Berkowitz, long-term Jewish executive, called the "old boys' network" of Jewish communal life.[199] Professors Susannah Heschel and Sarah Imhoff described the ubiquity of this culture at all levels of Jewish professional life:

> *Every woman can recount examples of being marginalized, patronized, and excluded by male colleagues. Women's scholarship is at times not cited by male colleagues, even when those men "borrow" directly from women's publications; women's innovative interpretations are ignored or treated as inconsequential – until a man says the same thing and people listen. As the sole woman at a conference can tell you, tokenism carries its own set of problems, which is why gender parity, not the inclusion of one or two women, is the goal.[200]*

Many interviewees described environments in which women were excluded. Helen, for example, who was molested by her professor-mentor, said that she stayed with him because there were no female professors to go to. "It would have been nice to have more women professors around. Someone who I would have felt safe asking to mentor me. Or telling her about it, about what was going on." But there were none.

Shlomit described how, at the fortieth anniversary gala of the school where she worked, "They honored only men. That was a big statement that forced me to say, 'It's the year 2000-something and we're still doing this?" That exclusion of women permeated her entire professional experience. "When the next head of school was chosen, there was no selection committee or process. It was the previous male head of school anointing the next king. And that was the attitude." From there, things only got worse:

---

[198] For a compilation of sources on this, see Elana Sztokman, "The Dynamics of the Jewish Patriarchy," *AJS Perspectives*, Spring 2019, https://www.associationforjewishstudies.org/images/defaultsource/publications/perspectives/patriarchy/elana-sztokman-infographic-ajs.png?sfvrsn=4

[199] Dreyfus, "New Allegations Against Robinson "https://jewishweek.timesofIsrael.com/new-allegations-against-robinson-include-a-minor/; Dreyfus, "After N.J. Camp Exec Sacked," https://njjewishnews.timesofisrael.com/after-n-j-camp-exec-sacked-last-week-more-womenalleging-sexual-harassment-come-forward/

[200] Susannah Heschel & Sarah Imhoff, "Where Are All The Women In Jewish Studies?" *Forward*, July 3, 2018, https://forward.com/culture/404416/where-are-all-the-women-in-jewish-studies/

> *The one who took over gained more power, and the gender bias
> became more apparent because this group of a boys' club, a
> group of rabbis basically, it was like this frat house. As a
> woman you just felt excluded because, you know, you weren't
> going to join the male party. It's the culture. You can't compete
> with that... Those male rabbis all had their own offices, but a
> female teacher who needed to nurse would end up nursing in
> the electrical closet because, 'Oh, we don't have room.'*

Although Shlomit worked in an Orthodox setting, even people who proclaim support for egalitarianism can also promote the exclusion of women. The rabbi of an egalitarian synagogue, for example, decided to celebrate an event with music and dancing in which he created an all-men's dancing circle. Rena, who attended with her female friends, got out of the way. "Then we were like, 'Why did we just do that?' We just opted out of that moment." Even places that purport to be feminist often exclude women.

Rena sees similar dynamics at professional conferences, another setting where she would have expected women and men to be treated equally, but often women are subtly excluded from panels, conversations, and even informal get-togethers. "It sets a tone for these other things. It's connected to us feeling like we have to fight our way in." One academic group she belongs to runs a popular lecture-panel series that often has no women lecturers. "That just shouldn't be happening. Like, we shouldn't have to bring it up all the time. I wish we didn't have to say all the time, 'Why are there no women on that panel?' It's like pushing your way into the dance."

Rena had many experiences of feeling excluded. Her mother had died a few years ago, and she has written scholarly articles about women's cultural experiences, including women saying the mourners' kaddish. At one conference, when only three people showed up to the egalitarian service, she had to attend the Orthodox service where a massive opaque curtain set up a women's corner. She could not say kaddish from behind that curtain, so she sat in an unobtrusive corner in the back of the room — and some men clearly expressed their dissatisfaction with her presence. Although she was able to say kaddish in the end, she left the experience shaken. She spent the rest of the year collecting stories from women saying kaddish and writing scholarly papers in her field about Jewish women's cultural experience around kaddish. She said that almost every woman she spoke to about saying kaddish had a story about being excluded.

Despite all her knowledge and research on the subject, her ideas were not valued in her own community, which was very painful for her When a visiting rabbi came to speak on kaddish, and the synagogue held a communal Shabbat afternoon meal, she wanted to share some of her research findings and personal insights, and she was summarily shut down:

Both rabbis started saying how the real reason that women don't say kaddish is that we don't want to. So, I said, 'Well, why would you think that? Why would you think that women wouldn't want to mourn the way the tradition tells us to mourn?' And then of course, where does it go? 'Well women were focused on their home life so they wouldn't have even wanted to participate in the minyans so this wasn't an issue. So, it's not us, it's not Judaism being a problem. It's that the women were content with their home life.' And there I was in this position where I had to either argue with the guest of honor, and say, 'Actually that's not true and let me show you the responsa I've been reading, and let me show you what I found in the Talmudic texts,' or take the other route. Which is that I just very gently said, 'That's interesting; I've heard a lot of different perspectives on it.' I said something very neutral.

As a result, everyone around the table thought that I agreed with this speaker. They all nodded and said, 'You see, Rena, it's not an issue. You don't have to be worried about this.' ...

This guy who was a friend of the rabbi was given the kavod [honor] and the platform and was assumed to be an expert on something he knew very little about... while my real knowledge and experience was seen as annoying interference. So those are small but they're big, and it's about having our perspectives heard.

There are many layers of gender discrimination in this story— from having a man declare expertise on women's history and women's feelings, to giving the honored seat around the table to a man who is *not* an expert in this topic instead of to the woman who *is* an expert, to the general cultural comfort with women being accommodating instead of assertive. The man sitting at the table is listened to over the woman and given credibility and voice, while the woman is not. Even when women have knowledge and experience, and even when the topic is women's feelings, history, and experience, that is often not valued as much as whatever it is that a man at the table has to say. As Leah said, "It's subtle. It's being in a room and saying something and being ignored and then a younger male colleague saying the same thing and watching him being called brilliant. Lots of that. I can give you hundreds of little instances." Rena risked being cast as difficult or disrespectful—as not knowing her place—if she shared her knowledge too loudly or emphatically. In this case, knowing the risks, she silenced herself rather than receive that backlash.

Making women small or invisible

The exclusion of women is connected to another dynamic, which is making women small. The comment I cited above, "There are no women of that caliber," to justify women's exclusion is a tactic for casting women as lesser — less capable, less smart, less deserving, just less. Women have to work many times harder than men to achieve even a fraction of the respect that men receive. In the case of the organization that had no women speakers or authors, they eventually invited Professor Tamar Ross to speak at an event, explaining to me that she was the only woman of the right "caliber" for their work. To be clear, Professor Ross is an internationally renowned distinguished professor of Jewish Philosophy with 50 years of scholarship and experience who has penned hundreds of articles and had many awards under her belt. Some of the male contributors to the book were thirtysomethings and most had a fraction of that expertise.

The intentional shrinking of women reminds me of the time I was working for an NGO and met with a local school principal we collaborated with in order to introduce him to our newest staff member, and he called her a "pretty young thing." She is a trained educational professional and excellent at her job, but was reduced to being a pretty child by a supposed colleague. "There are a lot of borderline things," Rebecca said, "where, like, you're at a meeting and the person running the meeting is a man and needs a photocopy and turns to the first person and hands the task to a woman because 'woman' looks like 'admin person.' That happens to me." Similarly, Carmela, who is a rabbi, says that people in her synagogue regularly ask her husband religious questions. Even when he says, "Ask Rabbi Carmela," she says, "it doesn't matter. He always gets the questions. People assume he has authority." She adds, "If you talk to any woman rabbi or cantor, you'll hear the same thing."

Another way that women are reduced is by erasing women's titles. One rabbi who works as the director of a large organization says, "My title position of rabbi freaks people out. This woman said I shouldn't be signing my name with 'rabbi' because I'm not a rabbi of the community. She said, 'We didn't hire a rabbi.' And I said, 'You *did* hire a rabbi.' I verified that other rabbis who were hired were never told not to use their title." Her story reminded me of the time I was working as Executive Director of a feminist (!) organization and the board chair asked me to take the "Dr." out of my email signature because it "sounds self-promoting." (I also wasn't allowed to talk about my books, not even when one of my books that was directly tied to the work I was doing won the National Jewish Book Council Award.) My experience is a reminder that women can *also* shrink other women.

"Speaking as a woman rabbi, when we are not referred to as 'rabbi,' and when people make comments that don't uphold the authority of our position and that objectify us, when this happens on a constant basis, the message from our community is one that we are not worth as much as men," says Rabbi Mary Zamore. This is not only a Jewish problem but it is definitely a gender problem. One study of medical conferences found that when women introduce a speaker, they use the person's title — man or woman — nearly 100 percent of the time. But when men introduce a speaker, they use men's titles nearly 80 percent of the time but women's titles only 49 percent of the time.[201] The impacts of women's titles being ignored include increased "isolation, marginalization, and professional discomfiture expressed by women faculty" in their fields.

There are also financial ways to keep women small, like offering women lower salaries, smaller budgets, tinier offices, and no support staff. Ricky shared a story about this dynamic:

> I was working for an organization, and I started the exact same time as a man in a side-by-side position, and over the two years of working together, the other person was given a big title and unlimited budget to try new things and six full-time staff, while I was given half a staffer and no available budget for programming. For me it was impossible.

Women most likely to succeed in this environment are perhaps the ones who know how to "play the game," which often means effectively shrinking themselves. Daliah, who was the assistant in a very large congregation for 11 years, certainly tried that tactic. "I used to say that the reason I was successful in my job was because I always knew when to roll over. I can know my place very well. I knew how to play that game. I knew how to be successful in that system." Or so she thought. When the senior rabbi left, she thought she would be in line for the job. She was in for a big surprise:

> It was just an awful experience, a real wake-up call. I had done all the right things, I had done everything that was asked of me, for 11 years, and it was really clear that they were never going to consider me for the position. At the end of the whole awful, awful process, they basically said, 'You're not senior rabbi material.' I heard a lot of things. I heard I was too female, I was too aggressive, I was too fat. I heard so much. I had been there for 11 years so I knew the congregation really well and they knew me really well. They offered the position to someone else who didn't want it. They never offered me the position.

---

[201] Julia A. Files, Anita P. Mayer, Marcia G. Ko, Patricia Friedrich, Marjorie Jenkins, Michael J. Bryan, Suneela Vegunta, Christopher M. Wittich, Melissa A. Lyle, Ryan Melikian, Trevor Duston, Yu-Hui H. Chang, and Sharonne N. Hayes, "Speaker Introductions at Internal Medicine Grand Rounds: Forms of Address Reveal Gender Bias," *Journal of Women's Health* Vol. 26, No. 5, Published Online:1 May 2017 https://doi.org/10.1089/jwh.2016.6044

They kept offering it to people who didn't want it. Just not me.
I had been made second.

No matter what Daliah did, the congregation did not envision her as senior rabbi. Another rabbi shared a similar experience and insight. "I definitely experienced gender discrimination from older male board members who made comments about my abilities to lead projects or understand legal and governance documents due to my gender, and speculation from other employees (male and female) about whether I advanced in my career due to flirting with older male leaders." There are endless ways to make women shrink down from their abilities and worth, based on speculation and gender assumptions. Women are often simply not seen as "leaders."

This kind of shrinking leaves an impact. As a result of these experiences, Daliah left the congregation and took a position as solo senior rabbi in a smaller congregation, where she has been for six years. She is happy, she told me, but she may never get the kind of position she wanted, which was to lead a large congregation. Similarly, Leah said, "As I age, it's clear to me that my career is not where it might have been in large part because of the patriarchy. I mean, as much as I am an outspoken, self-actualized woman, I think there has been a lot of sexism that has stood in my way as I've tried to build my career, ways in which men have put me down at work, ways in which I've been ignored while men have been advanced."

Verbal and emotional microaggressions

Sometimes women's gendered experiences devolve into verbal and emotional attacks and microaggressions.

Shlomit, who left the school she had been working at for nearly two decades because of gender abuse, described her head of school as abusive:

> *The old head of school was verbally and emotionally abusive.*
> *He had anger management problems. He might yell at a*
> *teacher in public, he would rip on people, he would demean*
> *people. He created an atmosphere of lying, no transparency,*
> *playing one person off of the other. You could never know if an*
> *agreement would be honored because you could just wake up*
> *the next day and it wouldn't be honored. I had carpal tunnel*
> *and he mocked me behind my back for it. His abuse was an*
> *open secret, and it was like, 'Well, that's just the way he is.'*
> *There was nobody to call him on it. So, you're caught up in*
> *this web. I was acculturated to this my whole life, this toxic*
> *masculinity, so at first, I accepted that this is the way it was.*
> *But the more work I started to do on myself and on being more*

connected to the outside world, the more I realized that this is
really messed up and I can't be part of this anymore.

Note how many tactics of abuse the head of school used: mocking, lying, intermittent reinforcement, isolation, and more.

Many respondents described toxic work environments — organizations, synagogues, conferences, schools — where emotional and verbal abuse were the norm. "Women leaders are routinely marginalized, intimidated, and gaslighted in ways that are not necessarily sexual harassment in its direct form," one respondent said. "I watched my former boss act in an extremely rude and intimidating way to a female rabbi who was a guest at a conference I organized. When I raised this incident with two different lay leaders, it was underplayed and never addressed."

Several respondents reported abusive interactions with their bosses. "When I asked to take a leave of absence or unpaid time to visit my stepmom in the hospital, I was told I could not go home unless she was actually going to die." Ruth described the director of her organization as a "bully" who "yells at people, yells at staff, berates them," and "thinks he can get away with it because, at this point, he knows so much about the organization they can't get rid of him."

Some aspects of this toxicity are not gendered. Bullies come in all genders, as do the people being bullied. Some respondents reported women supervisors participating in this kind of toxicity, like "Sara," the boss who encouraged Ruth to sleep with the potential donor. "She would say, 'I'm going to protect you from him,'" but in the end she did the exact opposite. Like my supervisor, Marjorie, who was the go-between for the abusive professor and the lowly staff, many women play both sides. Ruth said, "I think he puts her through a lot, and part of her own behavior has to do with what she was getting from the top. He was mean to her, too, he was mean to everyone, he was just a nasty person." This is again the dynamic of "kiss up-kick down," where the go-between (often a woman), transfers the abuse down the chain.

Verbal and emotional abuse is often comprised of microaggressions, or behaviors that seem almost small but carry with them an impact of controlling, demeaning, or hurting another person.

Melissa, for example, told a story from when she was Vice President of a Jewish organization on campus, dealing with microaggressions from her President. It was seemingly little things: he refused to share information with her about the location of an activity so she couldn't navigate herself and had to follow his car; he would tell her what to do without discussion — even how to sign her emails — and he would say things like, "You just have to listen to me," and "I know what's best and you don't." "It was not a discussion between two people who are in leadership positions who theoretically are on a board together. He was completely dismissive. 'No, no, no, we're doing it my way.'" She eventually quit her position, leaving behind her ambition of becoming President. Penelope explained that "when men yell at women and talk over women in an office setting, to them it's often just like a fun way to argue, and to us it feels real and immediate, and it's our experience of the world and our own lives that they are negating." Or what Carmela describes, "when everyone around the board room table looks to someone else as the authority, just not her — that's misogyny, that's microaggression. That's very different from flourishing."

Sexist commentary

Sexist commentary can set a tone in different ways. It can be direct, such as one respondent who reported, "I was called a cunt and a bitch." Sometimes the sexism is more indirect. Another respondent reported. "I was told if I got married my contract would not be renewed." Sybil Sanchez was told by the director of her organization to consider not coming back from personal leave "because they wanted to hire someone younger and cheaper than me." Indeed, sexism often has ageist elements to it, in which women who are not considered "young" are not considered smart, capable, or worthy. "I was asked by the CEO of my company to shotgun a beer, and when I responded that I didn't want to, I was told that I was being boring and no fun," reported a respondent.

Sexism also at times makes reference to women's appearance, as Daliah alluded to above in her congregation considering her "too fat" to be a head rabbi. Others had similar experiences. "A headhunter in the Jewish communal world referred to the limits of my candidacy for a position in terms of 'not wanting to send another pretty face' to the client," reported one respondent. Shlomit said that the head of school told one of the women teachers, "You have to dress cooler." Another reported that her female colleague struggles with job security due to her being obese, an experience backed by research on the persistent waistline wage gap.[202]

Most significantly for the purposes of this research, sexist commentary can also have sexual undertones, exemplifying the sometimes-blurry line between gender abuse and sexual abuse. "I was at a staff retreat with a supervisor asking me about my dating life, and he pressured me to look at my Tinder profile," reported a respondent. "That's sketchy, but it's not harassment. But I wanted him to like me, so I did this uncomfortable thing." Another reported that, "My boss told me, 'Good girls don't have their noses pierced.'" Ricky shared a story about her boss pressuring her female colleague to do a task that was not her job, and saying, "If you do this, you'll

---

[202] Virgninia Highes, "Why Do Obese Women Earn Less Than Thin Women (and Obese Men)?" *National Geographic*, Nov 3, 2014
https://www.nationalgeographic.com/science/article/why-do-obese-women-earn-less-than-thin-women-and-obese-men

be doing me a favor," with a wink. "There was a physical dominance in that he was towering over her. She came to me after it happened shaking in tears. It was creepy. That insinuation did not happen with the young man." Shlomit reported another creepy story about her head of school. "I went to an event at the school when my daughter was in twelfth grade, and we bumped into him on the staircase and he said, 'I'm stalking you the way yeshivah boys stalk girls.' He thought that would be a professional compliment." The comment also speaks to the question about connections between abusive staff behaviors and abusive school cultures that kids pick up. This head of school was "joking" about boys stalking girls — and not only did he fail to contain that, he thought it would be cute to engage in that behavior himself.

The connections between these behaviors are clear and seem endless. Sexist commentary sets the backdrop for sexist behavior, which opens the door to harassment and abuse, which in turn lingers uncontrolled and uncontained and contaminates the entire culture.

Economic inequality

All of these gendered behaviors go hand in hand with women's economic status — a situation in which dynamics in the Jewish world match surrounding cultures. The testimonies above about women's projects getting smaller budgets and smaller staff than men's projects reflect one aspect of this culture. Another key aspect is women's salaries in the Jewish world, where women executives are making 60 percent of what male executives make, and women rabbis make an average of $43,000 less per year than male rabbis. This reflects yet another aspect of treating women as "less" — less seen, less valued, less powerful. But it goes the other way around, too. These economic realities reinforce cultural dynamics, because if women have less financial security, they are less likely to be in a position to fight back or take financial risks like quitting and finding a new job. As Klara explained, "Women comprise the bulk of Jewish organization employment, yet rarely are they among the executives. This has enabled a situation of disregard for women to continue."

It is worth emphasizing that while these patterns mimic those in the broader culture, there is little if any research exploring these patterns in greater depth. For example, while gender wage gaps usually intersect with racial wage gaps — making women of color among the lowest earners in the American economy, for example — there is no research, to my knowledge, of the intersection of gender and race in wage gaps in Jewish communal work.

Interviewees shared how wage gaps, sexist cultures, and women's vulnerability to abuse are all connected. Ruth described how the economic inequality gave her a sense of being trapped in a sexist culture:

My first job in a Jewish nonprofit was in 2007. I liked the work but what I found was that I had no room for growth. It was right before the financial crisis – and then things got bad. They started cutting salaries, they started taking three people's jobs and having two people do it. They stopped giving bonuses or raises. I was offered less money for higher positions than I made there. This did not affect the very good jobs – we know this, women are not being chosen for those jobs. Women are being kept in middle-management, the middle-coordinator jobs where they are making $55,000 a year for twenty years, and they're not getting raises.

There were a lot of things I liked about the job, but the guy I worked for was a misogynist. For example, he told me that if I did a whole bunch of tasks that weren't part of my job, that I would get a $5,000 raise. I wasn't hired in a fundraising position, but by the end of the first year, I was doing all fundraising. I raised a lot of money for them – I was doing grants, I was doing events, I found myself working from 9:00 a.m. till 10:30 or 11:00 at night because they were understaffed. And at the end of the year, he said, 'Well, the board told me that I can't give you the raise. I'm sorry.' And I said, 'But you promised me, and I accomplished everything you asked me to.' I hit every benchmark, then some. And he said, 'Well, you know, you probably make more money than my sister ever made.' And I was like, what does that have to do with me? I don't know his sister. I don't know what she does professionally. I was making $53,000 a year. And this man was saying to me, you know, 'My sister, my sister never made that much money.'

Here, too, many gendered issues overlap to make women vulnerable – salaries, responsibilities, how women are treated overall, and how women's work is viewed. It's more "my sister" than "my top professional." Ruth worked long hours for low pay, doing work to raise money for the organization, being promised a better position, and despite doing great work, went nowhere. And, incredibly, all this was justified by the boss saying that none of the women he knows get paid well, so neither should she. It is patriarchy justifying patriarchy, a system perpetuating itself. As Ruth further explained:

Women are taken advantage of. The whole structure hurts women. Why are women who worked for 25 years unable to make more than $60,000? It doesn't make any sense... And then the boards create these mandates. They say, 'You can go out and raise tons of money for these projects. We're not going

to give you money, but you can find a donor who is more
passionate about this project than me. We don't have $5,000
for your project, but we want you to raise $100,000.'

Women often have responsibilities to raise the money for the work that they want to do, while receiving few if any, rewards and unfair salaries, no matter how long they work in a position or how good they are at their jobs.

Daliah adds that even in rabbinical school women are being prepped for lower-status, lower-pay rabbinic jobs. "Young women I know now being accepted to rabbinical school are being trained to run religious schools for $50,000 a year. That's what they are being ordained for, not to be senior rabbis or even assistant rabbis, but to run schools and earn even less than assistant rabbis." These are also positions with less voice and less authority that culturally sustain patriarchal cultures.

Disrespecting women's real lives

These forms of gender abuse coincide with other aspects of gender inequality that women face, especially issues of caring and motherhood. I remember on my first day of a new position, I was told by the program director, "Don't let me hear that you're the one leaving early to pick up your kids." Anne told a similar story about her first day on a new job in Israel where the head of HR called her into his office and interrogated her: "You have a very important job. You're married, right? You have children, right? You have a really serious job — what are you going to do when your kids are sick? Are you going to stay home?" She gave him her best answers, but he was never really satisfied and made her life miserable on that job. She eventually left and started her own business.

Sometimes the disrespect for women's lives intersects with body commentary. Ricky, for example, had traumatic experiences around pregnancy and working — in a Jewish educational setting:

> *I had been in my role for two years when I shared with my*
> *supervisor that I was pregnant. I was the first woman to hold*
> *that role. And they made a big deal about it when I applied for*
> *that job. The head of the organization then approached me in a*
> *very public place, and said, in front of a whole bunch of people,*
> *'Are you pregnant or planning on getting pregnant because I*
> *found a great maternity leave replacement for you.' And once*
> *I recovered from that comment, the follow-up comment was,*
> *'Well are you planning on taking maternity leave?' And that*
> *pressure implied not to. When I went to tell my supervisor that*
> *I was pregnant, the very first thing out of his mouth was, 'This*
> *is why we don't hire women in this position.'*

She did not go back to the job. They used the maternity leave as an excuse to push her out.

It isn't only pregnancy that is often an impediment to women's work. It can be parenting generally. As Rena, who is a single mother, experienced:

> They were paying me close to nothing for 10-12 hours per week, and they would expect me to be available nights and weekends. And I had to keep saying, 'Well, I'm a single mom, and you're not paying me enough to hire a babysitter, yet you're expecting me to be available.' It was a constant tension. There was this expectation that you have to care about what we're doing all the time, and the assumption was that you'll have someone else at home to cover for you, because that's what the men had. And when you don't have that, there was still an expectation that you would have that, without accommodating that people's lives look different.

Women are put in impossible roles — with communal pressures from early on to get married and have children but are punished when they do, even in Jewish spheres that claim to celebrate and encourage production of families. As Rena says:

> It's a mixed message we're getting, which is, on the one hand, you should have careers, and you should have careers in the Jewish community and be a Jewish professional and continue to devote yourself to Jewish academia and care about the community and devote yourself to the community – and also, you should get married and have a lot of Jewish babies, send them all to Jewish day school, and to Jewish camp, and belong to synagogues, and do all this stuff, and with no understanding that those two things don't always go together. There's no accommodation in either place for the other. I feel like that's part of the larger context of how women are treated and there's not a lot of space for the realities of our lives, especially those of us whose lives don't look like the community thinks they should look.

All of these tactics — keeping women small, pelting women with microaggressions and sexist commentary, paying women inadequately, and failing to give women support that they need to do their work — contribute to women's vulnerability. It is easy to imagine how women working in these conditions may not have the wherewithal to resist sexual harassment and abuse, and possibly risk their already fragile careers.

The political context: The Trump Effect

I would be remiss to describe the dynamics of gender abuse without referencing the particular political context that the Trump era ushered in during the period that I was conducting these interviews. This topic came up in a number of interviews and is worth including here.

Melanie, for example, was specifically triggered to recount an assault from forty years earlier just by watching the 2016 presidential debates. She disclosed the abuse for the first time right after watching the second debate on a big screen. "When Trump started stalking Hillary like a crazy gorilla, I grabbed my husband's knee and didn't let go. My heart was pounding in terror!"

For Shlomit, who left both her job and her synagogue as a result of gender abuse and sexism, the Trump culture played an important role. "I spent a lot of time being angry about gender, especially after Trump won, and the response of the Orthodox in my community, and I was like, I have to walk away from this, this is not healthy for me." The rabbi of her husband's shul is a vocal Trump supporter, and he has often used his pulpit to share Trump's views on women and other people.

> This rabbi talks about rape in crazy ways... The week that Trump moved the American embassy [to Jerusalem] and made the comment about the shithole countries, I said to my husband, 'He has spoken about women in degrading ways and has spoken about minorities in degrading ways and now he got up in shul and asked everyone to thank Trump.' I said, 'How can he do this? And my husband said, 'He did a good thing for us.' And since then, I just haven't gone back to shul.

The Trump backdrop exacerbated her already simmering feeling that the synagogue was not safe for her. The experience of listening to Dr. Christine Blasey Ford's testimony about being violently assaulted by now-Justice Brett Kavanaugh when they were in school contributed to that as well — and brought her back to the experiences of sexual boundary-breaking from her days in her Jewish high school. "The whole Christine Blasey Ford thing was so triggering. You're back in high school and you're thinking about all that, and then to have a rabbi now say to me, 'But he moved the embassy,' so okay, so you're saying girls' bodies are not important except to cover up." It was too much for her, and she left her community and shortly afterward her job as an educator in a religious school.

While Shlomit was being triggered by these events, Helen discovered that her abuser was becoming a famous talking-head in Israel and the United States — and was also a vocal Trump supporter. "[O]n his Facebook page...

he has a post defending Kavanaugh." These connections have been particularly difficult and triggering for some women. As Shlomit added:

> *Watching the Orthodox world get behind Trump, with the 'horseface' tweet [referring to certain women][203], watching them line up. I don't understand. And I can't be part of this with them anymore. Especially when we know the trickle-down effect. When he calls women 'horseface,' then we know, yeah, that this guy can say to me, 'I'm stalking you.' Who's going to stop him? It's normalized.*

Interplay between sexual abuse and gender abuse

Women face abuse in many different aspects of their lives — systematic exclusion within toxic environments and microaggressions, compounded by economic inequalities and a lack of respect for women's real lives. An atmosphere of gender abuse may or may not include sexual harassment, but when sexual abuse makes its way into an already abusive environment, the ground is ready. As Sarah Bronzite commented, these testimonies show how "mostly male perpetrators ignore all those 'right behaviors' that mostly male rabbis taught teachers to impress on girls and women, and then mostly male leaders ignore or erase all the boundary-crossing of their fellow males, and furthermore blame girls and women for the fact that the boundaries were crossed. If this isn't evidence of the patriarchy at work in sustaining sexual abuse, I don't know what is."

Yet, some people will hear these stories and say that they have nothing to do with sexual harassment, gender, or anything specifically Jewish. Rena said, "When the Steven Cohen story broke, we had all these older men on the Jewish studies listserv saying, 'There's no way he was affecting women's careers. If those women had wanted to build their careers, they could have absolutely done it. They chose not to.'" Rena asserted that this is not true at all. "It's like, no, there are ways that this is affecting people that you need to listen to."

Many women who work in the field of gender issues in the Jewish community see the connections clearly. As Rabbi Mary Zamore, Executive Director of the Women's Rabbinic Network explained:

> *Pay equity is the financial and employment dimension of gender harassment. Sexual harassment is the bodily*

---

[203] Meghan Keneally, "'Horseface, 'crazy,' 'low IQ': Trump's history of insulting women," *ABC News*. 18 October 2018 https://abcnews.go.com/Politics/trumps-long-history-calling-women-crazy-attacking-appearances/story?id=48348956

manifestation of gender abuse. If your body is being commented upon or inappropriately touched, it is a physical manifestation of gender harassment. These behaviors are on a spectrum. Sexist comments are not rape. Physical violence, like rape, is the most extreme example of sexual violation. But if we don't address the small things as part of the #MeToo-#GamAni movement, then we've overlooked an important part of the equation... There's a certain static with which women live every single day. And when we don't name it and address it, that anesthetizes us so that when the medium and big things start to happen, we don't react the same way.

Similarly, longtime Jewish feminist activist Shifra Bronznick, who founded Advancing Jewish Women Professionals, said to me in an interview, "Sexual harassment is happening because we don't have the power we deserve. The fact that we have a wage gap makes us complicit in a certain type of sexual harassment." Keren Herron, head of the #MeToo town hall project at Tikkun Olam Women's Foundation in Washington, DC, also explained that "these issues are linked — the way men view women, the way they think they can treat women, and it can all trickle down. We need to look at what the policies are in our society — things like paid family leave, policies that affect the workplace, like how men view women and even how women view women — to look at these issues and to see how these cross."

Respondents agreed with this assessment. Daliah shared that these cultures indeed "trickle down" to her community:

When women would come to the senior rabbi, if they were physically or sexually abused by their husbands, he would tell them it was okay. He wouldn't send them to our Jewish community abuse services. So, if the moreh d'atra [head of the community] is a man keeping the patriarchy established, that trickles down in so many ways — from how domestic violence and abused women are given pastoral counseling, to the way he made $250,000 a year and the women secretaries earned $32,000 a year. And this whole system was perpetuated by everyone. It's all connected.

Penelope concurs. "If we are going to come from this fundamental place of believing either women are inherently weaker and inferior no matter what we say, or believing women bring things upon ourselves, we are coming from a really problematic place."

The issues interact in another way: In an environment of gender abuse, victims of sexual abuse are less inclined to come forward. As Debbie Findling, who disclosed being abused by Len Robinson, said, "I was scared to be labeled as 'one of those women' and I was afraid I wouldn't get another job." She told the *Jewish Week*, "I am 54 now. I have found the courage to find my voice and speak out against this injustice. I'm redeeming the 23-year-old me."

One final observation: Even as conversations about sexual abuse have been making their way to the public arena, the underlying erasure and exclusion of women has maintained its stronghold. As I concluded this chapter, a story published by JTA celebrated "A journalist breaking Orthodoxy's biggest sexual abuse stories says he wishes he didn't have to." That there is a journalist (of any gender) exposing sexual abuse is good news. But the fact is that this male journalist's stories about sexual abuse were co-authored with a woman, journalist Shira Elk, whose name and work were rendered completely invisible, as if she was a mere invisible helpmate behind the scenes, as if we are still living in a *Mad Men* era in which men worked and women stayed in the background. The embedded cultures of erasing and disrespecting women, which create the very settings that allow sexual abuse to take place, may become even harder to root out than sexual abuse itself.[204]

Takeaways about gender abuse in the Jewish community

- **Gender abuse is a thing.** The Jewish community has a gender problem even before specifically addressing sexual abuse and #MeToo. The prevalence of inequalities, women's exclusion, sexist commentary, microaggressions, economic inequality, and the erasure of women's lives and experiences all contribute to a toxicity that undermines women's abilities to thrive and keeps women as a group vulnerable.
- **Gender abuse enables sexual abuse.** This patriarchal toxicity and women's vulnerabilities create environments in which sexual abuse easily finds a home and where women have difficulty coming forward or finding protections. The practices support each other. As Clare Hedwat wrote, "The Jewish woman is vulnerable because she is invisible in a way the Jewish man is not. The Jewish woman is unequal in a way the Jewish man is not." Cheryl Moore called "rich

---

[204] Rachel Kohn, "A journalist breaking Orthodoxy's biggest sexual abuse stories says he wishes he didn't have to," *JTA*, November 29, 2021, https://www.jta.org/2021/11/29/Israel/a-journalist-breaking-orthodoxys-biggest-sexual-abuse-stories-says-he-wishes-he-didnt-have-to?fbclid=IwAR2QHB0kAh0qLKFJhDEQGxHlvWG0qwJzcZQhQbdZatMWT6aoggqgQDSw2o0

male donors with wandering hands," and "public, outrageous and/or crude comments and behavior… *machismo at its core*."

- **It is also a problem among "progressives" and is done by women — even feminist women.** This can be a crushing insight, but it is the reality that clearly emerged here. As Heschel and Imhoff wrote, "What is striking is that many of the men who have not included women on their editorial boards or in their edited volumes are not right-wing, ultra-Orthodox scholars who might have a deliberate religious or political objection to working with women colleagues. On the contrary, most think of themselves as liberal and progressive, and they are often innovative leaders in the field, yet they, too, may overlook, ignore and exclude women. Even women in positions of power can be guilty of excluding and ignoring other women."[205]

- **It affects all genders in different ways.** All genders can be bullies and perpetrators, and all genders can be victims. While this is true, it does not contradict the fact that patriarchy constitutes a prevailing underlying gendered aspect of the toxicity, dynamics of men maintaining Jewish power hierarchies and women trying to live their lives. Certainly the culture spreads in all directions, and of course it is not all men. But it is often connected to toxic masculinities, in which "boys' clubs" and the exclusion of women created much of our communal cultures.

- **It is not *just* a Jewish thing, but it definitely *is* a Jewish thing.** The testimonies of women rabbis and cantors about synagogue cultures paint a damning portrait of Jewish culture on both organizational and communal levels. This is not something the Jewish community can simply dismiss as "the same as everywhere." There are particular Jewish cultural and social dynamics that sustain these abuses — which is the subject of the next chapter.

---

[205] Susannah Heschel & Sarah Imhoff, "Where Are All the Women In Jewish Studies?" *Forward*, July 3, 2018, https://forward.com/culture/404416/where-are-all-the-women-in-jewish-studies/

Part III: The Telling

What are the words you do not yet have? What are the tyrannies you swallow day by day and attempt to make your own, until you will sicken and die of them, still in silence? We have been socialized to respect fear more than our own need for language.

Audre Lourde

Chapter 8: Disclosing

When Rhonda Abrams was the Executive Director of a college Hillel, she was sexually harassed by a prominent donor to her organization over what was meant to be a work breakfast, according to her account published by the *Jewish Telegraphic Agency*. The abuse itself — in which the donor followed up on inappropriate body commentary by grabbing her behind, squeezing at her breasts, and then denying it and winking — was the easy part to get through, she asserted. Though she left the meeting shaking, her distress was only beginning. What came next were months of torment: What was she meant to do about the fact that a major stakeholder in the organization was on the prowl?

"I didn't know what to do," she wrote. "I felt the need to speak up, even though it might affect my standing in the community in several ways. I don't want my name tied to a scandal, and I also don't want other organizations finding themselves with holes in their budgets because I decided to say something." She was torn between speaking up and staying silent. "But while bringing attention to this issue could be costly, I can't afford to stay silent. Since that awful breakfast, I've been grappling with an ever-growing number of questions. What if this happens to me again? Or to a colleague? Do I want to meet a male donor alone ever again? How can I be more careful in the future? Is this my fault? Should I pretend nothing happened, shrug it off again, and carry on?"[206]

---

[206] Rhonda Abrams, "One of my donors harassed me. I couldn't afford to stay silent," *JTA*, December 21, 2017
https://www.jta.org/2017/12/21/opinion/one-of-my-donors-harassed-me-i-couldnt-afford-to-stay-silent

For many victims of sexual assault, the experience of assault is just the beginning of the torment.[207] Post-assault torment often arrives at a later milestone of the abuse: *disclosure*. Disclosure, the first time a victim tells the story about what happened, is sometimes described as a "lifelong process," and only in a small minority of cases takes place right away.[208] Many research studies describe complex impacts of disclosure on the victim, that can vary dramatically depending on the dynamics of the disclosure process. Victims who are able to safely disclose the abuse are found to have fewer negative psychological symptoms, such as depression and anxiety.[209] Not being believed, on the other hand, can have impacts that some victims consider more traumatizing than the original abuse, with a significant effect on the healing process.

There is still a lot of information that remains unknown about disclosure. Many researchers have found that significant numbers of children do not disclose experiences of sexual abuse until adulthood — and delays can range from 20 to 50 years — including high numbers of respondents whose first disclosure is to researchers.[210]

However, if the dynamics of disclosure in the *general community* are still not fully understood, the dynamics of disclosure in the *Jewish community* are even more blurry.

In 2017, Sara Zalcberg was the first researcher to examine disclosure patterns among victims of sexual assault in the Orthodox Jewish community. She interviewed 40 ultra-Orthodox men in Israel, ages 18-44, who were sexually abused by educational figures or religious leaders they knew. She found that 65 percent of the interviewees had not disclosed the abuse until the interview. To wit, one of her interviewees said at the end of the interview, "I feel better already." Zalcberg concludes that abuse in the Orthodox community is underreported compared to the general community.[211]

---

[207] Chanel Miller, *Know my Name*, (Viking 2019)

[208] Hunter, S. (2011). "Disclosure of Child Sexual Abuse as a Life-Long Process: Implications for Health Professionals. Australian and New Zealand," *Journal of Family Therapy*, 32(2), 159-172. doi:10.1375/anft.32.2.159

[209] Roberts, S. T., Watlington, C. G., Nett, S. D., & Batten, S. V. (2010), "Sexual trauma disclosure in clinical settings: Addressing diversity," *Journal of Trauma Dissociation*, 11(2), 244–259. doi:10.1080/15299730903502961; Hébert, M., Tourigny, M., Cyr, M., McDuff, P., & Joly, J. (2009), "Prevalence of childhood sexual abuse and timing of disclosure in a representative sample of adults from Quebec," *The Canadian Journal of Psychiatry*, 54(9), 631–636. doi:10.1177/070674370905400908; Nofziger, S., & Stein, R. E. (2006), "To tell or not to tell: Lifestyle impacts on whether adolescents tell about violent victimization," *Violence Victims*, 21(3), 371–382.

[210] Rosaleen McElvaney, "Disclosure of Child Sexual Abuse: Delays, Non-disclosure and Partial Disclosure. What the Research Tells Us and Implications for Practice," *Child Abuse Review* (2013), DOI: 10.1002/car.2280

[211] Sara Zalcberg (2017) "The Place of Culture and Religion in Patterns of Disclosure and Reporting Sexual Abuse of Males: A Case Study of Ultra Orthodox Male Victims," *Journal of Child Sexual Abuse*, 26:5, 590-607, DOI: 10.1080/10538712.2017.1316335

In 2020, a group of researchers led by Dafna Terer examined the particular dynamics of disclosure among religious victims of child sexual abuse in Israel. They concluded that disclosure is "nuanced and at times are even more complicated in cases of closed religious societies."[212] Issues such as whether the parents are supportive, what the community dynamics look like, and even levels of exposure to social media — which vary among religious communities — can impact how disclosure unfolds for the victim, which in turn has a major impact on the victim's recovery process.

Despite the significance of the disclosure process, there remains little research on the particular dynamics of disclosure of sexual abuse as a function of Jewish culture.

Barriers to disclosure

Many of my interviewees never disclosed at all until this research project or the period leading up to it. Their reasons for not disclosing varied.

For some, the reason not to disclose was *shame*. Eliana, who was assaulted by a client when she was a social work student, said, "I never told anyone — not my supervisor, not my boyfriend at the time, not my mother. I was too embarrassed to tell." Similarly, Nina, who was raped after synagogue by a man in her community walking her home, said, "I didn't share the story. I was ashamed." Hanna, who was assaulted by a rabbi-professor in rabbinical school and did not disclose until very recently, said, "It was more than 40 years ago and I still feel ashamed that I let it happen, that it didn't occur to me that it was not just happening to me, that I never told him how awful he made me feel years later when I could."

For some, the shame can be mixed with *self-blame*. Blima said, "I did not tell anyone. I was embarrassed and worried maybe it was partly my fault in a way. And I was a proud feminist at the time! But these things are so deeply ingrained." Nancy also explained, "If God forbid it's your boss and he grabs you, or makes an offer that you don't want him to make, you feel like it's going to create so much trouble if you say something about it."

It is also interesting to note that Blima was *less* inclined to report because she had a strong feminist socialization. Rather than provide her with skills, knowledge, and defiance, her feminist education made her feel inadequacy,

---

[212] Tener D., Marmor A., Weisrose E.L., Almog-Zaken A., Filtser T.M., Turjeman S. (2020) "Disclosing Sexual Abuse in Religious Communities in Israel: Lessons Learned by the Research Group on Child Sexual Abuse," In: Roer-Strier D., Nadan Y. (eds) *Context-Informed Perspectives of Child Risk and Protection in Israel Child Maltreatment* (Contemporary Issues in Research and Policy), vol 10. Springer, Cham. https://doi.org/10.1007/978-3-030-44278-1_15

guilt, and shame that she was attacked — believing she should have somehow "outsmarted" it.

Another barrier to disclosing is the expectation *to be "nice,"* so to speak. As Blima, who was attacked by her father's best friend while he was presumably helping her find a post-college job, said, "This was a 'family' member and I didn't want to cause trouble." Once again, this need to be "nice" overlaps with female gender socialization into a kind of submissiveness, not only when one is being assaulted but even after the assault.

For some women, the reason not to disclose is *fear*. Gloria, who was stalked and assaulted by a powerful congregant in her synagogue, said, "I would not confront him or take action against him because it would reignite his fire to destroy me." Tina, whose uncle molested her for years when she was a child, only began talking about it decades later as an adult. "It has taken me a lifetime to feel safe enough to tell my story," she said.

Some victims did not disclose because they *had no place to turn to*, or so they were led to believe. Helen, who you may recall was molested by her professor and mentor in graduate school in the 1980s, felt she had nobody to tell. Vivian also said that she didn't exactly have the knowledge or ability to tell anyone. "Women tended to keep quiet and to believe that each of us was the only one. And to whom exactly would I have complained — the male dean?" As with Vivian, for Klara — the Executive Director of a Jewish organization who was repeatedly harassed by her board chair — the feeling that there was no place to turn was intertwined with the fear. "I did not feel I would have any support. As a small agency there were no protocols and no HR department — just him. I'm afraid of a backlash or retaliation."

Some victims felt they *lacked the tools or language* to know what to do. Lara, who was molested by a family friend at home when she was a child, never disclosed to anyone because she felt her job was to hold back. "I feel bad that I wasn't able to go to the people I should have — my parents, the police — but in those days you stayed silent. You just held it. It was uncomfortable to even talk about, just verbalize it. To even say it to my parents, I didn't even have the language. I'm not sure they would have known what to do either."

Other victims did not disclose because they *convinced themselves that it was not so bad*. "It wasn't rape," one woman said. "My sister was raped at the age of 15, so I thought, maybe it's not so bad." Yet, here she is, decades later, still feeling the sting of the experience. This trope of "it wasn't rape" repeats itself in many places as victims try to make sense of their experiences and why it feels so traumatic.

Some did not disclose because they *chose to leave it behind* and get on with their careers. You may recall Vivian, for example, explaining that she needed her doctoral advisor for graduate school. Indeed, many of the stories in the chapter on workplace abuse were not disclosed due to fears of career implications.

For some, the reasons not to disclose — fear, shame, isolation, and others — coexisted with a strong *desire* to disclose. Risha, for example, a Jewish professional who was repeatedly harassed by a lay leader of her organization, said, "I did not do anything. I did not tell my brother until last year. The man who attacked me became a big shot attorney who was in the newspaper often and he died of cancer last year. I often thought about what I would do if he decided to become a politician or become a judge. I don't know if I would have had the courage to do what Dr. Christine Blasey Ford did. I don't know. Maybe?" Nancy similarly describes the competing voices in her head.

> *I'm 73, so maybe things are different now. But when I was brought up, girls had to be quiet and nice and not cause trouble and blah blah. It's hard even when you're on the subway and a guy puts his hand on your ass, to say, 'HANDS OFF! WHO DO YOU THINK YOU ARE?' That was really hard to do. Very hard to do. And then you'd leave the train feeling very pissed off at yourself even more than at him. Because why didn't I make a stink? Why didn't I embarrass him in front of everyone? And that was a pretty common story.*

Even when women were taught not to speak up about abuse, women perhaps still wanted to. Yet, these feelings of wanting to protect oneself and keep a desirable job often competed with other equally powerful feelings such as fear, shame, isolation, and self-blame. And as Blima indicated, even when women are taught to be strong and/or feminist, there are still many pulls away from that during an attack. Whether women are taught to be "nice" or taught to fight back, it can be very hard to resist an attack — and women are often left with complex feelings of self-blame and shame, both decades ago and today.

The ups and downs of telling friends

Some studies suggest that victims of sexual abuse are more likely to disclose first to a close friend. A Swedish study by Priebe and Svedin of 4,339 adolescents, of whom 1,962 reported some form of sexual abuse, 59.5 percent had not disclosed until asked by researchers, and of those who did disclose, 80.5 percent had told only a friend of their own age.[213]

---

[213] Priebe G, Svedin CG. "Child sexual abuse is largely hidden from the adult society: An epidemiological study of adolescents' disclosures," *Child Abuse & Neglect* 2008,32: 1095–1108.

Many interviewees described a kind of underground peer network for sharing stories of abusers. Avital, for example, who was sexually harassed by a Jewish academic, first disclosed to a colleague. "She said to me, 'What, nobody told you? Everyone knows to avoid him!' That tells you everything. That's horrifying." Avital added that she believes this was very common among women for years, even generations. "For a long time, women protected themselves through gossip. You couldn't talk about things publicly, but you could share whispers. Women used this to protect each other, although if you weren't in the chain you wouldn't know." Wendy, who never formally complained to anyone in her Jewish organization, said that while others might "joke around like this is funny, it wasn't funny to us women. We would all kind of discuss it behind closed doors about how gross this was." Nancy said that a similar kind of gossip-chain among women friends and colleagues existed about men in power in Israel . "Gossip protects people," she said. "Girls whispering to each other, 'Be careful of that guy.' Or 'Watch out for his hands.'" Significantly, she also added that "We never thought of it as gossip. We thought of it as passing along important information. This is not negative. This is positive. I wouldn't have thought of it as lashon hara. It is important information."

This role of gossip as protection stands in stark contrast to the rabbinic warnings not to expose abusers because of lashon hara. This idea of women quietly sharing gossip, is *the exact opposite of lashon hara*, as described previously. These testimonies point to the direct relationship between gossip, ignoring lashon hara prohibitions, and disclosure. It is *precisely* gossip that has protected women from sexual abuse for generations. Sarah Bronzite explained it to me this way: "Young people are raised to see the disclosure of abuse as lashon hara; of giving warnings to others as 'gossip.' But they should be taught that their talk is in fact a *to'elet* — that it is not gossip but, rather, speech for a constructive purpose — and therefore permitted."

Telling friends can also help in enabling the victim to validate her own story. Helen described that experience, although it took a process. "I told a male friend who I had once dated, who admitted that he did not believe me at first when I told him, but then he was having a private conversation with that professor, and he asked him, 'Do you know so and so?' and when he said yes, the professor said, 'Oh she's a bitch,' and then my friend realized it's all true."

Having a friend's support can be a positive, validating experience. Kayla, for example, was empowered when she told a friend about being molested by a rabbi whom they both knew. "When she and I talked it was the first time I truly felt validated." Similarly, when Helen told friends, she said, "they all believed me. Most of my friends were very sympathetic," even if they could not help her in any palpable way. Just being believed is very helpful to victims.

Sharing can also be preventive. For Wendy, all it took was one friend to protect her from an attempted assault. "I wouldn't have made it at all if it hadn't been for one friend who was also in grad school at the same time somewhere else. We'd talk on the phone and share all our bizarre stories and turn them into something where we could laugh." As a result, when she was considering a date with a particular classmate, her friend quickly warned her about his reputation for "not understanding consent," and she stayed away.

Still, disclosing to friends can be a mixed bag, and not all friends react in a way that victims find helpful. Leanne, for example, who was molested by her rabbi when she was 13 years old, was with a friend who was entirely supportive of her:

> It was a very scary situation because I was stuck there for Shabbat and could not get the guy to stop touching me. And my best friend noticed him touching me and said, 'Something isn't right,' and I was stunned. And we got back to our bunk Friday night, and I said, 'I don't know what to do,' but then she said, 'Oh, you're just being stupid.' She kind of recanted. But then she told the counselor... And nobody helped. ...[I]t made it a thousand times worse when I felt not helped by people who I wanted help from, who I wanted to count on.

Leanne's friend — who was, herself, all of 13 years old — was in some ways supportive. She both understood that something was "not right" and that they should tell someone and was also usure about what to do and how to help her friend. More significantly, the counselor — who was all of 16 years old and also Leanne's sister — was also unhelpful. She likely had no idea what this was and what she should do. The absence of knowledge and understanding about issues of touch and consent, along with the counselor's lack of willingness to help, left Leanne with scars for decades.

Charley, who is in her twenties, had similarly painful experiences when she tried to disclose to friend after she was raped on campus by a rabbinical student:

> I disclosed to a lot of friends, including people who had been in youth groups with me, including men who had been in the fraternity with him. The response I got from men, who I thought were trustworthy friends, was, 'You would have had sex with him anyway, though, right?' I was like, 'No, probably not the first time we hung out when he had a girlfriend, so, no.' I had I only had one sexual partner at that point in my life. There was a disconnect between what happened when I told guys versus when I told women.

Trying to disclose to peers left Charley in the midst of a campus culture in which her male friends automatically assumed she had consented and was quick to establish new sexual partners. Although she says, "I didn't have people who didn't believe me," she discovered that she did not have a lot of support in her social circle, especially among people who knew the man who raped her and were friends with him. "Either they didn't take me seriously or they didn't think it mattered." This is quite a different response from the "gossip chain" in which women believed one another even if they had little power to make change.

The promise and pitfalls of telling family

In theory, one might think that disclosure of abuse to close family members would be an important part of their recovery from abuse. Indeed, research suggests that for child victims in particular, disclosure to parents has a significant impact on the recovery process.[214] However, disclosure to family members also carries a risk of not being believed. In fact, children's reluctance to disclose to parents — which, again, is the case in the majority of victims, some of whom wait decades before disclosing to anyone — is a function of the fear of not being believed.

According to research by Irit Hershkowitz and her colleagues on CSA victims' disclosure to parents, fewer than half disclosed to their parents at all, and over 40 percent who did so did not disclose spontaneously but did so only after they were prompted. In addition, 50 percent of the children reported feeling ashamed or afraid of their parents' responses — and significantly, the parents of those who were afraid to disclose tended to blame the children or act angrily. They concluded that the "strong correlation between predicted and actual parental reactions suggested that the children anticipated their parents' likely reactions very well."[215]

Similarly, many of Zalcberg's ultra-Orthodox interviewees avoided disclosing to their parents out of "a sense of detachment that pervades their relationship with their parents, which prevents them from sharing personal topics, especially anything related to sex or sexuality. Isaac explained, 'To speak about these things is viewed as profanity. And this is why I was afraid to tell my father. I thought if I would have spoken about this, he would have

---

[214] Tener D., Marmor A., Weisrose E.L., Almog-Zaken A., Filtser T.M., Turjeman S. (2020) "Disclosing Sexual Abuse in Religious Communities in Israel: Lessons Learned by the Research Group on Child Sexual Abuse," In: Roer-Strier D., Nadan Y. (eds) *Context-Informed Perspectives of Child Risk and Protection in Israel. Child Maltreatment* (Contemporary Issues in Research and Policy), vol 10. Springer, Cham. https://doi.org/10.1007/978-3-030-44278-1_15
[215] Irit Hershkowitz, Omer Lanes, Michael E. Lamb, "Exploring the disclosure of child sexual abuse with alleged victims and their parents," *Child Abuse & Neglect*, Volume 31, Issue 2, 2007, Pages 111-123, ISSN 0145-2134, https://doi.org/10.1016/j.chiabu.2006.09.004.

beaten me.'"[216] Again, we hear the problematic echo of abuse being viewed as something *dirty* as opposed to *hurtful*.

This sentiment was echoed in many interviews. Gail, who was assaulted by her classmates, did not tell her parents out of concerns about their reactions, and out of shame. "The boys told me, 'If you tell you'll be sent to a place for bad girls, and everyone will know you're disgusting.' I was always sure I was disgusting and fat." As of the time of the interview decades later, she had not disclosed to her parents.

Other non-believing family members can also make disclosure a painful experience, especially when they actively side with the abuser. Abby, who was molested by her synagogue rabbi when she was 11 years old, disclosed to her family, but they "didn't want to hear anything about it" because "he is a great scholar." In fact, her sister dated the molester's son and "almost married him. My sister thinks [my abuser] is the most wonderful thing because he helped her get into college. I don't think she denied that he could do it because she knew how abusive he was to his children. But she didn't want to hear about this." Leanne also had a painful experience with her sister. She disclosed later in her interview that the "counselor" who did not believe her when she was molested at 13, was her 16-year-old sister. Thus, when she described her decades-long trauma of not being believed by the adults around her, she was including her older teenage sister who was meant to protect her but did not.

On the other hand, when family members *believe* the victim, this can have a very powerful effect and enable both healing and justice, even if it takes a while. Janice, who was assaulted by a gynecologist, was believed by her mother, which enabled her to come forward years later.

> *I told my mother and she believed me… Many years later, I read in the local newspaper that more than 20 women had come forward to accuse this same doctor. I then called the Board of Registration in Medicine to share my story, and I agreed to testify against him. Ultimately, his license was revoked.*

Janice is gratified by the ending of the story, though there was a major hiccup in the middle: Her primary physician did *not* believe her. "I also told the referring physician; he said it was my word against the gynecologist and no one would believe me because I was an 18-year-old girl and the gynecologist was a prominent doctor." She is upset that the doctor blocked the process of ousting the offending gynecologist. "If I had been believed when I was 18 years old, many other women would not have been abused by this man for so many years," she said.

---

[216] Sara Zalcberg (2017) "The Place of Culture and Religion in Patterns of Disclosure and Reporting Sexual Abuse of Males: A Case Study of Ultra-Orthodox Male Victims," *Journal of Child Sexual Abuse*, 26:5, 590-607, DOI: 10.1080/10538712.2017.1316335

Some people have different experiences with their parents. Ann's story is a powerful illustration of the impact of having parents who believe and protect:

> When I was six years old, my mother decided it was time for me to start Hebrew school along with the boys in the neighborhood, and my mother approached the teacher, Mr. Weissberg, who said he doesn't take girls. My mother said, 'Look it's not just my daughter, I can also bring you 4-5 other girls.' He said, okay, so we started, all of us. And he said, 'But you know the girls are starting a few weeks behind the boys, so I would like to see everyone for a few minutes before class to catch them up.' So, my mother would bring me about 15 minutes before the class started, and I would go in with Mr. Weissberg into his office and then go into his class. And after a week or ten days of this, my mother said, 'How's it going? What do you do with Mr. Weissberg?' And I was six, I didn't know anything, and I said, 'He takes me into his office, and I stand in front of him, and I read the letters, and if I read correctly, he squeezes me between his legs.'... I never saw my mother angrier. Two minutes, I was out, all the girls were all out of the class. I don't know what happened with Mr. Weissberg or repercussions, that wasn't discussed with me, but I know we were out of the class, and the search was on for an after-school program taught by a woman. That was my first experience. It wasn't the worst experience, but what was good was that I saw my mother's reaction and it was dealt with. I was clearly believed, there was no discussion, or 'You're making this up.' It was dealt with immediately and that was that.

When children are believed by their parents, the experience can preempt potentially years or decades of painful scars.

The experience of having one's trauma validated can help victims, even if nothing else happens. As Charley described:

> It took me a while, but I told my family. I was particularly worried about my father because he's a lawyer and I knew that would be how he wanted me to respond, and I had already decided not to go that route. A few different times I would watch with my mom shows like SVU, and she would say something like, 'So sad how often this happens,' and I'm wondering if she may have known something happened to me... The second time she said that, I said, 'It happened to me.' And then I told my dad with her there, and he did have the reaction that I expected. Either, 'I want to kill him,' or 'I want

> *to pursue legal action.' So, I said, 'I had rape kit done but it's*
> *not on the shelves anymore, but I appreciate that this is what*
> *you wanted to do.'*

Charley had started and abandoned the idea of pursuing legal action before she told her parents. They believed her, and her father even got into his fighter stance to protect her. She did not need that, but she said she appreciated that kind of reaction.

Leanne similarly described the relief of being believed, even if she was afraid that she would not be. She did not initially tell her parents about the rabbi molesting her at the day school retreats because "It felt very risky to tell them... I thought, if I tell them, either they are going to be super upset, which will be terrible, or they won't be, which will be worse." When she finally did tell them four years later at the age of 17, "it was good," she said: "I cried and cried and cried when I told them. I think they felt bad that I hadn't told them. Because I have great parents. I have wonderful parents."

Part of the lingering scar for Leanne was her relationship with her sister, the one who was her counselor and did not protect her from the abuse, even after she disclosed. "I was angry at her for a long time," she said, which her parents noticed. "My mom was like, 'Why are you so angry with her?' So, I finally told them." She and her sister were able to work through what happened. "Now I have kids around the same age that we were at the time, so I think about how painful that must have been for her. She was a child, too. How do you deal with this? How would you deal with this as a 16-year-old? And I feel protective of my sister, which is why I didn't share that detail initially. She feels terrible."

For people who were sexually abused *by a family member*, the process of disclosing to another family member can be particularly fraught. Hinda, for example, whose father sexually abused her for years when she was a child, was not believed by her mother, and has carried around that pain for decades:

> *I did tell my mother. She told me to shut up and not make*
> *trouble. I never brought it up to her again, and as soon as I was*
> *able to leave home, I fired my father, totally banishing him from*
> *my life. Later in his life he did try to reestablish a relationship*
> *with me, but I was only willing to try if he would go to therapy*
> *with me. He refused, and I never spoke to him again.*

The experience of not being believed by family members leaves long-lasting traumas and scars. "I am to this day plagued by the loneliness that is a result of so much that I have experienced in my life," Hinda recalled.

Similarly, Alyssa, who was also abused by her violent father, was not believed by her mother. "There were many hints to my mom that this was going on, but she didn't or wasn't able to see them. I knew she wouldn't believe me if I told her, and I was right because when I finally did tell her in my mid-20s, she didn't believe me. She believed my father's denials." This harrowing story of violent, life-threatening abuse by a father on his toddler daughter was made all the worse by the presence of a mother who did not protect or even believe her daughter. Alyssa's torment is still palpable in her text nearly fifty years after the abuse happened.

The challenges of telling an intimate partner

If telling parents and siblings is complicated, telling an intimate partner can be even trickier, especially for adult women who were groomed over a long period into unwanted sexual "relationships." But just as parents' belief or disbelief can have a powerful impact on the victim's process of dealing with the trauma, so, too, can a spouse's belief or disbelief.

For Melanie, who was attacked by a tour leader in Israel when she was 18, that process happened only decades after the abuse. You may recall that she was spontaneously triggered to tell her husband in 2016, during the presidential debates:

> Afterwards, I asked him if he understood. He manned-up and admitted no. 'I knew you were upset, but I wasn't sure why.' 'Duh!' I said, 'Because I was afraid that if she turned around and made eye contact, he would smack her!' So, there it is. I told my husband the core of it in the morning, how ashamed I was, how stupid I was for going with him. I put myself in this situation. How could I have been so dumb!

> I learned a lot about myself that weekend and hubby learned new things he had never suspected. I am a big, assertive gal and always have been, but finding that black hole of fear from that night in 1970 explained a lot to me. But that night was like the final exorcism. There is nothing more Mr. Sabra and his ilk can do to me now. It wasn't my fault! I have no shame anymore. I am a warrior.

The experience of sharing a 46-year-old trauma with her husband who believed her and supported her enabled Melanie to find the "warrior" in herself that no longer feels shame about her experience.

For women who are being sexually abused over time during a marriage, however, there is often a deeper fear and shame about sharing. For Brenda, telling her husband was the beginning of her healing process. "I had kept it from him for a long time," she said, "out of fear, or embarrassment, or some kind of feeling like I wanted to protect the rabbi." Once she told her husband

and he accepted her and supported her, she was able to move on, to report the abuse, and start healing. But that is not always the case. When Cindy, who was very actively pursued by her rabbi/boss, disclosed the grooming to both her husband and her mother, they believed her but did not initially help her when she needed it:

> When the rabbi first started making suggestive comments, I did not know what to do. I told my husband and my mother. My husband trusted me to ignore the comments, and my mother said, 'All men are the same.'

Neither of those responses helped her get out of the situation, which only escalated over months. Cindy eventually caved into her boss's demands for sex out of fear for her job and other issues. But she did not want this, hated the sexual coercion, and felt so ashamed about it that she kept it from her husband for a long time:

> After several years, I eventually told my husband. My guilt and shame made me a horrible wife. I would start arguments just so that he would get mad at me and yell at me. All along I was so deeply mad at myself, disappointed in myself... I wanted my husband to hate me, because I was sure I deserved it, so I would be awful in trying to make that happen. When I finally told him, it was like a lightbulb went on and he understood everything.

Cindy was so shamed, guilt-ridden, and angry at herself that she *wanted* her husband to punish her. But he lovingly saw through all that. "I thought he would find me disgusting, that he would leave me, that he would hate me. Instead, he hates the man that manipulated me, he saw clearly what happened."

As with other family members, then, spouses can also play a powerful role in the process of disclosure by believing the victim. That kind of support can help relieve heavy burdens of guilt, shame, and self-blame from the victim.

Supportive — or unsupportive — women

Another potential recipient of disclosure is often believed to be women. In fact, popular advice in self-defense classes for example, is that if you are in danger, find the nearest woman. This advice is based on the statistic that over 90 percent of all cases of sexual assault are committed by men.[217] Women are typically considered "safe."

Many interviewees disclosed to women around them, hoping for some of that "safe" response. Some interviewees received the support that they needed from women. One interviewee reported that, "I once told a female attorney over dinner about the man who put his hand on my thigh—and she alerted me to the fact that this was in fact harassment."

But some interviewees were disappointed to discover that women were not always "safe." When Leanne was being abused by one of the synagogue rabbis, she first went to the senior male rabbi, who dismissed her, and then went to one of the female assistant rabbis, who was "a really destructive person in all this." The assistant rabbi was offended that Leanne had not gone to her first, and as a result treated Leanne with a kind of jealous resentment. "I mean, the drama was just crazy. She resented that I had gone to the other rabbi. Her ego was too invested. She wanted to be the rabbi fixing it. I still smart from that experience with her. She played a really negative role in the whole thing, and in my whole path Jewishly."

In another one of Leanne's experiences, she also went to a woman for help. She wanted to write a letter to her old camp director who'd rehired the molesting guitar-playing rabbi even after knowing that he was "a problem." She first approached a woman rabbi whom she had thought of as an ally, but the rabbi emphatically discouraged her from writing. "She told me that most people haven't had these experiences so there was no good reason to start writing about them," Leanne said. This reaction shut Leanne down for some time.

Wendy reported that when she told "a couple of women in the department" about the harassment she experienced, "I got back that it was both my fault and not a big deal." As a result, she stopped talking about it. Drori said, "I'm a Jewish woman who was betrayed by others who were also Jews or women too."

Recall Ruth, whose female boss encouraged her to date a donor in order to secure a donation. Until that experience, her boss had said that she wanted to be Ruth's "mentor," but when Ruth needed her support the most, she did not receive it. Ruth felt that there was something else going on:

> The sense I had was that she felt a little bit envious that I had that conversation, like I had an in with [the major donor]. If he was joking around with me in that way, that meant he liked me or noticed me, and she didn't like that. She didn't want me

217 Michele C. Black, Kathleen C. Basile, Matthew J. Breiding, Sharon G. Smith, Mikel L. Walters, Melissa T. Merrick, Jieru Chen and Mark R. Stevens, "National Intimate Partner and Sexual Violence Survey 2010 Summary Report", November 2011, *National Center for Injury Prevention and Control Centers for Disease Control and Prevention Atlanta, Georgia* https://www.cdc.gov/violenceprevention/pdf/nisvs_report2010-a.pdf

> *to be under his radar that way. She wanted to be able to take*
> *the credit for anything that I brought in. That was the first*
> *time I saw that that was her way. But I just brushed it off.*

Later on, after the boss encouraged her to use sex to get the donation, Ruth started to rethink all her relationships with women in Jewish nonprofit work and reflect on what she saw as women's lack of supportiveness for other women over the years:

> *I have found in nonprofit that women are not supportive of*
> *other women. Part of the reason they are not supportive is*
> *because there is a competition and there is so little room for*
> *growth. So when they see another woman who is talented and*
> *who is growing, they will hold her down because there isn't*
> *room. I'm sure sometimes women are very nice in their real*
> *lives, but it becomes dog-eat-dog because of the pressure from*
> *the top... I came in there thinking, oh, we're going to sing*
> *kumbaya together, we're going to do great things together, and*
> *I think for me the most shocking thing is that it's not how it is*
> *at all.*

Other interviewees also described what they saw as women's dismissiveness. Anne said that when she went to talk to her co-workers about her experience, "The women execs couldn't care less and would not be particularly supportive... It was part of the job. It was something you had to learn how to deal with." Leanne also said, "It becomes, 'Well, I dealt with it, so you deal with it too.'"

There is possibly a generational divide driving some of this dynamic. Perhaps, just as some senior women may expect junior women to get through what they had to get through themselves, today senior women may also expect junior women to speak out more from the perception that times are changing. Avital complained about this dynamic in which she experienced "older women in the community who likely have their own stories and aren't going public but are happy to tell younger women like us that we should go public". She saw this several times:

> *I see 60s- and 70s-generation feminists who were lukewarm to*
> *this topic and were socialized to be more accepting. They got*
> *ahead and broke glass ceilings while being quiet about this, so*
> *they have been conditioned to let it roll off their backs. But they*
> *left it for us to deal with.*
>
> *Like, at one of the meetings about sexual abuse in the*
> *community, when the Steven Cohen story came out, someone*
> *said, 'Oh, he's been like that since grad school.' But I feel like*
> *saying, 'You didn't take that seriously then, and now it's 30*

> *years later and he's harassing a younger female colleague.'*
> *That's a generation gap in the discussion. The older women left*
> *a big mess for us, and not all younger women want to carry*
> *that load.*

Perhaps some women in power adopt their surrounding cultures and internalize patriarchy. Indeed, according to Fran Sepler, women are usually competing over scarce resources, they are socialized to be relational and not competitive, and take more covert tactics for bullying than men do. She adds that women are responsible for an estimated 40 percent of workplace bullying, but most of this goes underreported.[218]

Or perhaps a few unsisterly women block the view of the rest of the women who *are* supportive. Or perhaps women have more obstacles of their own to deal with, which complicate their ability to rescuer other women. As Penelope suggested, "Don't blame the women for the tools that they have had to use in a patriarchal, sexist and misogynistic society."

Takeaways about disclosure

- **There are many internal pressures not to disclose.** Victims face many internal barriers to disclosure, such as fear, shame, loneliness, self-doubts, and a desire to move on and focus on their lives and their work.
- **External barriers, too.** There are also many real lived experiences that prevent disclosure — not being believed, harming one's career, and being cast as difficult, problematic, or crazy.
- **Pressure around "niceness" is a major barrier to disclosure.** Socialization into being "nice" girls makes the world more dangerous for them. Pressure to always be "nice" are in many ways tormenting to women and girls, even oppressive.
- **Gossip is protection.** Whereas lashon hara threats are often used to keep victims quiet, the converse is also true: the sharing network is precisely what protects victims, and can even prevent assaults.
- **Disclosure to family can be terrifying.** Many victims are reluctant to share with family members. This may be counterintuitive to some people, as families are meant to be "safe spaces." But if parents know the abusers, if there is a history of abuse within the family, or if the family is not a place where dynamics of abuse are understood, the process of disclosing to family can backfire. Some also do not tell

---

[218] Fran Sepler, "The Bullying We Don't Talk About: Women Bullying Women in the Academy," in Kirsti Cole, Holly Hassel, eds, *Surviving Sexism in Academia Strategies for Feminist Leadership*, (Routelage, 2017), pp 296-303

parents out of internalizing the shame that their abusers lay into them.

- **It can also be healing and empowering.** However, some victims who were initially afraid of telling parents, or who even waited years before telling out of fear of being blamed or disbelieved, found themselves pleasantly surprised by their families' support. Victims who were believed by their families report that this was a key step in continuing their healing.

- **Abuse by a family is particularly damaging.** When the abuse takes place in the family, the absence of any kind of trusted safe space is especially devastating, in large part because the victim does not have any place in the world to be able to trust and begin to heal.

- **Some families side with the abuser.** When the family does not believe the victim, the impact has echoes of being abused by a family member. It destroys the victim's ability to trust anyone, even themselves, and thus blocks the process of recovery.

- **Telling the intimate partner can be fraught — or empowering.** When a clergy member abuses an adult over time, this is still often seen as an "affair." When victims of that kind of abuse tell their intimate partners, explaining this can be mired with shame and guilt. When the partner is supportive and understanding, that enables victims to start the healing process, much the way a believing family changes everything.

- **Women are not always a safe haven.** While women have had a "gossip network" of protection for generations, sometimes women are not as supportive as one might expect. When this happens, some victims feel an extra sense of betrayal.

Chapter 9: Reporting

> **In this chapter**
>
> **Why victims do not report**
> **Variations of reporting experiences**
> > Reporting to senior rabbis
> > Rabbis protecting rabbis
> > Reporting to rabbinical committees
> > Reporting in the workplace
> > Reporting to the community
> > Reporting to the media
> > Reporting to the police
>
> **Takeaways about reporting**

When Dr. Christine Blasey Ford testified in Congress that she was sexually assaulted by then-Judge Brett Kavanaugh, she was immediately badgered by the question: *If it's true, why did you not report it 36 years ago when it happened?*

The answer is complicated, but the reality is clear: an estimated 80 percent of sexual assaults are not reported, according to the Department of Justice.[219]

To be clear, disclosure and reporting are two different things. Disclosure is when the victim first tells someone they know what happened (e.g., parent, friend, or colleague). It is a validation that something happened. Reporting is telling someone in order to have what happened followed up by authorities. Reporting refers to a purposeful disclosure to a person or authority figure who in theory should be able and willing to take next steps in order to fix the situation. This may mean removing the abuser from their post, outing the abuser to their community, workplace, or denomination, or going to the police or legal authorities. If there is an expectation that the listener will *do something* about the abuse, that would make it reporting as opposed to just disclosure. Reporting may overlap with the disclosure process, but it is more likely to come at a later stage to a different person. Most victims usually need to have had conversations with friends or family before taking steps to report.

---

[219] Rachel E. Morgan, Ph.D., and Grace Kena, "Criminal Victimization, 2016," U.S. Department of Justice, Office of Justice Programs, *Bureau of Justice Statistics, Bulletin*, October 2018, NCJ 252121 https://bjs.ojp.gov/content/pub/pdf/cv16.pdf ,

This is somewhat counter-intuitive. Generally, when a person is a victim of a crime, the natural response is to report it to the proper authorities. And yet, sexual assault is the most underreported of all crimes. Countless studies have shown that only a small fraction of people who experience sexual abuse report to criminal justice authorities.[220] In the Orthodox community, Sara Zalcberg's research found vast underreporting due to cultures of "silencing in matters related to sexuality" as well as cultures that encourage "blind obedience," factors that are particularly salient in religious communities.[221] Researchers have found that reporting rates are even lower among male victims due to stigmas, myths, and stereotypes about men and sexual abuse and "the beliefs of the male victims themselves, who feel that being abused reflects personal weakness and a lack of masculinity.[222]

However, most of these statistics do not look at more "internal" reporting — that is, reporting to committees within institutions or denominations. The Takana Forum, for example, a once-secret committee within the Orthodox community in Israel, was set up in 2003 to deal with complaints of abuse in the community, especially against Orthodox rabbis.[223] When it was publicly discovered that the committee had heard testimonies that could have gone instead to the police, especially around the case of Moti Elon, there was an uproar.[224] "While Takana and similar bodies are an improvement to a situation in which all complaints are suppressed, they tend to prefer settling matters quietly, even if sex offenders go unpunished," the editors of the *Jerusalem Post* wrote.[225] Elon was eventually reported to the police and convicted of sexual abuse of students in his yeshivah, and Takana worked to become more transparent and collaborative with the authorities, aiming to comply with the laws of mandatory reporting.

One of the most difficult topics that emerged from this research is how challenging it can be to report sexual abuse in the Jewish community. Perhaps that should not be so surprising given what we already know.

The Orthodox community, for example, has particular mechanisms for blocking reporting. According to the organization Za'akah, which advocates for victims of CSA in the Orthodox world:

---

[220] See statistics collected by the organization RAINN for an overview of reporting numbers in the criminal justice system. *The Criminal Justice System: Statistics*
https://www.rainn.org/statistics/criminal-justice-system
[221] Zalcberg "The Place of Culture and Religion"
[222] Priebe and Svedin, "Child sexual abuse is largely hidden"
[223] http://takana.org.il/english/
[224] Tomer Zarchin, Yair Ettinger, "The Rabbi Elon Case: Sexual Abuse in the Zionist Orthodox Community. Allegations of abuse against Rabbi Moti Elon emerged more than five years ago via Takana – an organization that deals with sexual harassment in the community," *Haaretz*, Nov. 3, 2011 https://www.haaretz.com/jewish/1.5206161
[225] Jerusalem Post Editorial: "Takana's damage. The Takana Forum was created within the religious-Zionist community to combat this self-destructive pattern," *Jerusalem Post*, September 20, 2016, https://www.jpost.com/opinion/jerusalem-post-editorial-takanas-damage-468253

Survivors of child sexual abuse will recognize the universal
pressures that exist in every community to silence them from
speaking out against their abusers. These include:

- *Feelings of shame and guilt for having been abused*

- *Threats made either explicitly or implicitly by the*
  abuser against the victim or their family

- *Feelings of confusion about the abuse*

- *A desire to just move past it and hope that ignoring it*
  and moving on will make it go away

- *Inability to articulate, both internally and externally,*
  what exactly happened (which can be corrected with
  abuse prevention education curricula)

- *A general feeling that you're alone in your experiences,*
  and that no one will understand you or what happened
  to you

- *A general worry, often based on seeing other survivors'*
  experiences, that you won't be believed or supported if
  you come forward and might even be blamed for your
  own abuse.

Some of these norms are particular to Orthodoxy, such as pressures on dating, and tight-knit communities that are able to enforce "inside" and "outside" status. One ortho-centric issue that is particularly jarring when it comes to reporting is *"mesirah"*, the prohibition against reporting a fellow Jew to governmental or non-Jewish authorities. According to Za'akah, this concept is "often used to silence survivors who otherwise might come forward... Survivors who have reported abuse to the authorities in these communities have been evicted from their homes, have lost their jobs, their children have been expelled from their schools, and they have been completely ostracized from their communities and synagogues. Reporting sexual abuse in the Orthodox Jewish community can mean losing everything in the process."[226] Michael Lesher, in his book about sexual abuse in the Orthodox community, chronicles the networks of support that offenders may receive:

The dismal history of how far too many cases have been
assiduously concealed both from the public and from the police;
how influential rabbis and community leaders have sided with
the alleged abusers against their victims; how victims and
witnesses of sex abuse have been pressured, even threatened,

---

[226] Child sexual abuse in the Orthodox Jewish community. https://www.zaakah.org/child-sexual-abuse-in-the-orthodox-jewish-community

not to turn to secular law enforcement for help; how autonomous Jewish 'patrols,' displacing the role of official police in some large and heavily religious Jewish neighborhoods, have played an inglorious part in the history of cover-ups; how some Jewish communities have even succeeded in manipulating law enforcement officials to protect suspected abusers.[227]

While Lesher's research is particular to Orthodoxy, reporting does not always seem particularly effective in non-Orthodox Jewish communities and Jewish institutions in general. On the positive side, the Reform movement's Hebrew Union College-Jewish Institute of Religion (HUC-JIR) was the first denomination to conduct and release the findings of an independent investigation into sexual abuse in their rabbinical school campuses, in November 2021.[228] Two other Reform institutions later did the same. The Conservative movement's Rabbinical Assembly (RA) began to release details about their ethics processes around the same time, though they did not fully disclose whether suspensions were specifically for sexual abuse. The CCAR also released a female-led, trauma-informed investigation of their own reporting processes, also in late 2021.[229] In the Orthodox community, a handful of organizations have cropped up to deal with sexual abuse (listed in the Appendix).

Some organizations seem to lack effective reporting mechanisms altogether. For example, when the story broke about Len Robinson's decades of abuse at various JCCs, the JCC Association of North America released a statement renouncing Robinson's alleged behavior while claiming that "no complaints about Robinson were brought." But it seemed that "no official policy or procedure to handle concerns that arise from among the group's 29 member affiliates" existed, or was known about, the CEO told reporter

---

[227] Michael Lesher, *Sexual Abuse, Shonda, and Concealment in Orthodox Jewish Communities,* (Macfarland, Jefferson, North Carolina; 2014) pp 7-8

[228] Grace E. Speights, Sharon P. Masling, Martha B. Stolley, Jocelyn R. Cuttino, Ira G. Rosenstein, *Report of Investigation into Allegations of Misconduct at Hebrew Union College-Jewish Institute of Religion,* November 3, 2021 http://huc.edu/sites/default/files/About/PDF/HUC%20REPORT%20OF%20INVESTIGATION%20--%2011.04.21.pdf

[229] Jacob Magid, "Conservative movement publishes list of rabbis it has expelled or suspended. Rabbinical Assembly says move part of review of its handling of misconduct allegations; 9 listed, including rabbi arrested in Israel for performing non-Orthodox wedding," *Times of Israel,* 22 October 2021, https://www.timesofIsrael.com/conservative-movement-publishes-list-of-rabbis-it-has-expelled-or-suspended/; "The Rabbinical Assembly to Review Its Code of Conduct and Ethics Procedures," The Rabbinical Assembly, April 22, 2021, https://www.rabbinicalassembly.org/resources-ideas/ethical-guidelines/code-conduct/press-release; Rena Paul, Margaret Gandy, Rahel Bayar, "Report of Investigation of the Central Conference of American Rabbis Ethics Process", *CCAR,* December 21, 2021, https://www.ccarnet.org/about-us/ccar-ethics-system-report/

Hannah Dreyfus. "Reporting instances of abuse—sexual or otherwise—becomes a game of broken telephone... dismissed as 'insignificant' somewhere along the way up the chain of command," one employee said.[230] Similarly, when a complaint was filed in New York State against HALB about alleged sexual abuse by one of their first-grade teachers, the complaint revealed that HALB had no policies on student-teacher interaction in place, no regular supervision structure, and no training or reporting structure. As Asher Lovy says, "The reason these policies are so important is because schools that don't have these policies, or refuse to develop these policies, often foster environments that are friendly toward would-be abusers."

Moreover, there is a question about how victims are treated when they report. Dr. Guila Benchimol studied reporting of sexual abuse in the Jewish community and found that "Our community reinforces a culture of silence, and even when victims overcome it, we often blame the victims. All too often, when powerful individuals commit sex crimes, silence is the default reaction."[231] Fran Sepler, a consultant, investigator, and researcher who has been working with Jewish organizations for 30 years, said, "if the culture of the organization isn't proactively focused on respect and fairness and safety, it doesn't make a difference because these things will go underground."

According to many advocates, the importance of the reporting process in not only treating but also preventing future abuse cannot be overemphasized. As Asher Lovy said:

> The single biggest indicator of whether you're going to have a community that's rife with sexual abuse or not is whether there's a culture of impunity in that community. And that can extend to communities as large as a denomination of Judaism, or it can be as small as the culture within a specific synagogue or a specific institution. But the one thing that's true is that any time you see a culture of impunity where someone can assume that they can abuse and get away with it... there's going to be an increased prevalence of sexual abuse within that community.

To be clear, this chapter explores the topic of reporting in the Jewish community from the *perspectives of victims*. It is *not* a fact-finding investigation, nor is it a formal evaluation of processes and procedures. It is

---

[230] Hannah "Dreyfus, More Women Come Forward Against N.J. Camp Exec Alleging Sexual Harassment. She had always thought of him as a family friend — until he invited her to spend the night with him alone at his private residence in the Poconos," *Jewish Week*, April 18, 2018, https://jewishweek.timesofisrael.com/after-n-j-camp-exec-sacked-last-week-more-women-alleging-sexual-harassment-come-forward/

[231] Benchimol, Guila, 2016, "Sacrificing victims on the altars of silence and power,". *Jewish Week*, January 19, 2016 https://jewishweek.timesofisrael.com/sacrificing-victims-on-the-altars-of-silence-and-power/

a collection of testimonies on the issue exclusively from the point of view of interviewees. I make no claims on facts or evidence. I am simply bringing here what victims saw, heard, experienced, and felt, scaffolded by existing research and investigative journalism. A thorough investigation or evaluation of the actual efficacy and transparency of reporting mechanisms in the Jewish community is beyond the scope of this research. This is about what victims experienced and described in the context of reporting or potential reporting.

Why victims do not report

In 2018, a social media trend #WhyIDidntReport took hold in Israel. A study examining the texts of the people sharing their stories showed the five most common reasons why people do not report sexual abuse:

(1) Relationship between superior and subordinate

(2) Self-blame on the part of the victim

(3) Assumption that no one would believe the victim

(4) Minimization and repression of the abuse

(5) Feelings of disappointment after (one's own or others') experience of reporting.[232]

Some of these reasons resemble my interviewees' reasons for not reporting. As with disclosure, reporting can be fraught with fears and anxieties. Helen was once offered an opportunity to report her abuse, but she declined for a list of reasons. "I thought about it, but I said no because I thought nobody would believe me or that there would be repercussions on my career," she said. "Also, I thought, I don't want to hurt his wife and his cute little boy. Not that he was hurting him, but that I was hurting them. So, I never complained. I didn't want to go through with it." This last line about not wanting to harm the abuser, is a lashon hara rationale in plain English, as Leah explained earlier.

Reporting can also be damaging to the victim. One particular fear is that, by coming forward, the victim risks being blamed and shamed. Marion said she did not report because "I didn't want to bring shame down on myself or on my family, risk my marriage, or have to look at my father who would have used the story against me in twisted psychological ways. Lots of

---

[232] Michal Dolev-Cohen, Tsameret Ricon, Inba Levkovich, #WhyIDidntReport: Reasons why young Israelis do not submit complaints regarding sexual abuse, *Children and Youth Services Review*, Volume 115, August 2020, https://www.sciencedirect.com/science/article/abs/pii/S0190740920301067

deterrents." Helen did not report because "I thought a prosecutor would drag me through the mud and make me feel like a slut." Coming forward also often places the victim, instead of the perpetrator, in the spotlight, risking what Avital called "this old habit of making the person speaking up become the problem."

Indeed, Tali had such a bad experience with reporting sexual harassment that later on when she was raped, she did not report it at all. "There's no way in hell I'm going through that again. The one who loses out is the one who reports things." She added that when she told friends what happened many said, "Oh, that happened to me, too!" She heard "so many stories where women say, 'I've had this happen, but I don't want to tell anyone about it because it's not worth it.'"

These fears reflect potentially real-life consequences. In the Orthodox world, one may get "tainted" or become unable to get a "shidduch," or marital match. Yael said, "I didn't want to be tainted. I didn't want to be involved in anything that would have my name on it because I was orthodox and single, and I didn't want to hurt my shidduch reputation."

Orthodox rabbis — and possibly other leaders across denominations — may shun even the potential for reporting. As Shlomit said, I was very close with a prominent male rabbi in the Orthodox community. 'Any time you want me to tell you what happened with these men,' I said to him, 'let me know.' And he was like, 'Nope, I don't want to know.'" This is a purposeful block to reporting. Shlomit said it characterizes her community's culture. "The Orthodox world just doesn't care that much," she said. "The men rule the world. They don't have to listen. Who's going to make them listen?"

But it's not just in Orthodoxy. When Yael finally went public a few years later during the #MeToo movement — after she was married — she suffered consequences. "I wanted to identify with the women coming forward," she said, so she sent out a 140-character tweet alluding to her experience without mentioning names or identifying details. As a result, her life exploded. "I literally just tweeted that this happened to me, and suddenly I was being made into a story. And then [a journalist] published my tweet on Facebook saying I was just seeking publicity. It became such an ugly story." Yael began to experience the underbelly of coming forward. "After I tweeted that, there was such a storm. I tweeted in the evening, and in the morning, my phone was exploding with retweets and messages and Google alerts." Some journalists found out her personal details and shared them on social media as well. "One of the Israeli newspapers put my face on their front cover with my husband at a haredi wedding, and they dug up my whole life. This was beyond the pale. That was the hardest part for me."

Still, the Orthodox world seems to have its own particular tools for threatening victims. When Yael's husband's photo was shared on social media as part of the response to her coming forward, she said, "people were commenting that he should divorce me because I was raped, which would mean that I was tainted. I mean, it got completely out of hand."

That said, the potential damage to victims is not ortho-specific:

> I was being inundated with publicity that I didn't want. That really hurt me more than anything. Every single top news anchor was reaching out to me to interview me. Obviously, people were trying to get a name, but I was not interested in getting into that... We had a social function that weekend, and I remember being terrified to walk into the ballroom where it would be full of New York Jews and I knew people had talked about me. I felt like I was wearing a scarlet letter. I remember being in such a dark place that day. It was terrible.

Yael agrees that this issue is fraught for all victims, not just the Orthodox ones. "For me, the takeaway is not just what happened in a hotel room but also how we talk about it later," she said. "Because that was the most traumatizing. I didn't know how I would live through those few days." Other interviewees shared the fear of experiencing what Yael experienced. Tali, for example, said simply, "There is nothing good that comes from speaking out. It's very painful."

Workplace trainer Sarah Chandler said that "Why didn't you come out with the allegation sooner?" is an extremely common blame-shifting tactic in response to reporting:

> In our trainings, we teach that this is one of the top five 'no nos' of things to say when someone reports. The average reporting time is 16 months after the incident. If the person receiving the report belittles the victim, that will lead to the victim shutting down and not completing the report – or worse, not reporting at the time the abuse gets more severe.

As Joan Kuriansky, Executive Director of Wider Opportunities for Women and former head of Tikkun Olam Women's Fund, explained to me, "Why didn't women come forward sooner? Because it would compromise so many aspects of their lives."

Variations of reporting experiences

When victims do decide to report, they may have several different avenues open to them, depending on details such as the role of the abuser, the context of the abuse, and the relationship with the abuser. If the abuser is a rabbi, then the victim might go to a rabbinical committee. If the abuser is a boss, the victim might go through a professional reporting process in the organization. Other victims might choose to go public in the media or in social media, or tell community leaders. Each of these outlets for reporting has particular dynamics, although there emerged some surprisingly common issues to reporting that cross these contextual lines.

Reporting to senior rabbis

When victims decide to report on abuse in the Jewish community, one address for reporting is rabbis. This is especially the case if the abuse takes place in a setting where the senior person in authority is a rabbi — which may be not only synagogues but also schools, camps, rabbinical schools, or nonprofit organizations. A rabbi holding a supervisory position may be expected to have the power or authority to help alleviate the situation, while perhaps also offering pastoral care in the process, as well as validation.

For victims who were abused by a rabbi or who grew up with a rabbi as an authority figure, this can be a particularly complicated process. According to Sara Zalcberg, one of the key factors in underreporting among religious Jews is the tradition of obedience and respect for educational-religious figures. Some of her ultra-Orthodox interviewees were explicitly forbidden from reporting by their rebbes, for reasons such as "religion forbids doing these things." Some rebbes blamed the victims for the abuse, and some victims were expelled from their yeshivahs for reporting.

Indeed, many of my respondents reported to rabbis — and it often did not go well. Leanne, who was abused by several different rabbis over her life, has a litany of stories from her attempts to get help and support from other rabbis. Some 25 years after her abuse in summer camp, she wrote a detailed letter about her abuse that she sent to the two camp directors involved. "I remember feeling very nervous when I first wrote and sent the letter," she said, "but now reading it I feel stronger." She immediately received "heartfelt apologies [from one of the directors], and it gave me some closure. But [the other rabbi] remains a pillar in his community." The (female) rabbi who tried to stop her from writing is no longer a friend, and in fact Leanne thinks of her as being emotionally abusive, too.

Many respondents had difficult experiences when they reported to rabbis. Fay, an ultra-Orthodox woman who was sexually abused by her father, was told by her mother's rabbi not to report to the police "because it is not nice to air our dirty laundry with the goyim and we should not tell anyone, because it will hurt my shidduch chances." Note that her real-life experiences with reporting to a rabbi confirm the very fears expressed by the victims who did not report. The head rabbi of her community also forced her to meet with her father "even after they knew that he abused me. He said, 'I am the *rosh beis din*, so you have to listen to me.' I didn't go, and he thought I was disrespectful."

Brenda, who was abused by an assistant rabbi, eventually told the senior rabbi, a 40-year veteran in her movement. She says he "dealt with my situation horribly. This has been a really upsetting experience for me." You may recall that, despite her twenty years of service to the synagogue, the senior rabbi immediately sided with the junior rabbi rather than with her. In addition, rather than alleviate the situation, he immediately had the synagogue hire a lawyer to represent the *abuser.* "I was so distraught," she says. Brenda also appealed to other rabbis and got nowhere. "I have spoken to two dozen rabbis over the past two years, and they all felt that there was nothing for them to do. Which I found utterly disturbing."

Fran Sepler disagrees. I asked her about Brenda's conversation with the senior rabbi, and this is her analysis:

> I spend a lot of time teaching people how to receive complaints. And what you've just given me is an example of all the don'ts. That rather than seeking to understand what was going on and acquiring the perspective of the person coming to him and saying things like, 'Tell me more about this', and, 'How is this affecting you?' the rabbi did what people who believe their role is to conserve organizational integrity will do. He immediately started debating and arguing with a person... If he had really listened to what she had to say before jumping to conclusions, he might have been deeply affected by understanding that this was harming somebody who was valuable to his congregation, and would have then said, 'Well, we've got to do something about this.' So, this was a failure of complaint handling. It was a protective analysis rather than a compassionate analysis. And, it, it, it demonstrated a lack of knowledge and a lack of skill.

Many interviewees had experiences reporting to rabbis that made their situations worse and not better. Abby, a 30-year veteran of the rabbinate, had to continue to work with several rabbis in her denomination who were in senior positions and greatly revered, despite the many accusations against them:

> When I told colleagues [at the rabbinical school] about my rabbi who was a pedophile, I was told not to tell this story because it wasn't relevant to my personal growth. Or when people had asked me who my rabbi was growing up, I would say his name, and they would say, 'Oh, great scholar but a pedophile.' Everyone knew. Even people who went to school with him in the 1930s said, 'He was always a strange guy.' Never censured, went from congregation to congregation. There

was — at the time, in 1978 — there was no mechanism for anyone to do anything about him.

Everyone knew he was a pedophile, Abby says, but dismissed it because he wrote books. Similarly, an interviewee who is an assistant rabbi of a congregation and was harassed by a congregant, said, "I finally told her, the rabbi, that I was having a problem with this guy and he was being inappropriate, and I couldn't do my job. But her response was very 'conventional,' like, 'Were you being friendly to him?' It felt extra crushing to have this happen."

Even when people report, they may not be believed, or it may have no impact. To wit, Emily, a cantor who was molested by the husband of the synagogue president, immediately reported it to the rabbi, who said, "If he hadn't done this before, you wouldn't have been believed." This was a big shock for her. "I was floored! Why would I make this up? What would I have to gain? If this man had a history of being inappropriate with young women, why was he permitted to sit next to me? Why wasn't I warned about his behavior?" Previous reporting was ignored, she was not protected, and the rabbi she reported to admitted that he had not been inclined to believe her.

Indeed, reporting may have little impact, even when the victim is believed and some action is taken. Daliah described an experience of being asked to speak at a conference where the other main speaker was a rabbi who had been removed from his pulpit because of abuse allegations. "He was fired from his job, and it was all public, and the [movement umbrella organization] was investigating, but he felt completely comfortable signing up for this spirituality retreat," she said. "And when I spoke to the organizers, lovely rabbis involved in progressive Judaism, the act of alienating or turning away a rabbi doesn't seem like something they were willing to do. They preferred to favor the accuser. I was just — I couldn't believe it." Zelda similarly shared that the rabbi who abused her and was censured by his movement is still a frequent speaker and performer at Jewish conferences and retreats.

One question is how much all this has changed over the past few years. Abby believes that today things may be changing — "I mean, the times were different." On the other hand, many of these stories are from the past 5-10 years. Still, Abby believes that today, "People are taking seriously what it means to honor someone who has a bad history and trying to decide whether, or how you can recognize someone's contribution while recognizing this dark, awful side of him. I don't know what the answer is to that." To wit, Chaim Walder's books were taken out of bookstores when the extent of his pedophilia became known. But the Chief Rabbi of Israel still went to console his family instead of the victims after he died. Two steps forward, one step back.

Rabbis protecting rabbis

Some respondents believe that it is fundamentally problematic to have a reporting mechanism about rabbinic abuse conducted by other rabbis. Many believe that rabbis cannot be trusted to handle abuse of other rabbis.

For one thing, some argue, the abuse is too rampant among rabbis. Daliah, a rabbi and wife of a rabbi in one movement, and daughter of a rabbi from a different movement, says that from her life experience, the situation is so far gone that rabbis cannot be trusted to protect the public from sexual abuse by rabbis. When she was in middle school, her father "had an emotional affair with a congregant," although he stayed married to her mother for 31 years. "Growing up, I knew that my father's friends were having affairs with congregants," she says. "I knew about all this stuff." Ann, who is connected to a different denomination, shared a similar experience. "I'm the wife of a rabbi," she said, "and one of the things I'm always aware of, the cliché, rabbis who have affairs with the sisterhood president and get away with it. At best they move to another congregation."

The inequity of these "affairs" makes reporting abuse by rabbis to rabbis extremely problematic. "Affairs" between rabbis and their congregants are by definition not consensual given the structural, emotional, and power inequality, as I analyzed earlier, and yet, those understandings have not quite impacted the culture. "I still did not expect that the power structure in the movement would side so strongly with the perpetrators in terms of protecting them and moving them around. It's not exactly like the Catholic Church but it's not *Welder's* like the Catholic church," Daliah says. "People were knowingly moved around." Ann agreed, "They are never removed from the rabbinate."

There are many examples of this. The man who abused Manny Waks was quietly sent from Australia to America. Rabbi Norman Lamm protected abusive rabbis on his staff by quietly sending them to teach in Florida. Baruch Lanner was supported by his rabbinic supervisors for years if not decades. Reut said that the abuser-rabbi left his previous community under hush-hush circumstances that were never shared with her synagogue. "There's this whole thing of just shuffling people out of their institution, of getting rid of the problem by moving it on somewhere else without warning anybody about what the issues are. So, supposedly somebody at the shul was warned about the fact that there was something wrong with him from the previous community, and nobody stopped it from happening."

This dynamic of rabbis covering for other rabbis potentially undermines the entire reporting process. Rabbis who abuse are often also in positions of power within a network of other rabbis in power, some of whom may also be carrying out forms of abuse. Daliah said, "Rabbis will always side with the rabbi and never with the accuser."

Moreover, abusers tend to support other abusers. One of Moti Elon's biggest supporters is Shlomo Aviner, who has himself been accused of sexual abuse.[233] Similarly, the board president who supported Rabbi Jonathan Rosenblatt when he was found to have been abusing boys in the sauna is a man named Donald Liss, who was also accused of sexual misconduct.[234] One has to wonder whether rabbis who protect other rabbis have something to hide themselves.

It is also possible that this norm of cover-each-other-no-matter-what is at times encouraged in the profession of rabbis. Here is how Brenda described it:

> *My stepbrother and his wife have been rabbis for 20 years and are very well-respected. And over Thanksgiving, I finally told them what happened. I had been holding it back for a long time. They said to me, 'In rabbinical school, we were taught that you have to protect your colleagues.' They said that their number one job is to protect the other rabbis. I couldn't believe they were saying this! I said, 'Did they ever teach you what to do if a colleague was accused of harassment?' And they were like, 'No, no training.'*

It seems that, in some places, rabbis consider protecting each other to be part of their jobs, no matter what. One touches, another relentlessly pursues, another rehires the other, and yet another keeps the victim from telling her story. These work together and create an ironclad network. It is challenging if not impossible for a victim to report an abusive rabbi when he is, say, good friends with the camp counselor — or worse, dean of the rabbinical school. For victims, trying to achieve justice or even responsiveness within this network can be a daunting or even impossible task.

And it is worth pointing out this jarring discovery: The tendency for rabbis to back other rabbis arguably exists across all denominations. Considering how emphatically some Jewish movements try to distinguish themselves from one another; this commonality of protecting rabbis as the top priority is particularly striking.

---

[233] Nathan Jeffay, "A Sex Scandal Splits Orthodox Zionist World Between Silence and Action," *Forward*, February 24, 2010 https://forward.com/news/126324/a-sex-scandal-splits-orthodox-zionist-world-betwee/; Ruth Sinai, "When no one can hear you scream: After complaining that a senior rabbi harassed her, a settlement resident becomes an outcast," *Ha'aretz*. March 31, 2003 https://www.haaretz.com/1.4839853

[234] Andy (Avraham) Blumenthal, "Birds of a Feather," August 19, 2015, http://www.andyblumenthal.com/2015/08/birds-of-a-feather.html

Reporting to official rabbinical committees

Another format to report abuse to rabbis is a more formal context: that is, filing complaints with rabbinical committees, ethics committees, or the *beit din*—the rabbinical court. Take, for example the story of what happened when ultra-Orthodox Pearl Engelman's son, Joel, reported to their rabbinic committee that he had been molested at the United Talmudical Academy in Williamsburg when he was a child. According to the *New York Times*, "The school briefly removed the official but denied the accusation. And when Joel turned 23, too old to file charges under the state's statute of limitations, they returned the man to teaching. 'There is no nice way of saying it,' Mrs. Engelman said. 'Our community protects molesters. Other than that, we are wonderful.'"[235]

Many interviewees had experiences reporting to rabbinical ethics committees in their synagogues or denominational umbrella organizations. Rabbinical ethics committees of the various movements are meant to provide an avenue for victims. But many respondents often described difficult encounters.

Yittel filed complaints with her local beit din against the rabbi who raped her, but he is still running a huge educational institution. "He has not denied what happened but instead blames me and feels like I've harmed him by speaking out," she says. Kayla spoke to her local board of rabbis. "They said they knew about his behavior but could do nothing. Maybe he wasn't really a rabbi, they said, as he told them his papers were destroyed in Europe. They thanked me for being so courageous and for speaking up"—and then did nothing.

Similarly, Daniel, who was violently attacked by a rabbi-colleague, had what he called a "shocking" experience of "perfidy and cruelty" in reporting his experience to his denomination's ethics community. "The Ethics Committee deliberately assisted [the rabbi who assaulted me] in defeating my petition for a restraining order in court. This breathtaking breach of impartiality sounds wild, but I proved it in a procedural appeal that the Executive Committee sustained. The Ethics Committee found my claim 'supported' but sentenced him only to a confidential self-reflection." The committee was also working with the offending rabbi, sharing committee documents with him and his lawyer and not with Daniel. "For half a year I repeatedly reached out to find ways to restore my confidence in their ethics process, but the Ethics Committee ignored all of my inquiries. I cannot overstate the cruelty of giving the silent treatment to the legitimate concerns

---

[235] Sharon Otterman and Ray Rivera, "Ultra-Orthodox Shun Their Own for Reporting Child Sexual Abuse," *New York Times*, May 9, 2012,
https://www.nytimes.com/2012/05/10/nyregion/ultra-orthodox-jews-shun-their-own-for-reporting-child-sexual-abuse.html

of a sexual assault complainant." The committee seemed to be actively assisting the rapist and derailing the victim.

What Daniel suggests here is that even when the rabbinical ethics committee files a judgment of sorts against an offending rabbi, it may not have any real effect — because rabbinical committees may by default protect rabbis. Abby has a similar perspective:

> *I found out about a rabbinical student who was abusing congregants as an intern, and [the institution] said that we can't do anything until there are formal charges. So, they filed. The guy was found guilty, then let off on a legal technicality. The case was said to be retried, but three years later the families decided not to do it because the kids had moved on, so he was never retried. He applied for reinstatement and ordination, and [the institution] put together a panel and made an ad hoc ethics panel and read through the transcripts of the trial, and they felt that they evidence was there, so they refused to ordain him. But he got private ordination and now serves at a [movement] congregation. Even without formal ordination.*

Even when rabbis are censured, sometimes their careers continue anyway. Daliah discovered that a rabbi in her community was a repeat sexual abuser who was fired from his previous job for these actions but not censured by the movement. When this story leaked to the public, Daliah began getting calls from women he had abused over the years. "I became a recipient of all these victims' stories. I became a vessel for this. It was women from across the country. Some I had never met, and some were people in my own community."

Her first stop was to report this to the heads of her movement:

> *I kept pushing, writing letters to the president and the CEO [of the umbrella organization], 'What can we do about this? This guy is in our community! And I'm not comfortable with him working in our community.' And they kept telling me, 'There's nothing we can do.' I was told by people, 'Don't do it,' 'You're not the right person,' 'It's not the right time,' 'Shut up, you've said enough,' 'Back off.'*
>
> *Finally, the previous president of the [movement organization] offered me advice and said, 'If you have any connections to the board of his temple, contact them and tell them what you know.' The senior rabbi of his congregation, which was my old congregation, knew about the accusations and told me that it was none of my business and basically to shut the fuck up.*

The more Daliah tried to report, the worse her situation in the movement became. The hushing process continued. She contacted members of the board whom she knew and trusted. "They went to the senior rabbi. And I got reprimanded by the [movement organization]. Even though they were the ones who advised me to do this. And I felt terrible, and it was awful." Daliah was knocking on institutional doors and getting nowhere. It put her in a no-win situation. Eventually, she told the story to the media, under her own name—and then was further punished.

One of the most unsettling testimonies about rabbinical ethics committees came from Zelda, who spent a year trying to get the rabbinic committee of her abuser's movement to hear her—a process that involved sharing her intimate story multiple times with panels of strangers, most of whom she said were untrained in evaluating clergy abuse. She shared hundreds of pages of evidence, yet was shunned and shamed by the community before ever receiving justice. She first filed a complaint several months after she got the courage to get out of the abuse. "[The abuser] didn't even try to deny any of it, because in his mind, none of it was wrong," she told me. The committee initially censured him privately, asked her not to share that information, and let him continue in his post without telling the community—even though there was evidence that he was abusing many other women.

> He was censured, which is basically a letter that says, 'You did a bad thing, now go to counseling, and nobody has to know about it.' The censure was just an administrative slap on the wrist. And there is no incentive for him to go to counseling. I said, 'What if he doesn't go?' And they said, 'Then nothing.' There was no reason for him to comply with the counseling request because there was nothing to lose. I said, 'What is this? This is just you having his back. He's your buddy. This committee is just a bunch of other rabbis.' I was enraged.

She complained that the censure was meaningless, ineffective, and unethical, but she could not get the attention of the board or the ethics committee, who at a certain point stopped returning her calls. It took a team of lawyers, therapists, and allies who provided unsolicited testimony and supporting evidence—as well as some national media coverage and years of pressure—to finally get him suspended, though still not expelled. Even though they censured him, the synagogue did not receive any details from the rabbinical organization but only from Zelda. Meanwhile, the offender continues to be an in-demand speaker and performer at events and conferences around the country.

Zelda's story gets worse. During the ordeal, Zelda learned that her abuser had been abusing women for 17 years in his previous community—and possibly outside the Jewish community as well—that he was forced to resign from his prior synagogue in another state for sexual misconduct, and that he had been secretly reprimanded by his rabbinical association, which was never made public. This was the same rabbinical association that helped place him in her community, where he began abusing again almost immediately, and where he began abusing her within a few months of starting his new job. She was also all alone, despite the fact that he openly bragged about preying on many other women at the same time:

> It's mind boggling the level of negligence. I said to the committee, 'You had a chance in 2014 to stop him, and instead, you're also the organization that does placement for rabbis, and your placement chair knew that he had a sexual abuse problem and was made to resign from his temple, and yet you quietly placed him in the largest synagogue in the region, and nobody said anything.' The people at the former temple didn't say anything, and the [rabbinic body] didn't say anything. His wife told me that while he was transitioning into this job, he was still acting out sexually, going on to internet places that nobody should know about and finding strangers that he can have gangbangs with.

Some rabbinic organizations, it seems, lack the ability, skills, training, political interests, and/or willingness to bring justice in cases of clergy abuse. And the impact on the community is alarming. As Zelda asked, "I have to wonder how many women who go through these things don't live to talk about it." As Daliah said:

> The movement was covering up so much stuff. They knew about him for so long. Why wasn't he removed? How many people have to complain? There is such a lack of transparency that is really upsetting.... Clearly nobody wanted to do whatever it would take to stop this person from perpetrating in the Jewish community. It was more important to cover asses from the past than to protect the community in the present.

For Zelda, Daliah, Abby, Leanne, Brenda, Daniel, Carmela, and others, there is a sense that the ethics committees systematically side with the offenders and do whatever they can to silence victims. As Carmela explained, "It's about setting the bar really low and making women's tolerance of sexual harassment pretty high. The message is that this institution permits it. And that... leaves you very unempowered."

In other words, power structures within the denominations, coupled with overarching norms of power hierarchies, often combine to make it nearly impossible for victims to be heard by other rabbis. Daniel says simply that "ethics committees cannot be trusted." Brenda calls rabbinic organizations a "big wall of silence. I have spoken to two dozen rabbis over the past two years, all [in the same movement], and... they all felt that there was nothing for them to do, which I found utterly disturbing," she said.

With that, some initial signs of change may be afoot. The reports released in late 2021 are a first hopeful sign. The Central Conference of American Rabbis (CCAR) released the findings of an extensive, women-led, trauma-informed investigation into reporting processes in their institutions.[236] And Abby, for example, who has been in the rabbinate for over 30 years, said, "The good news is that I think the movement is taking itself seriously. The times were different when I was in school in the 1980s. Now, they are doing something about it."

Reporting in the workplace

For victims who work in Jewish organizational settings, reporting to people in positions of authority in their organizations is also a significant action following abuse. Unfortunately, that is not always effective. A 2018 study conducted by the Harris Poll on behalf of the AFP Foundation for Philanthropy and the Chronicle of Philanthropy found that respondents who have experienced sexual harassment by a donor and who told their organization, in most cases—71 percent of the time—no action was taken against the perpetrator after the incident was reported.[237] As Fran Sepler explained to me, reporting at work can be fraught, and can come back to haunt the employee:

> We find that at least half of employees going to their employer and saying, 'I'm being harassed, I'm being bullied', have experienced what I call the Employee Issue Triad — absenteeism, attitude problems, and performance problems — within the six weeks prior. So at least half of those people come forward to make a complaint to a board member about a senior staff member, and the senior staff member says to the board member 'Oh well, they're really screwing up their work and, you know, they're more of a problem than I'm ever going to be', and poof, you, you have you have taken advantage of the very destabilization you've proceeded to discredit a complainant.

My interviewees described similar dynamics. Many had difficult experiences reporting at work. Recall Ruth, who had been openly solicited

---

[236] Paul, Gandy, and Bayar, CCAR Report, https://www.ccarnet.org/about-us/ccar-ethics-system-report/

[237] AFP, "One-Quarter of All Female Fundraisers Report Sexual Harassment: Donors Account for Nearly Two-Thirds of Harassers," *AFP*. August 22, 2018 https://afpglobal.org/one-quarter-all-female-fundraisers-report-sexual-harassment?fbclid=IwAR15drXFmHnHTyrcmLuxoH2eHpnNcumDTMHFbhMnz841MT0_H0 5tfAQH2x8

to date a potential donor, reporting to her boss who said she should consider doing it because "it would be a shame to lose the donation." Although she is the only interviewee who was directly pressured by her boss to have sex with a donor, many interviewees were encouraged to stay in compromised or dangerous situations in order to protect their abusers.

Leanne, for example, who was abused by a camp counselor when she was a teen, said she came to a brick wall when she tried to the heads of the camp:

> *The entire administration and senior staff knew what was going on but they did not intervene... I went to the camp director, and I said, 'You can't have him this position, he's a risk.' He said, 'Well, you're not a psychologist so you don't know.' I said, 'He shouldn't be at camp, he's not a good person to be at camp.' And the director said, 'You don't know. He's lonely. And I'm lonely, too.' And I felt like I was complaining to someone who really aligned with the guy and not with me.*

When that director was replaced the next year, she went to the new director as well. "The new director said, 'I don't advise you to spend time with this guy.' And I was like, 'What do you mean? Why are you bringing him back?' And he said, 'Well he's a rabbi and has a lot to offer.'" Leanne quit shortly thereafter.

Similarly, when Daliah went to an organization to discuss how they hired a rabbi who had been accused and censured by his movement for sexual abuse, they ignored her. "They were completely comfortable hiring him," she said. As Sheila Katz, who was allegedly harassed by Michael Steinhardt, told *The New York Times*, "Institutions in the Jewish world have long known about his behavior, and they have looked the other way. No one was surprised when I shared that this happened."

Many interviewees described unhelpful encounters with professional staff when they went to report. Melissa faced a dead-end when she went to report abuse at camp. She was a teenager at the time and worried about her friend who was being abused. "I went to one of the advisers, and I said, 'Maybe can you check in on them?' And she was like, 'That doesn't happen here, they're good kids, blah blah blah.' I don't think anyone ever talked about this. I was so disheartened that I didn't even bother going to report it anywhere." When Janice tried to get the rabbi of her synagogue to protect her from a harasser, she did not get a response. But when she noticed that her harasser was also harassing the teachers in the synagogue school, she went to talk to the senior staff. "I was totally shut down," she says. The woman she went to, she said, "was completely unable to help me. She had all her own issues to deal with, and I think this threatened her."

Another time, when Melissa was facing gender abuse in her lay leadership role in her campus organization, she also tried to report to the professional leadership, with no success:

> I tried to reach out and say that this person was treating me in a way that was completely sexist. I was totally ignored... every time I tried to say something to someone about it, it was like, 'Just deal with it.' Or, 'We don't want to get involved,' or 'How could you say it's sexist?' There was a professor on campus who was assigned to the club, and when I went to him, he was like, 'I have to support the president that I put in.' And he was in denial that there was sexism. I also tried to reach out to the regional leadership, but when I tried to reach out to them, they were like, 'We had lunch with your president and we learned everything we need to know about it.' So, when you get these kinds of responses, you're not going to go back and reach out when something serious happens. This was like a low-key sexism. But when people are not willing to talk about this, why in God's name would you go to them for something more serious?

Rhonda Abrams had a different experience reporting sexual harassment by a donor to her superiors. As she wrote publicly:

> Thankfully, my local board, Hillel International, and my local Federation have proven to me what it means to do the right thing, the Jewish thing. My local board insisted that we cut all communication with this donor, despite the financial strain it may cause our organization. Hillel International offered extensive support, including a timely launch of materials for Hillel professionals to help in other situations of sexual harassment and assault. They also put their money where their mouths are, offering to help make up the lost funds. This week, my local Federation is convening constituent agency leaders to launch communal discussions around sexual harassment. All the professional leaders that I turned to believe that I should not only stand up for myself but also speak out so other Jewish professionals can realize that they will not be alone. This fight is necessary for us to see change.

Odelia also had a positive first experience with reporting but was anxious about going further. "I told my male colleague, and he wants to follow up. A response is pending from the community. It feels hard to tell others, like other staff, even though I think it's important."

Sometimes a positive initial experience of reporting goes nowhere. Lila, for example, shared that, "When I told the HR person, I did ask that he check the outgoing phone records from the office, but I never heard from HR." She never pursued it further. Other times the process seems too daunting and does not go any further, as with Helen's story above. Yona had a similar experience of reporting to her supervisor, along with another colleague who was also harassed, but then deciding not to report any further because it was too risky. "We both told our chair, who said we would need to be willing to say something officially. They couldn't act on our complaints otherwise. As untenured faculty, we simply couldn't take that risk. And while the actions were egregious, we doubted that anyone would care. We chose not to file complaints."

Tali is one of the few interviewees who went through a complete reporting process through HR. Initially, she was enthusiastically supported by the HR staff. But in the end, the process cost her they job and derailed her career:

> *I went to this professor for help, and I'm crying, and I'm like, 'I don't know what to do. I need this job. I have two kids, I'm a single mom, what is he going to do?' So, this professor said that this is sexual harassment. He said, 'I'll take care of it.'*

> *An hour later, I get a call from the dean, saying 'Come meet me.' I go to meet him and tell him the whole story, and he says, 'We are required by law to look into this. We can't just let it go.' And I was crying, and it was awful. And he says, 'You can go talk to the university representative for sexual harassment, the university lawyer.'*

> *So, I went to talk to her. I tell her the story, and by this time it's my fifth time telling the story and I'm finally not crying anymore. She says, 'Women should fight and not be afraid to report.' And they say they have to have an investigation whether I want to or not. So, it's going to happen.*

> *I go to talk to the dean, and I said, 'I'm going to lose my job, I don't know what to do.' And he says, 'I promise you, you won't lose your job. I will find you another lab to be in.' He says I should find a new building because it won't be nice working in the same building with this guy who's a creep. I say okay, and he says he'll get back to me. He comes back to me and says there's a guy in geology who's looking for someone in the same kind of position. So, I basically move from chemistry where I have a PhD, to geology, which is rocks. It was like, this is horrible. I also took a significant pay cut. And the case was closed with that same lawyer saying, 'Well, we feel it's in the gray zone. It may not be sexual harassment. He just took things on a personal level that you weren't comfortable with.*

And since both parties are happy with the way it was resolved, you found a new job, so, that's it, they closed it.'

That was pretty much it. After a year, I had to start again as a post-doc, with the pay cut. We agreed that I would stay there for a few months and then reevaluate. There's a whole bureaucratic process to move from post-doc to research fellow – and they said since I hadn't published because the guy took my name off all the publications of things I worked on because he was telling everyone I'm a bitch, I didn't have enough publications.

So, in the end, I just started looking for other things because I was blackballed … I started my own company and looked into the entrepreneurial world.

Now that I know all these implications, I think I could have been smarter about how I reported. I just figured, she said it's sexual harassment, she really must care about me. Then I realized that if they weren't going to make a legal claim against him and he was the star, it's impossible to do anything. He's the one who matters.

Tali's experience as a research fellow at a Jewish university being sexually harassed by her supervisor ended up with her losing authorship on papers, losing a place in the department (the whole building!) where her expertise is, taking a pay cut, and not being able to advance to the next level in her career. All because she *did* report at work and go through the "correct" process and was encouraged to "fight." There were no consequences for the abuser. But she ended up leaving academia altogether and working in the private sector.

Joan Kuriansky explained how reporting can harm women in the workplace:

To understand the impact of reporting, you have to look at the person who has been harassed and where they are in their power structure. Even people who had all the money in the world who still felt they had to comply – that is extraordinary. You move that to the lives of most women and the kinds of jobs that most women have, it would be so detrimental for them to speak out without a very large network of support. I mean, I have colleagues who were leaders in their fields of science and government, but when they brought complaints, even successful litigation, their careers were basically over. They had to start all over because their decision to pursue their rights was so detrimental to their careers.

In other words, even when there is a positive response to the first report, victims still struggle with the process. The same dynamics that keep victims from speaking out at all — shame, fear of retribution, lack of trust in the system, lack of protections for themselves, and underlying patriarchal structures — also keep people from making official reports. And there are also at times real consequences against the victim for reporting.

Reporting to the community

If reporting to other rabbis can be a brutal experience for victims, the process of telling the community is not necessarily easier. Indeed, one of the most painful aspects of reporting is when the community supports the abuser rather than the victim. This dynamic became prominent following the suicide of Chaim Walder, as I have shared. Although he was removed from some of his jobs, ultra-Orthodox celebrity figure Rebbetzin Tziporah Heller, for example, wrote a post praising Walder's books[238] and the chief rabbi of Israel visited Walder's family sitting shiva.[239] And in at least one case, parents were urged to "exercise extreme restraint when discussing this," again invoking variations of lashon hara to silence victims and protect abusers.[240]

Many abusers have continued to receive support from their communities, such as Moti Elon, who was convicted of abusing boys at his yeshivah but still has a strong following. Or the late Shlomo Carlebach, who is still celebrated despite decades of accusations against him, or Larry Bach and Marc Gafni, who have careers as spiritual teachers or guides despite years of allegations. Or Menachem Mendel Levy, who remains a respected and active member of London's Chabad community and who has received help and support from the wider London Orthodox Jewish community despite having been convicted and imprisoned for child sex offenses.

Fran Sepler, who has been investing, consulting for, and training Jewish organizations in reporting processes for 30 years, describes the process in which communities excuse the abuser as a "culture of exception":

---

[238] Rahel Bayar, "Too many chose to look away from Chaim Walder's crimes. We can make other choices now," *JTA*, January 6, 2022 https://www.jta.org/2022/01/06/opinion/too-many-chose-to-look-away-from-chaim-walders-crimes-we-can-make-other-choices-now; Tziporah Heller, "The Chaim Walder Parsha," 3 January 2022 http://www.tziporahheller.com/; Louis Keene, "She defended disgraced author Chaim Walder. Now a revered rebbetzin is facing a backlash of her own," *Forward*. January 6, 2022, https://forward.com/news/480478/tziporah-heller-chaim-walder-facebook-post-apology /

[239] Shira Hanau, "Chief rabbi slammed for Walder shiva call urges victims to speak out. Chief Rabbi David Lau was criticized for visiting the Chaim Walder funeral, Israeli haredi author accused by dozens of women of sexual abuse and rape," *JTA* December 30, 2021, https://www.jpost.com/Israel-news/article-690197

[240] Kobi Nachshoni, "After his suicide: Haredi rabbis support Chaim Walder, accused of sexual abuse," *Ynet (Hebrew)* 28 December 2021, https://www.ynet.co.il/judaism/article/bkt3ncdsk

> *I work with a lot of synagogues and there's all sorts of flaws in their cultures. One is the absolute obeisance to the wealthy. And another is the culture of exception. I saw it a lot during Covid – 'No bar mitzvahs in the shul.... but this member can have the bar mitzvah in the shul.' As soon as people see it, even that kind of exception, it's a culture of exception, which means, 'I'm going to hold some people accountable and other people not.' And the biggest slice I see is a legacy member, when a family has been with a shul for a long time. They're viewed as having more privilege in the shul and money.*

Sepler argues that this "culture of exception" protects abusers. Instead of being rebuked, the community says, "'Oh that's just so and so we make an exception for them because they're so talented or they're so they have such.'"

Many interviewees shared variations of this story. The abusive rabbi in Reut's synagogue who still retains a pulpit in the community received a letter of support from 70 other rabbis "talking about how wonderful a mentor he was and how he made such a difference in their lives." And people in the community still go to him as a rabbi. "It's just sickening that you can walk around here and then people have him be the *mesader kiddushin* at their children's weddings, come speak under the *huppah*," she said. She has lost many friends in the community because of the many ways they defend him and support him.

> *I can't talk to them anymore because they were just so vehemently in support of him and completely, they use the same words people use all the time. You know, 'It's a witch hunt,' or, 'Oh, it was a long time ago, and he doesn't do it anymore.' It's like it never happened. People are like, it never happened. Nobody seems to care.*

Many interviewees had very painful experiences reporting to their communities. Zelda, for example, after the harrowing process of getting the rabbinic committee to heed her complaint, then had to deal with the resistance of the community that worshiped her abuser. "Even after he's been suspended, nobody cares," she said:

> *People are like, 'He's still our Facebook friend, we don't understand what happened,' or whatever. While the congregation fired him because my rape allegation was plausible, they turned around and told the community that he had done nothing illegal and that the woman reporting him was not even a part of the community! Everybody thinks he is a good, safe guy, and there are women in the community that still trust him. They have no idea.*

Brenda was similarly shunned and disbelieved by her community. Her story was "outed" to the community before she knew it, when her private correspondence was shared with the board. By the time she went to report, the community and leadership had already decided that she was the problem, not the rabbi. This process was agonizing for her:

> *I wrote a letter to the chesed committee and said, 'How can I run a chesed committee with someone who had no chesed for me?' It was a call for help. I was desperate. 'Please somebody intervene, somebody help!' I pretty much got no reaction, not from the president or past president who is the HR person. Nobody responded to me. I said to my husband, 'Maybe I'm paranoid, but I think people are treating me differently, they're avoiding me now.' This whole time when I was crying and begging for help from these people, they all know he has a lawyer, and nobody said anything to me, or helped me. So, I'm going through hell, thinking, like, if someone would have just said something to me. It was just devastating; I felt so unsupported by my community.*

Other interviewees shared painful experiences of being disbelieved by their communities. After Yittel reported being raped by the rabbi who was counseling her for depression, she went public. The rabbi never denied the charges and simply claimed that she seduced him. "I, the virgin Bais Yaakov girl who'd never talked to boys, seduced *him*, the married *baal teshuva kiruv* rabbi. It was crazy." As a result, he received a job promotion to lead a large Orthodox Jewish organization, and she in turn was ostracized from her community. She has since moved thousands of miles away from her family and married a non-Jewish man.

In some cases, members of the community have gone on the offensive to cast the victim as unstable, unreliable, or crazy. Brenda, for example, was told by the senior rabbi that *she* is the abuser, not the rabbi. Reut described how one of the women who first broke the story about how the rabbi abused her son was dismissed and ousted by the community. "People called her a crackpot. She was not a crackpot. She's just trying to tell the truth, but the truth is nobody wanted to listen. So people thought if you can dismiss her, you know, as a crackpot, then you don't have to take anything that she's saying seriously." Similarly, Esther was cast out of her synagogue and community when the abuse became public, labeled vindictive and mentally unstable, while her abuser retained his high-profile position in the community.

In Reut's synagogue, the abuser's supporters openly attacked victims and the people who wanted the rabbi to leave the synagogue:

There was a letter circulating to get the rabbi to leave, but people were scared to put their names on it because they didn't know what was going to happen to them if they signed it, like who was going to start making ugly rumors about them. When the letter was published, one guy started his own blog where he went and tore apart every single person who signed that letter and said the most disgusting things about them. Like, this one woman who signed it, he said, 'And you should see how short her skirts are when she goes to shul. And the hooker heels she wore.' That's the kind of ugly, ugly, ugly things people said. The woman moved out of the community pretty soon after that because it was just so ugly.

Ultimately, the impacts of reporting to the community and not being supported can be devastating. As Daliah explained:

As a whistleblower, you're ostracized. That's what happens. That's what I felt. People from my old congregation who I had been rabbi to for 11 years would walk right by me and not make eye contact. It was real ostracization. They wanted me to not work in the high school anymore. It was really painful. It was so uncomfortable. I've gotten so comfortable with being uncomfortable. I walk around with my head held high and I did the right thing, but it has been very painful.

Brenda has also been ostracized from her synagogue — where she has been an active volunteer and donor for over 20 years — for filing a complaint about her rabbi. "I feel uncomfortable in my own community. It has been devastating to me."

Reporting to the media

Some women who are ready or even eager to go public choose to use the media because the media, as opposed to the rabbinic committees, can potentially be detached and less invested in the outcome of a story, and have a wide reach. The media is a form of reporting that uses the power of the crowd instead of one leader or one committee. The #MeToo movement brought a lot of change, and that was a clear, direct result of using the media to go public.

But going to the media does not always have positive impacts either. Daliah went to the media when her movement shunned her. She was motivated by the knowledge that the man whom she had reported to the movement was still in a position to abuse. "He was still working in the community, still working in the high school. I was also being contacted by people who said they had been students and cantors in his congregation and that they had been sexually harassed. The school knew. The movement knew. He had a huge file. Every time they sent him someone, he sexually harassed them. That was really, really terrible." For these reasons, when Daliah had the opportunity, she changed course and went to report to the media. When a newspaper contacted her about the accused, asking her if she would speak in her own name, she first refused knowing what this would mean for her standing and relationships in the movement. But then, she said, "It was right around High Holidays, so I did a lot of introspection, and the day before the article was about to be published, I said, 'Go ahead, use my name. And my life has not been the same since."

If Daliah was punished when she reported to the movement, it was even worse after her name was published in a large Jewish newspaper accusing another rabbi of sexual abuse:

> Being a whistleblower, I was ultimately rejected in my membership [in my movement's umbrella organization] after many years of being a full-paid provisional member. It was so awful, unbelievably awful. I lost friendships. Lost career contacts. They told the synagogue musician, 'We'll only give you a contract if you never work with [Daliah] again.' I lost a lot. It was not good. I was being contacted by other members saying that I'm a terrible person for ruining this man's life. That he just had an affair. Till this day basically I'm the vindictive bitch who 'made up lies' about this person.

Notice that all the items that I listed in "Stage 6" of the grooming process— in which the abuser works on the externalize the narrative, preparing the public for the revelations with mind-games and crazy-making spin— are showing up in these accounts. Abusers— and in some of these cases, their supporters and defenders— interweave lines such as "It was just an affair", "She is a vindictive woman", "It was no big deal", or "He is a good guy" to isolate accusers or whistleblowers while protecting offenders. This can be a very painful experience for those who choose to report. In Daliah's case, she wasn't even a victim of the sexual abuse—she was the accidentally appointed spokesperson for the victims. "Which is crazy because the newspaper would not publish two full articles about this person based on my ability to make up a web of lies. It's just been really awful."

Indeed, one of the issues that Daliah encountered—i.e., that newspapers tend to prefer publishing stories without anonymity—is an issue for some victims who want to come forward. Kayla said, "I told my story to a New York newspaper, but they said I needed more women to come forward before they would print it. At 12-step meetings women came up to me and said that 'Yes, he had been inappropriate with them and others,' but they would not come forward." Similarly, Yael, who is herself a journalist who was assaulted by another journalist, told a reporter, but the story never came out. "I told one friend who is also a journalist, and he referred me to a veteran female journalist who I met with. The reaction was all, 'That's horrible, that's disgusting, we'll never have anything to do with this person ever again.'" The story was never published.

Some women are ambivalent about the media, including Yael, who was relieved when her colleague decided not publish her story. "I didn't want to be tied to him publicly in any way. I mean, the guy is a gross guy who I don't respect in any way, and I didn't want my name attached to him. If I would have reported it, Google search results are forever. I did not want that. It would have been disgusting to me."

Yael was also gratified because "I certainly felt supported. It felt right, like that was enough." Again, for many victims, the experience of being believed and validated is all they need, even more than media reporting.

Just as some interviewees believe that the approach of internal ethics committees is changing, some also believe that the attitude of the media is also changing. As Carmela, who is involved in pressing for change in her denomination, told me:

> One of the benchmarks is when the newspapers don't need to investigate and adjudicate for us but are rather just reporting on the Jewish community policing itself. I think in this phase, right now, victims' willingness to come forward to illustrate what has happened to them is actually pretty important because it serves as a wake-up call to the Jewish community. That's what's happening in the world. The goal is not to out victims and force them to come forward. If this is healing and brings justice, then we should support that. But naming what is happening is very important, especially when the perpetrators are still in positions of power. That they are not dead.

Ultimately, going public can be empowering. As Wendy, who was hesitant about coming forward, said, "I thought I knew — I thought everyone knew — all that was going on." She was surprised at how empowering she felt about coming forward. "As this goes on, I realize that I don't know all that was going on. We all don't. So, let's keep talking. And going public feels good!"

Reporting to the police

Outside of faith communities, the first or most obvious form of reporting is probably the police. And yet, of my interviewees, only a handful ever spoke to the police, and for the most part, the process ended there.

The few interviewees who went to the police mostly had stultifying experiences. Dina, who was nearly raped in Jerusalem by a man who stopped ostensibly to give her a ride, said, "The police absolutely refused to do anything. They wouldn't even dust for fingerprints. I told them he licked me, and they would not dust my body. They just said go the next day to make a report. Which I did. And they said it was my fault because I didn't get the license plate." Drori, who was attacked by the Executive Director of a campus organization after sharing personal issues with the rabbi, said, "I spoke to the rabbi, and she just wanted to keep it quiet. I filled out a police report, but it went nowhere. I didn't get any results and there could be more victims. I've tried to report this a few times, and no one cares." Zelda also talked to the police and also got nowhere. "The police told me that this guy was just an abuser who manipulated me into a relationship. They didn't say it wasn't consensual but that was the implication."

Other interviewees actively avoided the police. For Fay, she was pressured not to go to the police in order to protect the community, as well as her "shidduch chances." For Lara, going to the police never even occurred to her.

Charley is the only interviewee who had an experience in which the police took care of her. Charley, who was raped by a rabbinical student, disclosed to a friend the next afternoon who encouraged her to go to the police:

> When I went to the bathroom, I saw that there was blood that shouldn't be there, so I showered. I was still very disoriented, and then I had a study session in the afternoon where I disclosed to a friend on the way to our dorm. She called her mom and decided that I should go for a rape kit. I called the college rape crisis center and a got an escort, and she told me to take my underwear so I could leave it with the kit and all that. The doctor said she would testify on my behalf if I decided to press charges because she saw the tearing.

Despite the fact that she had a rape kit and evidence, Charley ended up dropping the case. Her state had a law that rape victims had a year to decide whether to press charges before the police tossed the rape kit:

> I debated that year whether or not I was going to press charges, disrupt my life... I was certain that if I outed him, I would get blowback professionally because he was the most beloved staff person. Everyone worshiped the ground he walked on. And they had dating policies and this idea that all staff people who worked with teenagers should be role models and shouldn't be having premarital sex. And there was no interdating allowed; these were some of the policies in my contract. And it was in the same scope as doing something that was inappropriate — I was afraid I would be held to blame for putting myself in a compromising position and lose my job.

Here, again, the idea that assault is some kind of bad sexual behavior — "dirty" or unseemly, as opposed to a violent attack — keeps victims from being seen and heard. Ultimately, Charley decided not to pursue legal action because she was afraid of retaliation, losing her job, and being blamed for being raped. And because, perhaps predictably, she felt that the charismatic rapist still had more power and pull than she did. She was still vulnerable in so many ways.

Joan Kuriansky explained to me that Jewish activists and advocates are aware of the problems in police reporting, and that these problems run deep. "We found that when we created laws that enable police to make arrests in domestic violence, we had a terrible backlash of police arresting both men and women. Till we take one step ahead, there is going to be a response to take us backward. We are looking for attitudinal change, and that takes time." She said that the Jewish organizations she is working with in her community are "looking at responders like police or clergy and providing tools. We are not at that point yet to say we are responding effectively to sexual harassment. But preparing to look at all these different sectors" is the strategy for long-term systemic change.

Takeaways about reporting

- **Most victims never report.** Only a fraction of interviewees went through a reporting process, which is consistent with evidence from around the world on this topic. This is because reporting requires victims to fully face the trauma, and then to push through further difficulties around shame, fear, self-blame, guilt, and the possibility that they won't be believed, that they might be blamed, or face retaliation. For many, it is far more tempting to try to move on and shove the experience in a mental vault.
- **Nevertheless, reporting can be crucial.** The ability to report can have an impact not only on whether the perpetrator continues to abuse but also on whether the victim receives validation and the ability to heal and move forward. For some victims, the reporting process can be empowering, despite the challenges. It also has communal-wide impacts, as abusers who are not removed will likely continue to cause harm. Reporting is a key component in bringing about change, and can be an empowerment experience if the community supports it.
- **Reporting is often problematic in religious institutions.** Victims sharing problematic reporting experiences represented all Jewish

denominations. All the movements struggle with reporting, though there are some early signs that this may be changing.

- **Reporting is often responded to with silencing.** Many interviewees — again, from all denominations — described being actively silenced when they went to report. The silencing comes from many different sources, and in some case, even from the police. Different communities may have different nuances in their silencing mechanisms, but the effect is the same.

- **Orthodoxy is not exactly one "denomination."** In liberal settings, institutions often played a powerful role in silencing victims and enabling abusers to find a new locale. Orthodox interviewees did not have the same kind of experience because there is no singular Orthodox overarching body but rather mini-networs: a Hassidic rebbe, a beit din, or different rabbinic institutions representing particular subsets of Orthodoxy. But while Orthodox respondents described a very tight obedience to Orthodox norms and behaviors, liberal respondents described a tighter network of protecting one's *movement* . Control over victims in the Orthodox community tends to take place in a more grassroots, backdoor kind of way, with mini-networks. But all the movements suffer from the practice of rabbis supporting rabbis at all cost.

- **But Orthodoxy can be brutal.** That said, the control mechanisms within the Orthodox community, though not formally structured like the Catholic Church, can nevertheless be devastating. The scope of the sexual abuse networks in ultra-Orthodox communities that is alluded to in many interviews — described in greater detail by Michael Lesher — is way beyond the scope of this research.

- **Harmful responses are strangely similar across the community**. In many ways, the resistance of organizational leaders, rabbinic committees, and rabbis to support victims is remarkably similar. Reactions of disbelief, blame-shifting, silencing, and sweeping under the rug seem quite consistent among Jewish settings across denominations, communities, and contexts.

- **Overall, rabbis protect rabbis.** Throughout all the movements, there is a culture of rabbis protecting rabbisError! Bookmark not defined.. One interviewee even reported that she learned that her movement's rabbinical school actively trains rabbis to protect each other while failing to give any training about abuse.

- **There can be a very high price to pay for reporting.** Some lost their jobs, careers, friends, networks, communities, reputations, or their place within organizations.

- **In some organizations there seems to be no reporting mechanism at all.** Many Jewish communal organizations seem to not have any reporting or training mechanisms whatsoever. This research is not a comprehensive study, nor is it an evaluative study. However, the anecdotal texts that emerged from the interviews are very concerning and point to a need to check this issue across the Jewish community.

- **The media is the last stop**. A handful of interviewees went to the media, and not all of those experiences ended up in public stories. But contrary to some public perception, the media tends to be the last stop for victims, not the first. The experience with the media can cause shunning and ostracizing, but it can also be empowering, as the #MeToo movement demonstrated.

- **Some of this may be in the process of changing**. Some interviewees believe that these systems are getting better. And there are currently some programs to train organizations to combat abuse in the Jewish world. As Joan Kuriansky said, "We can't talk about naming victims without support for them and giving them the choice to come forward. That does not mean that you ignore what has happened, but you look at ways to support them—that's why women coming together in a particular workplace makes a difference in how these issues are addressed."

Chapter 10: Jewish Responses

When the *New York Times* broke the story in March 2019 that Jewish megadonor Michael Steinhardt had been reportedly harassing women for decades, one of the most bizarre if perhaps predictable reactions was in the comments section.[241] A long list of reactions claimed that the article was nothing more than *anti-Semitism*. Commenters were fuming that the *Times* chose to put the descriptor "Jewish" into the headline and emphasize his Jewish-connected philanthropy in the story.

"This article is plain and simple anti-Semitism!" wrote one commenter from Texas, a sentiment that was repeated in at least a dozen other comments. "No other people accused of sexual harassment were identified by their religion. This flames anti-Semitism," wrote someone named "Abby." "In this volatile and divisive time, please use your heads!" wrote Edward of London. One commenter from Hartford called the article a "hit piece," and added that it "appears to be the side door entrance from the BDS [Boycott, Divestment and Sanctions] movement." Significantly, the commenter continued to dismiss sexual harassment in general by saying, "These women are so threatened by a few jokes with sexual innuendo from one of the most well-known Jewish philanthropists at the same moment J Street is promoting its alternative 'viewpoint' trip to Israel. It is all very convenient." And

---

[241] https://www.nytimes.com/2019/03/21/nyregion/michael-steinhardt-sexual-harassment.html?action=click&module=Top%20Stories&pgtype=Homepage#commentsContainer

someone with the moniker WiseNewYorker wrote "The headline of this news story is blatantly antisemitic [*sic*]... An apology is owed to the entire readership of this paper."

At the risk of stating the obvious, I would like to suggest that women sharing their stories of abuse are unlikely motivated by anti-Semitism and more by the desire to tell the truth about their traumas and promote justice and safe spaces. Moreover, it is worth pointing out that the victims are all Jewish themselves, which makes the anti-Semitism article a bit absurd. It also implies that the Jewishness of the accused is more significant than the Jewishness of the accusers. It casts a broad insider-outsider structure of Jewish connection in which the accused are *inside* the Jewish collective – and thus able to receive the collective's support and protections – and accusers are *outside* of it.

These reactions illustrate a crucial aspect of sexual abuse in the Jewish community. That is, there are uniquely Jewish codes for supporting, reacting to, and handling accusations. From the rhetorical excuses to the power games, there are elements to this story – such as ignoring a massive exposé with a flippant "Anti-Semitism!" – that could only take place in a Jewish setting. This chapter aims to explore some of those particular Jewish elements.

This chapter reflects on the previous two chapters about "the telling" and examines aspects of this process that have particularly Jewish aspects to them. It looks at Jewish rationales for covering up abuse, Jewish structures that support abusers, and Jewish values that are co-opted to keep victims silent.

Forms of denial

Several Jewish-centric tactics support the denial process. Perhaps the oldest is the myth that "It doesn't happen to us." Blima, who was abused by her synagogue rabbi, said, "Many still believe it doesn't happen in our community." Drori similarly said, "It's a mistake to think you're safer in a Jewish environment." Hinda concurred that, "There still, to this day, exists the myth that alcoholism and sexual abuse do not exist in Jewish families, that somehow we are above all of these issues." She "heard that expressed over and over," and as part of #MeToo, "I specifically want Jewish women to know very clearly that they are not alone."

The realization that one's own community is not safer than the outside world can be jarring. Nicole, who was attacked by a Jewish man in her community said the experience "changed me dramatically":

*I always felt safe dating in my community. I've been sheltered.
And naïve. The men I knew were 'nice Jewish boys.' Even the
ones who rubbed me the wrong way or were arrogant or
misogynistic. I learned the hard way how naïve I've been. Our
community is not safe from abuse and harassment. We never
were. But we feel otherwise.*

The myth that "it doesn't happen to us" also blocks efforts to address the problem. As Lucy said, sexual abuse "happens at Jewish summer camp. It's happening in our institutions, where our children should feel safe and joyful. We have to be more vigilant and teach young men what not to do." Interestingly, Charley reported that right after a major scandal with the rabbi in her community, she was impressed that "they were really great about creating support systems and offering lots of resources," while at the same time, "I think unfortunately the community usually only steps up that way when there is a crisis, and does not acknowledge that there is an ongoing crisis of a lack of consent education and healthy attitudes toward sexuality."

Another particularly Jewish aspect of this denial comes in the form of denominational comparisons. Thus, while the notion that "it doesn't happen in our *community*" may be fading in some places, it is sometimes replaced with, "it doesn't happen in our *movement*."

In the Orthodox community, for example, there is a common misconception that laws of body-cover for women (so-called "modesty" or "*tzniut*") somehow "protect" women and girls from being abused. Popular Orthodox blogger Avi Shafran wrote as much in *Tablet*, claiming that sexual abuse in the Orthodox community is "rare" because of the laws of modesty and enforced segregation of the sexes.[242]

Orthodox actress Mayim Bialik, who dresses according to Orthodox norms of body-cover in her roles, made a similar argument in a *New York Times* op-ed, suggesting that she was never assaulted by Harvey Weinstein because of her adherence to "modesty" — as well as her lack of physical attractiveness: "I have also experienced the upside of not being a 'perfect ten.' As a proud feminist with little desire to diet, get plastic surgery or hire a personal trainer, I have almost no personal experience with men asking me to meetings in their hotel rooms. Those of us in Hollywood who don't represent an impossible standard of beauty have the 'luxury' of being

---

[242] Avi Shafran, "A Safer Space for Women in Orthodox Judaism's Rules for Sex: 'Do we really imagine that true respect for women can survive, let alone thrive, in a world where standard "entertainment" is saturated with their objectification and all too often actual abuse?'" *Tablet*, October 17, 2018 https://www.tabletmag.com/sections/news/articles/a-safer-space-for-women-in-orthodox-judaism

overlooked and, in many cases, ignored by men in power."[243] Bialik was pilloried in the media for that op-ed, and she spent a week apologizing all over the internet. The anger was not only about the assumption that "ugly" women do not get harassed, but also that a woman's attire has something to do with sexual assault. She gave several interviews in which she admitted that women's clothing choices actually do nothing to cause or prevent sexual abuse.[244]

Charley was particularly outraged by Bialik's article:

> I used to act professionally as a kid, but I stopped when I was on an audition for a laundry detergent ad where they wanted me to be topless, and I was only 13, and I was by myself because my mom was home with my newborn brother. And I said to them, 'No!' Luckily, I had the wherewithal to say no. It was just a time when Calvin Klein ads were all with girls wearing nothing. It was the era. But I was just like, 'Fuck you.' And then I told my mom that I don't want to do this anymore, and she was like, 'Yeah, that makes sense.' So, I'm familiar with this idea that if you have breasts then some casting agent is going to want to see them. But this whole idea that the way I dressed impacted whether I was sexually assaulted was just so naïve. Terribly naïve.

Nevertheless, the idea that Jewish laws "protect" women from sexual assault is pervasive. One of my interviewees, Yael, an Orthodox woman who complies with Orthodox norms of body-cover and gender separation, was also mistakenly under the impression that these behaviors somehow "protected" her. You may recall that while she was being pulled into a hotel room by a colleague sexually assaulting her, she was screaming, "Don't touch me, I'm religious!" and "I'm shomer negiya" — that is, she abides by the religious rules not to touch men. The attack shattered her belief that this would not happen to her because she was religious. "To be frank, I was — I am — a frum [religious] girl so there was an additional kind of thing, like, I don't want to be touched, I'm untouchable." She literally thought that she was "untouchable" because she is religious.

Helen also thought that Orthodox rules would protect her. When she converted via the Orthodox rabbinate in Israel, she began dressing modestly with "all the safeguards." She said that it "was part of the attraction to me. It felt like it might protect me." It came as a bit of a shock that "I was also

---

[243] Mayim Bialik, "Being a Feminist in Harvey Weinstein's World," *New York Times*, Oct. 13, 2017 https://www.nytimes.com/2017/10/13/opinion/mayim-bialik-feministharvey-weinstein.html
[244] "Mayim Bialik on Feminism and Harvey Weinstein." *The New York Times, Opinion Section* https://www.facebook.com/nytopinion/videos/1890320664316214/

harassed when I was dressed all modestly, all covered." So ingrained was her idea that Orthodox rules "protect" her that even after she was harassed, she decided that it must have been *her fault* somehow. "I also blamed myself for that. I thought it was my fault because I wasn't raised Orthodox and so I sometimes hugged the rabbi-type man. So, I thought it was my fault."

Despite these perceptions, the Orthodox community is hardly "safe" from abuse. Chavi Eisenberg, an Orthodox blogger, wrote a response to Avi Shafran's piece, pushing back against this common misconception among Orthodox Jews that "modesty" protects women from sexual abuse. She argues that "there is more sexual assault in ultra-Orthodox society" than elsewhere, but "it doesn't get reported. Instead, the abuser gets protected." The Orthodox women she knows who have been abused while keeping the laws of modesty and gender segregation were certainly not "protected":

> I studied at a very religious seminary for two years after high school. There was a rabbi there whom I admired who was later accused...[of] taking advantage of his position and having 'inappropriate relationships.' Even those who are religiously observant should consider themselves lucky if they have not been victims. But it is disrespectful to victims to deny that it happens in our community, yes, even to those who keep the halacha. Just because a given individual may not have had this personal experience does not mean it isn't true. I believe scientific data and I believe the women who have been abused, yes, even in my own communities. We are not immune.[245]

Shana Aaronson, Director of the organization Magen that advocates for sexual abuse victims in the Orthodox community fully agrees that these rules do not currently protect women and girls — although maybe they could. The problem is not the laws, she says, but in the fact that women are taught that important men can break them:

> Not only is it wrong to say that we are protected by these laws, but it is not about that at all. Sexual assault is not about how the victim dressed or acted. It's about a predator who makes a decision to take advantage of someone in this way. Which is ironic, because in theory those laws are there for precisely this purpose — to keep things like this from happening. The reason it's not working is because even though women and girls are trained from an early age to keep these laws, they are also trained to listen to their rabbis and authority figures

---

[245] Chavi Eisenberg, "No, Rabbi Shafran, modesty won't prevent sexual assault People don't want to know that there are some terrible things that all the precautions in the world simply won't prevent," *Times of Israel,* Oct 26, 2018 https://blogs.timesofIsrael.com/no-rabbi-shafran-modesty -wont-prevent-sexual-assault/

> *no matter what. So, if a rabbi comes and says, 'It's okay to break yichud with me,' they go with that rather than refusing or telling anyone else about the interaction. The view of rabbi as ultimate knower of all things and an ultimate authority stymies their ability to experience these rules as protection.*

In other words, the story of Avital who was fully empowered to push away her attacked because she is shomer negiya may be the exception rather than the norm.

In addition, not only does Orthodox body-cover not protect women, it may make women targets. One interviewee, Dina, who is confined to a wheelchair, said that she felt *less* safe dressed in skirts than in pants:

> *I dealt with so many instances of men stalking me in Israel that it became a big joke among my friends that I had all these crazy wild stories. But after that, I realized that it was dangerous for me to wear skirts. Even though it was supposed to be 'modest,' it risked my safety. I thought that when I wore pants I would get harassed more, but it was exactly the opposite, because I learned that haredi men look for single religious women who they see as an 'acquisition.' So, when I stopped dressing like a 'virgin,' it stopped.*

> *One day in Jerusalem, I happened to have a skirt on, after a year of wearing pants, and this old Hassidic man came up to me and started chitchatting with me about his grandchild, and then after he asked for my number because he and his wife wanted to welcome me for Shabbat, I gave him my number, he then asked me if I would be willing to go to the mikveh and have sex with him. It came as such a shock. How could you imagine an old religious guy making such a proposition? You don't expect it from someone who is making a statement with what they wear to say, I'm a religious person. And when their actions don't match their appearance, it is so disturbing and makes you feel like you can't trust anyone... Any time that sexual harassment and abuse occur and is perpetrated by someone who is outwardly appearing to be a religious person, it's that much more harmful and hurtful.*

Dina's experience suggests that Orthodox attire sends a message to certain predators that a woman or girl is vulnerable, perhaps even an easy target.

The idea that "my denomination is safer than the others" works in all directions. As Melissa said, "Coming from the Reform movement, we like to point fingers at the Orthodox movement and say, 'You don't handle this very well!' But we have our own skeletons in our closet." Daliah concurred: "I don't think Reform is any less patriarchal than Orthodoxy. It's just a non-halakhic patriarchy. For so many years we pointed fingers at Orthodoxy, but the true reckoning should be with ourselves." In fact, she claimed, in the Reform movement it is harder to expose the abuse because "the Reform movement is a bit like the Catholic Church mixed in with Hollywood. The rabbi really is treated like a rock star. You can't question."

To wit, it is worth pointing out that hookup culture in Jewish youth groups refers to non-Orthodox settings, as well as descriptions of "huggy" Jewish events, are exclusively descriptions of non-Orthodox settings.

Sexual abuse exists in all denominations, but sometimes people find it surprising that it exists in their own community. Brenda, for example, who was abused by the rabbi in her Conservative synagogue, belongs to an interdenominational support group for Jewish women survivors of clergy abuse, where she has met Reform and Orthodox women who have experienced almost identical dynamics, including "the same kind of dismissal" and victim-blaming within their communities. She concludes that, in the end, her Conservative movement is "not worse" but also "not better" than the other movements.

Victim-blaming around Jewish constructs of "femininity"

The question of whether Orthodox rules of women's dress and gender segregation "protect" women goes to another issue, which is the construct of female identity and power in Jewish life. Several interviewees grappled with this issue.

Yael, for example, who was attacked even while she was screaming, "I'm religious!" nevertheless continued to maintain that religious rules protect women. She wrote an essay in which she argued that partitions and yichud – rules of gender segregation in private spaces – are tools for women's "empowerment." "I wrote about this in the aftermath of Harvey Weinstein after the Mayim Bialik thing, and I said that that yichud could help us. I said that we can reclaim yichud as protecting our personal space." Like Mayim Bialik, Yael received a lot of negative pushback for that suggestion. "I got criticized by a lot of feminists for that article, but I think I made a good case for reclaiming yichud as a feminist power."

The notion that yichud is a protection – a concept partially adopted by former Vice President Mike Pence, who apparently never eats with women alone – is part of the problematic Ortho-centric narrative that suggests that women who keep all the laws of gender segregation will never be sexually assaulted. It also has the effect of limiting women's entry into locations of power while blaming women for being assaulted and once again letting the perpetrators off the hook. As feminist thinker Jessica Valenti said about Pence's "rule," "The underlying message is the same one that's taught to teens in abstinence-only education classes: men can't control themselves when alone with women. It's an insulting view of men, a limiting role for women — we're there to either entice or domesticate — and an archaic take on gender roles more generally."[246]

Some of my interviewees agree. Charley, for example, was one of those adamantly opposed to Yael's suggestion. She recalled an exchange she had with an Orthodox rabbi she works with who "really thinks it's possible to teach consent and lessons through traditional modalities like yichud.":

> It's so corrupt and problematic to perpetuate those tools as lessons of consent because it says, 'if you're not following those rules, if any of those rules are broken, or if you as a girl or woman 'allow' any of those rules to be broken, you can be held accountable for having failed in the situation.' And it still prevents women from coming forward by reinforcing those norms... To say modesty protects you from sexual assault is false. Sexual assault is not about attraction and desire; it's about power and control. When one claims that the halakhot can protect themselves from assault, the underlying implication is that those who were victims should have taken more precautions, that they were assaulted because they failed to do something... Which is victim-blaming.

Nevertheless, the pervasiveness of the idea that women who conform to the "rules" are "protected" has affected many interviewees. Dina, for example, actively changed the way she dressed in order to appear different to potential attackers, as I mentioned earlier. "At first, I thought I needed to dress modestly, even though both times I was attacked I dressed extremely modestly. But every single thing you do, you think, will this cause me to get assaulted or raped? Will wearing a skirt cause me to be assaulted?" After experimenting with these changes, she realized that she was actively trying to figure out what Jewish men were seeing when they looked at her, an exercise that she ultimately decided was unhelpful.

The practice of trying to prevent abuse by conforming to male expectations of correct womanness is flawed, as Dina explained:

---

[246] Jessica Valenti, "Mike Pence doesn't eat alone with women. That speaks volumes," The vice-president's rule is insulting for men and limiting for women. But let's not let Pence's sexism distract us from his whole party's sexist agenda. *The Guardian*. 31 Mar 2017 https://www.theguardian.com/commentisfree/2017/mar/31/mike-pence-doesnt-eat-alone-women-speaks-volumes

In the Jewish community, especially the Orthodox community, there is too much focus on wearing a strict uniform that men have determined based on their own ideas of what is immodest, instead of placing importance on what women feel more comfortable in and safer in and more modest in. So often, women are dictated how to live by a man's opinion and what they think is right and what is safe for us. The whole idea that we should follow tzniut laws and cover our heads so that we aren't attacked and we aren't raped – that's coming from a man's opinion. Maybe we should start listening to women more, listening to our stories and why we feel one way or another. If a woman is wearing pants, there may be a reason why she is doing that, and we shouldn't place judgments on her because she is not following laws that a man made out for her.

This troubling dynamic, in which ideas about sexuality rely on men's views about women's "correct" appearance and behavior, found expression in other issues as well.

For instance, the perception that a woman's job in Jewish life is to "make babies" also impacts attitudes about sexual abuse. The connection between views of women as baby machines and sexual abuse was highlighted with the discovery that Steven M. Cohen is a sexual predator and has been assaulting women for years. As one of the top Jewish sociologists, he was often called upon to lead communal policies about topics such as "demographics", all the while chasing women. He was, in theory, a progressive thought leader. Yet throughout his career, his research and policy recommendations were tinged by a particular kind of a misogyny, one in which women are babymakers and objects serving the male-led Jewish collective rather than whole, independent people.[247] As Clare Hedwat wrote, "As a community, we unthinkingly granted an academic the power of a policy maker, who told women, in effect, to fill Jewish baby carriages, and led a movement that prioritized reproduction over meaningful Judaism. Chauvinism has distorted those we choose to laud, those we're able to hear; the thinking we're exposed to, and the ideas that shape our community."[248]

These constructs of women/girls as potential babymakers has particularly infiltrated informal educational environments, as we saw in the

---

[247] Gary Rosenblatt, "Cohen's Fall Tests Border of Demography And Sexism: In wake of sexual harassment allegations against sociologist, throw out the baby with the bath water?" *The Jewish Week.* August 1, 2018 https://jewishweek.timesofIsrael.com/cohens-fall-tests-border-of-demography-and-sexism/

[248] Clare Hedwat, "The Jewish World's #MeToo Crisis is Much Deeper than Ari Shavit and Steven Cohen," *e-Jewish Philanthropy*, August 3, 2018, https://ejewishphilanthropy.com/the-jewish-worlds-metoo-crisis-is-much-deeper-than-ari-shavit-and-steven-cohen/

"perpetuate the Jewish people" excuse to justify the abusive hookup cultures in summer camps. A 2018 *Washington Post* story about Jewish summer camp cultures in the wake of #MeToo demonstrated how language of "Jewish futures" — that is, the idea that Jews who attend Jewish camps are more likely to have Jewish-centric adult family lives and marry other Jews — is used to encouraging kids from young ages to "build Jewish relationships," or couple up. "I want Jewish grandkids," one interviewee said. Les Skolnick, who was a camper in the 1990s, told the *Post*, "It was very much in the mission of the Jewish camps at that point. Very cliche: Perpetuate Jewish babies." Realizing that these ideas also support some abusive behaviors, the Foundation for Jewish Camp eventually launched the nationwide Shmira Initiative to stop this trend by training their staff in issues of consent and healthy relationships — or "dismantling the culture."[249] Charley, who conducts similar trainings in other organizations, agrees that "the pushback about women as prioritizing women as Jewish babymakers is very important."

Perceptions of Jewish women's bodies and identities as instruments for the purpose of serving the Jewish people are part of the cultures and settings in which sexual abuse take place. These ideas about women needing to be covered and as future babymakers form the backdrop to communal conversations, programming, and vision.

Jewish networks to support abusers

Another issue that interviewees described as part of the backdrop to sexual abuse is the interconnectivity of the Jewish community. For most people, concepts of "community" and "connection" elicit positive cultural dynamics. But in the context of sexual abuse, these concepts can serve a different purpose.

In the Jewish community, lines are often blurred between the personal and the professional. As Avital explained, "So much of what Jewish professional life is about breaks those traditional boundaries between the personal and professional. Boundaries are not clear." As an example, she said, when she graduated college and went to work at a Jewish day school, "People would ask me, first thing, 'Would you like to meet someone?' I was very offended at the time. I was trying to see myself as a professional, but I

---

[249] Zauzmer, Julie, "#MeToo goes to Jewish summer camp, a traditional place for teenage romance", *Washington Post*, July 14, 2018. https://www.washingtonpost.com/local/social-issues/metoo-goes-to-jewish-summer-camp-a-traditional-place-for-teenage-romance/2018/07/14/05c1fb28-86b8-11e8-8f6c-46cb43e3f306_story.html?utm_term=.9fe2b8c11aa6

think that they thought they were being welcoming and helpful and friendly. The boundary can be blurry."

Yona described how the man who harassed her talked to her as if they were family members. "My senior colleague was also Jewish and, when he was not commenting on my body or my professional choices, would often try to bond with me about our Judaism. The lack of boundaries — being in the same "tribe" — can become an excuse for engaging in abusive behavior. As Rena explained:

> *The gender problem plays out differently in Jewish contexts. People start asking all kinds of questions that in other contexts would be inappropriate, but they think that because we're all part of this Jewish family they can ask these questions. You wouldn't have people asking personal questions like people in the Jewish world feel like it's okay to ask. It's like, yes, but we're supposed to be professionals here.*

Karen Herron, who coordinated a town hall on sexual abuse for the Tikkun Olam Women's Foundation in Washington, DC, said that one of the issues with sexual abuse in the Jewish community is that "everything is based on creating community. And part of our mission is about community — people expecting hugs and kisses even from rabbis. How do you allow for community but not allow for harassment? In that way it's different than in a regular workforce." As Rena said, "the same people you see at your kids' school, are the same people you're working with — you're at shul together, you're at school together, you're in the community together, you're on the boards together. So, it's very hard to figure out the boundaries. I think that allows for a very slippery slope."

This lack of boundaries can create discomfort and preempt people's abilities to say "no" to behaviors that are unwanted. Recall Rena's comment about the Jewish professional conferences where hugging is expected. Shifra Bronznick agreed. "It's very hard, in the family-like atmosphere, where there are no professional boundaries," she told me. As Jewish educator and researcher Sarah Bronzite said to me:

> *People outside the Jewish community may not know just how deep the interconnectedness goes... Our numbers are small and everyone knows everyone, and everyone in the Jewish nonprofit sector has worked with everyone else, and your colleague is your aunt's first boyfriend from twenty years ago, and your boss shared a room at college with your cousin's best friend, and your main contact at the charity you're carrying out research for used to go to the same synagogue as the person you invited to give the keynote speech at your departmental*

*conference, and so on. This tight web of social connections can
make it harder to speak out when something does not feel right.*

The elaborate connectivity can also cause harm to victims because it sullies many aspects of their lives. Zelda, who was abused by her synagogue rabbi, ended up losing her entire social and spiritual connection to Jewish communal life. Similarly, when Brenda was abused by the rabbi at the synagogue that she had been affiliated with for over twenty years, she felt her entire life fall apart. "I can't go to services when he is leading them. I think to myself, 'I'll *daven* by myself.' I'm now almost at a point of emotional detachment. I've had to compartmentalize my religious life in these terms." When she turned to the community for help, she said, "I felt so unsupported by my community," which further pained her. "The way the synagogue handled it and has refused to respond in any meaningful way has been devastating to me." Rabbi Mary Zamore explained. "The fact that we are such a small, intertwined community perpetuates some of the culture because the victims are concerned about ruining their reputations in the community, and we are not strong enough in standing up to abusers because they are members of the communit, friends or family."

"Community" means that abusers are almost always beloved by someone — often high-profile community members. Shira Berkovits of Sacred Spaces, one of the leading experts on this issue, explained that, "The abusers never look the way you think they are going to look. It is never the overtly 'bad' guy. It's always someone's neighbor or best friend or college roommate or father-in-law's business partner. There is so much overlap, and that's one of the reasons why abusers get so much support." This is the dilemma of Jewish communal life. Everyone is interconnected, and these connections are encouraged. But they can be a nightmare for someone experiencing sexual abuse.

When this happens — when members of one's community fail to protect victims out of commitment to the abusers — that "hurts more," says Anne. Moira said, "it breaks your heart more than when it happens in Hollywood. It takes a bigger emotional toll." Anne elaborated:

*My expectations of Judaism are different. I expect us to be
better. And maybe that's wrong, too, but I think it ends up
hurting more when I realize that we're no better, we're just as
capable of doing this. It hurts more when frankly it's people
we're idolizing, people we look up to, when our leaders are
behaving this way... We need to be telling leaders that they
are going to be held to a standard of behavior. Or should be.
What really hurts more is the willingness to look aside. When
the head rabbi is told over and over that there was a senior staff*

> *member who was abusing children and he hires him again, that*
> *hurts more.*

The community culture is one in which people who are considered too valuable to lose will be able to get away with abuse.

The long-term damage of one's own community protecting abusers is perhaps not fully appreciated. At Cheryl Moore wrote:

> *It has often been said that for bad things to happen, good people*
> *have to stay silent. Until staffers and volunteer leaders of*
> *organizations step up and call people out for disrespectful and*
> *inappropriate behavior, it will continue. Until the dignity of*
> *one young woman is equal to the million-dollar donation (and*
> *even all of the people that will benefit from that donation), it*
> *will continue. Until people accept that the generous but*
> *handsy guy needs to be more closely watched, it will continue.*
> *It is too late for me though. I'm never coming back.*

Finally, a recurring theme about how the Jewish community envelops abusers is in what several interviewees described as "the bystander" phenomenon. The silence surrounding abuse — as illustrated by the 200 people who witnessed Steinhardt's public harassment, or the people sitting at Cheryl Moore's table while she was being pressured to sleep with a donor — is hard to comprehend. It reflects this notion that certain abusers are too valuable to lose, and the fearfulness in the face of power or status. For some interviewees, the bystander silence was even more painful than the abuse itself.

In fact, several people mentioned that it's the culture of enabling that has been most hurtful. When victims come forward, if they are believed and supported, that opens up a path to healing and functionality. However, if the people to whom they disclose respond with disbelief, blaming, accusations, or worse (e.g., getting fired), this can often lead to years of secondary trauma and PTSD that may interfere with basic functioning such as holding a job or maintaining marriage and relationships. This is consistent with the larger issue of sexual abuse. As Shira Berkovits explained to me, when victims of sexual abuse come forward, the response that they receive upon disclosure can create a secondary trauma that is at times worse than the trauma of abuse itself.

Co-opting Jewish values to silence victims

Another uniquely Jewish aspect of sexual abuse is how Jewish values are co-opted to protect abusers.

Anti-Semitism

The language of anti-Semitism is a uniquely Jewish idea that is at times used to silence victims and protect abusers, as I brought up in the introduction to this chapter. It can also be a tool to lure victims by creating a sense of "togetherness." One interviewee described how her attacker, the only other Jewish person in the office, tried to bond with her over their need to find protection from anti-Semitism in the office. That bonding, in his mind, meant going to his hotel room alone after hours.

It may also instill in some women a fearfulness about the world, and the message that Jews need to be silent in the fact of threats. When Lena, for example, a child of Holocaust survivors, was being attacked, she didn't scream or yell, or even make a noise:

> I think some of that is my upbringing. We were taught non-verbally not to call attention to yourself. But I didn't run out or get my father... I didn't scream. I didn't want to call attention. My message growing up in my environment, I got this message that as a woman, as a Jewish woman, I was not supposed to be vocal. I was not supposed to express the deepest searches of my soul, could not pursue my passion of music, all these things were suppressed because my parents came from a different era, a different country, and their values were different. I internalized being quiet. So, I never called out. Never screamed, just shriveled up inside in the moment

The idea that the world is a fearful place for Jews — especially Jewish women — can be deeply embedded in victims, and tragically support terrified silence.

Another related theme is that victims must stay silent for the survival of the Jewish collective. This idea is sometimes expressed as the need to protect Israel. In one head-splitting comment on the Steinhardt article, for example, the commenter with the BDS conspiracy theory wrote, "Support for Israel will remain strong despite your attempts to chip away at it and make anti-Semitism okay again." This may sound like a crazy rambling troll who hates women, liberals, and non-Jews. But the notion that accusations need to be silenced for the sake of Israel is real. When an aide to then-Israel Prime Minister Bibi Netanyahu was accused of sexual abuse, for example, the story quickly went away. "The last thing the state of Israel needs is for the person representing us to be a slimeball," one interviewee commented. "This is in the worst interest of Israel. We have to live above all reproach. We cannot have anything that can ever bring us bad publicity. It speaks for the entire country." (In Israel, at least, it is worth mentioning that the top offender — former president Moshe Katsav — went on trial for rape and was convicted and served a jail sentence.)

The idea that victims of abuse by high-profile Jewish offenders should stay silent so as not to endanger Israel or the Jews is a very real trope. Perhaps it is about a generations-long fearfulness and need to control the external narrative about Jews. Or maybe it is just an excuse to protect abusers. As Felicia, who was abused by an Israeli professor, said, "I share this story in a Jewish context partly because this is Israel, a real place, with real, fallible people, and American Jews should stop idealizing Israel. Just as we should stop idealizing the Jewish community as one big happy family and admit that sexual assault and harassment happen here too."

Lashon Hara

One of the primary Jewish concepts used to silence victims is the principle of *"lashon hara,"* the prohibition against speaking ill about another person. Lashon hara is frequently invoked, especially in the Orthodox community, when victims come forward in a way that can damage the offender's reputation. In research by Sara Zalcberg on sexual abuse in the Orthodox community, lashon hara was cited as one of the key factors preventing victims from disclosing their abuse.[250] Malka Leifer, for example, who is on trial in Australia for sexually abusing students in the Australian yeshivah where she worked as headmistress, was protected in her ultra-Orthodox community for a long time due to, among other things, socialization around lashon hara.[251]

But it isn't just the Orthodox community. This precept lies behind an entire practice of protecting the reputations of abusers. As Leah explained, "Lashon hara is just a way of shutting people up. It's the same as when they say about young men, like Brock Turner, 'Don't ruin this poor guy's life.' It's basically just devaluing victims."

Significantly, there is a direct link between the willingness to violate lashon hara rules and the ability to protect people from sexual predators. As Rachel Sadalow-Ash wrote in a 2017 article in *Lilith* called, "In Defense of Lashon Hara":

> [G]ossip keeps us safe. When I was a sophomore in college, an acquaintance of mine saw me leave a party with a male classmate whom I had just met. That acquaintance texted a mutual friend that he was worried about me; the mutual friend, in turn, texted me, 'I lived on the same freshman hall as Dave, and a couple of women on our hall told me that he's pretty bad

---

[250] Sara Zalcberg, "Culture and Religion in Patterns of Disclosure"

[251] Sam Sokol, "Child advocates blast systemic failures in Israel's handling of sex abuse cases. Political culture, stringent slander laws, inadequate sentencing and a taboo against reporting make it difficult to prosecute suspects, critics say," *Times of Israel*, 3 July 2019 https://www.timesofIsrael.com/child-advocates-blast-systemic-failures-in-Israels-handling-of-sex-abuse-cases/

> *about consent.' When I received her text, just before I got to Dave's dorm, I told Dave that I was tired, turned around, and left. I will never know for sure, but my friends' and classmates' gossip may have prevented me from being sexually assaulted that night… Because women gossiped, they helped protect not just their friends, but also women whom they did not know… [G]ossip undeniably reduces harm.*[252]

While the *idea* of lashon hara — whether those precise words are used or not — is often invoked to protect abusers, the willingness to break with those norms is what protects victims and potential victims.

It isn't just lashon hara. Other Jewish ideas that are rooted in Orthodoxy are carried into many other settings to protect abusers. Values such as "*kavod harav*" — respecting rabbis; "*shalom bayit*" — maintaining peace in the home; and even "teshuva" — the ability to repent, are easily invoked in the process of silencing victims. These values, which sound lovely when they stand alone without context, can take on sinister implications when a rabbi or communal leader has been abusive and members of the community want to speak out.

Teshuva

Indeed, the Jewish concept of teshuva has been gaining traction in protecting abusers well beyond Orthodoxy. The idea that a community may decide to "forgive" the abuser and keep him in his job because they trust that he feels bad about it, is being echoed even outside of Jewish circles. Calls for engaging in communal teshuva have also been sounded by activists promoting restorative justice.[253]

Such is the language, for example, that the congregation led by Rabbi Jeremy Gerber used in defending their decision to keep him on after he admitted to having sexually pursued a congregant — who is married, as was he at the time. He was working together with his victim on a synagogue project, and he used that connection as an opportunity to pressure her to have sex with him. She reported this, he was censured by the Conservative movement, and then the synagogue voted to keep him on as rabbi because they said he did teshuva.[254]

---

[252] Rachel Sandalow-Ash, "In Defense of Lashon Hara," *Lilith* April 25, 2017 https://lilith.org/2017/04/in-defense-of-lashon-hara/

[253] Alissa Ackerman and Guila Benchimol, "Restorative Justice and Teshuva Following Sexual Misconduct," *e-Jewish Philanthropy*, September 12, 2018, https://ejewishphilanthropy.com/restorative-justice-and-teshuva-following-sexual-misconduct/

[254] Arno Rosenfeld, "How a rabbi suspended for sexual abuse gets to keep his pulpit," *Forward*, Feb 9 2022, https://forward.com/news/482269/rabbi-suspension-sexual-misconduct-gerber-conservative-rabbincal-assembly/

Abuse survivor Rakhel Silverman, who was given a pamphlet on forgiveness by a rabbi while she was in trauma recovery, described the torment that language of teshuva gives her and other survivors:

> *Why are we more focused on making victims forgive than we are on supporting and validating them?... We must recognize the harm that teshuvah and its forgiveness rhetoric can do to survivors of any kind of mistreatment. We must also be accountable to how Jewish customs can be used to perpetuate victim blaming... So, survivors... [y]ou have nothing to apologize or repent for. Do not let anyone tell you that you must focus on your abuser. What happened to you was not your fault, so please forgive, accept, and love yourself.*[255]

Rabbi Danya Ruttenberg put it succinctly: "Forgiveness is up to the victim and the victim alone. Atonement is up to God."[256]

How does Jewish culture compare?

Most of the testimonies highlighted in this chapter described what interviewees believe to be uniquely Jewish aspects of sexual abuse — forms of denial, Jewish constructs of femininity, the interconnectedness of the community, and the co-opting of Jewish values like anti-Semitism, lashon hara, and teshuva. But is Jewish culture different than all other cultures when it comes to sexual abuse?

The answer is yes and no. While abuse happens everywhere there are nevertheless uniquely Jewish aspects, Leah said, for example. "We do have these silencing mechanisms and we do have these powerful people. The Jewish community does have its own dynamics of silencing, but everyone does; they are just different dynamics."

Several interviewees felt strongly that the Jewish world is "behind" the rest of the American community in terms of addressing sexual abuse. Sarah reflected that, from her experiences training Jewish organizations, "In the Jewish nonprofit world, there can be some glossing over some of these bigger issues. I've trained at synagogues where people can be like, 'We have a

---

[255] Rakhel Silverman, "The Harm of Tshuvah: A Letter from an Abuse Survivor," *Jewish Women's Archive*, September 12, 2018, https://jwa.org/blog/harm-of-tshuvah-letter-from-abuse-survivor

[256] Danya Ruttenberg "Famous abusers seek easy forgiveness. Rosh Hashanah teaches us repentance is hard," *Washington Post*, September 6, 2018 https://www.washingtonpost.com/outlook/famous-abusers-seek-easy-forgiveness-rosh-hashanah-teaches-us-repentance-is-hard/2018/09/06/c2dc2cac-b0ab-11e8-9a6a-565d92a3585d_story.html

female cantor so we're so progressive,' but they treat their women staff terribly." Rena, who lives in a small midwestern Jewish community, concurs that her community "is probably 20 years behind the more progressive places in the country. Around Jewish issues, around gender issues, around all the places where they intersect. There is just no awareness. And the conversations happening elsewhere are very different from the conversations happening here."

Without a comprehensive, comparative quantitative research study, there is no accurate way to know exactly how the Jewish community fares vis a vis other communities. But what emerges from this qualitative study is that there are uniquely Jewish codes and norms that contribute to the problem — Jewish cultural ideas and practices that protect abusers, silence victims, and inhibit healing and justice.

Takeaways about Jewish responses

- **Anti-Semitism and Israel are easy cards to play**. Defenders of the accused use these rationales with great ease to discredit victims.
- **Orthodox practices offer excuses, not protections**. "Modest" dress and prohibitions of touch can serve as rhetoric for victim-blaming, suggesting that womena and girls who segregate and cover-up do not get abused. But this is merely rhetoric aimed at further hurting victims, and in fact those rules do not protect women from being abused. In fact, they can make women and girls targets, making them appear pure, innocent, or easy prey for certain abuers.
- **Yichud may restrict women's risk, but that is also victim-blaming, potentially oppressive, and not a solution**. The suggestion that "yichud"—a prohibition against a woman and a man being alone in a room together—protects women from abuse is not uncommon. But this argument is a red herring, and as a practice, severely limits women's movements as well as professional opportunities, and does not protect victims. Nevertheless, it is quite telling that not only patriarchal men (like Mike Pence) but also some Orthodox women who have experienced abuse see this as their most viable protection. It is as if to say, gender segregation is women's best solution. This is a dangerous fallacy and a self-defeating set of instructions that remains alive in the culture.
- **Jewish constructs of femininity also hurt victims**. Perceptions of women as babymakers who should be modest, demure, and in servitude of the Jewish collective also play into cultural dynamics that support abuse.

- **Religious men are not more "safe" than others**. Religious dress is one of many codes that are intended to make some people appear "safe." But this, too, is a dangerous fallacy.
- **All denominational communities have dangers**. It is common for people to believe that abuse happens in "other" denominations, but they are all misconceptions. It happens everywhere. And many codes that are assumed to be Orthodox have versions that are found nearly everywhere, such as lashon hara and teshuva.
- **Lashon hara remains a powerful silencing technique across communities**. The pressure not to speak out is often couched in this religious prohibition not to "gossip." Even in non-Orthodox settings, this precept is cast as not "airing dirty laundry" or not damaging the abuser's reputation, the community, or Israel.
- **Excessive Jewish connectivity blurs boundaries.** Jewish abusers often have deep communal support networks that make it difficult for victims to come forward. Abusers are usually "involved" and "connected," and as such it can be hard to hold them accountable. There can also be a lack of boundaries in communal spaces that make it easy for abusers to act on their predilections.
- **The community still values donors above all.** As Cheryl Moore wrote, the donor is far more likely to get community support than the person who was victimized by them.
- **The Jewish community seems to be behind**. Many interviewees feel that Judaism is behind the rest of the Western world on this issue. We do not have hard data on that, but perhaps it would be helpful to know how we measure up in terms of protecting our communities from abuse. The need for more information about all these issues is urgent.

Part IV: The Impacts

I just want to sleep. A coma would be nice. Or amnesia. Anything, just to get rid of this, these thoughts, whispers in my mind. Did he rape my head, too?

Laurie Halse Anderson, *Speak*

Chapter 11: Impacts on the Victims

Much has been written about the impacts of sexual abuse on victims. A 2017 meta-review of hundreds of papers on this subject found the impacts on the victims are likely to include the following:

- **Emotional wellbeing and mental health** Emotional distress, trauma/PTSD, anxiety, depression, retraumatization

- **Interpersonal relationships:** Reduced relationship satisfaction and stability, issues with intimacy and parent-child relationships

- **Physical health:** Physical injuries, weight/food struggles, problems related to childbirth, unexplained medical problems
- **Religious and spiritual belief:** Disillusionment with religion when the abuser is from the religion, or alternatively intense religiosity as a coping mechanism
- **Externalizing behaviors:** Substance misuse, 'risky' and inappropriate sexual behaviors, offending
- **Socioeconomic:** Lower educational attainment, higher unemployment, financial instability, homelessness
- **Vulnerability to revictimization:** Sexual revictimization in childhood and adulthood, other types of victimization.[257]

There is some research specifically on how these factors play out in the Orthodox Jewish community. One 2021 study of 372 Jewish community members found that people who experienced CSA showed significantly higher anxiety and depression as well as negative religious coping than those without CSA.[258] Another 2015 study of impacts of CSA on Orthodox men found that those who experienced abuse (25 percent of the sample) were more likely to have depression and hypersexual activity.[259] One study of sexual abuse among married Orthodox women found that women who experienced abuse (26 percent) suffered more than the sample group with depression, marital issues, and other emotional or psychological issues for which they sought treatment.[260] Another study of Orthodox women's experiences with ritual immersion before sexual activity found that women who had a history of sexual abuse struggled more with the practice than women who did not.[261] A 2015 study of Orthodox and secular Israeli women found that those who suffered sexual abuse exhibited similar trauma

---

[257] Cate Fisher, Alexandra Goldsmith, Rachel Hurcombe, Claire Soares, "The impacts of child sexual abuse: A rapid evidence assessment," *ICSA Research Team*, July 2017
https://uobrep.openrepository.com/bitstream/handle/10547/624859/iicsa-impacts-child-sexual-abuse-rapid-evidence-assessment-full-report-english.pdf?sequence=2

[258] Miriam D. Korbman, Steven Pirutinsky, Eva L. Feindler David H. Rosmarin, "Childhood Sexual Abuse, Spirituality/Religion, Anxiety and Depression in a Jewish Community Sample: the Mediating Role of Religious Coping," *Journal of Interpersonal Violence*, March 17, 2021, https://doi.org/10.1177/08862605211001462

[259] Fagin, C. Gabriel, "The Moderating Effect of Religion and Spirituality On the Relationship Between Childhood Sexual Abuse And Negative Outcomes Among a Sample of Orthodox Jewish Men," *Doctoral dissertation, Yeshiva University*. 2015
https://www.proquest.com/openview/950f5ee8ce84e36ac604a07ab171f4a1/1?pq-origsite=gscholar&cbl=18750

[260] Yehuda R, Friedman M, Rosenbaum TY, Labinsky E, Schmeidler J. "History of past sexual abuse in married observant Jewish women," *Am J Psychiatry*. 2007 Nov;164(11):1700-6. doi: 10.1176/appi.ajp.2007.06122030. PMID: 17974935.

[261] Naomi Rosenbach, Michael J Salamon & Leora Levine (2021) "What impacts Jewish orthodox women's mikvah experience?" *Journal of Religion & Spirituality in Social Work: Social Thought*, 40:3, 239-251, DOI: 10.1080/15426432.2021.1912687

impacts.[262] A literature review of sexual abuse in the Orthodox Jewish community also found that the impacts of abuse resembled impacts among the community at large.[263] In short, victims of sexual abuse in the Orthodox community seem to struggle with many of the same trauma responses as everyone else.

To my knowledge, there are no studies specifically on impacts of sexual abuse in Jewish communities outside of the Orthodox community. The question of why this is so deserves some communal attention and checking of attitudes.

Almost all of the trauma impacts described in the research found expression with my interviewees, suggesting that when it comes to the impacts of abuse on victims, the Jewish community is roughly like everyone else, give or take, with a few unique aspects.

Emotional Impacts

Interviewees' testimonies were replete with emotional impacts, mostly similar to those experienced in the population at large.

Anger

Many interviewees expressed anger at different issues. Abby, who experienced many forms of abuse over the course of her career as a rabbi, was angry at feeling silenced, powerless, and infantilized. She said, "It makes you so angry. And you have to be polite and not say anything. Because I was a professional and couldn't say anything. But there's so many moments like that and you just want to scream, and you can't. Or if you do, you get, 'Well, isn't that cute,' demeaning your concerns about those kinds of statements. I had all those kinds of feelings." Odelia said, "It has made me more wary, and angry. It's emotionally exhausting."

These are reminiscent of descriptions I brought up in previous chapters about the crushing impact of having to be "nice." Again, socialization into "niceness" can be oppressive and even dangerous.

Some people were angry at the sexism and double standards. As Abby said, "There's times when you know that there is no way that they would ever say those things to a man." Similarly, Gail said, "I am so heartsick at all

---

[262] Feinson MC, Meir A. "Exploring mental health consequences of childhood abuse and the relevance of religiosity." *J Interpers Violence*. 2015 Feb;30(3):499-521. doi: 10.1177/0886260514535094.

[263] Lusky-Weisrose E, Marmor A, Tener D. "Sexual Abuse in the Orthodox Jewish Community: A Literature Review," *Trauma Violence Abuse*. 2020 Feb 13:1524838020906548. doi: 10.1177/1524838020906548. .

this. Because our stories just don't count. They don't matter." This anger is at the entire system that allows abuse to happen.

Perhaps the #MeToo movement has allowed space for anger to emerge. As Helen suggested, "I think women are getting mad, and I think many men did not realize that pretty much every woman they know has gone through some kind of harassment or sexual assault or something."

Guilt and shame

Another emotional impact is the feeling of guilt or shame, feelings that seem to be connected, and which were already present in the discussion about why victims don't report. "I was a total wreck," Brenda said. Kayla, for example, said, "I felt such shame… thinking it was my fault somehow as he thought I was a liberated woman, and tremendous shame because he was a rabbi." Similarly, Melanie said, "how ashamed I was… how stupid I was for going with him… I put myself in this situation… how could I have been so fucking dumb!" Marion said, "As a repetition of the conditioning I got from my father, I thought everything must have been my fault." Hannah said, "You wonder what you did to deserve it even though you know better; there is still a place where you wonder… my fault, my shame." Cheryl Moore, in her essay about years of sexual abuse while working as a Jewish communal volunteer, wrote, "Each of those interactions left me feeling ashamed and wondering what it was about me that projected that I would go along."

Leanne also felt guilt about being abused and felt the need to protect her abuser:

> When I was 13 on that religious school retreat dealing with the inappropriate teacher, one of the major feelings I had that guided my behavior was guilt. Was I being fair to HIM? How could I complain about his behavior without saying something to him directly? I felt like I was betraying HIM! It made me feel terrible. Was I being a bad person because I told someone about the behavior rather than say something to him? I was 13 and he was 30, and I was uncomfortable and he was being inappropriate in his physical and verbal behavior to me. I was in terrible distress, and yet one of my biggest concerns was whether I was being fair to him. I remember this feeling like it was yesterday.
>
> It amazes me as I look back on it, because I know I am a product of a 'himpathetic' culture, how women [feel we] are responsible for men's behavior and actions.

"Himpathetic culture," a term coined by feminist scholar Kate Manne, is the centering of men's needs, even men who are abusive or violent.[264] A classic illustration is Leanne's worry for the man who hurt her, shrouded in guilt and responsibility for what happened, and enmeshed in shame that she has all these feelings.

Brenda, too, kept her story to herself "partly because I didn't want to embarrass the rabbi. Partly because I had my own mixed feelings about it. Partly because it had a sense of confidentiality about it, it felt private. Maybe I felt guilty, I don't know." Even today, years later, victims still struggle with feelings of shame and guilt.

These "himpathetic" feelings are possibly a result of a combination of factors: the grooming tactics of gaslighting, the socialization into female niceness, and the particular way Jews are socialized to revere rabbis. Victims, no matter what they are going through, so often seem to be concerned about the rabbi. And as a result, they so often doubt themselves and blame themselves. The victims' frequent sense that rabbis don't do this sort of thing, or the cognitive dissonance of "This feels weird, but I can't explain why," is a function of being told both by the community and by the abuser that this can't be right, that the rabbi isn't abusing them, that there is something wrong with their thoughts and feelings. It is often an entire community and an entire culture that "himpathizes," that puts the needs and reputation of the abuser over and above those of the victim. When it comes to rabbi-abusers, victims are reporting gaslighting—himpathizing on a communal scale. And thus, the impacts of all that on the victim—guilt, shame, anger, confusion—make complete sense.

For Orthodox women, there can be added layers of self- blame due to cultural norms, especially around gender. As Yael explained:

> *Even if you're not touched, the fact that a man might pursue you, you might be perceived as asking for it, that you presented yourself in a certain way that was inappropriate. Or you shouldn't have been in that situation. You shouldn't have been on your own. You shouldn't have this career. You shouldn't be at a hotel. You shouldn't have been talking to a man. In the evening. Even though it was a work-related conversation. That is the attitude.*

In Orthodoxy, there are so many added rules of gendered behavior that these can pile on to the feelings of guilt and self-blame.

---

[264] Kate Manne, *Down Girl: The Logic of Misogyny*, Oxford University Press 2017 p 200

Anxiety

Many victims struggle with forms of anxiety for years or even decades after the abuse. Rhonda Abrams described "great distress" right after her abuse and said, "I was shaking." Other people described prolonged anxiety. Leanne, for example, said, "I had a lot of anxiety, trauma responses, that I worked through in college. But there have been hard times. The experiences created a lot of self-doubt, a lot of sadness, a lot of feeling like there was something wrong with me." Marion said, "The event threw me into depression and shame."

Lara described ongoing anxieties:

> The end result of all these experiences is my terrible paranoia. When I walk down the street, if I'm anywhere where I'm walking, I'm always turning around. If there is a man behind me, I have a terrible paranoia of what's going on behind me, a fear of someone coming up behind me and immediately putting their hands on my breasts.

Depression, suicide, and PTSD

Connected to anxiety, many interviewees described variations of PTSD, depression, and suicidal ideation.

Dina, who was nearly raped by a religious-looking man in Jerusalem, said, "I definitely had PTSD from this, and every time I saw a man in a white shirt in Jerusalem, I was terrified." Drori said, "I don't feel safe anymore. I've had mental health diagnoses of depression, PTSD, and suicidal ideation." Hinda, who was sexually and emotionally abused by her father, said, "I suffered from what we now know as PTSD. I was afraid to talk to strangers, even on the telephone, for fear of once again becoming a victim. Although very successful in college, earning two bachelor's degrees, two master's degrees, and a small part of a doctorate, I had little or no feelings of self-worth, with the notable exception of when I was teaching." Lucy described it as follows:

> For a long time, this was a trauma I deeply embedded in my psyche and told no one. I ended up with PTSD that came to the surface when I was a sophomore in college from abuse I suffered when I was 12. I didn't know what was going on, who to talk to, or even what had really happened. I suppressed it for many years. After a lot of therapy and some meds, I was able to manage my anxiety and speak publicly about my assault at Take Back the Night in 2006. I am now a proud survivor and speak about it often.

For some victims, everyday survival is a struggle. Esther disclosed that she had been hospitalized for depression only a few months before our interview. "I went to residential treatment for trauma in February and to an intensive outpatient program in March. I struggle to survive, every day."

Cindy was suicidal as a result of her abuse and was saved only by thoughts of her children. "I contemplated suicide to get out. I thought about how I could land myself in the hospital just to get away. I considered checking myself into a psychiatric ward. I fantasized about getting in my car and driving forever, but I could not do something so horrible to my children."

Alyssa, who was also abused by her father, said, "The sexual abuse has made my life a terrible struggle. I suffer from complex PTSD, Major Depression Disorder, and Generalized Anxiety Disorder. I also have an eating disorder. I cannot hold a full-time job. I actually think that, given the torture I experienced for so many years, I think I'm doing pretty well overall."

The experience of not being believed upon disclosure is potentially so devastating that it is referred to as "secondary trauma" or "retraumatization." Research shows that when victims experience retraumatization, it can have long-term impacts, especially on issues of trust, hypervigilance, depression, and suicide.[265]

A common trigger in retraumatization is around not being believed. Zelda described severe retraumatization after reporting to the rabbinical ethics committee. When she finally gained the courage to come forward to committee, "the investigation was more harmful to me than the abuse itself. I almost killed myself during this investigation." The reason she became suicidal, she said, was because "when the fact-gathering team sent me their final report, they said that I said I enjoyed the rape." She added, as if she needed to defend herself against the claim that she enjoyed being raped, "I never said that!" Telling a victim that they wanted the abuse is mind-numbingly gaslighting. "They also said that they viewed the relationship as consensual, and that this goes against everything we know. I even talked to researchers at Yale University about sexual abuse by clergy," Zelda added. "They have published papers titled, 'It's Not an Affair—It's Abuse.'" Zelda, like so many victims, spent a lot of time having conversations with herself to remind herself of what she knows, in order to avoid drowning in retraumatizing triggers.

---

[265] See for example, Stephanie J. Dallam, "A model of the retraumatization process: A meta-synthesis of childhood sexual abuse survivors' experiences in healthcare," Submitted to the graduate degree program in Nursing and the Graduate Faculty of the University of Kansas in partial fulfillment of the requirements for the degree of Doctor of Philosophy. 2010 https://kuscholarworks.ku.edu/bitstream/handle/1808/6373/Dallam_ku_0099D_10726_DATA_1.pdf?sequence=1&isAllowed=y

Self-concept

Many victims described damage to their own self-concept or sense of self. As Sybil Sanchez wrote about years of sexism in her career as a Jewish professional:

> [I]t all took a toll. I was never happy or secure. I chronically doubted the impact of my efforts. I worked on my vision as a leader, but it felt shallow as all I could see was a minefield of obstacles... A senior colleague casually joked that I had a penchant for the intractable. He had no idea how true that rang nor how deeply it stung... I was fighting too many battles alone and on too many fronts, and I felt like I was spinning my wheels.

Cindy said, "As a young woman I really thought I knew myself. I really thought I had a grip on who I was, where I came from, and where I was going. I got blindsided and derailed."

Wendy stopped speaking up. "When I told my family and a couple of women in the department and got back that it was both my fault and not a big deal, I stopped wanting to share. I feared it made *me* look inappropriate or slutty or like I didn't belong. That's a big part of the power with these things. It comes from men not being comfortable that you're there, and you end up really getting the message." Similarly, Sybil Sanchez said, "I was affected. I never took all the space in the room or at the table. I always had a lot of self-consciousness about my role in anything I did. I swallowed a lot of negative comments and negative dynamics and just took them as de facto."

On the other hand, Wendy also feels that the work she did on herself after the abuse made her a better person and better member of community:

> I became more thoughtful and inspired about creating spaces that are healthy and learned a lot about how an overall environment that undervalues humans plays out along these structurally placed fault lines of gender, class, race. I was able to pursue interests in other areas and perhaps am being guided toward somewhere else, a different life or purpose more suited to my needs or to the world's. I also was directed more toward my own health and relationships. Overall, I'm a better person. I think the costs of being able to participate in a demoralized competitive system are also high. I like my life and I am often glad that I left.

Perhaps it is true that what doesn't kill you makes you stronger. But this sounds like a tormenting path to get there.

Impacts on relationships

In addition to emotional impacts such as anxiety, depression, and PTSD, many victims also struggle with relationships — especially intimate relationships and sex.

Dating

Some women changed their behavior vis-à-vis men after their abuse. You may recall that Nicole said that she changed her dating habits and no longer prefers Jewish boys because that was, in her words, "naïve." Charley also said that "one of the reasons to date Jews is that they have the same values as you, and if that's not accurate, I wasn't any safer in the Jewish community, so there was no reason not to explore outside of the community." Nancy, said, "I was extremely cautious of men I didn't know. It didn't help me with men I did know. I was extremely cautious being alone with a man or being in a room with a man I didn't know." Similarly, Dina described the impact on dating:

> When I was raped, it completely changes the way that you live, the way you behave, and the way you interact with other people, especially men. I started never being alone with a man, even if it's a good friend, because the guy who assaulted me the first time was a good friend. I would not drink to the point of intoxication around another man because it makes you more vulnerable. I had made great male friends in Israel who would invite me to go on a road trip or whatever, but I told them that sounds great, but I simply do not go out alone with another man anywhere unless I'm dating that person, in which case the benefit outweighed the risk. I completely changed my lifestyle.

Sex

Not surprisingly, several respondents reported difficulty in sexuality following experiences of sexual abuse. Marion said, "I felt toxic, that my body was a neon sign for predators. I went numb from the waist down for a couple decades. Lots and lots of therapy. Lots of it. More than lots." Hinda said, "I have never been able to maintain a healthy sexual relationship. Many years of therapy have helped me come to appreciate myself and allowed me to finally make a number of good, long-standing friends, but I am to this day plagued by the loneliness that is a result of so much that I have experienced in my life."

Other women described abstinence or difficulty in sex, even with their husbands. Hallel said, "This nightmare has haunted me all my life, seared into my mind, polluting my memory and affecting every adult relationship

I've ever had." Lila's marriage was also affected. "I found I couldn't trust men, including my husband. I feared that he, too was mistreating women and not realizing it." Zelda said, "I can't even fathom sex because it just makes me think that I'm an object. I can't even have sex with my husband. I've been abstinent since the whole thing. I'm so screwed up from all this."

Risha was also affected in not knowing how to trust the sexual intentions of men. "My attitude toward men changed. My father was very empathic, compassionate, kind, and generous. However, on the other hand, I saw my brother and his friends use women as 'fuck objects.' So, I saw both 'kinds' of men, the best and the worst. And then I was attacked by one of the worst who saw me as a 'fuck object' and felt he was entitled to attack me and rape me." As a result, it was hard for her to know what "kind" of man she would encounter.

Some women changed sexual behaviors in other ways. Charley said, "I really like sex and sexuality, I like to talk about it and teach it. But I'm now much more careful how I talk to men about it."

Loneliness

Related to the traumatic impacts around dating and sexuality is loneliness. Some of this started at the time of the abuse. Zelda's abuser purposely isolated her in her own community. Esther's abuser did the same. Daniel, who was assaulted by his rabbi, said that his suffered from isolation after coming forward. Kayla similarly reports that "For the next 16 years I moved all over the country, running from my feelings. When I came home to New York, I got clean and sober and the memories of what had happened with Rabbi X surfaced. I initially wanted to do something drastic. I have never married." For some victims, the loneliness is palpable. Alyssa said, "I am 50 years old and have never married or had children, though I wanted those things very much for myself."

Losing trust and faith

Sexual abuse that takes place within a faith community can have devastating effects on trust issues, especially when there is secondary trauma, but not only. As Chuck DeGroat writes in his book, *When Narcissism Comes to Church*, "Spiritual abuse bears a particularly sinister twist, as principles and maxims of faith are wielded as weapons of command and control."[266]

An abundance of research on sexual abuse in the Catholic Church points to a direct impact of abuse on victims' faith. The most outstanding impacts are loss of trust— although, perhaps counter-intuitively, some victims strengthen their faith by looking toward their faith for help and guidance in healing. A meta-analysis of 34 studies examining the impact of sexual abuse on spirituality and religiousness that looked at a total of nearly 20,000 participants found that religiousness and faith are often deeply impacted by the abuse. In 14 studies, sexual abuse led to a decline in religious belief or spirituality. Survivors reported that they were distrustful of God, felt more distant toward God than non-abuse survivors, and believed that God was harsh and critical. In addition, a number of participants also reported that they wondered if God still loved them after abuse had occurred. In 12 studies, some victims experienced a decline in religious beliefs.[267] Research on impacts in the Jewish world are less comprehensive at the moment. A 2010 study of Orthodox Jewish women who experienced sexual abuse, called "Losing my Religion," found that nearly 50 percent moved toward secularization as a result of the abuse.[268]

Comparable quantitative research specifically on how sexual abuse by rabbis impacts the victim's relationship with Judaism does not, to my knowledge, exist.

Losing faith in rabbis and Judaism

The overall theme of losing trust emerged in many interviews. The loss of trust was often directed in ways that reflected the identity of the abusers. Blima, for example, said the assault made her "more cynical and less trusting of men in general." Similarly, Janice said, "my naïve assumptions about the world were shattered with regard to powerful men in general." Ann described the feeling of "pushing people away." Dina, who was assaulted several times in different contexts and different countries, said, "I stopped trusting anyone. Whether he looked harmless or old, I just couldn't trust anyone because my safety was at risk. It changes you into a person who simply can't trust another man no matter who that is and often you couldn't

---

[266] Chuck DeGroat, *When Narcissism Comes to Church: Healing you community from emotional and spiritual abuse.* Illinois: Intervarsity Press, 2020 p 125

[267] Walker, D. F., Reid, H. W., O'Neill, T., & Brown, L. (2009). "Changes in personal religion/spirituality during and after childhood abuse: A review and synthesis," *Psychological Trauma: Theory, Research, Practice, and Policy,* 1(2), 130–145. https://doi.org/10.1037/a0016211

[268] Ben-Ezra, M., Palgi, Y., Sternberg, D., Berkley, D., Eldar, H., Glidai, Y., Moshe, L., & Shrira, A. (2010). "Losing my religion: A preliminary study of changes in belief pattern after sexual assault," *Traumatology,* 16(2), 7–13. https://doi.org/10.1177/1534765609358465

trust really good people because I was too afraid that I could get harmed or hurt."

When the abuser is a rabbi, especially one whom the victim trusted, the impact on trust in rabbis can be intensified. Kayla, who was molested by a rabbi to whom her parents sent her for guidance, said, "I felt such a mix of emotions and completely alone. Injured. A rabbi could do this?" Indeed, victims whose abuse was connected to rabbis described their belief systems and communal lives being affected. The fact that the abuser presents himself as the gatekeeper to religion left them with a severe spiritual and emotional crisis.[269]

Tanya, who was molested by a rabbi who would become famous, said he would visit her home for Shabbat when he was a 20-year-old college student. When he finally stopped abusing her, this is how she reacted:

> I would no longer be badgered by [his] teshuvah rhetoric, would no longer be forced to hear about his tormented struggle with his perverse sexuality and his Judaism. But I was no longer part of the normal, oblivious world of my friends and classmates. I was now set apart from them in a way that none of them knew or, as far as I could imagine, would ever know. I could not feel connected to anyone, or to my school or synagogue.
>
> The spiritual world of my earlier childhood had been taken from me. Shabbat was now connected to a nightmare. The concept of teshuvah was forever corrupted for me. I began to see hypocrisy and absurdity in a world that I once innocently felt was home. I was no longer anchored.

Similarly, Lisa Rabinowitz Dunn who was abused by Baruch Lanner said that his use of Jewish ideas "closed the door for religion" for her:

> His behavior was so hypocritical, singing about the wonders of Hashem and then chasing young girls. For me, it closed the door for religion, and while I have no sense of revenge, I feel that he took advantage of an innocent soul, and you can never get that innocence back.[270]

Leanne also changed her relationship to Judaism after her abuser was allowed to lead services. "How were we supposed to take his divrei torah

---

[269] Victor I. Vieth, Basyle Tchividjian, "When the Child Abuser Has a Bible: Investigating Child Maltreatment Sanctioned or Condoned by a Religious Leader," *Centerpiece*, Volume 2, Issue 12: 2010, NCPTC https://www.zeroabuseproject.org/wp-content/uploads/2019/02/e8299da4-centerpiece-vol-2-issue-12.pdf

[270] Rosenblatt, "Stolen Innocence," https://www.bjpa.org/content/upload/bjpa/stol/Stolen%20Innocence%20-%20Gary%20Rosenblatt%20-%20Jewish%20Week%20-%20Sexual%20Abuse.pdf

seriously or daven with him as *shaliach tzibur* when we were also told to watch out for him and to avoid being alone with him? Do you see how this makes no sense?" For Zelda, the fact that her abuser was still running the synagogue left her so deeply distrustful of the world that she felt suicidal:

> When I saw that he was still on the bima after his censure, seeing him in all white and the prayer shawl talking about justice and compassion and respect, and I know he's kicking holes in the wall and hitting his wife and verbally abusing her in horrible ways, and here he is in all white talking about forgiveness, it made me sick. I couldn't do it, I felt like I couldn't live in the world. I wanted to commit suicide... The despair of seeing duplicity of that depth and an utter and complete disregard for human life and the sacredness of sexuality, a complete and total absence of soul. I witnessed a darkness and emptiness that was so extreme, profound, and severe that it was traumatic in and of itself. I never thought such a thing existed in this world. I'm so screwed up from all this.

The source of her trauma and pain was up on the podium being revered by the community. "He destroyed my trust."

Cindy similarly said, "If a rabbi esteemed in his community can be like this, then really nowhere is safe." Esther said, "Because my relationship with the rabbi and my relationship with God had become one and the same, losing my relationship with one meant losing my relationship with the other. I still cannot separate the two. Every time I reach out to God in love, I find the rabbi and his betrayals, the scapegoating by the community, and the sheer pain and loss of those many years, right in the center. It breaks my heart."

Brenda, who spent 20 years as a senior lay leader in her synagogue, had a similar experience of spiritual crisis after watching the hypocrisy of her abuser as the spiritual leader. "He's giving this whole talk about chesed, and like, I almost lost it, because everything he said was so filled with hypocrisy, it was exactly how he was not treating me," she explained. It was tormenting for her:

> I would go hear his sermons and my head would explode from the hypocrisy coming out of his mouth. I hate to go when he's there leading services. Like, he's not my shaliach tzibur... I am really struggling. I just want to get through the year — my term as a trustee will end in May, and done, I've been on the board for 14 years straight... I feel bad leaving it, but I need space and healing for myself.

Leanne avoids rabbis entirely. "I don't hang out with rabbis at all. I switched synagogues, and my younger daughter, to get ready for her bat mitzvah, I didn't even have a single meeting with the rabbi. We can't be shocked at all these stories." Charley has started going back to synagogue again, but only one that does not have an official rabbi. She says her synagogue has rabbis as congregants, and she is okay with that. "I want to know their whole humanity and not just the face they put forward as a leader because that doesn't feel real to me."

The abuser preaching with power from the pulpit while abusing congregants often causes a deep spiritual crisis for victims and often ends up isolating the victim instead of the abuser.

Losing trust in community

Many victims have distanced themselves from the Jewish community, its institutions, and its practices. Daniel, a rabbi who was assaulted by another rabbi and not supported in the reporting process, was affected in terms of communal trust and organizational trust. "One of the most painful things has been the loss of professional relationships — all for being a victim-survivor who wants to be the last. The movement absolutely can never again be trusted until they do some serious organizational teshuva around leaders tainted by misconduct, cruelty or incompetence resign." Leanne, who was harassed, stalked, and molested by several different rabbis during the course of her life, eventually left the synagogue, stopped reading Torah, and did not return to camp. She spent much of her life avoiding rabbis and Jewish communal life, which meant losing connections and spiritual and communal outlets.

Shlomit, whose abuse took place in the religious school where she worked as well as in her synagogue, also lost faith in her religious community. "I don't feel like the Orthodox community will ever protect my body or my rights the way I need to be protected. And I'm tired of giving them the chance and tired of apologizing for it and I will never ever give them the opportunity to hurt me again." Reut said that after her community continued to back the rabbi, "We basically immediately stopped going to that shul." Other people moved out of the neighborhood. "People who used to live here have moved away, including friends who and are still very disturbed by the fact that they left behind a community that hasn't been cleaned and cured of this plague."

Yittel, a formerly haredi woman who was raped by her rabbi when she was 21, made perhaps the most radical changes. "What he did to me has negatively affected the course of my life. I'm married to a non-Jewish man and have no religious affiliation."

Esther summarized the connections among these different aspects of trust: "I have no faith in God where once my faith was profound. I have no tie to a Jewish community that was once my life breath. I no longer sing, or pray, or trust other people. My dream of becoming a rabbi has long since died; I am now 60 years old. I have lost my people, my religion, my family, my vocation, and my belief in God."

Socioeconomic impacts

Career losses

For many victims, especially those whose abuse took place in a workplace, the abuse can have a devastating impact on work and career.

A 2018 study conducted by the Harris Poll on behalf of the AFP Foundation for Philanthropy and the Chronicle of Philanthropy found that among fundraising professionals who have experienced sexual harassment by a donor, more than one-third (35 percent) have felt a negative impact on their career through revealing their incidents of harassment. [271] But it isn't just fundraisers who are impacted. Marion, for example, who was abused while pursuing a music career, said, "I didn't pursue my composing or performing career any further. I felt toxic... I went numb... for a couple decades."

> I left the PhD program and the field, and the intervening years were plagued by doubt and underemployment. I've had a hard time imagining taking on a fresh intellectual challenge and having a different experience than the one I had before. Having my contribution not only not taken seriously but distorted into someone's sexual fantasy was profoundly humiliating. I suffered for years with exaggerated perceptions of others not speaking or listening to me as if I mattered. This made it impossible to think about gathering the confidence, mentorship, or resources to attempt a new endeavor that mattered. I have largely floated between odd jobs, and I panic whenever asked 'What do you do?'

Similarly, Vivian said, "I remained on the margins of academia for my entire career, not wanting to subject myself to playing the game for high stakes." Helen, who was abused by her professor and mentor in pursuit of an advanced academic degree in Middle Eastern studies with plans for an Israel-centric career, also dropped her ambitions as a result of the abuse:

> I lost my confidence. He gave me the feeling that I wasn't good enough. I can't prove that this made me not have a career. I

---

[271] AFP, "One-Quarter of All Female Fundraisers"https://afpglobal.org/one-quarter-all-female-fundraisers-report-sexual-harassment?fbclid=IwAR15drXFmHnHTyrcmLuxoH2eHpnNcumDTMHFbhMnz841MT0_H05tfAQH2x8

*had this master's degree in Middle Eastern studies, and I
ended up in secretarial jobs and as an English typist. I can't
blame it all on him. But I lost my confidence... Like if I was
taking a course and needed help from a male professor, I would
be wary of going into his office and asking for help. I think it
affected my career adversely, the career I never really had.*

Tali, who was pushed out of her job after reporting abuse, also lost her professional tools:

*Afterward in my new work setting, I was petrified to make
personal connections. I didn't want anyone to think I was a
slut, or that I wasn't smart enough, or I wasn't a competent
enough scientist. So, it affected my ability to make other
connections at work. Constantly proving yourself. I had to
prove myself professionally and socially. That my self-worth is
dependent on other people making up lies about me.*

For some victims, exiting their careers felt like their only option. Nancy, who was assaulted by a colleague, said, "The easiest thing for a woman to do in that case is leave. I think that is what women do. Among other things. You hide. Or you leave. Keep it mostly to yourself. Especially if he's your boss."

Shlomit feels she lost her career because of larger communal sexism that sent her down a gendered path she didn't want. "I had other dreams, I wanted to be a political journalist. I sacrificed them so I could be the good Jewish wife. I sacrificed a tremendous amount, and this betrayal is too much."

Some women's careers and ambitions were affected not because their abuse took place in a work or academic setting but because they were simply affected in their ability to function. Esther said, "I am disabled by trauma [that keeps me] from working. I have not held a full-time job in many years."

Fran Sepler explained the cycle of abuse and job loss. She connects it to what she calls "victim blamability," which is a real phenomenon:

*Victims are very blamable. Victims become blamable by the
process of being victimized. They act up. They quit roles that
they have. In the workplace we see this amazingly. I call it the
Employee Issue Triad: absenteeism, attitude problems, and
performance problems. We start seeing that people start
staying away, they start calling in sick, they start spending the
day on the internet because they can't engage with anybody
because they were vulnerable. And of course, that gets them a
talking to. 'You're not showing up when you're supposed to
be showing up', 'You were supposed to be at that meeting. Why
weren't you at that meeting?' which destabilizes the person*

and then they develop an attitude, because they're angry and scared and so they may get withdrawn and so on, or they may get really angry and circle the wagons with other equally unhappy people. They may get snarky. They may get mean. And now their colleagues are all seeking distance because that, that looks and feels kind of dangerous. And they're also getting feedback, 'What's the problem with your attitude? You used to be such a good employee. You got an attitude problem.' If you get a performance review, they get nicked a little bit, and then you get to people starting to fail at their job. It's really easy to say to a complaining employee who looks like that, 'Oh well, she's, she or he is just trying to keep their job. They're just you know they're just raising this because they couldn't handle the work environment.'

Victims are not always perky and eager to please. In fact, they are often struggling and distant. The trauma itself makes it easy for them to be distanced and disbelieved, and cast as poor workers or community members.

The crushing portrait of women leaving communal jobs as a result of abuse raises critical questions about the overall impact on the community. There is currently no research that asks this question about how the community overall is impacted by women rabbis leaving as a result of abuse — that is, until now. In the following chapter, I turn these interviews around, including the voices of women rabbis, to ask about the impacts of all this on the *community*. For now, let's continue with the impacts on individuals.

Financial insecurity

Connected to losing work and career is loss of financial stability. Tali, for example, a post-doctoral scientist who reported the sexual harassment at her workplace and followed all the protocols, experienced steep financial impacts:

The financial implications of all this — I took a pay cut, didn't get published, had to switch fields, eventually quit, plus doing four jobs including sewing lessons and baking cakes in order to pay the rent. I was literally working every single minute of the day to pay the bills. I understand women who don't want to report things. It's not simple. The important guy can't be fired. It's easy to be at the end and say, okay, I found something else to do. But it doesn't excuse them just pushing me out.

Other victims did not land on their feet at all. Hinda said she was "forced to go before the board of regent of my state's university system and convince them that I was a financial orphan, after which I was given loans that I could pay down by teaching in certain schools."

These testimonies about the impact on career, finances, and socio-economic status are very important. The connection between abuse and work is not necessarily intuitive. But trauma and abuse seem to affect virtually every aspect of a victim's functioning in the world.

Other personal changes

With all these damaging impacts of abuse, some interviewees also expressed positive changes that resulted from the entire process.

Education and parenting

Experiences of abuse made some people take different approaches to parenting or education. Uriah said, "I always made sure my daughter had money for transportation, and a car of her own so she would NOT hitchhike." Nicole also said, "I see things differently for my daughter. I teach my son with more passion. And I warn others."

Deeper Jewish involvement in religion

Interestingly, several interviewees said that they came closer to religion as a result of the abuse, an outcome that is consistent with some of the research on clergy abuse. Although most research shows a crisis in faith following religious-based abused, some people who are abused come to rely *more* on faith to get them through their darkest time. This phenomenon appeared with several interviewees.

Alyssa, who was violently assaulted by her father, found refuge in a new religious community.

> Judaism and Israel and the Jewish community where I live is what kept me going during the worst times when I first started dealing with the abuse in my mid-20s. I am so very thankful that I am Jewish. It's the best part of my life. My entire family cut me off and believed my dad. I had no money, and a rabbi family took me into their home for a few years. Saved me. When I moved out, the Jewish Federation loaned me money, and I went to the Jewish Food Pantry for food. Having a community at synagogue was a lifesaver. My Jewish friends stood by my side. Eventually, I got a job at the JCC. Spiritually, emotionally, practically, physically, in so many ways, the Jewish community was there for me. Internally, I gained strength and hope from being Jewish. From reading Jewish

books, including the bible. From understanding how we as
Jews grieve and handle loss and very painful challenges.
Whenever possible I looked at my situation through the eyes of
Judaism and it brought me much knowledge and comfort.

Tina, who was alienated from her community for many years is working her way back to the Jewish community, mostly for the sake of making change. "I am practicing forgiveness and working on being a member of the community." This is very important to her because "I have always identified with being Jewish and I love the Torah and Hashem and it has been my saving grace despite all hardships... I am glad I can be among my sisters and brothers again in my faith and community despite how hard it has been."

Zelda, who was sexually abused by her liberal rabbi and alienated from her community as a result, has also sought out refuge in synagogue – but in an Orthodox synagogue, where she feels "safe":

It's hard enough when you were sexually abused, raped, by a
rabbi. A male rabbi, to be in a shul with a male rabbi is very
triggering. Very hard... But the local Hassidic rabbi... I went
for services during the high holidays and I was really amazed.
He never said anything to me [about the abuse, which was
reported in the local papers] and looked at me very kindly. He
gave me the space that I very clearly showed people I wanted,
and he gave a great prayer service.... I thought it was a good
service, but it was still hard for me. I was still in shul and with
man leader. But I will say actually sitting in a women's section
was nice for me, and also not having to shake men's hands and
have that respected, it was like, I'm asserting a boundary and
the men here respect that. So, I think I might hide out in the
Orthodox world for a while because I like those very strict
boundaries that I can use right now.

Some victims/survivors of abuse find ways to turn around their experiences, work on themselves, and even contribute to the community. Nevertheless, these "silver linings" cannot change the very real and deep impacts that abuse has on the community. The loss of real people with talent and gifts, along with the damage to what Jewish culture means and consists of — these are often unseen effects of sustained abuse and communal protection for abusers.

Takeaways about impacts on the victim

- **Victims of abuse in the Jewish community share most impacts with victims generally**. Most of the dominant emotional impacts of abuse that appear in the wider literature about abuse—depression, anxiety, shame, self-blame, etc.—showed up in this research. This is true also for other impacts, such as loss of job and financial stability, difficulty in relationships and with sex, and loss of faith and trust. One area of impact that did not particularly show up in the research is substance and alcohol abuse—either because it is not a dominant feature of the community or because interviewees did not report it or did not considerate significant.

- **With an addition of communal "himpathy."** Experiences of communities siding with the abuser—especially when the abuser is a rabbi—add layers of trauma and can result in loss of faith, loss of religion/spirituality, and loss of Jewish connection.

- **Retraumatization can be worse than the abuse.** The process of not being believed upon disclosure can have an even more devastating impact than the abuse itself, according to many interviewees, to the point of suicidal ideation.

- **Again, it's not an affair; it's abuse.** The misuse of language for labeling abuse—such as calling it an "affair" or "relationship"—also adds to the victims' experiences of being abused, then blamed, then shunned. The gaslighting causes deep, inner torment

- **Traumatic reactions can look like emotional instability, which is just more victim-blaming.** Victims of abuse are often blamed for their own traumatic reactions or cast as crazy or unstable, rather than being understood as having been abused. This, too, is emotionally destabilizing

- **There can be a serious financial impact to abuse.** The financial trauma, which is often counter-intuitive, is both a cause and effect of abuse. As a cause, abuse is often entangled with economic insecurity because women who have less financially security and job security to begin with and are thus more vulnerable. As an effect, the inequality in financial leverage between abuser and abused becomes a factor in who receives communal support, and who is valued. Since many abusers are in positions of power in the workplace, women can be ousted or blacklisted from their industries when the public takes the abuser's side. And finally, the many other impacts of abuse on the victim— such as PTSD, anxiety, depression, and self-doubt— can impact victims' ability to successfully pursue their dreams and passions, and build the careers that they want and deserve.

- **'What doesn't kill you makes you stronger?'** Maybe, but it shouldn't have to. Certainly some victims have used their experiences to become powerful advocates and have created activism towards communal change — *but that is too big a price to pay.* People should not have to dedicate their great talents to issues of abuse instead of the creative passions that they were engaged in when they were abused.

- **There is no research on communal impact.** While many Jewish workplaces, synagogues, and communal organizations seem to have problems with sexual abuse that leave community members, staff, and other participants often disillusioned and distanced from the community, there is virtually no research looking at how the estrangement of victims impacts the wider community. .The Jewish community has access to great resources in the people who dedicate their lives to Jewish causes, but the community then loses them when they find themselves abused in the process and veer off into other directions. This is the topic of the next chapter, which has, to date, never been adequately researched or studied.

Chapter 12: Impacts on the Jewish Community

In this chapter

Communal losses
    Loss of Jewish connection
    Loss of Jewish professionals
    Loss of women rabbis
    Loss of dedicated volunteers
Cultural damage
The silver lining: Building new cultures
    Women helping women
    Building new institutions
    Changing institutional cultures
Takeaways about impact on the community

The previous chapter exposed many difficult impacts on victims, including alienation from religion and community, difficulty in relationships, and loss of jobs. But these impacts do not only affect individuals. The loss of members and the loss of professional talent are trends that affect the community at large. Yet, while there is some research on impacts of sexual abuse on individuals in the Jewish community, there is almost no research examining the impact on the community as a whole, or how the community is damaged by the fallout. Even in communal discussions that call for changes around this issue, the focus is generally on changes to institutions in order to make sure that abuse does not take place, *for the sake of victims*. But there is another aspect to why abuse is bad: it also *damages the entire community*.

For instance, Rabbi Michael Melchior and Manny Waks called for communal attention to sexual abuse, writing that "until we put the interests of our children first — their safety and well-being — and the welfare of victims and survivors who have endured sexual abuse as children, we will not make the sustainable progress that we so desperately need within the Jewish community globally." This is an important point about how sexual abuse harms the Jewish community's "progress." But even here, the writers do not explain what kind of "progress" is stunted by the presence of sexual abuse. They continue: "A child who is harmed in a place where they should feel the greatest security, in all likelihood will find it difficult to ever find a secure place in this world. Simply put, often these are life and death issues."[272] Again, in this view, the damage done to individuals needs to stop for the sake of ensuring that children do not get hurt. All of that rings true. But it does not answer the question about how the community itself is actually harmed when abuse is rampant. How, indeed, does the presence of abuse impact the community culture on the whole?

This is an important if subtle distinction. Focusing on individual struggles with abuse implies that this is merely a scattered problem. The premise of this research, however, is that there is room — and even an urgency — to view this is a cultural-communal issue. Although we do not have quantitative data about how widespread abuse is in the culture, the portraits that emerge here indicate that the problem is not just one of a few scattered bad apples, so to speak. Many practices and behaviors that enable abuse, keep victims vulnerable, silence criticism, or block reporting are culture-wide and community-wide. The story being revealed in the research is not about a few individuals who need to figure things out on their own. It is about an ugly stain on the culture that is otherwise beloved to many. And it is about the loss of vital members with passion and contributions who fall out or walk away.

Yet, this is not an idea or perspective that I have seen reflected in any current research. In my many searches for existing research on the impacts of sexual abuse on the community, I came up nearly empty. Unlike, by contrast, the reactions when a deadly virus is spreading, there has been no systemic attempt to examine the communal or global impact when a devastating culture is spreading.

The only scholar I found who analyzed the impact of rabbinic sexual abuse on the community is Professor Rabbi Rachel Adler. In the Spring of 1993, she wrote what can only be described as a prescient article on this topic, in which she called the impact of abuse on a congregation "disruption of cosmic disorder:" "Unethical sexual conduct by rabbis seriously harms congregants who experience it. It divides congregations and destroys their trust. It damages the reputation of the rabbinate," she wrote.[273] The article was published in the *CCAR Journal*, but it did not have any particular impact. "Nobody really listened to me," Professor Adler told me nearly 30 years later.

---

[272] Michael Melchior, Manny Waks, "Confronting sexual abuse in the Jewish community," *Jerusalem Post*, July 7, 2015 https://www.jpost.com/opinion/confronting-sexual-abuse-in-the-jewish-community-408279

[273] Rachel Adler, "A stumbling block before the blind: Sexual exploitation and pastoral counseling." *CCAR Journal* : A Reform Jewish Quarterly, Spring 1993, , 13-54pp 18-19

Many interviewees reported impacts that can easily be construed as individual experiences. Issues described at length in the previous chapter, such as changes in career direction, financial losses, and walking away from synagogues, can be viewed simply as individuals' decisions about their personal lives. But if we zoom out on these descriptions, we can look at these patterns as profoundly impacting communities. It is a story about loss of talent, loss of membership, loss of affinity, and a thinning out of the group as a direct result of abuse. It is, oftentimes, particularly in reference to those survivors who had dedicated their professional and volunteer lives to building up the Jewish community, the very people who were trying to support the faith who ended up being forced out of it. And, as Professor Adler says, it is also about the "reputation" of the community — how the culture is perceived by those inside of it and those on the edges, what the culture *looks like*, what it *signifies* to its members, and ultimately what it *is*.

In this chapter, I am doing something different with the interviewees' narratives. I am shifting the location of my lens, so to speak. Instead of analyzing the texts as a collection of individuals' stories, I am analyzing them from the perspective of group membership. I am doing so because the narratives about these issues — the ways in which experiences of abuse cause victims to walk away from Jewish community, Jewish work, Jewish leadership, or Jewish involvement — offer a vital glimpse into how the presence of sexual abuse impacts the community at large. And it also offers crucial insight into how the culture is understood and defined by people who once intensely belonged to it but who have been rendered invisible within it.

As Shira Berkovits explained to me, "Reports of child sexual abuse — especially in instances where Jewish institutions have mishandled or enabled the abuse — breed distrust throughout the community in our Jewish institutions. Moreover, in any given community, roughly 20 percent of adults will have had their own experience of CSA. Victim-survivors — whether child, teen, or adult — are watching from the sidelines, and how we respond sends a critical message about where we stand and whether our institutions are safe for them."

Communal losses

The previous chapter, which described the many ways that victims suffer, painted a portrait of loss on only on the individual level, but also on the communal level.

Loss of Jewish connection

As we saw in the previous chapter, many respondents reported a loss of faith and religious connection, which is characteristic of clergy abuse across religions. As Marion said, "It took me thirty years to want to step foot in a shul again." Tina said, "It alienated me from my community for many years." Together, this can be seen as an invisible dropping out, or dropping off. It is a loss of membership that nobody seems to be counting or even noticing. As Shlomit said:

> I just stay far away. I don't feel like the Orthodox community will ever protect my body or my rights the way I need to be protected. And I'm tired of giving them the chance and tired of apologizing for it and I will never ever give them the opportunity to hurt me again. I just don't feel comfortable there anymore. And I'm no longer going to be an apologist for it, like, 'Oh, it's okay, it's not a big deal that women doing do anything or that women are silent.' It's not okay, it's clearly not okay, you took advantage of us.

Moreover, many of those dropping out – including Shlomit – had dedicated immense efforts to communal building before they left. "I wanted to remain in the community to which I had moved. I had a home there and put together a life for myself," Esther mourned. "But I could not live in the same small town with my abuser, so I fled." She called this "shattering" as everything she had built "on which I'd lived my life for so long had also disintegrated." Her community lost a vibrant resource. She is effectively out.

This is also a loss of Jewish social networking. Charley, for example, said that after she was raped by a rabbinical student, "I expanded my circle outside of the Jewish community." Her current partner is not Jewish. Melissa, who faced abuse while she was volunteering for Jewish organizations on campus, also disconnected Jewishly after her experience:

> I took a step back from the Jewish community at college. I found my support group in my major and in my friends. I studied abroad. I found different ways to make Jewish observance part of my life. I made Shabbat dinners, and I have great memories of bringing non-Jewish friends into the Sukkah and having our own little meal on the floor. So, I found ways to make Jewish observance work for me that bypassed the official stuff.

Melissa effectively created a Jewish community of one, using all her knowledge and creativity in private, far from the broader community. Ten years later, she said she is starting to wind her way back, but not in the same way. "I don't like Jewish institutions, but I like Judaism. But now I'm starting to see positive things that can come out of Jewish institutions, which is not something I have felt for, like, ten years. I'm taking baby steps back to Jewish institutions." The community lost ten years' worth of Melissa's contributions, and may never fully get them back.

Community by definition is a collection of people coming together, and the prevalence of abuse damages that by sending people away. Shlomit said, "I don't identify as Orthodox anymore. I don't find denominations useful. It's too painful," she said. "I just identify as Jewish. I happen to keep Shabbat and keep kosher and my entire family is Orthodox, so it would be very hard to leave. But I'm creating the community I want." Shlomit's dropping out represents not only a loss of numbers. It is also a loss of knowledge, insight, creativity, and passion.

When victims leave communal organizations and synagogues, the decision affects the community in both size and quality. This exit has not, to my knowledge, been statistically quantified. That is, the number of people leaving Jewish communal life as a result of abuse is currently unknown. But the interviewees here paint a clear picture of communal exit as a result of these traumatic experiences in a Jewish context. Although there is some anecdotal evidence pointing to a connection between sexual abuse and decisions to leave ultra-Orthodoxy, there is still currently no other research on this.[274] Nobody seems to notice that this is happening, or to care.

Loss of Jewish professionals

Just as people who are abused in communal or congregational settings often respond by leaving Jewish settings, victims of workplace sexual or gender abuse often leave their jobs as Jewish professionals. The abuse itself often pushes out talented and dedicated professionals and volunteers. This process sometimes starts with the onset of abuse — whether it's the mentor who turns his graduate students into secretaries or personal assistants while they are desperate for academic support, or the board that is more interested in the cantor's hair than in her abilities, or the high-status policy-maker who molests researchers during meetings that were meant to be about their professional contributions to communal policy-planning. These are not just cases about individual choices to walk away from Jewish organizational life. This is a tragic saga about sexual abuse that drains the community of vital resources and talent.

---

[274] Even the 2016 groundbreaking Nishma study on why ultra-Orthodox Jews leave their communities did not bring up sexual abuse as a cause – though they did find that the status of women was the number one predictor. "Starting a conversation: A pioneering survey of those who have left the Orthodox community," Nishma Research, 2016
http://nishmaresearch.com/assets/pdf/Press_Release_Survey_of_Those_Who_Left_Orthodoxy_Nishma_Research_June_2016.pdf

These kinds of movements, in which the trauma of sexual abuse in a Jewish professional setting led to an exit from Jewish professional life, permeated the interviews as well as published accounts of abuse. Sybil Sanchez, in her essay about two decades of abuse as a Jewish professional in several different settings that ultimately led her to quit Jewish professional life altogether and embark on a new career, describes her exit:

> When I look back upon that decision with some distance, I see someone who when harassed spoke out of concern for others rather than herself. Who was silenced rather than offended when a board member crossed the line… Now I know better. I learned, as a friend once advised, to get strategically mad and stand up for myself. Sadly, I had to change careers to do this.

The pervasiveness of abuse in Jewish work settings is causing people to leave. Shifra Bronznick, who has been working with women in professional leadership roles in the Jewish community for many years, similarly told me that she knows many women who left after being harassed at a job in a Jewish organization and ended up in a completely different career. "Many people have told me that story." Indeed, Sanchez says that, "According to our communal drop-off rate of women in positions of leadership and glaring lack of female executives, I am in good company."

Where are these talented but abused professionals going? Many becoming independently employed — which comes with freedom and workplace safety but also great financial/career risk. Anne, who was sexually solicited by her boss, was nudged out and started her own business. Although becoming independent can be empowering, it is not necessarily a *desired* form of employment when it is a result of fallout from abusive experiences. As Katie said, she became a freelance consultant to both Jewish and non-Jewish organizations after 20 years of Jewish professional work because she was "tired of being told, 'That's a great idea but it will never happen,' or 'Yeah, nice idea but we can't do that.' No matter how senior I was — I was at a VP level in my last job — no matter what I was doing, I was never given the support and resources I needed and deserved to fulfill my job to the best of my ability." The feeling of constantly being shunned pushed her to become independent. "I decided I wanted to work for myself. It is a huge step, terrifying and exciting at the same time. I felt that the only option I had was to go on my own."

Becoming independent benefits some women, but it carries a lot of risk, and for women who are abused, it is not necessarily what they wanted. Tali, who was demoted after reporting, left academia altogether and started her own business. It was going well for a while but she did not get enough funding, so she closed a few years later and became a technical writer in a hi-tech firm. Lili, who was fired after reporting, eventually left the field of education and went into publishing. Moreover, although according to Bronznick many women "ended up having a great career" outside of Jewish communal life, that is not always the case. Wendy, for example, left academia entirely in the midst of a PhD program following repeated abuse, and she struggled to build a new career due to being "plagued by doubt and underemployment." All of these women wanted to be working in the Jewish community, and wanted to dedicate their passions and skills to their people. But the abuse crushed all of that.

The persistence of sexual abuse and gender abuse in Jewish professional life keeps talented and dedicated women out of the spaces that need them, spaces that would benefit from their knowledge and dedication. Yona, for example, said that the abuse "encouraged me to avoid large segments of my departments," limiting her ability to function, advance, and grow. Similarly, Helen said, "The experience made me afraid to go to, like, if I was taking a course and needed help from a male professor, I would be wary of going into his office and asking for help."

Indeed, even when seemingly "nothing happens there can be immeasurable unseen and undefined damage. When the abuser holds the keys to the victim's future, encounters like this can have an intense residual effect by blocking important life passages and opportunities. As Julie explained following public revelations about Steven M. Cohen:

> Careers are built on a combination of skill and talent, education and opportunity, luck and determination, creativity and collaboration. They are not made or broken with a single conversation. But the Pandora's box that was opened recently made me think about what might have happened if that day had gone differently. If I had felt more comfortable with him, would I have chosen to pursue the research projects he had suggested? Would I have made useful connections, had the opportunity to publish in higher-profile journals, been part of conversations I would have liked to be part of? And just as importantly, would I have had something interesting to contribute to those conversations, brought ideas and perspectives that weren't otherwise represented?

The abusive gatekeeper effectively damages the entire Jewish communal professional world by keeping talented women out, especially those who are abused while seeking work as researchers or seeking a mentor. "The gatekeeper dynamic," as one interviewee explained, is when a woman walks out of a potential work experience and says, "That was creepy and I don't want to work with him." Dr. Gila Silverman, a Jewish sociologist, wrote an essay about the loss of talent, especially female talent, due to abuse:

> *I find myself wondering, how many women's ideas have we lost to situations like these? What intellectual contributions have we missed because women's insights were ignored or silenced or co-opted? What community-changing policies were never pursued because women walked away from professional situations that were uncomfortable or unsafe?*
>
> *For far too many women, our complex professional calculations and negotiations had to include whether we felt safe with our colleagues, and how much sexual innuendo or unwanted physical contact was a deal-breaker.... And I am pondering all of the complicated ways in which gender has affected my own professional trajectory.[275]*

The loss of women who were harassed is not just damaging in terms of loss of talent. It also damages the *entire Jewish culture*. Wendy, for example, said that she "lost respect for the entire field." Across the board in Jewish organizations, many women are making decisions about whether they are interested in working in such a flawed and hurtful environment. As Professors Susannah Heschel and Sarah Imhoff wrote, the everyday sexism and abuse that women experience impacts the entire field of Jewish studies in terms of both loss of talent and the culture that it foments:

> *Women with an interest in entering the field will wonder: Will I be welcomed and mentored by the men who dominate the senior levels of the field? And if I bring innovative ideas and interpretations, will they be dismissed, or treated with respect? They will see many serious, respected women scholars whose work is admired by their colleagues in adjunct fields but too often not cited, invited or published by men in Jewish studies. If this is the state of the field, perhaps we should urge women not to enter it.[276]*

The prevalence of abuse affects the Jewish academic field both in practice and in name. Potential contributors may be reluctant to walk in the door because they are not sure they will like what they find there, or unwilling to return once they have fled. Ruth, who lost her job after being encouraged to sleep with a donor, describes this damning impact. "I always wanted to work in nonprofit but I thought the salaries are so low. But I thought, okay, I was looking for work that was meaningful." She left behind a lucrative career in finance thinking she would find purpose and belonging. Instead, she was nearly pimped out to a donor for money. "The most shocking thing is that

---

[275] Gila Silverman, "In Judaism, Death, as Life, is with People," *HBI Blog*, May 18, 2018
[276] Heschel & Imhoff, "Where Are All The Women",
https://forward.com/culture/404416/where-are-all-the-women-in-jewish-studies/

it's not how it is at all, and the Jewish nonprofit world is a cesspool." The loss is not only that a talented, dedicated member left. It is also that the Jewish professional world can be described as a *cesspool.*

Heschel and Imhoff draw a direct connection between the gender abuse or sexism that Jewish professional academics experience, the loss of talent to their fields, and the overall state of Jewish professional culture:

> *Why does this matter? Excluding women is damaging to their scholarship and careers; it is also nasty and unethical. It affects hiring, salaries and grants – all of which have very tangible effects on women's careers....[N]ot to include younger female scholars in conferences and anthologies limits women's career paths and will ultimately diminish the debates that make a field vibrant. Moreover, the exclusion of women from so many areas of Jewish studies hurts the field: Not only do we intellectually limit ourselves when we fail to hear from women scholars, but we also make the field of Jewish studies look ridiculous in the eyes of our academic colleagues.*[277]

Given the sexual abuse, gender abuse, and sexism in the field of Jewish professional and academic life, the terms some women associate with those fields are "ridiculous" and "cesspool." Jewish professionalism and academia should be pillars in which our community can take pride, but words like that paint a portrait of a very flawed culture.

Loss of women rabbis

Perhaps the greatest professional, cultural, and communal loss due to rabbinic abuse is the loss of women rabbis. Women rabbis are often trapped between abusers and victims, or by members of the pulpit who may be abusing them. Abby described this trap:

> *Women in the rabbinate, especially those of us from the early years, we all have stories about jobs we didn't get because they weren't ready for women. There was a position where I was clearly the front runner and they really liked me, and I was told blatantly that they were not ready for a female rabbi. The person they hired ended up having a nervous breakdown. Instead of hiring me. If you were a rabbi in a congregation that had a female cantor, you wouldn't get the job because they wouldn't have two women on the pulpit. That was a big concern in the early days. It was very hard to prove that you could be the rabbi for everyone.*

---

[277] Heschel & Imhoff, "Where Are All The Women"
https://forward.com/culture/404416/where-are-all-the-women-in-jewish-studies/

Women rabbis often comport themselves in order to survive in their roles. Abby also dressed, spoke, and behaved in ways that people were willing to see in a woman rabbi. "People speak to women in the clergy in ways that they would never speak to men. The tone, the arrogance, the aggressiveness. They would never speak to men the same way," she said. In response, she dressed differently. "One of the things I learned was that I would show up in pink and lady-like suits, and then I could say anything, because they couldn't get mad at the lady in pink. They were so flabbergasted so they wouldn't spend their time trying to shut me up." She also changed her hair, to make it less appealing. "I would learn never to have my hair done on Friday because then nobody would listen to my sermon. They would say, 'Oh, your hair looks so cute.' You want to be looked at for who you are and what you're saying. That's part of being a female professional that's common across the board."

She would also be very contained in the way she could speak. "The cardinal was coming to meet with the board members, and I get a special phone call to make sure I wouldn't embarrass them by asking provocative questions. And you have to be polite and not say anything because I was a professional and couldn't say anything. But there's so many moments like that and you just want to scream and you can't." Klara said, "I do not ever want to work directly for a man again." Barbara also reported that she "avoids powerful men."

The comportment of women rabbis deprives the community of rabbinic talent, while sustaining a rabbinic culture of abusive patriarchy. Abby, who says that "despite all this I became a rabbi," is no longer willing to work for a synagogue for longer than an interim period. "It makes you so angry." She left her last position because of these dynamics and is not entirely sure what is next. "I am now taking a bit of a sabbatical and figuring out what I'm going to do. I'm applying for some interim positions. I don't have it in me to fight those battles. I don't have the energy to keep fighting and banging my head against the same wall. I'm just, I'm just done." Abby says she is not alone in making the decision to step back from her rabbinic career:

> I know just a lot of women who got to a point in their careers and decided that they were done fighting and took positions and created lifestyles that were less 'successful' because they were without titles and positions, but they were tired of the fight. I'm one of those people.

The loss of rabbinic talent and the sustaining of unsafe cultures trickles down to congregations. As women rabbis themselves do not have enough safe spaces, that impacts the entire community, making communal life worse for everyone. Just as female rabbis avoid certain activities to avoid abuse, so do congregants. Women rabbis do more pastoral care than male rabbis, and a lot of congregants — especially women — rely on that. When there are fewer women available, members of the congregation are less likely to get what they want and need from their rabbis. And people like Leanne, did not participate in the planning of her daughter's bat mitzvah because it involved meetings with the rabbi. Those are layers and layers of loss.

The abuse has a deeply destructive impact not only on women rabbis but also on communal life and deprives people of pastoral care as well as religious and communal belonging.

Loss of dedicated volunteers

Just as unpaid abusers are an invisible arena in Jewish life (see Donors, Board Members, and Congregants), the dropping out of volunteers and lay leaders as a result of abuse is also barely noted. Unpaid workers are often not part of official reporting and configurations. And yet volunteers often constitute a major force in Jewish life. Most Jewish organizations rely heavily on boards, committees, and other volunteers who do everything from setting up the kiddush in synagogue to organizing multi-million-dollar campaigns and fact-finding missions.

The impact of abuse on volunteerism was described by Cheryl Moore, who resigned from high-powered lay leadership positions as a direct result of relentless sexual harassment.

> I have no experience as an employee of the Jewish communal or academic worlds. I have extensive experience, however, as a volunteer in the Jewish communal world. I have held leadership positions in local, regional, national, and international organizations, and at every level, I have experienced #MeToo moments, hours, months. The cumulative effect of these, primarily intense shame, led to my exit from 90 percent of my Jewish communal leadership roles… After six months of confusion and shame, I walked away from a project on which I had been very excited to work.

Similarly, Zena, who was assaulted at an international board meeting, said that she "never went back to another Board of Governors' meeting or any other national or international Jewish board meeting. I never wanted to expose myself to that again. Twenty-five years later, I can still recount the story, the faces, the names, just like it was yesterday." Brenda, who has been a high-level lay leader in her synagogue for years and has held a lot of leadership positions — on the Board of Directors, the rabbinic search committee, head of the chesed program, as well as volunteering in other ways like inviting new visitors for Shabbat meals to her home — was very hurt not only by the abuse but also by her own community's failure to support her. She also felt that nobody appreciated all the unpaid work that she had done or the tens of thousands of dollars she had donated over the years. As a result, she nearly stopped showing up to synagogue. "I'm now almost at a point of emotional detachment. But I still hate when he's there leading services, I have this thing in my mind, I'll daven by myself. I've had to compartmentalize my religious life in these terms." Although she has not yet fully left the community, she is gradually dropping out.

Brenda's story also emphasizes the often-unspoken gender hierarchies in synagogue life. Brenda was giving her whole personal and professional self to the synagogue and to the rabbi — fulfilling a very hard unpaid job, which does not provide her with money but with a whole range of intangible rewards for her such as community, religion, meaning — and he, because he has official status and title and a pulpit, has all the power where she has none. She gave her sincerity and all her energies for free, and he got a powerful podium, salary, and adulation. He was able to get everything he wanted while the things that mattered to her most— community and belonging — were lost for her. That is the gender hierarchy of the synagogue that enables abuse.

As Shlomit, who hasn't gone to synagogue "in years," described her exit, "I'm out. These aren't my values. I'm not playing with you guys." She left the synagogue as well as the idea that it reflects her core belief system — as a direct result of how she and other women are treated. "I just don't feel comfortable there anymore. And I'm no longer going to be an apologist for it. It's not okay, it's clearly not okay, you took advantage of us."

Similarly, Melissa, who was volunteering for a Jewish organization on campus, said, "Why would I put myself through this? I didn't want to go to rabbinical school, I didn't want to become a Jewish professional. I was doing it because Jewish life was something I cared about. But I was like, this isn't fun, and it isn't enjoyable. I decided, I'll dedicate myself to other things."

The exodus of women as unpaid workers and participants in synagogue and communal life is often invisible. Women leave for many reasons — social, spiritual, and emotional. Many who leave do so as a result of shaming experiences or as a result of pervasive sexism. And most of them have never had an experience of being asked to come back. Their talents and contributions to the community are simply lost. So often, when women drop out of synagogue life, nobody even seems notice.[278]

Charley, who has left Jewish communal life after she was raped by a rabbinical student, mourns her own loss. "The truth is, I would have made a great *rebbetzin* [rabbi's wife] in life. I love reading Talmud, I'm very good with *teshuvot* [responsa] and writing," she said. But today, that future is no longer on the table. Cindy, who moved far away from synagogue life after

---

[278] Elana Sztokman, "Why Are Women Dropping Out of Synagogue Life?, *Lilith*," October 10, 2017 https://lilith.org/2017/10/why-are-women-dropping-out-of-synagogue-life/

being sexually abused by her rabbi/boss, said, "I would rather walk away from any job, sell off all I own, and do whatever is necessary to survive and support my family before I will ever, ever, ever compromise my values again. There is a real freedom in having finally moved away from this man and his manipulations. Freedom to choose — understanding that free will exists — is the most life-altering freedom there is."

The silver lining: Building new cultures

There is a kind of "silver lining" to these reactions to abuse. Some of the people who are rejecting abusive, patriarchal cultures are working to build new ones.

Women supporting other women

One of the most difficult aspects of this research is the discovery that women are not "safe" the way some of us were taught to believe. However, there are people working to change that.

As a result of her sexual assault, Gloria became active in rape crisis centers in order to help other women. "I am 74 years old and belong to the generation that took male sexual harassment for granted as part of life. I certainly don't anymore, and I love the #MeToo movement. I hope it finally reaches our harasser-in-chief." Yona, who was nudged out of her job for getting pregnant, said, "It encouraged me to become particularly protective of junior colleagues who are pregnant." Similarly, Dina said, "If we listen to women and understand what men do to us and how it makes us feel, maybe they would adapt their actions. I just think women need a much bigger voice in the Orthodox community."

Janice also used this experience to help other women. "I felt empathy and an affinity for other women who experienced abuse and trauma. When I sensed that someone was struggling with some form of trauma, I would share my story with them to let them know they were not alone." Similarly, Tina said, "I am still trying to heal and find my way in the Jewish community and also support other survivors and help others so they don't have to go through what I went through."

Building new institutions

One of the major ways that victims of gender abuse and sexual abuse in the Jewish community are making change is by rejecting institutional patriarchal practices and working to replace them with better ones.

Shlomit left the school where she had been abused and eventually opened up her own school. "My choice was to create the world I wanted. I was thinking about this school for seven years. And at a certain point I said, if [Trump] can be president, I can make my school. That's why I chose this time. There were other factors, but I was like, I'm not going to be helpless anymore. Forget these awful men who are never going to protect me the way I need to be protected. I'm 48 years old and I'm so tired of waiting for the system to be working for us."

Changing institutional cultures

Hanna, a rabbi who was sexually harassed by a senior rabbi in rabbinical school, vowed to change cultures in her congregation:

> It prepared me for setting up clear boundaries as a congregational rabbi. The experience readied me to sniff out inappropriate words and behaviors that had nothing to do with me and everything to do with a culture that tries to put women down through harassment and intimidation. I vowed to be an ally to other women suffering similar fates.

Charley, who was raped by a rabbinical student while in college, is tackling male cultures on campus. "I mentor men. I got very involved with Take Back the Night at college and stayed on mentoring a few men in the organization afterward. The truth is, I went to work on campus eventually because I wanted to improve the atmosphere on campus and be a resource. That was important to me."

Cultural damage

In all of these cases, there are two main aspects of damage to Jewish communal culture as a result of abuse: loss of dedicated or talented members, and the lessening of the value of the culture.

In terms of loss of talent, this finds expression in the many ways described above— loss of rabbis, pastors, professionals, volunteers, congregants, and all the creative and dedicated intelligence and energy that comes along with that.

In terms of the quality of the culture, there is an unspoken damage to the reputation of the culture, as well as how it is experienced. When abusers stay and their victims leave, then abuse becomes the norm, in many ways.

Interviewees expressed this damage to the culture in many ways. When they leave the community, that is a rejection of the very notion that the Jewish community is a good place to be. When they opt out of working in the Jewish community, that is a damning assessment, and another vote with the feet. One interviewee called the communal culture a "cesspool".

Susannah Heschel and Sara Imhoff said that the community comes out looking "ridiculous".

When Jewish culture is one in which abusers have power and find a stranglehold, then people who have a different idea of what makes a culture attractive walk away. Those who want the culture to provide safe spaces eventually realize that they will not find that in their culture. When abuse and the protection of abusers is the cultural norm rather than the exception, the culture itself is no longer the "light unto the nations" that some would have us believe.

Takeaways about impacts on the community

- **Spiritual abuse is a Jewish communal issue.** Judaism is not just a religion but a community with social, cultural, ethnic, and historic ties. As such the impact of what is considered "spiritual abuse" because it takes place in a faith community goes deeper. It leads to not only spiritual alienation but also social and cultural disconnection. Put differently, when community members are hurt by their spiritual leaders, the entire religion becomes a source of harm rather than one achieving lofty aims.
- **Clearly the community is losing invaluable talent.** For many victims, loss of community and loss of profession are devastating. But it is also a big loss for communal institutions that lost talent— often unappreciated talent, as well as members and connections. There is a lot of discussion among community talking heads about Jewish engagement and retention. And yet, this issue of losing members because of abuse is not discussed anywhere.
- **There is almost no research about communal drop-out as a function of sexual abuse.** In the sociological and demographic research about Jewish communal life, there is almost zero attention to the connection between sexual abuse, gender abuse, and victims dropping out, whether among volunteers, congregants, participants, or professionals. Yet, these were dominant themes among interviewees. Victims dropped out of communal life, professional life, and volunteer life as a result of abuse in Jewish contexts. Yet, nobody is even counting them.
- **Women rabbis are often on the frontlines.** Women rabbis are often at the intersection of these issues— victims, observers, potential enablers, and potential change-agents. But they, too, are at high risk of dropping out as a result of abuse coming from all directions. This dynamic also deserves communal attention urgently.

- **Jewish culture is damaged by all of this**. The presence of abuse, the victory of abusers over victims/survivors, and communal dynamics that protect abusers, all contribute to the detriment of Jewish culture as a whole. It turns Judaism into a place that tolerates or even supports abuse yet does not tend to victims or people who are vulnerable. The culture becomes a mockery of itself, "ridiculous", or even a "cesspool." These are costs that thought leaders, spiritual leaders, or policy makers in the community do not seem to even notice. "Who are we" or "what are we" as a Jewish community or culture when abuse is allowed and enabled are questions that have not yet been asked on a communal level.
- **But the community is not paying a big *financial* price, apparently.** Not one interviewee said that as a result of the abuse they will stop donating to particular causes. Many said they would stop working, volunteering, practicing, or showing up Jewishly. But none described using money as a reaction. This stands in stark contrast to the prominence of donors as abusers and the dynamics in which donors are often protected because of financial leverage. This begs exploration about connections between money, power, and abuse.
- **There are a few hopeful signs.** Victims/survivors are also on the frontlines of making change. They are helping other potential victims, they are changing cultures around them, volunteering in some difficult places like rape crisis centers and mentoring men, and sometimes even creating new institutions with difficult cultures and values. But again, this is a huge price to pay in order to get all that talent to work for improving the world. Going through abuse should not be the way to get people to work for the betterment of the community.

Part V: Conclusions

I can be changed by what happens to me,
but I refuse to be reduced by it.

Maya Angelou

Chapter 13: Pulling it Together

In this chapter

Jewish social hierarchies
    Rabbis, power, and charisma
    Other Jewish leaders
    Donors
    Vulnerable populations
    Deeply embedded patriarchy
    Female clergy

Jewish codes in grooming, reporting, and impacts
    Jews as a "family" or "people"
    Jewish exceptionalism
    Spiritual bypass and spiritual narcissism
    Jewish ideas: Teshuva, lashon hara, and others
    Gender and sexuality

Gaslighting the community
    Communal cover-ups
    "It's someone else's issue"
    It's abuse, not an affair
    "Nothing happened"
    The "good guy" defense
    Cultures of impunity

So, how do Jews compare?

This research on sexual abuse in the Jewish community, based on over 80 interviews with victims, survivors, and advocates, is hard. It was hard to listen to, hard to write about, and hard to read. Each story is jolting in and of itself, and the pain of many victims is palpable. The cumulative effect of hearing all these accounts coming out of the Jewish community — my own community, the spiritual-cultural space where I have dwelled my entire life — is staggering. The process of conducting this research has shaken me to my core and permanently altered the way I see my own community.

But it is also crucial in that it reveals dynamics that are often unseen, ignored, or denied, dynamics that ruin people's lives and sully the community and the culture. The research revealed parts of our community that, understandably, many people would prefer not to look at. But looking away will not make these dynamics go away. Looking away will only make it worse, causing more pain to survivors while protecting abusers and enabling these horrific things to continue. This book is an exercise in *not* looking away. In staring straight on at these terrible things.

In that effort to shine light on parts of the culture that have been in the dark, the primary question is this: *What does sexual abuse in Jewish culture look like?*

Below are some of the answers that emerged from this research.

Jewish social hierarchies

To answer that question, the first topic I would like to expound on is structural. I would like to look at the ways in which the culture creates social hierarchies so that certain people are deemed powerful — such as rabbis, leaders, and donors — while others are cast as vulnerable. The culture makes those determinations, and thus sets the backdrop for abuse.

Rabbis, power, and charisma

A significant segment of my research focused on rabbis across denominations and communities. Whereas clergy abuse in other religions has at times been broadly researched (think Catholic priests), this is the first attempt, to my knowledge, to characterize rabbinic abuse. What I found is that rabbis of all backgrounds, from all denominations, in all positions, in all roles, and of all ages, genders, shapes, and sizes, can be abusers. Wherever the rabbi is revered as a source of knowledge, authority, and/or power, the rabbi is assumed to be someone who will care, protect, and *not* violate. The "rabbi" title also awards access, intimacy, and most of all, trust. This combination of assumed authority, trustworthiness, and intimate access, is extremely dangerous and attractive to predators.

To an extent, these dynamics are quite like abuse by members of clergy from other religions who use the tools at their disposal to have their way — permission to be alone with potential victims, assumptions of authority and reverence, and meetings with people at their vulnerable moments. They also share a broad profile of personality traits, such as charisma, narcissism, and a need for control. The grooming tactics also fall into the same categories, such as targeting the vulnerable, feigning interest, false intimacy, coopting spiritual language, spiritual bypass and manipulation, giving prizes and love-bombing, and endless gaslighting. Rabbis, like priests are also surrounded by structures like entrenched patriarchy, and similarly receive an astounding degree of high-profile support and communal support, even after the abuse is revealed. The impacts of abuse by rabbis and other clergy members are also similar. Victims experienced not only the litany of emotional, physical, financial, and social traumas that victims everywhere go through, but also often a loss of faith, loss of trust, and loss of connection to their communities, congregations, and religion. Religious leaders who abuse have enormous structures and mechanisms to protect them.

According to the research, one of the items that distinguishes Jewish clergy from other religious leaders is how Jewish culture defines "charisma". Jewish culture across denominations places rabbis on a pedestal for their abilities to hold a crowd and wow audiences. Whether this means skill in giving a sermon, singing a moving prayer, articulating uplifting words, playing the guitar, or comforting and inspiring people, rabbis are often venerated for their charisma on stage and in private. A rabbi who is adept at finding the words people want to hear is revered, idolized, and protected across denominations. It's a starstruck combination of entertaining performance, scholar, and inspiring, feel-good camp leader. Jewish notions of charisma are not, by contrast, like evangelical preacher who speaks loudly and with great animation and elicits many "amen"s. They are also not monotonous, distant, choral leaders who build on fire and brimstone. The Jewish version of "charisma" is funny, personable, flirtatious, musical, sincere, personally engaging, intelligent, handsome, inspiring, and caring. The Jewish leader knows how to get their own audience gently nodding and feeling good, whether with words of comfort, a guitar, or a good joke. It's a form of religious cultural performance. And when done well, it gains ardent supporters and loyalists.

Unfortunately, those very qualities that define charisma overlap with the same characteristics that make rabbis dangerous. Charisma and the ability to manipulate an audience are among the most common character traits of a pathological narcissist. And according to many interviewees, Jewish communities, rabbinic selection committees, and even rabbinical schools fall into this trap of valuing the charismatic performance above all else. It is a very risky process.

I recognize that this is a very specific definition of leadership and charisma, and may not even apply to every corner of Jewish life, not every ethnic tradition, and certainly not every moment of Jewish history. This research reflects a particular time and place reflected in these interviews. Jewish cultures in other eras or in locations not represented by the interviewees may reflect other norms. But this is what is happening right now in this particular cultural space.

Interestingly, the profile of the abuser shares characteristics regardless of religious affiliation, but each will also use the codes and language of their specific sub-group. While an Orthodox abuser may use words such as "mitzvah" or "holiness", a Reform abuser may use words such as "tikkun olam" or mysticism. The codes may differ slightly, but the abusers are all using the tools at their disposal for the same tactic — emotional and spiritual manipulation for the purpose of gaining their victims' trust and making their victims more pliant. It is an identical approach with some customized adaptations.

It is troubling to realize that the qualities valued in the rabbi are similar to those of the narcissist — love of performance, ability to manipulate others, insatiable ego, comfortable being center stage, belief that they are better than others and even a representative of God.[279] This is a difficult finding, for sure. Yet, I would like to suggest that it is entirely possible that the rabbinate actually *attracts* people who have narcissistic personalities and who lack the capacity for real empathy. When charisma is of highest value, observers and audiences can get trapped in the wrong place, falling in love with a public performance and not with the real person and what they are doing behind closed doors.

Moreover, when a rabbi is on a pedestal, like a celebrity idol, pushing back against rabbis can become *posnisht* — not done. Many interviewees described an internal block against talking back to the rabbi, what you may recall Zelda described as, "I could hear my mother telling me to invite the rabbi in — how could I not?"

In that sense, this research breaks a very important barrier by allowing critique of the rabbi personality and calling into question the ways in which unquestioned reverence opens the way for abuse. The research encourages people to rethink cultural ideals about what constitutes a worthy person, what constitutes "leader."

Other Jewish leaders

The profile of the abusive rabbi shares qualities with non-rabbinical Jewish leaders. In many Jewish settings, charisma is valued, as is the concept of "leadership", which is translated as power to hold a crowd, or an organization, or a budget. The person who can speak, entertain, or perform, the one who others sit up and listen to, or the one who can most effectively solicit donations, is the one who is most protected, no matter how abusive that person may be.

The grooming tactics among communal leaders are also usually similar. The sense of entitlement crosses all kinds of boundaries, the invasiveness, the bold tactics for getting into the victims' intimate space — these are common across abusers as well.

---

[279] Darrel Puls, *Let Us Prey: The Plague of Narcissist Pastors and What We Can Do About It* . Cascade Books 2020; Chuck DeGroat, *When Narcissism Comes to Church: Healing you community from emotional and spiritual abuse*. Illinois: Intervarsity Press, 2020

Power structures are also similar, even if they look different at first glance. Positions of leadership come with auras of respect and reverence. The person in power holds something that people want — such as a job, a salary, mentorship, status, connection, support, or opportunities. Just as congregants often support their rabbi because of what the rabbi does for them, so, too, workers and students often submit to abuse or look away at abuse because of the power that the abuser holds over their lives and over things that are dear to them.

The overlap between the profile of the rabbi abuser and the profile of other leaders who abuse is very telling about Jewish culture. This is a culture that places leaders on pedestals, that gives leaders pulpits, promotions, and powerful positions from which they gain a kind of untouchable status. While much of this may not be *unique* to Jewish culture in the sense that other cultures may do this as well, it is important to note how prominent this dynamic is in the culture described here — and how big of a part it plays in both the perpetration of sexual abuse and its aftermath.

Donors

One of the most glaring manifestations of the pedestals given to certain personalities is around the donor. Donors may receive the most communal reverence of all, with buildings and institutions literally named after them. Donors have such revered status across the community that they can be blatantly, publicly, and repeatedly abusive and not be censured at all. The role of "donor" is at least as powerful as the role of "boss" or "teacher" or "rabbi" in terms of the ability to engage in abusive behavior with impunity. Even victims who are publicly harassed may continue to revere the megadonor. And in one case, a woman was actually encouraged by her boss to sleep with a donor because it would be a "shame" to lose the donation. The Jewish community's policies, procedures, and laws on sexual harassment do not address this. The connection between money, philanthropy, and sexual harassment needs more attention and clarification in our community.

These dynamics reflect cultural norms and priorities. If charisma is the ultimate value of a rabbi, money is the ultimate value of a donor. If a person's monetary power is prioritized over all else — over the well-being of staff and volunteers — this creates a cultural setting ripe for abuse.

Communal structures and hierarchies reflect a culture's priorities. The communal structure is such that the people with certain traits — ability to perform, ability to charm, or ability to donate — are at the top of the pyramid. That set of priorities finds expression throughout this research. This is what Fran Sepler calls the "culture of exception," in which the person who gives the biggest donation or is revered for some other reason is excused for their abuse. They are the most valued, the highest on the social pyramid.

The next question, then, is: who is *not* valued? Who is at the *bottom* of the pyramid?

Vulnerable populations

This research highlighted not just the qualities of the most powerful people in the culture, but also the qualities of the most vulnerable. People who dwell on the lowest rungs of the internal social-cultural hierarchies are often favored targets for abusers.

In some ways, the people most vulnerable resemble those targeted by abusers in faith communities everywhere. That includes people experiencing uncertainty, shakiness, questions of faith, or pain. Similarly, people who have recently experienced loss, death, divorce, illness, or trauma are also vulnerable to being targeted. Ironically, research has demonstrated that those who have experienced sexual abuse are among the most likely to experience it again — and this is why. Like cracks in armor, the trauma makes them vulnerable and susceptible to repeat offenses. Many interviewees shared the experience of being revictimized by a rabbi while they were still struggling from previous abuse experiences.

There are also some Jewish-specific categories of vulnerability. Some interviewees shared that people who lack a specific place of belonging, a specific status in a synagogue community, or who felt that they did not have the Jewish "credentials" of having gone to Jewish day school or camp, baalot teshuva — those who became religious later on — or converts, are all in an inferior social-cultural position. A Jewish cultural emphasis on "family" often creates an adult version of high school cliquiness — who is "in" and who is "out", who is well connected and who is not, who knows important people and who does not. Their lack of "in"ness, combined with the feeling of not "knowing" things or perhaps not knowing the right people, contributed to their sense that they are cast as inferior in the social hierarchies and thus increased their susceptibility to exploitation and abuse. For someone feeling that kind of inferiority, a rabbi's "special attention" can feel like a godsend — until it isn't.

Moreover, for people who are vulnerable and underrepresented in Jewish workplaces, relationships with bosses, teachers, or potential mentors can be fearful, and have very real consequences, such as losing a job or derailing a career. And for women and other people who are disadvantaged in endemic Jewish patriarchal work structures, these consequences can be devastating. These power structures are critical to unpack in order to understand how abuse happens.

Physical issues also make some people vulnerable in the Jewish social order. Physical disability, for example, emerged as a factor that made interviewees feel like lesser members of the community. Other issues such as body size, physical appearance, and marital status were also issues "lesser" members of the community.

Or course, some victims/survivors have none of these issues. Some people are targeted for no apparent reason at all, or for reasons known only to the predator, such as Daniel. For others, the only category they fall into is that of being a woman. Brenda, for example, should have been considered in the class of "legacy family" that Fran Sepler described— a big donor, an "important" member of the synagogue, who should have benefited from "exception culture." Instead, none of that mattered. She was targeted by the rabbi, disbelieved by the senior rabbi, shunned by her peers, and left to fend for herself as she slowly left the community. Had she been a man, probably none of that would have happened.

The underlying patriarchy also contributes to social hierarchies. Women are often less valued by default, as evidenced by their underrepresentation in locations of power across the culture. This has other implications as well. For some women, just being alone as a single woman can feel vulnerable. When that aloneness is combined with any of the other points of vulnerability here, that can make a woman an easy target for a sexual abuser who grooms by making the victim feel special, wanted, and cared for.

These underling social hierarchies — in which certain people are revered at the top of the pyramid while others are relegated to the bottom — is the social-cultural setting in which abuse takes place. Thus, when abuse happens, the culture looks not at the abuse itself but at the location of the abuser and the abused within the social order. And that is how the cultural group often determines who is worthy of being heard, believed, valued, and supported.

Put simply: In this culture, rabbis, CEOs, charmers, and donors matter. Many others do not.

Deeply embedded patriarchy

Not all sexual abuse is about patriarchy. People of all genders can be narcissistic abusers, and people of all genders can be victims. That said, patriarchal culture is a clear contributing factor in many cases, and that backdrop is crucial for understanding much of how sexual abuse takes place in Jewish settings.

This is not always an obvious connection. Some advocates for CSA, for example, do not view it as a gender issue, since, according to some estimates, up to half of child victims are boys, the issue is not about gender. Similarly, although 90-95 percent of sexual abusers are men, the fact that women can also be abusers neutralizes the gender issue for some.

However, it is a mistake to ignore the gendered components of sexual abuse. Sexual abuse is about power and control, but it can also be about gender dynamics and hierarchies. Often, these issues overlap. In workplaces or organizations where men have more status, power, money, and prestige than women, those dynamics contribute to who is capable of abuse and who is more likely to end up a victim. These issues also connect because the profile of the narcissistic abuser includes traits that are also valued in Jewish leaders—charisma, charm, ability to speak publicly, confidence on stage, love of talking, and ability to manipulate a crowd. If Jewish organizational structures are rooted in patriarchal hierarchies, then male abusers are effectively given tools of abuse by virtue of communal structures and norms. Patriarchy and abusive relationships reinforce each other in Jewish cultural settings.

The issues of gender abuse, everyday discrimination, and sexism, is part of the cultural backdrop that enables abuse. This dynamic was echoed by many interviewees in different ways. Some of this is overt, such as salary differentials and women's lack of representation in locations of power. But much of it is subtle: The pressure to be a "nice girl," which had a powerful deterrent effect for many women who felt that they could not or should not say "no"; issues of financial dependency and needing the job; the "himpathy" factor, in which men are assumed to be more deserving of sympathy than women; or what Sybil Sanchez called the "implausibility bias" leveled against women in so many settings — they all contribute. This kind of patriarchal context creates a setting that exacerbates the gendered power dynamic when abuse takes place, and in the disclosure processes afterward.

Moreover, where gender abuse is normalized, sexual predators have an open playground in which to prey. Abusers commit rape because they were never stopped anywhere along the path from gendered norms to harassment to small assaults (an arm around the shoulders) to bigger assaults/abuse (the sexist jokes, the visual objectification of women, the casual unwanted brush against a body, the in-built assumption that men's needs and goals are more highly valued, the gendered expectation that masculinity means pushing for more, and so on). Not calling it out when the "small stuff" happens empowers perpetrators to continue their damaging behaviors.

Female clergy

Women rabbis and cantors are often in a double bind. In many liberal synagogues and a handful of Orthodox ones, women have taken active, central roles in the past generation or two, making women more visible and active in congregational life. The impact of women's presence within the traditional patriarchal structure in terms of clergy sexual abuse is twofold. On the one hand, they are often targets of abuse, sometimes relentlessly. On the other hand, they can potentially be part of the solution—or the lack of a solution. Women clergy serve on rabbinical ethics boards and share the same responsibilities as the men on the boards. Are female rabbis victims, protectors, enablers, fighters, or change agents? Perhaps some of the above. Perhaps none of the above. Some may be more than one simultaneously. Indeed, the (male) rabbi who abused Zelda was also found to have been concurrently abusing eight other women in the congregation, including two rabbis. Women rabbis are standing right at the center of the tornado of sexual abuse in Jewish communal life and culture.

They also have unique power. It is possible that, in some places, women bring new understandings about abuse that can bring change both publicly—as in from the pulpit, from their teaching—and privately, in the way reporting is handled and cultures are shifted. Certainly, the historic public release of the HUC-JIR report on abuse must be credited to the women rabbis of Reform Judaism such as Rabbi Mary Zamore and all the women she is hearing and protecting.

Women rabbis are in many ways standing at the center of this whole story.

Jewish codes in grooming, reporting, and impacts

Another major question that this research looked at was about how Jewish ideas and values played a part in cultures of abuse— specifically around grooming, reporting, and impacts of abuse. Jewish code-sharing can be used to target, groom, and break down boundaries across many different settings and contexts. It can also be used in a tactic of spiritual bypass, in which abusers use spiritual codes or ideas to avoid being held responsible, or to manipulate victims or bystanders.

What I found was that abusers across all denominations use tools at their disposal to prey on their victims, and that Jewish codes and ideas can be twisted and turned to protect abusers and keep abuse happening. This could be Sheldon Zimmerman's use of Buber's "I and Thou" to charm his teenage victim; Larry Back's use of Kabbalah ; Barry Freundel's insistence that his victims do a "practice immersion" in the mikveh; or labels of holiness and purity used by Ezra Scheinberg. Many interviewees shared similar stories. Jewish abusers often know well how to twist Jewish concepts and values in order to cajole their victims, conjure fake intimacy, and break down their resistance.

This is a crucial point. Abusers do not come from only one sub-culture, and it is not the culture itself that creates abusive people. Rather, abusers use whatever tools they have at their disposal to lure and groom their victims. They are social-cultural chameleons in that they know what terms to adopt in order to manipulate their prey. It is a mistake to think that one group has a monopoly on churning out abusers, as if their cultural codes do that. The abusers simply adapt to their surroundings and use whatever they can to get their way.

Below are a few of the Jewish codes that I found most prominently in dynamics of grooming, reporting, and impact.

Jews as "family" or a "people"

One of the core Jewish values co-opted by Jewish offenders for grooming is familial and communal connectivity. Abusers know how to break boundaries — sometimes gradually and sometimes all at once — in order to get close to a victim and break down that person's self-guard.

This takes many forms. It can be expectations of closeness among the only Jews at an event. It can be a Jewish coworker inviting themselves to sleep over. It can be too much hugging (although not in Orthodox settings), too-quick familiarity, or even more sophisticated rhetoric around protecting the Jewish people or anti-Semitism. The assumptions of, "We're in this together," or "We're like family," invite and allow invasions of boundaries. These can set the stage for unwanted sexual commentary or leering, allow "flirtation," and make it difficult for victims to stay at arm's length.

The breaking of boundaries around common Jewish "peoplehood" or "family" seems almost commonplace, but it also works to protect abusers while offering opportunities to prowl. The expectations of hugging at Jewish conferences or after-services events, for example, make it difficult to say "no" to unwanted touch. In Jewish workplaces, boundary-breaking behaviors seem to easily slide from body commentary to jokes to grabs to physical assault. Once the boundaries are crossed with small violations, the bigger violations can easily follow. This "sliding in" creates a cultural environment that supports patriarchal power and body impositions more than it supports consent and bodily autonomy. As Sarah Bronzite explained, "It's a hallmark of someone who carefully and deliberately considers their actions, who wants to be able to say, 'I was just being friendly, they seemed fine with it...'."

This dynamic extends beyond grooming. The emphasis on "community" also makes it difficult for victims to come forward, as the pressure to preserve community is used to protect leaders who are abusers rather than to create a space for victims, which might be seen as threatening to the collective. "The Jewish People" is also co-opted as an excuse and a cover. This has variations in both the Orthodox and non-Orthodox sectors. The Orthodox sectors will hush victims so as not to "air dirty laundry" or make a "shonda," or scandal for the community. In other places, if a victim wants to report a donor, for example, she may be told that the donor is too valuable for the existential survival of the organization or cause. We also saw anti-Semitism and support for Israel being co-opted in this dynamic as an excuse not to expose offenders.[280] One person becomes an exception, in order to keep the Jews exceptional. It creates a standard in which the supposed "needs" of the Jewish People come before the actual needs of the victim.

Thus, the very structures that are meant to members of the community may also do them harm. The myriad of ways in which Jewish people are connected can also mean that victims, abusers, and their protectors all have intersecting lives. Abusers are always on someone's PTA, shul committee, or baseball team. These entanglements can be difficult both in the grooming process, when abusers have an "in" with their targets, and during the reporting process. As Carmela said, "The fact that we are such a small, intertwined community perpetuates some of this. We're so concerned about ruining their reputations in the community, and we are not strong enough in standing up to abusers, because they are members of the community and friends and family." Abusers are always someone's "friend" — and they count on that.

Jewish exceptionalism

Another related issue that came up, which also impacts both grooming and reporting processes is the idea that Jews are "special" — God's chosen people, a light unto the nations, or just righteous.

In the grooming process, many victims are shocked that a person so trusted and revered would abuse them. The discovery that the place that they trusted most and considered their home is so sullied — or that a person who is a rabbi can be an abuser — negates everything they were taught to believe about Jews. Remember when Zelda let the rabbi into her house the first time and he proceeded to rape her, "I couldn't comprehend that he didn't deserve my trust and respect, because in my mind he inherently deserved it because he's a rabbi." This comment explains so much of how Jewish exceptionalism serves abusers' grooming impulses. The idea is that Jews are special, rabbis are the penultimate Jews, and they cannot possibly do anything wrong.

This idea of Jewish exceptionalism also protects abusers after the fact. People believe that the community needs to be "protected" from outside forces that seek to damage the "reputation" of Jews. The "chosen people" need to be taken care of and preserved. Individual members of the flock? Not so much. As Sarah Bronzite said, "It goes to the heart of Jews having to acknowledge that Jewish men (and some women) are not somehow 'better' than any other group of men, as our culture would have us believe." Jewish

---

[280] Elana Sztokman, "Don't use 'anti-Semitism' to protect sexual abusers: On the Steinhardt allegations: Why should the needs of the Jewish People come before the wellbeing of Jewish women?" *Times of Israel*, March 21, 2019 https://blogs.timesofisrael.com/dont-use-anti-semitism-to-protect-sexual-abusers/

exceptionalism makes people vulnerable, inhibits the process of saying no, and makes the damage all the more intense.

This Jewish exceptionalism also adds layers of torment to the healing process. For people whose identities are defined by the premise that being Jewish is special, the discovery of abuse by rabbis or other leaders can upend their entire lives. It is an ultimate betrayal of trust. It can engender loss on multiple levels— loss of community, loss of connection, loss of meaning, loss of trust, and loss of identity.

Spiritual bypass and spiritual narcissism

Jewish religious or ethical codes often play a key role in the grooming process. This process, which is a form of spiritual bypass, is used often by narcissistic abusers, who are experts at homing in on victims' needs and desires, and know how to comport their predation around what victims will respond to. This can be words of Torah at a funeral, sharing a book about Buber, or for the truly adept abusers, it can be what Zelda described as, "'Oh Kabbalah! I'm touching your boobs!' shit." Many victims are in places where they are seeking out religious or spiritual connection, and this manipulation of Jewish ideas can be very confusing and hard to see through.

This dynamic can also take over the reporting process. Spiritual narcissists are also master manipulators of their flock, and know how to use spiritual language to move their audiences in their direction. We saw many examples of this— abusers branding themselves as "spiritual guides," abusers giving lofty speeches even after they have been outed while their victims cringe in the back, or even being revered as spiritual masters for even decades after they are gone (e.g., Shlomo Carlebach) .

The experience of having Jewish texts and ideas used for abuse can have a particularly tormenting impact on victims and survivors. The sense of the good wrapped up in the bad makes it difficult to hold on to that which is meaningful. This can have an effect of uprooting their ability to reconnect with their own tradition and heritage. Many interviewees do not go to synagogue, many left religious practice, and several left Judaism altogether. For some, it is a deep, psychic, and indescribable violation, a theft of something precious and irreplaceable.

Jewish ideas: Teshuva, lashon hara, and others

Certain Jewish concepts gain particular prominence during the reporting process.

"Teshuva," or repentance, an idea that has been unfortunately gaining traction in response to #MeToo and the attempts by abusers to have "comeback," has meant that even admitted abusers are often given a "second chance" under the guise of Jewish values of forgiveness -- for example, Ari Shavit, Steven M. Cohen, and Jeremy Garber.

Similarly, lashon hara, a prohibition against gossip, is used to keep victims silent. This is given a different cover in different denominations — not to "air dirty laundry" or to protect predators' reputations. In Orthodox circles, other ideas are also sometimes used to protect abusers, such as mesirah, prohibitions against reporting a Jew to non-Jewish authorities, or hillul hashem, not to do something that embarrasses Jews (although these concepts did not appear in my interviews nearly as much as lashon hara did). In some cases, language of protecting marriage prospects, or shidduch, is also invoked as a variation of the same theme. Nevertheless, these are all part of the same dynamic to block reporting and maintain existing power hierarchies through silence.

These dynamics can be devastating for victims/survivors. They are part of a spiritual bypass in that they co-opt Jewish ideas in a sinister way, with all that implies for victims' spirituality. Lashon hara, in particular, is often considered one of the highest values in Jewish interpersonal behavior. The discovery that it is also a silencing technique can be torture.

Moreover, the language of forgiveness can also be tormenting to victims, who may find themselves under pressure to "forgive," or let the abuse "go." Abuse survivor Rakhel Silverman, who was given a pamphlet on forgiveness by a rabbi while she was in trauma recovery, described the torment that language of teshuva gives her and other survivors. "Why are we more focused on making victims forgive than we are on supporting and validating them? . . . We must recognize the harm that teshuvah and its forgiveness rhetoric can do to survivors of any kind of mistreatment." She says that calls for teshuva can perpetuate victim blaming. "Survivors," she writes, "do not let anyone tell you that you must focus on your abuser."[281]

Gender and sexuality

Female interviewees from across the denominational spectrum pointed to underlying ideas about gender as contributing factors to their vulnerability. Some of this is denomination-specific, but much of it isn't.

During the grooming process, for example, socializations into sexuality at times interfered with victims' abilities to recognize what was happening to them. Many women reported that their socialization to be "nice" severely inhibited their ability to deal with abuse. Some were socialized to be caring or compassionate, and respond to the needs of the person making all kinds of claims on their bodies. Many felt guilt or shame for not being "nicer" to their abuser as he encroached. Some were so worried about expectations that

---

[281] Rakhel Silverman, "The Harm of Tshuvah: A Letter from an Abuse Survivor," *Jewish Women's Archive*, September 12, 2018

they be sexually "pristine" that it took some time for them to realize something was off.

Similarly, boys assaulted by men are often so shamed about the implications of their incorrect sexuality ("I'm not gay!") that those socializations impede the victim's ability to say, "This is abuse." Socialization into gender roles is sometimes so subtle that it is taken as normal.

This is not just Orthodox-specific, and cuts across gender socialization everywhere in different ways. Orthodox women may be more susceptible than others, as Yittel claimed as a former Bais Yaakov girl who did not understand anything about sex when her rabbi started to come on to her. Or they may be *less* susceptible than others, as Yael was when she screamed "Don't touch me! I'm shomer negiya!" and would not let her attacker near her. But women of all backgrounds described vulnerability to grooming based on socialization into sexuality and expectations of pleasing and serving.

Certainly, in Orthodoxy, the culture of punishing incorrect sexuality is enforced with a particularly gendered intensity. Orthodox culture around female body-cover and segregation—tzniut, negiya, and yichud—are co-opted to both keep girls in their place and to absolve religious men of accountability when they abuse. Also, concepts of tzniut place the onus on girls to be desexualized and to protect themselves with excessive body-cover instead of teaching people not to objectify others, judge others, or attack others. As Sarah Bronzite said to me, "Young Jews are told that Judaism protects them through the mechanisms of modesty and separation but of course, abusive rabbis and other Jewish community leaders — who definitely know that they're breaking religious rules — cross those boundaries anyway. And at the same time, perpetrators perpetrate in the knowledge that their victims will not disclose because they know *they* will be blamed for not having been modest or separate enough. So negiya/tzniut acts as a triple bind for victims: they are proffered as a false promise of safety; they are used as a justification for not providing the education that could help to protect young people from, or to report, harm; and they are harnessed by perpetrators to control disclosure." That is a powerful triple whammy.

But gender roles permeate throughout Jewish society, not only in Orthodoxy, in ways that enable abuse and neutralize resistance. Constructs of girls/women as baby machines, and the purposes of informal settings to find a Jewish marriage partner, can have an overly sexualizing impact and heavily pressure both girls and boys to engage in actions that they might not want to. This also finds expression in Jewish camps and Jewish schools, which at times have overly sexualized cultures, even among peers. We saw Jewish schools, camps, youth groups, and other informal settings where "hooking up" created expectations of abuse both among peers and between adults in charge and the teenagers they were meant to be looking after. Even in some Orthodox schools that supposedly enforce gender segregation and no touching, sexual abuse between peers seems to be an issue.

These issues bring out a kind of chicken-and-egg question. Do oversexualized and boundariless student cultures create a place for adult predators to prowl, or are oversexualized student cultures a result of teenagers internalizing and mimicking the behaviors of some of the adults around them? Put differently, are schools attractive to sexual predators because sexual boundaries seem blurry and undefined among kids, or are boundaries undefined in schools because sometimes the people meant to be enforcing the boundaries are sexual predators themselves? Either way, the presence of abuse in Jewish schools by both peers and teachers is alarming from many perspectives. And they form one aspect of a very problematic and often gendered socialization into sexuality that sets a particular backdrop for abuse.

Distorted socialization into sex also seeps into the reporting process. Often, the surrounding culture casts abuse as some kind of wild sexuality or pornographic – incorrect Jewish femininity, or incorrect sexuality – instead of as violent assault. When observers silence the stories by saying things like, "This is filth" instead of "This is abuse", what they are basically saying is that abuse is a function of girls or women not properly containing their sexuality, as well as a host of other heteronormative patriarchal assumptions. It casts abuse as the victim's fault for being "dirty" rather recognizing it as violent assault. This is a function of Jewish culture more concerned with keeping people sexually controlled than with protecting people from being abused. And that language of controlling sexuality can become part of the already easy process of assigning blame to victims. And can be an ultimate silencing tool.

In addition, concepts of sexuality inform community reactions via practices of communal "himpathy", in which the strongest drive was to support a man, even if he is a narcissistic abuser.

Mostly, despite some sub-cultural nuances of difference, most of these dynamics cut across sub-cultures, and reflect an underlying double bind or hypocrisy that women and girls face across Jewish communities: Be modest, but have sex with demanding men. Keep the rules, but break them when you are pressured to. Protect your bodies, but make them available for the needs of the Jewish people. It's your responsibility to protect and serve the needs of the Jewish collective, but if you experience abuse, don't expect the collective to protect you or serve *your* needs. In fact, a woman's needs or desires are nowhere in this entire Jewish discourse about women's bodies and sexuality.

All of these Jewish codes and norms that I described above that are entangled in the abuse process – Jewish connectivity, Jewish exceptionalism, Jewish values like lashon hara or teshuva, and even Jewish ideas about gender and sexuality — do not *create* abuse. Rather, they are Jewish-specific ideas that are used by abusers to *support* abuse. Judaism is not the reason for abuse, but just a tool used by abusers who dwell in this culture. They are used as tools for luring victims, creating intimacy, breaking barriers, and gaining communal support. Abusers across different cultural settings are basically the same, using the same types of manipulations and strategies. But they know how to use the language and ideas that they have in common with their victims in order to gain trust and have their way.

Gaslighting the community

It is worth taking a moment to look closely at one of the most painful and difficult aspects of communal responses to reporting, which is the verbal assault on victims, or what I see as communal gaslighting. Victims are often left to feel that nobody believes them, that they are to blame for their own abuse, or that they are losing their minds. Although gaslighting—the process in which an abuser makes a victim feel crazy by changing reality or claiming that truth is false and lies are true—is a common tactic for making victims feel like they are losing their minds, there are some particular variations of gaslighting that emerged from this research which dominated in many Jewish settings.

Communal cover-ups

One of the most agonizing aspects of this research was how brutal reporting can be in so many Jewish settings — whether reporting to trusted clergy members, rabbinic committees, rabbinic supervisors, bosses, or even the general public. There seems to be a stubborn resistance in Jewish communal life and culture to believing victims—especially when the accused is someone in a position of power. Many suffer terribly for coming forward, leading to intense traumas of revictimization. Many respondents said that the aftermath was worse than the abuse, an assertion famously made by Chanel Miller as well, the woman who was raped by Brock Turner.

Take Steinhardt, for example. People around him knew about his alleged behavior. According to the *New York Times*, people running his organizations knew. People taking his money knew. Occasionally, they would pay lip service to victims. More often, victims were nor heard or heeded in any meaningful way. This is the real disease in our community: knowing that sexual abuse is happening and doing nothing.

The dynamics of power relationships in covering up abuse in the Orthodox Jewish community have been well-documented by others, but it is still jarring. Covering up is done in many ways, from moving abusers to different congregations, enforcing silence, and alienating victims to providing high-profile supporters of abusers. Some victims who spoke to me were petrified about people finding out that they were sharing.

But it is not just the Orthodox community that has a problem with communal cover-ups of people in power. The HUC-JIR report pointed to cover-ups that had taken place sometimes over decades in their institutions. My interviewees similarly shared accounts from different communities and denominations about cover-ups, being disbelieved, and at times losing relationships and even jobs. The prioritizing of people in power is a problem throughout the Jewish community.

While covering up sexual abuse isn't a strictly Jewish problem, Jewish patterns do arise when attempting to hide or ignore it. When a victim is told, "Don't ruin his reputation," that is the same idea as lashon hara. When a victim is told, "Don't go to the authorities; we will deal with this internally," that is the same concept as mesirah. Interestingly, almost none of my interviewees ever bothered reporting to police. This is consistent with research that shows that a very small percentage of incidences of sexual abuse get reported to the police. Some of this is because of the gap between how people experience abuse and how laws define it. The legal system often places undue burdens on victims and makes it difficult if not impossible to seek justice. The same can be said for internal reporting processes that are at times out of sync and at other times non-existent. Moreover, for most people, it takes time, even years or decades, to fully process what happened. Some are too preoccupied with the shame, guilt, and fear to come forward at all. Or they are afraid of the consequences—losing jobs, careers, or their reputations. But many *did* report to internal authorities nevertheless, such as ethics committees. This suggests that ideas about mesirah—that Jews should deal with things hush-hush in-house—has quite a broad cultural impact, even among people who may not be familiar with the term. Certainly, it is not the only reason why Jewish victims do not go to the police. But it is a compelling finding.

But almost none of the interviewees got justice. Or when then did, it was after years of torment.

Ultimately, these dynamics point to troubling cultural norms to protect the most powerful people in the community, no matter what the impacts are on victims of abuse.

"It's someone else's issue"

One of the most compelling findings was the popularity of the thought that the problem is somewhere else, in someone else's culture, denomination, synagogue, or community.

The Jewish exceptionalism trope mentioned above — "It doesn't happen by us" — when used to deny that the abuse happens, is a form of communal gaslighting. A common variation of this denial that came up in my research is, instead of "It doesn't happen in *the Jewish community*", is "It doesn't happen in *my movement.*"

Thus, for example, in the Orthodox community, there is a common misconception that practices of tzniut—modesty; women's body-cover or gender segregation for women —somehow "protect" women and girls from being abused. Mayim Bialik famously wrote that in the *New York Times*, for which she was pilloried, as did my interviewee Yael who pushed her assailant out with "I'm shomer negiya!". But the idea has sticking power, despite its obvious fallacy. [282]

Meanwhile, on the other end of the spectrum, non-Orthodox Jews often seem to think that abuse only happens in Orthodox spaces. Some readers of an early version of this manuscript commented to me, "Your interviewees are obviously mostly Orthodox." Another early reader said to me, "Your interviewees are mostly non-Orthodox." These exchanges, which came within days of each other, tell me that the "The problem is over there" trope is alive and well.

To be sure, all the major movements are implicated by this research. Rabbis described come from all the denominations. And the descriptions of grooming, reporting, and impacts are shared by different sub-cultures, despite certain nuances of difference. Both Orthodox and non-Orthodox Jewish settings have their own problems with sexual abuse

In non-Orthodox settings, the many testimonies from summer camp "hookup cultures," reports from women in rabbinical school, and huggy Shabbat services, all point to the fact that sexual abuse happens throughout the Jewish community. Yet that stereotype—that it's an Orthodox problem—pervades.

To wit, in the research literature about sexual abuse in the Jewish community, the only sub-group that is ever singled out is ultra-Orthodoxy. There are at least 13 studies on that community, as well as several books. But there is not a single book or peer-reviewed article that examines abuse in an exclusively non-Orthodox Jewish setting (to my knowledge). This suggests that while Orthodoxy is seen as problematic, no other movement is. As if to say, Orthodox groups are strange and exotic and messed up when it comes to sexual issues, and therefore that's where the problem lies.

But none of these assumptions are confirmed by my research. There is enough messed-upness in the Jewish community to go around. If Orthodoxy

---

[282] Chavi Eisenberg, No, Rabbi Shafran, modesty won't prevent sexual assault. People don't want to know that there are some terrible things that all the precautions in the world simply won't prevent. *Times of Israel* , Oct 26, 2018 https://blogs.timesofIsrael.com/no-rabbi-shafran-modesty-wont-prevent-sexual-assault/

is plagued by excessive emphasis on female body-cover and sexual abstinence, liberal spaces are plagued by hookup cultures, sexual "games" between campers and counselors, few boundaries, and people like Steven M. Cohen and Michael Steinhardt pushing cultures of women as sex objects and baby-makers in service of the Jewish collective.

The point is that no group has a monopoly on abuse. It happens everywhere. Moreover, as I keep pointing out, it is not the codes of a particular group that *cause* the abuse to happen. Tzniut does not *cause* sexual abuse any more than women in rabbinical school do. These cultures merely *enable* abuse by providing abusers with tools to manipulate and control their victims. Sexual predators exist across *all* communities and *all* denominations — whether Orthodox, Reform, Conservative, or other — and will use whatever they have at their disposal, whatever their cultures provide for them.

The "It's out there and not in here" misconception also contributes to the dynamics of cover-up. It provides excuses and language to dismiss allegations of abuse with a flick of a hand: "It's not like that," or "We're not like that" or "There's obviously more to the story" or "But he's really a good guy." It's all based on the idea that if the abuser is "one of us," then the allegations cannot be true. The message that victims sometimes hear is very simply, "The person complaining is not part of our culture or our community. We are good. She is not. She's not one of us."

There are so many ways to otherize victims and embrace abusers, especially when the abuser is held up as an icon of the culture.

That's where the problem lies. It's not just in the actual practices of tzniut, though those are problematic in their own right. The problem is that cultural norms create avenues to allow in abusers. And the thought that "we are good" and "they are bad" occludes reality. That very thought enables processes of denying, dismissing, excusing, and covering up for abusers — and that thought is not specific to any one group.

It's abuse, not an affair

Another form of gaslighting is the reaction that the victim wanted it. This is especially relevant to adult victims/survivors who are easily questioned and doubted. Sometimes women are cast as mentally unstable, or vindictive, or dismissed as having an "affair" with their abuser.

The tactics of grooming between adult victims and child victims are strategically the same, even if they often *look* different. While children may receive "candy" as a lure, adults may receive a raise, a promotion, or coveted attention. Abusers know how to target their victims' vulnerabilities. For children, that may mean special outings for a child of divorce, while for an adult that may mean special attention to a woman who is recently widowed or lonely. One victim was raped by her rabbi in the funeral chapel after her grandmother's funeral — a story that is extremely telling about how predators work. Narcissistic abusers are masters at this kind of emotional manipulation, and they know how to find people's weaknesses and prey on them, whether the victims are adults or children.

This is important to recognize. Because when adults are targeted by abusers, from the distance it may not *look* like abuse. It may look like care, attention, or even a kind of twisted courtship. Maybe the rabbi has an open marriage. Maybe he's into polyamory and just wanted to invite her. Maybe lots of people in his congregation are doing it. Or maybe he was just trying to help her, to make her less lonely. There are many ways abusers are adept at making it look like what he was doing was natural and not predatory.

Moreover, victims are so often, as Fran Sepler pointed out "blamable". People are not at their best after experiencing abuse, and their post-traumatic reactions are easily cast as unlikability. This is doubly punishing victims for being abused.

Victims of ongoing sexual abuse by rabbis, as with other clergy predators, struggle with perceptions that these are affairs, despite the fact that rabbis have many tools of persuasion and power to get their way over women's objections. The "affair" narrative lacks an understanding of the roles of narcissism, charisma, authority, and power in the sexual abuse dynamic. It may also take victims time to realize what they want, to understand the dynamic they are in, to unpack the rabbi's God language and charm, and to learn to say "no." This can be an agonizing process, and by some estimates it takes an average of four years to emerge from. In that time, the abuse may seem consensual from the distance — or perhaps the predator has convinced the victim that it is consensual. But there is arguably no such thing as consent within a rabbinic relationship that is charged with so many hidden hierarchies.

Male victims may also feel shame, weakness, or self-blame, as well as feelings of inadequacy in physical prowess in their lack of success fending off the abuse, feelings that may be reflected in reactions of disbelief. These reactions of doubt and disbelief are part of the retraumatization process. The lack of awareness or understanding that adults can be victims can exacerbate the damage and healing process. Adult victims should not be blamed or shamed for the abuse.

"Nothing happened"

Another form is communal gaslighting is the dismissal of forms of sexual abuse in which the abuse was less obvious. Many people still tend to equate sexual abuse with touching, but it is not always that way. Take Barry Freundel, for example. He was convicted and served jail time for placing cameras in the mikveh and watching and photographing women in the bathroom, shower, and immerse, nude in the ritual bath. He never touched his victims. In fact, the victims did not even *know* that they were victims until the police called them in to identify themselves in photos. For some, their first moments of being mortified were when they were standing in a squad room where a group of police officers were staring at their naked bodies on a screen. Yet, the fact that they were never touched does not alleviate the devastating impact of the experience.[283]

Many victims are not touched by their abusers. Incessant body commentary, sexual innuendo, propositions, jokes about their sexuality or fertility — all of these can leave damaging impacts. They can cause shame, instability, or feelings of being unvalued for anything other than their sexuality. These experiences affect victims' self-concept, community belonging, and career moves — which can also affect financial stability. And, of course, they can also affect victims' relationships with their bodies, their sexuality, and their partners. Non-contact sexual abuse is so often dismissed as if nothing happened — but it is not nothing.

The "good guy" defense

Another gaslighting tactic worth highlighting is the "good guy" defense — where an abuser gets away with it because he — or others around him — say "but he's such a good guy." This has two potential meanings. One is that the abuser is so "good" that they cannot possibly have done this — which essentially casts the victim as a liar, someone making things up about a beloved member of the community. The other potential meaning is that the abuser may have done it, but they should be forgiven because they have so many other points of merit. They *know* but they don't *care.* They like him, and that's it. End of discussion.

Victims struggle immensely with the "good guy defense for a few key reasons. One is that it sets up a social hierarchy in which the abuser is valued and the victim is not. Another is that "good guy" becomes a definition of behavior that completely excludes sexual abuse. In other words, a person can be deemed "good" for a zillion other reasons — political opinions, public speaking, or volunteering at a homeless shelter. After all, every abuser has redeeming qualities, often very public performative ones. But the fact that they are *also* be a narcissistic sexual predator is not considered relevant. The message is: Sexual abuse *doesn't matter.*

Mostly, it's a gaslighting tactic that completely erases the victim's experience. It reinforces the idea that not only may the victim be fabricating their reality, but that even if they aren't, it is not important. The victim's life

---

[283] Elana Sztokman, "Stop minimizing Freundel's actions by saying he is nonviolent," *Forward,* May 21, 2015, https://forward.com/life/308634/stop-minimizing-freundels-actions-by-saying-he-is-nonviolent/

is not worth discussing or even considering. That can be an extremely painful and head-spinning message to grapple with.

Ultimately, it is a powerful silencing tactic. The victim says, "He abused me," and the reaction is, "No, no, he's not an abuser" — and the entire conversation is over.[284]

Cultures of impunity

The enabling of "small" offenses is what Asher Lovy referred to as "environments of impunity." This insight—that "small" and often gendered offenses pave the way for larger offenses—was also reinforced by the HUC-JIR report that dedicated its opening pages to detailed descriptions of gender abuse, working on the assumption that those practices are a contributing factor in the broader issue of sexual abuse generally. Many aspects of abuse are exacerbated by ongoing gender issues and inequalities. Dynamics in which women's concerns are dismissed by the community, the public humiliation of women, the exclusion of women from leadership, the objectification of women clergy and congregants, and the frequent failure to even see women as whole people all contribute to a culture that allows sexual abuse to fester. "What hurts more is the willingness to look aside," Ann said. "When [a school principal and rabbi] is told over and over that there was a principal who was abusing children and he hires him again, that hurts more. My expectations of Judaism are different. I expect us to be better. And maybe that's wrong, too, because I think it ends up hurting more when I realize that we're no better, we're just as capable of doing this. It hurts more when frankly it's people we're idolizing, people we look up to, when our leaders are behaving this way."

So, how do Jews compare?

One of the dominant questions from this research is whether the Jewish community is different from other communities when it comes to sexual abuse.

To be sure, a precise answer to that question would require a comprehensive cross-cultural study that includes both qualitative and quantitative measures and looks at large samples from several different faith groups. This research is a qualitative study of only Jewish settings, which is a starting-off point for the discussion. So, my answer to this question is limited.

---

[284] The 2022 Netflix series, "Anatomy of a Scandal", offered a very effective treatment of the "good guy defense." The accused kept saying, "I'm not a brute", which everyone around him agreed with. Hence, he was able to get away with it.

The question itself is also not necessarily important. It may not matter how rabbis compare to imams or priests. The question itself may be a deflecting tactic, an opportunity for people to say, "See, we're not so bad! Look over there—that group has it much worse!" How the Jewish community fares on this issue compared to other faith communities may be not only irrelevant but also an effort to stymie change.

Perhaps the only useful note regarding other religions and organizations is that there are, indeed, similar patterns in most structured hierarchies.

Nevertheless, here are a few key similarities between abuse in Jewish culture and that of other faith communities that emerged:

- **Spiritual narcissism.** Like other clergy members who abuse, rabbis who abuse also seem to be associated with narcissistic personality disorder, in particular with spiritual narcisissm. They act like they think they are God, with all that goes along with that.
- **Spiritual bypass.** The tactics of spiritual bypass, in which the abuser uses religious codes and ideas in order to place himself as outside of the norms of the rest of the world, is also present. Religious abusers will apparently use whatever tools at their disposal for grooming, abusing, and cover-up.
- **Using pastoral care to prey on the vulnerable.** Rabbis and other religious figures use their positions as pastorial carers to target the people who need them most—those who are vulnerable, insecure, or in personal crisis. They use these settings as opportunities to break barriers and insert themselves into victims' intimate lives.
- **Protecting the institutions.** As with the Catholic Church, Jewish institutions also often protect their own rather than "out" the abuser. And just as the Catholic Church has a history of shifting abusers around from one place to another, many Jewish institutions seem to have behaved in a similar pattern when faced with abuse in their midst. As with the Catholic Church, these experiences can be retraumatizing and even terrifying for victims in Jewish communities as well.
- **Spiritual impacts on victims.** As with victims in other faith communities, Jewish victims similarly face crises of faith when the abuser represents the community. This can lead to severe depression, isolation, and distrust, and has a myriad of social, spiritual, and economic implications.

There are likely more. But this list should give the community some keys for understanding that Jews are very much like everyone else, that rabbis are clergy with all that implies, and that the dangers of abuse and impacts of abuse in our community share enough with other faith communities as to make us stand up and take note.

Ultimately, sexual abuse in Jewish culture is not about one particular religion, tradition, or denomination. Abuse takes place not because of particulars of denominations or attitudes to halakha. These experiences cut across the board in Jewish life, as with all other faith communities. Abuse takes place when the culture allows it.

Chapter 14: What Now

In this chapter
Looking for solutions
Policy changes
       Encourage safe speaking out
       Protect victims/survivors
       Fix reporting processes
       Hold abusers accountable
       Train and hire rabbis differently
Cultural changes
       Support victims/survivors
       Educate for changing cultures
       Fix gender socialization
       Challenge hookup culture
       Remember that money isn't
          everything
       Reframe some core cultural concepts
       Revisit what community means
Hopes for the future

We now know a bit about impacts of abuse on victims — traumatic scars such as PTSD, anxiety, shame, self-blame, fear, anger, depression, eating disorders, difficulty in relationships, difficulties in work, instability, and even suicidal ideation, which plague victims everywhere. Jewish victims seem to closely resemble other victims of sexual abuse. But when abuse happens in a Jewish setting, there is more. There is also the potential for spiritual crisis and the loss of faith and the betrayal of trust. In Jewish communities, where the rabbi is often the gatekeeper to communal life as well, the impact on victims can also be the loss of communal connection. For victims for whom the synagogue has been a central part of their lives, the abuse can lead to a loss, a complete detachment from some of the aspects of life that the victims hold most dear. There is also a particular risk of shame and self-blame when the abuser is a rabbi because of the image of the rabbi as pure and unassailable. This sometimes takes the form of misplaced concern for the rabbi-abuser instead of self-care and protection.

The devastation cannot be understated.

Yet, these crushing impacts are only the tip of the iceberg. They do not only impact the victims but also have effects on everyone around them, whether they know it or not. Taken together, these impacts cause great damage to the entire community and culture — yet hardly anyone is paying attention.

For decades, Jewish sociologists focused on topics like Jewish continuity, connectivity, and engagement. These were the keywords in Jewish communal research, education, outreach, policy, and funding priorities for at least a generation. And yet, none of that research, to my knowledge, has explored the impact of abuse on communal changes and dynamics. That has been a massive oversight.

My research started to fill that gap by looking at the connection between abuse and the community itself. The research emerged with two key areas of communal impact: loss of members or loss of "talent", and deterioration of the culture.

In terms of loss of members, this has many forms. Victims — who include professionals, scholars, teachers, volunteers, participants, congregants, and even rabbis and cantors — often leave. They take their wealth of skills, creativity, passions, and intelligence, and use them elsewhere. Many spent years or decades honing their Jewish knowledge and building networks and organizations. Some left other lucrative jobs to dedicate their passions to the spaces that they thought would afford meaning and connection. Many had devoted their entire lives to serving the community.

Sexual abuse destroys all of that. Many of those people are now gone.

People who are traumatized largely distance themselves from the people and places where the trauma took place. Victims in Jewish settings leave synagogues, schools, communities, and career paths. When a Jewish person is abused in a Jewish context by a Jewish leader or gatekeeper, it can affect the victim's entire relationship to Judaism. That can mean Jewish communal or social life, Jewish spiritual life, Jewish work, or Jewish volunteering.

Yet, they are so often invisible. They are unseen and uncounted. The community moves on. Abusers stay in place while victims drop out. It is a huge waste. A tragedy.

Significantly, this entire dynamic takes a significant toll on the culture itself. The Jewish community is left with the abusers in its midst — sometimes in positions of leadership — while those who once filled seats are absent. These values filter down— who is valued (people with charisma or money) and who is not (people without charisma or money); what norms are tolerated (abuse) and what norms are not (speaking out about it); who merits support (those with power) and who does not (those with no power). That becomes the culture. Every time an abuser is given a podium and a position while victims are left to fall off, the culture itself is affected. And yet I could not find anywhere in the communal thought leadership where this idea is being discussed, researched, or analyzed.

There is a connection between the presence of abusers in communal leadership and the cultivation of communal values. While Steven M. Cohen, one of the leaders in Jewish sociology for decades, was sexually harassing women who would be his successors, he was also receiving communal funds to set communal policy. Often his funding came from a megadonors who had abusive, sexist predilections. Together, they determined that "continuity" was a priority — that is, the need for Jews to hook up with other Jews and make Jewish babies — as opposed to, say, ensuring that the community was a safe place for everyone. Cohen was part of the problem that was being ignored. His own abusive and sexist tendencies directly cultivated the communal culture, values, and priorities, with lots of help along the way.

This admitted harasser also had a role in keeping out women who could have helped make change. Cohen was systematically abusing women in his field as they tried to develop professionally. During meetings about their careers, he would try to kiss them or sexually solicit them. Some of those potential scholars also left. The damage this did not only to potential researchers but also to the field of Jewish scholarship is unfathomable. While he was ignoring one of the most important issues to the community — and to women — he was also blocking the very people who might have seen this. He was blocking them *and* sexually abusing them at the same time.

And he is the one we know about. How many more like him are out there?

All these issues are connected. Abusers are given platforms and control policies and cultures, patriarchal ideas dominate funding priorities and researchers, abusers are given massive grants to do research and determine communal direction, donors who abuse are celebrated, abusive donors fund programs in which patriarchy is spread and where "hookup culture" that can lead to abuse is nonetheless celebrated as "Jewish continuity," and the cycle goes on and on.

When Jews are being hurt this way in Jewish spaces and choose to leave, the entire community suffers as a result. It is a loss of talent, a loss of relationships, a loss of connections, and a loss of humanity. What's worse, when the abusers are left in positions of leadership while victims slowly slip away, we become a badly stained community, one in which abusers are more valued than anyone else.

These patterns within Jewish culture demand attention. The connections between Jewish engagement, sexism, and sexual abuse are screaming to be fixed.

Looking for solutions

If all this is happening, it is because the surrounding cultures and organizational structures allowed it all to happen. Children need to be protected, and if they are being hurt, then their protectors are not doing their jobs. Adult victims/survivors and potential victims also need attention. As one of my interviewees said, "There is a *third party* in all the abuse: the surrounding institutions." Wherever abuse takes place, there are people around who could have stepped in to stop it, whether they are staffers, lay leaders, colleagues, fellow congregants, professional peers, bosses, witnesses, or family members. As long as the abuse continues to happen all around the community, these third parties are bystanders, with all that implies.

Protecting children, as well as everyone else in the community, means taking actions that are not necessarily easy — especially when the abusers may be donors, board members, congregants, or volunteers who are not supervised or monitored. This requires *policy* change.

Moreover, perpetrators of abuse are often celebrated, no matter what they do — whether it's sexual abuse or art theft. It is worth remembering that all abusers have redeeming qualities — fundraising, leading services, or finding words of wisdom at difficult times. Every abuser has some redeeming qualities. All abusers are beloved by some people. Nevertheless, if the Jewish community is going to be safe and whole, changes need to take place in communal settings in order to protect people from abuse. This requires *cultural* change.

Both forms of change are necessary. Policy change is vital and desired. But policy change can only go so far without work on the cultural side. Both culture and policy inform each other and impress on one another. They need each other to work.

My interviewees shared many thoughts about what can be done to prevent sexual abuse, or to protect victims after the fact. Below is a compilation of some suggestions, though it is a sampling and not nearly a comprehensive list. As I said at the outset, my work is not a formal evaluation of any kind. And thankfully, there are many organizations working hard at this (See the Appendix for a list of communal organizations involved in this work.). What I bring here is some ideas for both policy change and cultural change that were brought up by some of my interviewees.

Policy changes

Encourage safe speaking out

Speaking out is one of the greatest powers that victims have. Debbie Findling, who spoke out in the media about being abused by Len Robinson decades earlier, told the *Jewish Week* that, "My hope is that my experience will help empower other women in the Jewish community to speak out... Your voice will enable our community to stop a terrible cycle of sexual harassment and complicity." The exposure of so-called "modesty squads," for example, the Satmar gangs that are violent toward women considered to be "improperly dressed," was the result of a victim coming forward about sexual abuse by Nechemya Weberman.[285] This is an example of how coming forward, when it works, can lead to real change. And the #MeToo movement has arguably changed the playing field, giving victims more credibility and power than they have ever had.

Still, as this research shows, victims who come forward also take great risks. The damage from reporting — including being blamed, judged, shamed, and disbelieved, or even losing their jobs — can lead to even greater trauma to the victim while having zero impact on consequences for the abuser or change in surrounding cultures.

Communities need to make it safe to speak out and report. This will take enormous, directed, purposeful work. It is not enough to tell victims/survivors to speak out. The rest of the community has to ensure that they will be protected in that process as well.

Protect victims/survivors

Believing victims/survivors is one part of supporting them. Another is protecting them from retaliation. Retaliation can come in many forms. For Leanne, it meant that when she told her parents about the "creepy rabbi," she was no longer given Torah reading assignments. For Tali, it meant being moved to a different building and department, completely derailing her career. For Ruth, it was a quiet firing a few months after she refused to date the donor. Retaliation can also be public. It can be a smear campaign or social media posts calling the victim names.

---

[285] Hella Winston, "Trial Exposes Shadowy Chasidic 'Modesty Committees': Young woman's testimony reveals tactics of freelance 'purity' guardians in Satmar community," *Jewish Week.* December 6, 2012, https://jewishweek.timesofIsrael.com/trial-exposes-shadowy-chasidic-modesty-committees/?fbclid=IwAR3EQXS1O4gyePcWpD0PvNKQfrur6UhnNUTyM1RmgKtQS-ATP4AlSjGu9rw

People going through retaliation need support. This can be public support, social media support, or private checking-in. Every positive connection matters.

Organizations and communities need to advocate for victims on all fronts, not only from abuse but also from what comes afterward. The issue of sexual abuse in the Jewish community needs more passionate advocates. When passionate advocates outweigh and culturally overpower those who support abusers, real change will take place.

Fix reporting processes

A clear take-away from this research is that overall, reporting processes are a mess. That is not to discount the very real work that some institutions are doing to fix this. But it is notable that not one interviewee had a truly positive and effective experience with reporting. Most of the stories about that were agonizing. And they were in the minority of interviews. The overwhelming majority of interviewees never went through the process of reporting. In fact, the concerns that most interviewees had about reporting were confirmed by the experiences of those who did report.

The importance of fixing reporting processes cannot be overstated. In the long run, the safety of reporting mechanisms is what makes the difference between a safe community and an unsafe one. As Fran Sepler explained, "Somebody can do bad things anywhere, even in the greatest organization. But in great organizations, it's addressed and stopped. And, and in fact very often it's addressed and stopped early enough that it doesn't end up ruining people's lives... and people can go on with a bigger better relationship."

Shira Berkovits, in a paper based on her practical experience with reporting processes in the Jewish community, lists some characteristics in Jewish settings that are problematic in the handling of sexual abuse cases: (1) cognitive dissonance, as in, denials of the problem; (2) cognitive distortions, such as "all-or-nothing thinking" or labeling; (3) discounting victims' disclosures; and other issues, such as lack of organizational transparency.[286]

Synagogues need training as well. As Rabbi Daniel Pressman, chair of the RA's *Va'ad Hakavod* (Ethics Committee) told me:

> The congregation is a secondary victim. This can play out in many ways. There are always those who will defend the rabbi no matter what, so the congregations divide into factions. People lose trust in rabbis in general, making life difficult for the next rabbi. When the leadership mishandles the matter, key members will quit. And, of course, when the synagogue is strongly identified with its charismatic leader/abuser, it is shaken to its foundation. We need our denominations to step

---

[286] Berkovits, "Institutional abuse", 12-22

> up in early intervention to prevent congregations from making
> common mistakes, provide support for the victims, and tend to
> the healing of the congregation."[287]

Sura Jesselson, who has been fiercely advocating for change in her community in response to Jonathan Rosenblatt's years of abuse, has a vision for communal organizations:

> Just as we have a code for cleanliness and sanitary conditions
> in restaurants, we should aim for a code describing the work
> conditions at various Jewish institutions. This would cover
> issues such as salary equity, advancement opportunities, and
> general tone of an institution.
>
> We also need a union for workers at Jewish institutions, which
> would act as clearinghouses for issues of pay, working
> conditions, benefits, and personal safety.
>
> We also need a mechanism where people applying for jobs show
> certification that they are not criminals or ethically challenged.

Organizations on the frontlines of exactly these kinds of processes deserve communal support and resources.

Hold abusers accountable

There is also a need to deal directly with abusers. Berkovits recommends dealing with the problematic *behaviors* rather than focusing on individual *abusers*. But many interviewees disagree. Reut said directly, "I want the abusers to be punished for what they did." Rena also said about the report about abusive donors, "You want to hear people saying, 'We're not going to take that donor's money.'"

Many interviewees would have liked to see their abusers actually lose their jobs or their pulpits, or be ousted from the congregation or the board — rather than the victims being ousted. In some movements, rabbis can lose their certifications, and some interviewees pushed for those processes, although with very little effect.

In some cases, it is hard to know exactly what accountability looks like. What does it mean to hold a volunteer accountable? Or a donor? It is not always clear, but from these testimonies, it is clear what accountability does *not* look like. It is *not* inviting the known abuser to speak, to teach, to counsel, or to run a singing prayer session with fancy singing or guitar. It is *not* whitewashing the story or bullying victims to stay quiet. Accountability is the opposite of all that.

---

[287] For a brief description of a model, see https://abuseresponseandprevention.ca/clergy-sexual-misconduct/for-the-congregation-impacted/

Sarah Bronzite adds that there is a need to "hold abusers accountable through passing information to other, and future, employers and connected organizations. Organizational responsibility, especially in such a close-knit community, should extend to protecting our wider community and not just the small number of people in one particular setting, about how this needs to be seen as a *to'elet* — useful and beneficial to the community — rather than as lashon hara."

Train and hire rabbis differently

There is a need to rethink what the community expects from rabbis, as well as what qualities are esteemed in rabbis. When the emphasis is on performance, and the training is toward receiving positive reviews as performer, the position becomes open to corruption and narcissism.

Brenda, who almost entirely dropped out of communal life, is staying in one position: the rabbinic search committee. "I can't leave. I'm not quitting now when I finally have some power in the community. I think about all these issues all the time when I'm looking at all these individuals applying. I need to stay on that committee." Despite her emotional strain, and the community's lack of understanding of her abuse or appreciation of her contributions, she has found a way to use her experience to prevent it from happening again. Both the training and the hiring of rabbis needs to be refocused and to ask different questions about what it means to be a rabbi.

In particular, one of the key take-aways from this research is the real danger of valuing charisma and performance over all else. As Fran Sepler explained:

> I'm doing a lot of guidance for search committees hiring rabbis now, especially around implicit bias and how to avoid it. And I'm trying to move people away from, "I felt a personal connection to this person,' or 'We like this person,' because those are terrible ways to pick a rabbi. But that's also the traditional way of picking a rabbi. The people who bring the rabbi on feel an 'affinity.' They feel 'affection.' And that decision comes out of all sorts of problematic biases that. What does a rabbi look like? 'Oh, they're authoritative. They are particularly masterful. 'They have charisma.' These are all things that attach to certain kind of sociopathy — not always — but those are characteristics where you're much more likely to find somebody with a bunch of pathology going on.

The community should be engaging in deep questions about redefining what makes good character, what the purpose of "charisma" is, and how much of cultural expectations revolve around superficial, star-gazing, immediate gratification. The way the culture stands, the qualities most valued may be the ones that are most likely to cause harm.

Breaking these patterns will take introspection, humility, and honesty on the part of the community. Because, as Sepler points out, most people are not so eager to hear that their feel-good reactions were all wrong, and that the person they were excited about is abusing people. "The last thing, members of a congregation want to do is notice that, because it means that there's toxins flowing in the institution, and that reflects on them. It means that all this love and faith and trust they've invested in somebody was wrong and they were wrong which people don't want to admit. 'You know I'm a great judge of character, I couldn't possibly....'"

The first step is the willingness to admit that maybe something here is wrong. Maybe the star-struck fans of the charismatic rabbi have made a big mistake. Maybe the entire process of finding leaders needs a cultural overall.

Cultural changes

Support victims/survivors

There is a need to look deep into the culture and see how victims are valued versus how abusers are valued. This goes against how our culture is designed, which is to first assume that victims of sexual assault are lying.

Yet, there are many wonderful advocates out there who stand up for victims. Some of my interviewees demonstrated great courage in speaking out in their communities, in the media, or to reporting agencies. As Reut, a fierce advocate for victims, said, "When the story broke" about her rabbi abusing boys, "I believed the victims immediately. Why would somebody want to bring this on themselves?"

Unfortunately, Reut's compassion is not necessarily the norm. Sympathy for the accused often runs deep, as does Fran Sepler's "culture of exception." The media also often participates in skewing public opinion in a way to doubt victims, such as with the use of "allegedly" and the use of flattering photos of the accused.

The first step in making change is cultivating allyship is believing victims, and caring. There are ways to respond to the media bias as well. Sheila Katz and Rabbi Danya Ruttenberg recommend several practices to demonstrate believing those who report abuse. One is to share testimonies of victims without sharing the photos of the abusers, so as not to trigger victims. They recommend using a picture that says "believe survivors" to accompany posts. "This can be a way to show your support, center victims, and help reduce trauma for those most affected."

The community can create more ways to support victims/survivors.

Educate for changing cultures

There is a glaring need for policies, procedures, and training across Jewish organizations and communities about how to recognize and deal with abuse on a systematic level. As Fran Sepler said, "We need to ask questions like, 'Why does this happen in organizations?' and 'What are the cultural building blocks that are either present or absent, that allow this behavior to occur?'" Early reporting is a key issue that protects victims and organizations, and communities need to ensure that their cultures support that. As Shira Berkovits, in discussing the importance of systemic reporting processes, told me, "Institutions too often view reports or complaints as personal attacks and a breach of trust. We need to depersonalize and standardize. We follow X, Y, and Z steps regardless of whom we're talking about."

In other words, change begins with seeing this issue as a systematic, community-wide issue, and addressing it as such. Sheila Katz and Rabbi Danya Ruttenberg urge people in institutions to observe their own actions in response to abuse:

> *The true test of an institution that participates in harm is whether and how well it takes responsibility. If you're a stakeholder, can you be part of the project of holding your synagogue, camp, or other organization to accountability by making sure that it follows best practices? Some of these may include, but are not limited to, conducting a thorough and impartial investigation allowing survivors access to the investigation report; making funding for victims' therapy or other mental health needs available; and making a statement that you believe the survivor, are grateful for them coming forward and will be following up on their claim. Push your organization toward tangible actions and concrete measures of accountability. Remember that others are watching and if the institution remains silent, even if there is a legal situation, that silence is easily taken as support for the perpetrator.*[288]

Fix gender socialization

The cultures that see women as less powerful or less leadership-like are but one part of a larger socialization into Judaism and gender. The ideas about women as baby-makers and Jewish camps as places to hook up—are just some of the myriads of troubling ideas that contribute to objectifying women's bodies that need to be revisited. The objectification of girls' bodies,

---

[288] Sheila Katz and Rabbi Danya Ruttenberg, "What to remember when abuse stories break in Jewish communities," *Baltimore Jewish Times* September 1, 2021, https://www.jewishtimes.com/opinion-what-to-remember-when-abuse-stories-break-in-jewish-communities/

sometimes when they are very young, with ideas about tzniut and overall appearance, also contributes to this culture.[289]

Shana Aaronson, Director of Magen, believes that the problem is not necessarily body-cover but more the ways in which women and girls are socialized to put their own needs and desires aside when a man in authority tells them to. She proposed a cultural-educational shift for women and girls in the Orthodox community based not on doing away with body cover but rather using the rules to protect women, as she believes the rules are intended:

> We can be using laws of yichud and tzniut to protect women and girls who want to live by these halakhot. We have to teach them to listen to themselves, and to trust their own feelings and knowledge, and not to trust a rabbi – or anyone, regardless of how lofty a position they hold – who says, 'Break these rules for me. It's okay because I say so.' We can be training women that when a rabbi or any person does that, that is a red flag. If you feel like a line is being crossed, it probably is. And teach them to trust their instincts and feelings, while they are using these laws as protection.

The socialization into giving into authority despite one's own body needs or spiritual needs is not unique to tzniut or to Orthodoxy. Is arguably also connected also to the culture of niceness — expectations on women and girls to be sweet and caring and not make a fuss or a scene.[290] These social expectations that contribute to keeping victims from resisting or standing up to the abuse The entire Jewish culture and community needs to rethink some of these ideas and needs a revamp of gender socialization.

This is especially true now that we know about the connections between Cohen, Steinhardt, Birthright, and many other informal settings and youth groups in which girls of all backgrounds are pressured to give into sexual demands of boys, which are rooted in gendered ideas about female servitude that come from donors and policy makers. Ideas about gender and sex that the community took as sacred for so long are actually toxic. This whole culture needs to be revisited. It's not just girls who need a difference kind of socialization. Everyone does.

The patriarchy runs deep. It causes damage on many levels. One issue that came up in interviews was about how women are seen and heard. As Ruth made some suggestions:

---

[289] My late friend and colleague, Dr. Chaya Gorsetman, and I wrote a book about this in 2013. The book, *Educating in the Divine Issues: Gender issues in Jewish Day Schools*, is replete with the ways in which gender socialization instills problematic ideas. This research is the other end of that story – it is about what our culture has been turning out as a result of not addressing those issues effectively.

[290] Garland and Argueta, pp 10-20

It feels like an old boys' club. The women are saying we don't feel comfortable, so what would make us feel more comfortable? What can be different? There's the basic thing of having your ideas respected, being brought into conversations because you have something to offer. If there's a project, people usually bring in their same old boys' network on the project, and the rest of us don't get brought in, so we don't have work. What would need to be different is for us to feel like, as Jewish scholars and scholars of Judaism, that we were respected and treated as equals in our field. A lot of it comes down to people's attitudes and these subtle body things that they're doing. These things all add up to how you feel in the community. They add up to the cultural issue that needs to be addressed that I don't have words for. I would just like to feel different. I would like to be talked to differently by colleagues.

Many respondents described the need to listen to women and to pay attention to the ways in which that often does not happen. One respondent, describing a popular podcast run by two men and a woman, said, "I just am fascinated by the way the two men and often the guest talk over Stephanie. She has developed this surgical response: she'll wait it out and then dish a zinger that all the women in the audience will roar at, because we all recognize it as a strategy. You can't talk over them, so you have to be clever and subtle and use humor as a tool to point out the sexism." Still, that is not necessarily changing the culture. "The fact that we all are sharing and know and recognize the behavior, I don't know if that changes the behavior."

Ultimately, what this research shows is that there are certain underlying cultures in Judaism that support abuse. The backdrop of patriarchy in almost every aspect of communal life sends many messages about who is valued and who is not, and who deserves power and who does not. Those hierarchies enable abuse when the abuser is in a valued demographic and the victim is not.

The community needs direct, intentional, multi-layered interventions for uprooting patriarchal cultures.

Challenge hookup culture

One of the most dangerous cultural patterns to emerge from this research is "hookup culture" and its prevalence in spaces that are meant to be safe for Jewish youth. We now know that "jokes" about making Jewish babies are not only not funny — they are dangerous. Jokes about bodies are also not just offensive — they also put certain people in jeopardy. The community needs to have a zero-tolerance policy for rape jokes, fertility jokes, fat jokes, body jokes, and anything that objectifies one group of people and/or pressures teens to engage in unwanted sexual activity.

Thankfully, a group of young women is taking the lead on that process. Madeline Canfield, Lila Goldstein, Ellanora Lerner, Lilah Peck, Maddy Pollack, and Dahlia Soussan, are on it, writing and speaking about these issues and creating programs for awareness.[291] These young people, and people like them who are pushing back against destructive cultures, deserve the community's fullest support. And we can all learn from what they are saying.

Remember that money isn't everything

One of the most jarring findings in this research was how protected donors are. As one interviewee told me, "In organizational life, the second someone is dangling a big donation in front of you, everything else easily falls to the side."

Fran Sepler, in her work training Jewish organizations to create safe cultures, has a teaching tool she and her associates developed called "That's just so and so." In this tool, she trains people to recognize the "culture of exception" that is so often used to protect abusers. Her tool includes language such as, "Oh they have a heart of gold," or "Their bark is worse than their bite," or "You just have to learn to work with them," or "Ignore their personality." She said that while "we want a culture of civility, one person is relationally pulling people out in the community and we're turning our backs." She has dedicated her life's work to calling out these cultures and training people to do things differently.

This culture of exception, especially for donors, needs to change if there will ever be safe spaces. The kind of change is cultural, deep-rooted, and difficult. It requires hard conversations, self-awareness, and leaders who are willing to take risks in order to do the right thing. Those qualities sometimes seem to be in short supply.

Yet, this is exactly what is urgently needed right now. The look-away reverence for donors or other kinds of celebrities is at the core of so much of how abuse is enabled. Only an honest assessment of cultural practices around donor-reverence and celebrity impunity will enable the necessary changes. The community must begin asking what kinds of values — *midot*, if you will — *actually* deserve reverence.

Reframe some core cultural concepts

There is a need to reframe some of the Jewish cultural concepts that enable grooming, false intimacy, and protection of abusers.

---

[291] Madeline Canfield, Lila Goldstein, Ellanora Lerner, Lilah Peck, Maddy Pollack, and Dahlia Soussan , "For Continuity's Sake? Addressing Hookup Culture in Jewish Youth Groups," *e-Jewish Philanthropy*. https://ejewishphilanthropy.com/for-continuitys-sake-addressing-hookup-culture-in-jewish-youth-groups/

Lashon hara, for example, needs to be taught differently. The wider Western culture is engaged in reframing "secrets," teaching kids that sometimes sharing is the mitzvah. Yael Leibowitz wrote a very powerful essay about this following the Walder affair, in which she followed the evolution of approaches to kids' secret-keeping and adult disbelief through changes at *Sesame Street*.[292] She recounts how when Mr. Snuffleupagus made his first appearance on *Sesame Street* as Big Bird's friend in 1971, the running joke was that he always disappeared when adults were in the room, and hence nobody believed he was real. But in the 1980s, the producers decided that this was a problematic dynamic because it encouraged kids to think that their parents would not believe them if they told the truth. Hence, in 1985, they created the "Snuffy reveal" as a message to believe kids.

Leibowitz argues that Jewish education needs its own "Snuffy reveal" moment to upend generations of messages that harm victims of abuse and fail to protect kids. These messages may include issues such as lashon hara, tzniut, and even the way problematic texts are taught, such as the story of David's rape of Batsheva, which is often taught along with the Talmudic text that says that David did nothing wrong. She says that when students hear these messages, they may connect them to what is going on in their real lives. "The producers of *Sesame Street* understood that education goes way beyond the ABCs," and she urges Jewish educators to rethink some of the messages of Jewish education as well.

The community needs to reframe some other concepts as well—such as mesirah, anti-Semitism, and even family. Mesirah should be revisited in order to enable people to communicate with non-Jewish supporters and authorities. Anti-Semitism should be revisited in order to understand that often the enemies are within and that protecting Jews from being hurt by other Jews is *also* a crucial value. Jewish family concepts should be revisited and separated from sex cultures at camp and from ideas of Jewish women's fertility responsibilities to the collective. And this is just a start.

Revisit what community means

The concept of "community" itself needs some adjustment. For one thing, community as an unquestioned value above all else creates many risks of harm and opens doors to abuse. Community may be nice in some ways, but without definitions and understandings of ethics around community, it puts people at grave risk.

In addition, community creates boundaries of "in" and "out," of who counts and who does not count. And currently, some of these unspoken

---

[292] Yael Leibowitz, "Big Bird, Chaim Walder, and the power of nuance. Traditional explanations of difficult texts can turn harmful for students who may be sensitive for a whole host of reasons. Jewish educators can teach better." *Times of Israel*. Dec 30, 2021

assumptions create painful hierarchies that leave the most vulnerable people—the people who perhaps need community most—outside.

What appears to be a communal overemphasis on money, status, and prestige rears its head and keeps people seeking locations of power and money and hanging on tight to their seats. I say this with responsibility, as well as with trepidation. When I shared this particular finding in a social media post, I was called a "Nazi" for promoting the anti-Semitic idea that Jews are obsessed with money. I can assert that my motivation for sharing this observation is anything but anti-Semitism and comes from a great deal of pain having come upon this dynamic repeatedly throughout the research. The communal cultures that support abuse are deeply wound up in some very troubling values that desperately need attention and change, I am very sad to report this, but here we are. In so many cases, attachment to money and status was far more important than protecting people from sexual abuse. I find that immensely tragic.

At the same time, what is missing from our concepts of community are ideas about how community members support each other. Community seems to be implying that the leaders demand support and co-religionists have no boundaries.

Ultimately, home, family, and community are meant to be safe spaces, and yet at times they hold the darkest secrets of pain and abuse. In a culture in which the "Jewish home" is meant to be sacred, these stories are powerful illustrations that the culture does not always live up to what it claims to be. That constitutes a violation of trust for everyone.

As I said, as long as sexual abuse is happening in places that purport to be nice, fun, caring, protective, holy, or sacred, nothing in the culture can be trusted to be what it says it is—and no place is truly safe.

Perhaps a better definition of community would be that I care about my co-religionists' pain, I am there to help, and my leaders deserve respect so long as they have true character and at the very least are causing no harm. That in itself can be a revised conceptualization or definition of community that would be worth embracing— and protect all its members from abuse. We can be framing community not in terms of *what I get* from belonging to one, but *what I give* in order to create a culture that I want to belong to.

Hopes for the future

It's possible that some of these cultures are currently in the process of changing. One study showed that fundraising professionals believe that the culture within the profession is changing with respect to sexual harassment. More than nine out of ten believe that sexual harassment allegations in fundraising are more likely to be taken seriously today than ever before. The majority observe the #MeToo movement having a positive influence on the general workplace environment. [293] It is quite possible that we are in the midst of a major cultural shift around these issues. But it is perhaps too early to say for sure. After all, social advances are not always a linear process. Perhaps only in another decade or another generation will we know for certain whether we are currently at a turning point.

What we can say for certain, however, is that research helps us understand the dynamics of a problem — and can be used as a powerful tool to create cultural change.

Some survivors have used their experiences to become powerful advocates and have created activism toward communal change. But needing to fall into victimhood in order to be inspired to act is too big a price to pay. Nor should people have to dedicate their talents to issues of abuse instead of the creative passions that they were engaged in when they were abused. The Jewish community has access to great resources in the people who dedicate their lives to Jewish causes, but the community is at great risk of losing them to abuse.

If we really care about Jewish people— the culture, the community, and continuity— then healing the plague of sexual abuse in our midst is of the highest importance.

Personally, despite everything compiled here, I still believe in the power of the human spirit. And culturally speaking, the Jewish people are well-trained in willing things into existence. If we can *imagine* a changed future, maybe we can, in fact, *create* it.

---

[293] AFP, "One-Quarter of All Female Fundraisers", https://afpglobal.org/one-quarter-all-female-fundraisers-report-sexual-harassment?fbclid=IwAR15drXFmHnHTyrcmLuxoH2eHpnNcumDTMHFbhMnz841MT0_H05tfAQH2x8

Epilogue

A lot has changed in the world since I embarked on this research in 2015. Back then, the #MeToo movement had not yet exploded into consciousness and victims/survivors were more likely to hold their secrets in the dark. The world had not yet grappled with an attempted rapist on the Supreme Court or an admitted sexual groper elected as President. Serial abusers were still in locations of significant power and influence to control public opinion and public policy, including news anchors, governors, and Hollywood moguls.

We didn't know it then, but we were on the cusp of a massive cultural shift. As a consequence of #MeToo, the media began to eagerly print accounts of sexual assault rather than wait for dozens of victims to come forward to validate each claim. Organizations began holding abusers accountable and removing them from their positions. Gender inequality in spaces of leadership and decision-making became a topic on the cultural agenda. In the year following Harvey Weinstein's arrest for rape, over 200 men in senior or publicly-known positions were outed as predators, many lost their jobs, and a decent portion of those were replaced by women. This is all significant.

Yet, too quickly, the pendulum has already started swinging back the other way. Today some of the public chatter is focused on forgiveness, comebacks, and how to hold space for the poor, unemployed abusers. To wit, Louis C.K. — the comedian who was outed in 2017 for sexual harassment and subsequently lost some work — has had such a successful comeback that he quietly won an Oscar in 2022, just days before I am writing these words. In the time I have been working on this book, the culture around sexual abuse exploded — and then to an extent retreated.

The Jewish community has been a few steps behind the rest of the world in this journey. It took some time before the Jewish community began taking accusations seriously. Most notably, even when the *New York Times* and *ProPublica* wrote an exhaustive essay about alleged abuse by Jewish megadonor Michael Steinhardt, nothing happened. Not a single Jewish organization with which he is connected uttered a peep.

That said, as I was completing this book, some communal dynamics seemed to shift. The story of Chaim Walder, for example, had a very different ending to what the community was accustomed to. The ultra-Orthodox author and celebrity was discovered in December 2021 to have been sexually assaulting both children and adult women for decades. For the first time ever, ultra-Orthodox businesses and media outlets disassociated from the abuser in their midst, removing his books from shelves and cancelling his appearances and contracts. That was completely new, and many advocates commented on how this potentially signaled a cultural shift. Unfortunately, even this moment was marred by the backlash, as leaders including the Israeli Chief Rabbi spent considerable effort consoling Walder's family after his suicide. By contrast, there were no parallel efforts to tend to his victims. Other ultra-Orthodox leaders used the event as an opportunity to go on victim-blaming rants, going so far as to blame secular Jews for Walder's actions. Even now, as the specter of real change can be seen on the horizon, there is a lingering sense that progress is held back by those protecting the offenders. Again, two steps forward, one step back.

I have been personally affected, too. Just as this book was going to print, my own story of having experienced abuse and harassment at an organization where I worked nearly a decade ago blew up. I am referring to the Jewish Orthodox Feminist Alliance (JOFA) where I worked as Executive Director in 2012-13, and the revelations of abuse by its former president, Bat Sheva Marcus. After nearly a decade of silence, I made my charges public for the first time in April 2022, by sharing some of the traumatic experiences I had while I worked there. I had long put this story behind me and moved on with my life. But I came forward (due a series of events beyond my control), along with my successor, Dr. Sharon Weiss-Greenberg, who had also experienced severe abuse in the position as well as the painful forced silencing.[294] In coming forward, I was inspired by the courage of others who done the same in similar situations, such as Dr. Keren McGinity, and I felt that the time had come to speak my truth.

So I did this. I spoke up — and it had a powerful impact. JOFA is currently under scrutiny, several of its top lay leaders have resigned from volunteer jobs, Marcus was removed from her board position elsewhere (she had already been removed from JOFA), and she has been largely discredited as a sex therapist. In some places in the community, the charges have spurred on a genuine conversation about what constitutes abuse, about the traumas of non-contact abuse, and about the prevalence of non-sexual toxicity in our

---

[294] Details of the story are publicly available in a series of media stories about Bat Sheva Marcus, JOFA, and abuse, such as JTA here: Andrew Lapin, "Jewish feminist group in turmoil after Orthodox sex guru Bat Sheva Marcus, a founder, is accused of harassment", *JTA*, April 13, 2022 https://www.jta.org/2022/04/13/united-states/jewish-feminist-group-in-turmoil-after-orthodox-sex-guru-bat-sheva-marcus-a-founder-is-accused-of-harassment (the rest are easily searchable). You can also read my story in my Substack newsletter here: Elana Sztokman, "If your board vice chair sends you a vibrator, your workplace is probably toxic" https://elanasztokman.substack.com/p/if-your-board-vice-chair-randomly?s=w , or watch me tell the story in this Youtube video "Conversation with Elana Sztokman on JOFA and abuse in the Jewish Community" here https://www.youtube.com/watch?v=CW3sMEODkkE

organizational cultures. These are all positive outcomes, even if it is unclear how deep they will go or how long they will last.

I probably wouldn't have initiated the process without prompting. I was fully prepared to leave the story behind me and continue on with my other work, including the anthropology that I love. I would much rather do that than talk about my own past traumas. Nevertheless, the JOFA experience showed me the power of speaking out loud, and in public. It showed me that every story matters. Rumors and whispers — the "open secrets" that generations of women used as a tool for protecting one another -- ultimately have much less impact than public testimony in potentially bringing about change. When change happens, there is usually a courageous victim in the picture who has been willing to come forward.

Still, while telling my story has been liberating and impactful, the experience of coming forward has left me with a continued dilemma around the role of public sharing, or "outing" an abuser. Coming forward with one's own name and identity may have the most visible ripples, but it often comes with a cost for the victim/survivor.

To wit, JOFA was neither my first nor last abusive trauma in my working life. In the Prologue, I recounted some of the experiences of abuse that I've had during the course of my life. In the introduction to the chapter on gender abuse, I also shared some traumas that I experienced at my first Jewish communal job, at an organization where I stayed for four years because I did not value myself enough to say, "No." I have not yet outed the man who terribly abused me there, nor his boss who created an oppressive culture for everyone. And there's more. I have also not shared a particularly tormenting experience I had in another Jewish organization that I was involved with for a year while writing this book. I was conducting these interviews, collecting information, analyzing dynamics, recognizing terrible things around me — all while working with an institution where I was being actively and aggressively tormented. I still have not talked publicly about this, even though it is a story that needs telling, nor have I outed the people who purposefully played with my mind, disarmed me, and caused serious damage to my sense of self-worth as well as to my career. These are some of the stories I'm still carrying. And despite everything I know about the power of personal testimony, I'm still hesitating to tell these stories publicly.

Why am I still holding back? Even given my recent experience with the JOFA story and my full awareness of how important and powerful the telling is?

It's complicated. Obviously, I want to encourage the transparency, accountability, and justice that relies on public disclosures of abuse. But this process unfairly burdens victims/survivors with the responsibility of leading the fight. And it is *always* a fight. Because as I also learned in this work, high-profile abusers *always* have high-profile supporters. And that has implications for the person sharing publicly.

Coming forward forces the victim/survivor to be held under a microscope. There is, for example, no way for me to share this story without a long public sidebar about my professional skills, my career trajectory, my identity, my personality, and the inevitable doubting voices directed towards me. (*Maybe she wanted it? Maybe she deserved it? Maybe she was just being difficult? Maybe she doesn't understand? Maybe there is more to the story?*) Even in the best of circumstances, that is a lot to carry. In making the decision to speak out, I also had to be willing to put my entire life on hold for a few weeks as I dealt with it — fielding media calls, responding to a steady flow of commenters, writing updates as different parts of the story emerged. For one whole week, I didn't sleep at all, as social media was on fire and I dealt with it in real time.

More than that, this story is now an indelible part of my life story. No matter what other accomplishments I have, I will also be "the one with that JOFA sexual abuse story." I feel like some day, someone will write my obituary and it will be in there. That is not what I would have chosen to be remembered by.

Imagine if I started to dwell on each of my trauma stories that way – I might lose my ability to function. And if I came forward about all of them, that would become a 24/7 job. It would take up my identity. Everything else that I want to do in this world would be overshadowed. Is that the life story I dreamed of? Is it anyone's?

It's not just a dilemma for me, but for anyone who has been abused. It's a tug of war between wanting accountability or justice, and wanting to rebuild your life freely and far from that thing that was done to you that you don't want any part of. Certainly, some survivors make a powerful career out of advocacy, and the world is better off for that work. But that requires a decision to turn the abuse you experienced into your life's work. It is patently unfair to expect that kind of sacrifice from victims/survivors. Isn't enough that they were traumatized, with all that goes along with that? Should they also be then expected to put all their dreams on hold in order to "save" the community? Wouldn't it be fairer for someone *else* to take that work and free the victims/survivors to finally live their lives?

I suspect that everyone I interviewed shares this dilemma to some extent. As I said in the Prologue, I know that many people I meet — especially women who are Jewish communal professionals — are holding on to many stories. Rabbi Sharon Brous said that when she started recalling her stories of #MeToo, she reached 27 different events and then decided to put her pen down. Those are a lot of stories and a lot of scars. The background noise of gender abuse, emotional abuse, and sexual abuse from our youth and our adulthood continues until this day, for me and others. We have all had to figure out how to just live our lives, working hard to stop these stories from defining us.

For me, then, anthropology is not only a field that I love; it's also a powerful medium for social change that doesn't unfairly put the onus on victims/survivors. I want people to be able to share their stories without having to radically change their lives, risk their reputations, or out themselves as victims. For now, instead of focusing on my own experiences — or any one abusive situation — I am devoting my energy to collecting stories, drawing connections, and painting detailed cultural portraits. If I am successful in shining a light on these challenging dynamics and the ways in which they hurt people, we will have more tools. With more specific language to name what we see, we can more safely call out abuse and create the change we need to make our communities safer. In this way, story by story, systemic change may come.

On the most basic level, I hope that this book is helpful to all who have experienced abuse and trauma. I hope it offers comfort to know that you are not alone, and that what happened to you is not your fault.

Ultimately, I hope that this book informs our understandings of our culture, gives us language to name what we see, and empowers us to actively work towards the real change that will make our communities better and safer for us all.

Appendix: Resources

Emergency Services

If you are currently experiencing harassment, abuse, threats, or triggers. contact your local emergency service:

In the US and Canada

The National Sexual Assault Hotline
1-800-656-4673/1.888.407.4747
Open 24/7

The RAINN National Sexual Assault hotline
Call 1-800.656.HOPE (4673)
https://www.rainn.org/

SOVRI Helpline for Orthodox Jewish Sexual Abuse
Support for Victims of Rape and Incest
1-888-613-1613
All calls are confidential and anonymous. The helpline is open Monday-Thursday, 9:30 am-5:30 pm and Friday, 9:30 am-1:30 pm and is under the auspices of the Victim Services Program of Mount Sinai Beth Israel Department of Social Work.

Ending Violence Canada
For a list of emergency services in your province, go to:
https://endingviolencecanada.org/sexual-assault-centres-crisis-lines-and-support-services/

In Israel

Association of Rape Crisis Centers in Israel Hotlines
Call 1202: Women | 1203: Men
04-6566813: Arab Women
02-6730002: Religious Women | 02-5328000: Religious Men
Open for calls 24/7
https://www.1202.org.il/en/

Muganot Hotline
https://muganut.org.il/
1700-700-848 Operates 24/7
merkaz@muganut.co.il

Magen Hotline
02-372-4073
https://magen-Israel.org/

In the UK

Rape Crisis National Freephone Helpline
Call 0808 802 9999
https://rapecrisis.org.uk/get-help/want-to-talk/

Migdal Emunah Confidential Text Helpline
https://migdalemunah.org.uk/
Text "TALK" to 82228

In Australia

1800 RESPECT
1800 737 732
https://www.1800respect.org.au/

In South Africa

Rape Crisis Hotline
021 447 9762
https://rapecrisis.org.za/

Jewish social services, advocacy, and training

For non-immediate assistance, contact one of these services:

In North America

Amudim
https://amudim.org/
CEO: Zvi Gluck
646-517-0222
info@amudim.org
Confidential resource center esp in the Orthodox community, to provide assistance, support, and direct referrals for individuals and families impacted by sexual abuse, neglect, and addiction, and other crisis-related matters, as well as education and raising awareness.

Asap
https://asap.care/
Provides therapy funding grants for victims of abuse, as well as programs for professional training, and summer camps.

The Bayar Group
https://www.thebayargroup.com/
Principal: Rahel Bayar
917-473-0197
info@thebayargroup.com
Provides impactful training and consulting on abuse and harassment prevention for Schools, Camps, Faith-Based Institutions and Corporate Workplaces.

Fran Sepler and Associates
https://www.sepler.com/
President: Fran Sepler
1-952 646-6181
info@sepler.com
Provides services and advice to organizations interested in creating the most respectful workplaces possible, assists in fact-finding missions when there has been a claim of misconduct, offers coaching and education.

Jewish Survivors' Forum
https://www.jewishsurvivorsforum.org/
hello@jewishsurvivorsforum.org
Provides peer-to-peer support for abuse survivors

Jewish Teens for Empowered Consent
https://www.jewishteensforempoweredconsent.org/
Consent Education programming that unpacks hookup culture, comprehensive surveying of youth group members, alumni, and prospective members who chose not to attend youth groups to understand the pervasiveness of hookup culture and the like.

Jewish Women International

https://www.jwi.org/
CEO: Meredith Jacobs
202 857 1300
Prevention programming for youth, engaging men and boys as allies, supporting advocates with training and peer forums, providing survivors and their children with shelter and resources to build economic security, legislative advocacy and coalition building.

Sacred Spaces

https://www.jewishsacredspaces.org/
CEO: Dr. Shira Berkovits, Esq.
info@jewishsacredspaces.org
Provides Jewish institutions with the professional services necessary to develop robust policies and training to prevent opportunities for abuse and guide them responsibly should abuse occur.

Safety, Respect, Equity (SRE) Network

https://srenetwork.org/
Executive Director: Elana Wien
info@srenetwork.org
Provides training and grants to support justice and safe communities

Survivors to Superheroes

https://www.survivorstosuperheroes.org/
President and Founder: Julia Tortorello-Allen
info@survivorstosuperheroes.org
Created by a mother-daughter team in response to abuse, offers support for young survivors as well as education, political activism, and a literary journal.

Ta'amod: Stand up!

https://taamod.org/
CEO: Nicole Nevarez
nicole@taamod.org
Equips institutions and individuals with the resources they need to build healthy, safe, and equitable workplaces.

Women's Rabbinic Network

https://womensrabbinicnetwork.org/
CEO: Rabbi Mary Zamore
Provides resources and support for victims of harassment and abuse

Za'akah

https://www.zaakah.org/
Director: Asher Lovy
888-4-ZAAKAH (492-2524)info@zaakah.org
Seeks justice for survivors of sexual abuse. Offers advocacy for victims/survivors, information, a Shabbos hotline, and connections to various organizations that offer direct assistance.

In the UK

Migdal Emunah

https://migdalemunah.org.uk/
Founder: Yehudis Goldsobel
+44 (0) 20 3773 9998
info@migdalemunah.org.uk
Support service for Jewish victims of sexual abuse and their families, practical and emotional support for victims, raising awareness, and challenging the myths and taboos surrounding abuse.

In Israel

Amudim Israel
https://www.amudim.org.il/
Director: Yosi Golberstein
02-374-0175
office@amudim.org.il
Supporting those in crisis, especially in the Orthodox community with social services.

Association of Rape Crisis Centers in Israel (ARCCI)
https://www.1202.org.il/
Call 1202
Executive Director: Orit Sulitzeanu
Combatting sexual violence at the individual and regional levels by providing services and support for individual victims of sexual violence and working to raise awareness in their local communities.

Magen
https://magen-Israel.org/
Executive Director: Shana Aaronson
support@magen-Israel.org
Advocating for survivors of sexual abuse and exploitation within their communities, institutions and through the justice system in Israel; Raising awareness and promoting child-safety through educational events; Creating and publishing resources for parents and educators, and media; Supporting survivors of sexual abuse with therapeutic and communal resources.

VoiCSA (Voice Against Child Sexual Abuse)
https://www.voicsa.org/
CEO: Manny Waks
info@voicsa.org
Offers advocacy, awareness, and victim support.

Glossary

baal (ot/ie) teshuva	newly religious (women/men)
bashert	meant to be, holy match
beit din/beis din	rabbinic court
bima	podium
chesed	charity, lovingkindness
chavruta	learning partner
chochem	smart person
daven/davening	prayer or praying
day school	full-time Jewish elementary or high school
edah	group, division, tribe, or flock
frum	religious
halakha/ot	Jewish law/s
haredi	ultra-Orthodox
hillul hashem	desecrating the name of God
hineni	"here I am"
huppah	wedding canopy
kaddish	mourner's prayer
kavod	honor
kavod harav	honor for the rabbi
kiddush	social gathering after services, or the blessing recited on the wine on Shabbat
kiruv	bringing people into Jewish religious practice
kumsitz	singalong campfire
landsman/woman	fellow Jew
lashon hara	prohibition against speaking ill of another person
macher	expert, manipulator, or mover and shaker
mensch	literally, a "man", a good person
mesader kiddushin	the rabbi performing a wedding
mesira	prohibition against turning a Jew into the authorities
midot	good character
mifgash/mifgashim	encounters or meetings
mikveh	ritual bath
minyan	prayer quorum, or small gathering for prayer
moreh d'atra	esteemed rabbi of the community
negiya	literally "touch", prohibition against touching

oneg	Friday night social
posnisht	not done
responsa/ teshuva	rulings on religious issues
rosh	head
seudah shlishit	afternoon meal on the Sabbath
shabbaton	a weekend retreat
Shabbat	the Sabbath
shaliach	representative from Israel sent to Jewish communities to encourage Jews to move to Israel
shaliach tzibbur	cantor, or leader of the prayer service
shalom bayit	peace in the home
shidduch	a match for the sake of marriage
shiksa	derogatory slur for a non-Jewish woman (literally, a female cockroach)
shlita	an honorific reserved for ultra-Orthodox rabbi considered to be scholarly giants
shomer negiya	prohibitions against touch between males and females
shonda	an embarrassment to the family community
shuckling	bowing back and forth during prayer
shul	synagogue
talmid chochem	Torah scholar
tefilla	prayer
temple	synagogue
teshuva (h)	penance, or can also mean a responsa
to'elet	usefulness or purpose
tzitzit	ritual fringes
tzniut/tznius	female body-cover, or so-called "modesty
yahrzeit	anniversary of a death
yichud	prohibition against males and females being alone in a closed room

Abbreviations

BBYO	Bnai Brith Youth Organization
BDS	Boycott, diversity, and sanctions
CCAR	Central Conference of American Rabbis
CSA	Child sexual abuse
CSM	Clergy sexual misconduct
DSM	Diagnostic and Statistical Manual of Mental Disorders
HALB	Hebrew Academy of Long Beach
HUC-JIR	Hebrew Union College-Jewish Institute of Religion
JCC	Jewish Community Center
NCSY	National Council for Synagogue Youth
NFTY	National Federation of Temple Youth
RA	Rabbinical Assembly
RAINN	Rape, Abuse and Incest National Network
RCA	Rabbinical Council of America
NPD	Narcissistic personality disorder
URJ	Union for Reform Judaism
USY	United Synagogue Youth

Bibliography

ABC News, "Malka Leifer: Melbourne woman awarded $1.27m in damages over ultra-Orthodox Jewish school abuse," *ABC News*, 16 Sep 2015 https://www.abc.net.au/news/2015-09-16/malka-leifer-abuse-allegations-melbourne-woman-awarded-1.27-mill/6780040 .

Abrams, Rhonda, "One of my donors harassed me. I couldn't afford to stay silent," *JTA*, December 21, 2017, https://www.jta.org/2017/12/21/opinion/one-of-my-donors-harassed-me-i-couldnt-afford-to-stay-silent.

Ackerman, Alissa and Guila Benchimol, "Restorative Justice and Teshuva Following Sexual Misconduct," *e-Jewish Philanthropy*, September 12, 2018, https://ejewishphilanthropy.com/restorative-justice-and-teshuva-following-sexual-misconduct/ .

Adler, Rachel, "A stumbling block before the blind: Sexual exploitation and pastoral counseling," *CCAR Journal: A Reform Jewish Quarterly* (Spring 1993) pp. 13-54, pp. 18-19.

Adults Abused by Clergy, "The Silent Majority: Adult Victims of Sexual Exploitation by Clergy," *Adults Abused by Clergy*, http://www.adultsabusedbyclergy.org/ .

AFP, "One-Quarter of All Female Fundraisers Report Sexual Harassment: Donors Account for Nearly Two-Thirds of Harassers," *AFP*, August 22, 2018, https://afpglobal.org/one-quarter-all-female-fundraisers-report-sexual-harassment?fbclid=IwAR15drXFmHnHTyrcmLuxoH2eHpnNcumDTMHFbhMnz841MT0_H05tfAQH2x8.

Amborski, Amylee Mailhot, Eve-Line Bussieres, Marie-Pier Vaillancourt-Morel, and Christian C. Joyal, "Sexual Violence Against Persons with Disabilities: A Meta-Analysis," *Trauma and Abuse*, March 4 2021, https://journals.sagepub.com/doi/10.1177/1524838021995975.

American Psychiatric Association, *Diagnostic and Statistical Manual of Mental Disorders, 5th Edition*, (American Psychiatry Publishing, 2013)

Bayar, Rahel, "Too many chose to look away from Chaim Walder's crimes. We can make other choices now," *JTA*, January 6, 2022, https://www.jta.org/2022/01/06/opinion/too-many-chose-to-look-away-from-chaim-walders-crimes-we-can-make-other-choices-now .

BBC, "Harvey Weinstein scandal: Who has accused him of what?" *BBC*, January 10, 2019, https://www.bbc.com/news/entertainment-arts-41580010 .

Becker, J. V., "The effects of sexual assault on rape and attempted rape victims," *Victimology* 7, no. 1-4 (1982), pp. 106–113.

Ben-Ezra, M., Y. Palgi, D. Sternberg, D. Berkley, H. Eldar, Y. Glidai, L. Moshe and A. Shrira, "Losing my religion: A preliminary study of changes in belief pattern after sexual assault," *Traumatology* 16, no. 2 (2010), pp. 7–13, https://doi.org/10.1177/1534765609358465 .

Benchimol, Guila, "Sacrificing victims on the altars of silence and power," *The Jewish Week*, January 19, 2016, https://jewishweek.timesofIsrael.com/sacrificing-victims-on-the-altars-of-silence-and-power/ .

Berkovits, Shira M., "Institutional Abuse in the Jewish Community," *Tradition: A Journal of Orthodox Jewish Thought* 50, no. 2 (Summer 2017), pp. 11-49, https://www.jstor.org/stable/26879501 .

Bialik, Mayim, "Being a Feminist in Harvey Weinstein's World," *New York Times*, October 13, 2017, https://www.nytimes.com/2017/10/13/opinion/mayim-bialik-feminist-harvey-weinstein.html.

Bialik, Mayim, "On Feminism and Harvey Weinstein," *New York Times Opinion Section*, Oct 16, 2017, https://www.facebook.com/nytopinion/videos/1890320664316214/.

Bina Abuse, "If one of Rabbi Bina's student commits suicide, will the Jewish community say they didn't know what was going on at Netiv Aryeh?" https://binaabuse.wordpress.com/

Birch, Adelyn, *30 Covert Emotional Manipulation Tactics: How manipulators take control in personal relationships*, (Createspace 2015).

Bishop, Katie, "'Love Bombing' Is the Scary Control Tactic Narcissists Don't Want You to Know About—FKA twigs has accused Shia LaBeouf of this form of manipulation—here's why it can be so hard to spot," *In-Style*, February 23, 2021, https://www.instyle.com/lifestyle/love-bombing .

Black, Michele C., Kathleen C. Basile, Matthew J. Breiding, Sharon G. Smith, Mikel L. Walters, Melissa T. Merrick, Jieru Chen and Mark R. Stevens, *National Intimate Partner and Sexual Violence Survey 2010 Summary Report*, November 2011, National Center for Injury Prevention and Control Centers for Disease Control and Prevention Atlanta, Georgia, https://www.cdc/gov/violenceprevention/pdf/nisvs_report2010-a.pdf .

Blumenthal, Andy (Avraham), "Birds of a Feather", August 19, 2015, http://www.andyblumenthal.com/2015/08/birds-of-feather.html .

Blumenthal, Andy (Avraham), "Leadership, Technology, Life And Faith," August 19, 2015 http://www.andyblumenthal.com/2015/08/birds-of-feather.html

Blumenthal, Andy (Avraham), "SAR — Safe Haven for Sexual Abusers, Not for Kids," September 20, 2019, https://andyblumenthal.wordpress.com/2019/09/20/sar-safe-haven-for-sexual-abuse-not-for-kids/

Blustain, Sarah, "Rabbi Shlomo Carlebach's Shadow Side", *Lilith*, March 9, 1998 https://lilith.org/articles/rabbi-shlomo-carlebachs-shadow-side/

Boigon, Molly, "'This was no coverup': Inside the investigation of Rabbi Sheldon Zimmerman," *Forward*, May 17, 2021, https://forward.com/news/469213/sheldon-zimmerman-sexual-relations-rabbis-investigation/

Bronfman Fellowship Board of Directors, "A Message from the Board of Directors of The Bronfman Fellowship," October 21, 2021, https://bronfman.org/october-2021-message-from-the-board-of-directors-of-the-bronfman-fellowship/?fbclid=IwAR1HmIONR-Cp-SQhr6J2hIQSvZBpt7sQexiXoc2wowDUwG77d8QoDetLLb0 .

Bronfman Fellowship Board of Directors, "A Message to the Bronfman Community from the Board of Directors," March 15, 2022, https://bronfman.org/2022/03/a-message-to-the-bronfman-community-from-the-board-of-directors-march-15-2022/

Brous, Sharon, "#WeToo: Discomposing our culture of toxic masculinity: The epidemic of sexual assault and harassment thrives on many layers of cowardice and indifference, all too abundant in our culture of complicity. Now we must attune our ears to the stories told not by those with external power, but those with inner strength," *Yom Kippur* 5779 (2019) https://ikar-la.org/wp-content/uploads/YK-Brous-5779-WeToo.pdf.

Brownmiller, Susan, *Against our Will: Men, Women and Rape*, (Ballantine Books 1993, originally printed in 1973)

Buchhandler-Raphael, Michal, "Sexual Abuse of Power" (February 15, 2010). *University of Florida Journal of Law and Public Policy*, Vol. 21, p. 77, 2010, https://ssrn.com/abstract=1612195

Canfield, Madeline, Lila Goldstein, Ellanora Lerner, Lilah Peck, Maddy Pollack, and Dahlia Soussan, "For Continuity's Sake? Addressing Hookup Culture in Jewish Youth Groups," *e-Jewish Philanthropy*, September 3, 2020 https://ejewishphilanthropy.com/for-continuitys-sake-addressing-hookup-culture-in-jewish-youth-groups/ra

Capps, Donald, "Sex in the parish: Social-scientific explanations for why it occurs," *The Journal of Pastoral Care* 47, no. 4 (1993), pp. 350-361.

Carlsen, Audrey, Maya Salam, Claire Cain Miller, Denise Lu, Ash Ngu, Jugal K. Patel And Zach Wichter, "#MeToo Brought Down 201 Powerful Men. Nearly Half of Their Replacements Are Women," *New York Times*, October 29, 2018, https://www.nytimes.com/interactive/2018/10/23/us/metoo-replacements.html .

Centers for Disease Control and Prevention, "Adverse Childhood Experiences (ACE) Study: Major Findings," (2006) http://www.cdc.gov/violenceprevention/acestudy/about.html .

Chaves, Mark and Diane Garland, "The Prevalence of Clergy Sexual Advances toward Adults in Their Congregations," *Journal for the Scientific Study of Religion* 48, no. 4 (2009), pp. 817-824.

Cohler-Esses, Larry, "The Gender Gap At Jewish Non-Profits Is Bad — And Getting Worse", *Forward*, December 11, 2017, https://forward.com/news/389448/the-gender-gap-at-jewish-non-profits-is-bad-and-getting-worse/

"Conversation with Elana Sztokman on JOFA and abuse in the Jewish Community" https://www.youtube.com/watch?v=CW3sMEODkkE.

Craig, Elaine, *Putting Trials on Trial: Sexual Assault and the Failure of the Legal Profession* (McGill-Queen's University Press; Canadian First edition, 2018).

Dallam, Stephanie J., "A model of the retraumatization process: A meta-synthesis of childhood sexual abuse — Survivors' experiences in health care," Submitted to the graduate degree program in Nursing and the Graduate Faculty of the University of Kansas in partial fulfillment of the requirements for the degree of Doctor of Philosophy, 2010, https://kuscholarworks.ku.edu/bitstream/handle/1808/6373/Dallam_ku_0099D_10726_DATA_1.pdf?sequence=1&isAllowed=y .

Darkness to Light. "Grooming and Red Flag Behaviors," https://www.d2l.org/child-grooming-signs-behavior-awareness/ .

Davidson, Steven, "How Much Do Top Jewish Non-Profit Leaders Make?" *Forward*, December 11, 2017, https://forward.com/news/388240/how-much-do-top-jewish-non-profit-leaders-make/

Davies, Emily, "'It is with shame, and it shouldn't be': Dozens sue Yeshiva University High School over alleged sexual abuse," *Washington Post*, August 23, 2019, https://www.washingtonpost.com/nation/2019/08/23/yeshiva-university-high-school-sexual-abuse-lawsuit/ .

DeGroat, Chuck, *When Narcissism Comes to Church: Healing you community from emotional and spiritual abuse* (Illinois: Intervarsity Press, 2020)

Denney, Andrew S., Kent R. Kerley, and Nickolas G. Gross, "Child sexual abuse in protestant christian congregations: a descriptive analysis of offense and offender characteristics," *Religions* 18 (2008), pp. 1-13.

Dolev-Cohen, Michal Tsameret Ricon, Inbar Levkovich, "#WhyIDidntReport: Reasons why young Israelis do not submit complaints regarding sexual abuse," *Children and Youth Services Review*, vol. 115, August 2020, https://www.sciencedirect.com/science/article/abs/pii/S0190740920301067.

Donegan, Moira, "I Started the Media Men List," *The Cut*, January 10, 2018, https://www.thecut.com/2018/01/moira-donegan-i-started-the-media-men-list.html .

Doxey, Cynthia, Larry Jensen & Janet Jensen, "The Influence of Religion on Victims of Childhood Sexual Abuse," *The International Journal for the Psychology of Religion* 7, no. 3 (1997), pp. 179-186, DOI: 10.1207/s15327582ijpr0703_6.

Dreyfus, Hannah, "After N.J. Camp Exec Sacked, More Women Alleging Sexual Harassment Come Forward. She had always thought of him as a family friend — until he invited her to spend the night with him alone at his private residence in the Poconos," *The Jewish Week*, April 18, 2018, https://njjewishnews.timesofIsrael.com/after-n-j-camp-exec-sacked-last-week-more-women-alleging-sexual-harassment-come-forward/ .

Dreyfus, Hannah, "Can rabbinic ethics committees police their own? Recent cases test rabbinic ethics panels in the age of #MeToo," *The Jewish Week* (2019), https://jewishweek.timesofIsrael.com/recent-cases-test-expertise-of-rabbinic-ethics-panels/.

Dreyfus, Hannah, "Harassment Allegations Mount Against Leading Jewish Sociologist: Women academics cite long pattern of sexual improprieties at the hands of Steven M. Cohen, who has expressed 'remorse' for his actions," *The Jewish Week*, July 19, 2018, https://jewishweek.timesofIsrael.com/harassment-allegations-mount-against-leading-jewish-sociologist/.

Dreyfus, Hannah, "More Women Come Forward Against N.J. Camp Exec Alleging Sexual Harassment — She had always thought of him as a family friend — until he invited her to spend the night with him alone at his private residence in the Poconos," *The Jewish Week*, April 18, 2018, https://jewishweek.timesofIsrael.com/after-n-j-camp-exec-sacked-last-week-more-women-alleging-sexual-harassment-come-forward/ .

Dreyfus, Hannah, "New Allegations Against Robinson Include a Minor. Joanna says she was sexually abused by Len Robinson when she was 17," *The Jewish Week*, April 11, 2019, https://jewishweek.timesofIsrael.com/new-allegations-against-robinson-include-a-minor/ .

Dreyfus, Hannah, "Reform rabbinic giant disciplined for inappropriate relationships now accused of 'sexually predatory behavior,'" *Forward*, April 27, 2021, https://forward.com/news/468535/reform-cover-up-rabbi-sheldon-zimmerman-sexually-predatory-behavior/ .

Dreyfus, Hannah. "Riverdale Again Hit With 'Shocking' Abuse Case. Child porn charges against an SAR principal like an 'earthquake,' parent says," *The Jewish Week*, September 17, 2019, https://jewishweek.timesofIsrael.com/riverdale-again-hit-with-shocking-abuse-case/.

Dreyfus, Hannah, "Women academics cite long pattern of sexual improprieties at the hands of Steven M. Cohen, who has expressed 'remorse' for his actions," *The Jewish Week*, July 19, 2018, https://jewishweek.timesofIsrael.com/harassment-allegations-mount-against-leading-jewish-sociologist/ .

Eisenberg, Chavi, "No, Rabbi Shafran, modesty won't prevent sexual. People don't want to know that there are some terrible things that all the precautions in the world simply won't prevent," *Times of Israel*, October 26, 2018, https://blogs.timesofIsrael.com/no-rabbi-shafran-modesty-wont-prevent-sexual-assault/ .

El-Or, Tamar, *Next Year I will Know More: Literacy and Identity among Young Orthodox Women in Israel* (Wayne State University Press, 2002).

Evans, Patricia, Controlling People: How to Recognize, Understand, and Deal with People Who Try to Control You, (Adams Media, 2003).

Fagin, C. Gabriel, The Moderating Effect of Religion and Spirituality On the Relationship Between Childhood Sexual Abuse And Negative Outcomes Among a Sample of Orthodox Jewish Men, Doctoral dissertation, (Yeshiva University, 2015), https://www.proquest.com/openview/950f5ee8ce84e36ac604a07ab171f4a1/1?pq-origsite=gscholar&cbl=18750.

Feinson, M. C. and A. Meir, "Exploring mental health consequences of childhood abuse and the relevance of religiosity," *J Interpers Violence* 30, no. 3 (February 2015), pp. 499-521, DOI: 10.1177/0886260514535094.

Feldman, Ari, "Reform rabbi was secretly censured for affair with congregant," *Forward*, June 3, 2018, https://forward.com/news/402226/reform-rabbi-was-secretly-censured-for-affair-with-congregant/

Files, Julia A. Anita P. Mayer, Marcia G. Ko, Patricia Friedrich, Marjorie Jenkins, Michael J. Bryan, Suneela Vegunta, Christopher M. Wittich, Melissa A. Lyle, Ryan Melikian, Trevor Duston, Yu-Hui H. Chang, and Sharonne N. Hayes, "Speaker Introductions at Internal Medicine Grand Rounds: Forms of Address Reveal Gender Bias," *Journal of Women's Health* 26, no. 5, May 1, 2017, https://doi.org/10.1089/jwh.2016.6044 .

Filipovic, Jill, "The Problem With 'Feminist' Men," *New York Times*, May 8, 2018, https://www.nytimes.com/2018/05/08/opinion/schneiderman-abuse-feminist-men.html .

Findling, Debbie, "Is The Jewish Community Perpetuating Sexual Harassment?" *The Jewish Week*, March 20, 2018, https://jewishweek.timesofIsrael.com/is-the-jewish-community-perpetuating-sexual-harassment/.

Fischer, Elli, "On 'hard' and 'soft' charisma in Jewish education: Toward a taxonomy of risk," *Times of Israel* blog, June 23, 2016, https://blogs.timesofIsrael.com/on-hard-and-soft-charisma-in-jewish-education-toward-a-taxonomy-of-risk/?fbclid=IwAR0lrENThMr6GrQrJs8IUtZbgh6TkouX5JLMUxiKI0wjImVq6hCqPLoLti0 .

Fisher, Cate, Alexandra Goldsmith, Rachel Hurcombe, Claire Soares, "The impacts of child sexual abuse: A rapid evidence assessment," ICSA Research Team, July 2017, https://uobrep.openrepository.com/bitstream/handle/10547/624859/iicsa-impacts-child-sexual-abuse-rapid-evidence-assessment-full-report-english.pdf?sequence=2 .

Forward Staff, "Yeshiva U.'s Rabbi George Finkelstein Acted Inappropriately Even After Ouster after he was forced out of the high school in 1995 because of inappropriate wrestling with boys," *Ha'aretz* March 1, 2013, https://www.haaretz.com/jewish/yeshiva-u-s-rabbi-george-finkelstein-acted-inappropriately-even-after-ouster-1.5232101

Fox, Nina (trans. Elana Sztokman), "Early release for sex offender: 'Ezra Sheinberg continues to abuse us, and he will hurt other women.'" *Ynet* [Hebrew], August 20, 2021, https://www.ynet.co.il/judaism/Article/bkuoaufet .

Francis, Perry C., and James Stacks, "The association between spiritual well-being and clergy sexual misconduct," *Journal of Religion and Abuse: Advocacy, Pastoral Care and Prevention* 5 (2003), pp. 79–100.

Friberg, Nils C. and Mark R. Laaser, *Before the fall: preventing pastoral sexual abuse,* (Collegeville: The Liturgical Press, 1998).

Garland, Diana R. and Christen Argueta, "How clergy sexual misconduct happens: A qualitative study of first-hand accounts," *Social Work & Christianity* 37, no. 1 (2010), pp. 1-27.

Genesis Women's Shelter and Support, "The profile of an abuser," https://www.genesisshelter.org/the-profile-of-an-abuser/ .

Glaser, Karen, "Yehudis Fletcher: speaking out on sex and marriage: Yehudis Fletcher campaigns against ignorance and abuse in her Charedi community — after she courageously gave evidence against a man who assaulted her," *The Jewish Chronicle*, January 06, 2021, https://www.thejc.com/lifestyle/family/yehudis-fletcher-speaking-out-on-sex-and-marriage-1.510427.

Golan, Ori, "Washing away the trauma of abuse: Dassi Erlich, who says she suffered sexual abuse in an Australian ultra-Orthodox community, tells of her long journey, accuses former community of not taking steps to protect the next victim," *Jerusalem Post*, July 6, 2017, https://www.jpost.com/magazine/a-new-life-498946

Gorsetman, Chaya Rosenfeld and Elana Sztokman, *Educating in the Divine Image: Gender Issues in Jewish Education* (Brandeis University Press, 2013).

Gorsetman, Yedidya and, Gary Rosenblatt, "Has The 'Tough Love' Rebbe Gone Too Far?" *Jewish Week*, January 24, 2012, https://www.jta.org/2012/01/24/ny/has-the-tough-love-rebbe-gone-too-far

Gregory, Christina and Krista Soriano "Tell Me All I Need to Know About Narcissistic Personality Disorder," *Psycom*, https://www.psycom.net/personality-disorders/narcissistic/

Hanau, Shira, "Chief rabbi slammed for Walder shiva call urges victims to speak out: Chief Rabbi David Lau was criticized for visiting the Chaim Walder funeral, Israeli haredi author accused by dozens of women of sexual abuse and rape," *JTA*, December 30, 2021, https://www.jpost .com/Israel-news/article-690197.

Hanau, Shira, "Israeli politician sued two women for libel after they accused him of sexual harassment," *Forward*, May 9, 2021, https://forward.com/fast-forward/469246/dov-lipman-sued-two-women-for-libel-after-sexual-harrasment-accusations/.

Hébert, M., M. Tourigny, M. Cyr, P. McDuff and J. Joly, "Prevalence of childhood sexual abuse and timing of disclosure in a representative sample of adults from Quebec," *The Canadian Journal of Psychiatry* 54, vol. 9 (2009), pp. 631–636, DOI:10.1177/070674370905400908.

Hedwat, Clare, "The Jewish World's #MeToo Crisis is Much Deeper than Ari Shavit and Steven Cohen", August 3, 2018, https://ejewishphilanthropy.com/the-jewish-worlds-metoo-crisis-is-much-deeper-than-ari-shavit-and-steven-cohen/.

Heller, Tziporah, "The Chaim Walder Parsha," 3 January 2022 http://www.tziporahheller.com/

Hershcovis, Sandy and Julian Barling, "Comparing Victim Attributions and Outcomes for Workplace Aggression and Sexual Harassment," *The Journal of Applied Psychology* 95 (2010), pp. 874-88, 10.1037/a002 0070.

Hershkowitz, Irit, Omer Lanes, Michael E. Lamb, "Exploring the disclosure of child sexual abuse with alleged victims and their parents," *Child Abuse & Neglect*, Vol. 31, iss. 2 (2007) pp. 111-123, ISSN 0145-2134, https://doi.org/10.1016/j.chiabu.2006.09.004 .

Heschel, Susannah & Sarah Imhoff, "Where Are All the Women In Jewish Studies?" *Forward*, July 3, 2018, https://forward.com/culture/404416/where-are-all-the-women-in-jewish-studies/ .

Highes, Virginia, "Why Do Obese Women Earn Less Than Thin Women (and Obese Men)?" *National Geographic*, November 3, 2014, https://www.nationalgeographic.com/science/article/why-do-obese-women-earn-less-than-thin-women-and-obese-men .

Hoffman, Sarah Ruth, "Rabbinic Abuse: 26 Power & Control Tactics," *Times of Israel* blog, March 30, 2019, https://blogs.timesofIsrael.com/rabbinic-abuse-26-power-control-tactics/?fbclid=IwAR0zdlcbJ0Udr2PksiyOvwUe9tTmi9hhlECNnn2wD1Neuw Cp5_TbajFI45k .

Hoffman, Sarah Ruth, "Rabbinic Sexual Abuse and Patrilineal Descent," *Times of Israel* blog, December 12, 2108, https://blogs.timesofIsrael.com/rabbinic-sexual-abuse-and-patrilineal-descent/.

Hoffman, Sarah Ruth, "Recognizing Human Trafficking: Difficult Up Close", *Times of Israel* blog, Jan 3, 2022, https://blogs.timesofIsrael.com/recognizing-human-trafficking-difficult-up-close/.

Hogan, Mary Beth and Tricia Sherno, *The Report of the Independent Investigation*, February 17, 2022, https://urj.org/sites/default/files/2022-02/URJ_Investigation_Report.pdf.

Hopper, Jim, "How Reliable Are the Memories of Sexual Assault Victims? The expert testimony excluded from the Kavanaugh hearing," *Scientific American*,

September 27, 2018, https://blogs.scientificamerican.com/observations/how-reliable-are-the-memories-of-sexual-assault-victims/.

Hunter, S., "Disclosure of Child Sexual Abuse as a Life-Long Process: Implications for Health Professionals," *Australian and New Zealand Journal of Family Therapy* 32, no. 2 (2011), pp. 159-172, DOI:10.1375/anft.32.2.159.

ICASA, *Acquaintance Rape*, https://icasa.org/uploads/documents/Stats-and-Facts/acquaintancerape.pdf .

Jacobs, Andrew, "Orthodox Group Details Accusations That New Jersey Rabbi Abused Teenagers," *New York Times*, December 27, 2000, https://www.nytimes.com/2000/12/27/nyregion/orthodox-group-details-accusations-that-new-jersey-rabbi-abused-teenagers.html .

Jay, Alexis, Malcolm Evans, Ivor Frank and Drusilla Sharpling, "Child protection in religious organisations and settings," *Investigation Report*, September 2021, A report of the Inquiry Panel, https://www.iicsa.org.uk/key-documents/26895/view/child-protection-religious-organisations-settings-investigation-report-september-2021.pdf.

Jeffay, Nathan, "A Sex Scandal Splits Orthodox Zionist World Between Silence and Action," *Forward*, February 24, 2010, https://forward.com/news/126324/a-sex-scandal-splits-orthodox-zionist-world-betwee/

Jerusalem Post Editorial, "Takana's damage. The Takana Forum was created within the religious-Zionist community to combat this self-destructive pattern," *Jerusalem Post*, September 20, 2016. https://www.jpost.com/opinion/jerusalem-post-editorial-takanas-damage-468253

Jerusalem Post Staff, "Berland murder case: Benny Ze'evi revealed as second man accused. Ze'evi is the second man indicted for the 1986 murder of Nissim Sheetrit that was connected to the 'Modesty Guard' of the 'Shuvu Banim' sect," *Jerusalem Post*, December 5, 2021, https://www.jpost.com/breaking-news/benny-zeevi-son-of-rehavam-zeevi-is-the-accused-murderer-in-berland-case-687884 .

Jerusalem Post Staff, "Senior London rabbi removed from position after having affair. The rabbi was faced with harsh criticism, many of which claimed that in his rank and position, he is held to a higher moral standard," *Jerusalem Post*, April 14, 2019, https://www.jpost.com/diaspora/senior-london-rabbi-removed-from-position-after-having-affair-586751.

John Jay College of Criminal Justice, "The nature and scope of sexual abuse of minors by Catholic priests and deacons in the United States 1950-2002," *The City University Of New York For The United States Conference Of Catholic Bishops*, February 2004 http://www.usccb.org/issues-and-action/child-and-youth-protection/upload/the-nature-and-scope-of-sexual-abuse-of-minors-by-catholic-priests-and-deacons-in-the-united-states-1950-2002.pdf.

Joyce, Kathryn, "She Said Her Husband Hit Her. She Lost Custody of Their Kids," *Longreads*, July 2020, https://longreads.com/2020/07/08/domestic-violence-custody-family-court-disputes/.

JTA Staff, "Dutch Jews investigate Brooklyn rabbi on molestation charges. Action taken after local newspaper publishes two accusations against Mendel Levine dating back to when he worked as a youth counselor," *JTA*, January 8, 2018, https://www.timesofIsrael.com/dutch-jews-investigate-brooklyn-rabbi-on-molestation-charges/

JTA Staff, "In a shift, Conservative movement publicly lists the rabbis it has expelled and suspended," *JTA*, October 25, 2021, https://jewishjournal.org/2021/10/25/in-a-shift-conservative-movement-publicly-lists-the-rabbis-it-has-expelled-and-suspended/.

Judah, Jacob, "Prestigious Jewish schools in London reel over allegations of sexual abuse. Dozens of users on the British website Everyone's Invited share stories of rape, assault, and harassment, but some former students say fear of anti-Semitism are holding more back," *Times of Israel*, April 30, 2021, https://www.timesofIsrael.com/prestigious-jewish-schools-in-london-reel-over-allegations-of-sexual-abuse/.

Katz, Sheila and Rabbi Danya Ruttenberg, "What to remember when abuse stories break in Jewish communities," *Baltimore Jewish Times*, September 1, 2021, https://www.jewishtimes.com/opinion-what-to-remember-when-abuse-stories-break-in-jewish-communities/.

Katzenstein, David and Lisa Aronson Fontes, "Twice Silenced: The Underreporting of Child Sexual Abuse in Orthodox Jewish Communities," *Journal of Child Sexual Abuse* (2017), DOI: 10.1080/10538712.2017.1336505.

Kaufman, Scott Barry, "The Science of Spiritual Narcissism. Self-enhancement through spiritual practices can fool some of us into thinking we're evolving and growing when all we're growing is our ego," *Scientific American*, January 11, 2021, https://www.scientificamerican.com/article/the-science-of-spiritual-narcissism/.

Keene, Louis, "She defended disgraced author Chaim Walder. Now a revered rebbetzin is facing a backlash of her own," *Forward*, January 6, 2022, https://forward.com/news/480478/tziporah-heller-chaim-walder-facebook-post-apology/.

Keneally, Meghan, "'Horseface, 'crazy,' 'low IQ': Trump's history of insulting women,"*ABC News*. 18 October 2018 https://abcnews.go.com/Politics/trumps-long-history-calling-women-crazy-attacking-appearances/story?id=48348956

Kennedy, Margaret, "Exploitation, not 'affair,'" in *When pastors prey: overcoming clergy sexual abuse of women*, ed. Valli Boobal Batchelor (World Council of Churches Publications, 2013), pp. 26-35.

Klein, Amy, "A creepy abusive Jewish day school teacher? I'm not surprised. The sickening news that a New York principal was arrested for child porn brought me back to my own junior high experiences—and not in a good way," *Times of Israel* blogs, September 26, 2019, https://blogs.timesofIsrael.com/a-creepy-abusive-jewish-day-school-teacher-im-not-surprised/.

Kohn, Rachel, "A journalist breaking Orthodoxy's biggest sexual abuse stories says he wishes he didn't have to," *JTA*, November 29, 2021, https://www.jta.org/2021/11/29/Israel/a-journalist-breaking-orthodoxys-biggest-sexual-abuse-stories-says-he-wishes-he-didnt-have-to?fbclid=IwAR2QHB0kAh0qLKFJhDEQGxHIvWG0qwJzcZQhQbdZatMWT6aoggqgQDSw2o0.

Korbman, Miriam D., Steven Pirutinsky, Eva L. Feindler David H. Rosmarin, "Childhood Sexual Abuse, Spirituality/Religion, Anxiety and Depression in a

Jewish Community Sample: the Mediating Role of Religious Coping," *Journal of Interpersonal Violence*, March 17, 2021, https://doi.org/101177/08862605211001462 .

Lapin, Andrew . "Jewish feminist group in turmoil after Orthodox sex guru Bat Sheva Marcus, a founder, is accused of harassment", *JTA*, April 13, 2022 https://www.jta.org/2022/04/13/united-states/jewish-feminist-group-in-turmoil-after-orthodox-sex-guru-bat-sheva-marcus-a-founder-is-accused-of-harassment

Leibowitz, Yael, "Big Bird, Chaim Walder, and the power of nuance. Traditional explanations of difficult texts can turn harmful for students who may be sensitive for a whole host of reasons. Jewish educators can teach better," *Times of Israel*, December 30, 2021, https://blogs.timesofisrael.com/big-bird-chaim-walder-and-the-power-of-nuance/ .

Lesher, Michael, *Sexual Abuse, Shonda and Concealment in Orthodox Jewish Communities* (Jefferson, North Carolina: McFarland and Company, 2014).

Levisohn, Jon A., "Eros and (Religious) Education," (2017), http://hillelofficeofinnovation.org/sites/default/files/ooi_salons_eros_and_religious_education_jon_a_1.pdf .

Levisohn, Jon A., "Passion in Religious Education," *e-Jewish Philanthropy*, February 20, 2017, https://ejewishphilanthropy.com/passion-in-religious-education/ .

Liberty, Patricia L., "It's difficult to explain — The compromise of moral agency for victims of abuse by religious leaders," *Journal of Religion & Abuse* 3 no. 3/4 (2001), pp. 81-90.

Lundstrom, Marjie, "Female Victims of Clergy Abuse: Female victims often overlooked in horror stories of clergy abuse," *Sacramento Bee,* March 21, 2002, https://www.snapnetwork.org/female_victims/females_often_overlooked.htm.

Lurie, Rabbi Alan, "The Allure of Narcissistic Spirituality. The desire to control others in order to create a 'perfect' environment that nurtures our sensitivies is a calling card of spiritual narcissism. True spirituality takes place in the holy messiness of the world," *Huffington Post* blog, January 6, 2011. https://www.huffpost.com/entry/the-allure-of-spiritual-n_b_803415

Lusky-Weisrose, Efrat, Amitai Marmor, Dafna Tener, "Sexual Abuse in the Orthodox Jewish Community: A Literature Review," *Trauma, Violence, and Abuse*, February 13, 2020, https://doi.org/10.1177/1524838020906548.

Magid, Jacob, "Conservative movement publishes list of rabbis it has expelled or suspended Rabbinical Assembly says move part of review of its handling of misconduct allegations; 9 listed, including rabbi arrested in Israel for performing non-Orthodox wedding," *Times of Israel*, October 22, 2021, https://www.timesofisrael.com/conservative-movement-publishes-list-of-rabbis-it-has-expelled-or-suspended/

Manhattan D.A., "D.A. Vance: Michael Steinhardt Surrenders 180 Stolen Antiquities Valued at $70 Million. Seized Artifacts will be Repatriated to 11 Countries. Steinhardt Agrees to Unprecedented Lifetime Ban on Acquiring Antiquities." *Manhattan DA*, December 6, 2021, https://www.manhattanda.org/d-a-vance-michael-steinhardt-surrenders-180-stolen-antiquities-valued-at-70-million/?fbclid=IwAR20PvO1Dh5A0H28P9b_8kI3dxq8qasyiYG8iwMThoYAjs6raUSeUbxdesQ .

Manne, Kate, *Down Girl: The Logic of Misogyny* (Oxford University Press, 2017)

Martin, David S., "Rape victims say military labels them 'crazy,'" *CNN*, April 14, 2012, http://edition.cnn.com/2012/04/14/health/military-sexual-assaults-personality-disorder/index.html.

McElvaney, Rosaleen, "Disclosure of Child Sexual Abuse: Delays, Non-disclosure and Partial Disclosure. What the Research Tells Us and Implications for Practice," *Child Abuse Review* (2013), DOI: 10.1002/car.2280.

McGinity, Keren R., "American Jewry's #MeToo Problem: A First-Person Encounter," *The Jewish Week*, June 21, 2018, https://jewishweek.timesofIsrael.com/american-jewrys-metoo-problem-a-first-person-encounter/ .

McLaughlin, Barbara R., "Devastated spirituality: The impact of clergy sexual abuse on the survivor's relationship with god and the church," *Sexual Addiction & Compulsivity* 1, vol. 2 (1994), pp. 145-158, DOI: 10.1080/10720169408400039 .

Meek, Katherine R., Mark R. McMinn, Todd Burnett, Chris Mazarella, and Vitaliy Voytenko, "Sexual Ethics Training in Seminary: Preparing Students to Manage Feelings of Sexual Attractions," *Pastoral Psychology* 53 (2004), pp. 63–79 .

Melchior, Michael and Manny Waks, "Confronting sexual abuse in the Jewish community," *Jerusalem Post*, July 7, 2015, https://www.jpost.com/opinion/confronting-sexual-abuse-in-the-jewish-community-408279 .

Miller, Chanel, *Know my Name* (New York: Penguin, 2019).

Moehlman, Lara, "What's the Best Way to Say #MeToo? In the small, insular Jewish professional world, people are often reluctant to come forward with sexual harassment allegations — especially against 'big machers.' That's beginning to change." *Moment*, October 8, 2020, https://momentmag.com/whats-the-best-way-to-say-metoo/.

Moore, Cheryl, "#metoo in the Jewish Community," *e-Jewish Philanthropy*, September 17, 2018, https://ejewishphilanthropy.com/metoo-in-the-jewish-community/.

Morgan, Rachel E., and Grace Kena, "Criminal Victimization, 2016," U.S. Department of Justice Office of Justice Programs, Bureau of Justice Statistics, Bulletin, October 2018, NCJ 252121, https://bjs.ojp.gov/content/pub/pdf/cv16.pdf .

Musleah, Rahel, "Navigating the Fallout from Sexual Harassment Claims in Synagogues," *Hadassah Magazine*, March 2021, https://www.hadassahmagazine.org/2021/03/02/navigating-fallout-sexual-harassment-claims-synagogues/

Nachshoni, Kobi, "After his suicide: Haredi rabbis support Chaim Walder, accused of sexual abuse," *Ynet* [Hebrew] December 28, 2021, https://www.ynet.co.il/judaism/article/bkt3ncdsk .

Nathan-Kazis, Josh, "J Street Comes Under Fire for Quiet Handling of Ari Shavit Sexual Misconduct Claim," Forward, November 1, 2016, https://forward.com/news/353099/j-street-comes-under-fire-for-quiet-handling-of-ari-shavit-sexual-misconduc / .

Nathan-Katzis, Josh, "'Super Creepy' Game Hands Out Points for Hooking Up at Youth Group," *Forward*, November 30, 2017, https://forward.com/news/388645/underground-hookup-game-at-jewish-youth-group-awards-points-for-making-out/?fbclid=IwAR3LGsv918uaGzgr7Eg5hePjXqitWOXYFAx4osQ3tkcW8fXRM5R1KDg8Zu8 .

National Intimate Partner and Sexual Violence Survey, *2010 Summary Report*, https://www.cdc.gov/violenceprevention/pdf/nisvs_report2010-a.pdf

Neustein, Amy ed., *Tempest in the Temple: Jewish Communities and Child Sex Scandals* (Brandeis University Press, 2009).

Neustein, Amy and Michael Lesher, "Justice interrupted: How rabbis can interfere with the prosecution of sex offenders — and strategies to stop them," in Neustein's *Tempest in the Temple*, pp. 197-229.

Newman, Andy and Sharon Otterman, "Debate Over the Rabbi and the Sauna," *New York Times*, May 29, 2015, https://www.nytimes.com/2015/05/31/nyregion/fresh-debate-over-whether-a-rabbi-acted-inappropriately.html .

Newman, Marissa, "The ex-aides of a messianic, sex-convict rabbi fight from within to cast him out. Bratslav hasidic leaders have issued a rare ban on Eliezer Berland, a cult leader seen as a modern 'Sabbatai Tzvi'; the rest of the Haredi world is proving reluctant to follow suit," *Times of Israel*, September 5, 2018, https://www.timesofIsrael.com/the-ex-aides-of-a-messianic-sex-convict-rabbi-fight-from-within-to-cast-him-out/.

Nishma Research, "Starting a conversation: A pioneering survey of those who have left the Orthodox community," *Nishma Research*, 2016, http://nishmaresearch.com/assets/pdf/Report_Survey_of_Those_Who_Left_Orthodoxy_Nishma_Research_June_2016.pdf

Nofziger, S. and R. E. Stein, "To tell or not to tell: Lifestyle impacts on whether adolescents tell about violent victimization," *Violence Victims* 21, no. 3 (2006), pp. 371–382.

O'Malley, Katie, "What's 'Love Bombing' and How to Tell If You've Been a Victim of It. From showering you with gifts to messaging you non-stop throughout the day, we delve into the worrying behaviors of a 'love bomber,' who might have convinced you they're 'the one.'" *Elle*, August 2, 2017, https://www.elle.com/uk/life-and-culture/culture/news/a37470/what-is-love-bombing/

Otterman, Sharon and Hannah Dreyfus, "Michael Steinhardt, a Leader in Jewish Philanthropy, Is Accused of a Pattern of Sexual Harassment," *New York Times*, March 21, 2019, https://www.nytimes.com/2019/03/21/nyregion/michael-steinhardt-sexual-harassment.html

Otterman, Sharon and Ray Rivera, "Ultra-Orthodox Shun Their Own for Reporting Child Sexual Abuse," *New York Times*, May 9, 2012, https://www.nytimes.com/2012/05/10/nyregion/ultra-orthodox-jews-shun-their-own-for-reporting-child-sexual-abuse.html .

Papalia, Nina and James Ogloff, "Child sex abuse survivors are five times more likely to be the victims of sexual assault later in life," *Jakarta Post*, July 29, 2020, https://www.thejakartapost.com/life/2020/07/29/child-sex-abuse-survivors-are-five-times-more-likely-to-be-the-victims-of-sexual-assault-later-in-life.html .

Paul, Rena, Margaret Gandy, Rahel Bayar, "Report of Investigation of the Central Conference of American Rabbis Ethics Process", *CCAR*, December 21, 2021, https://www.ccarnet.org/about-us/ccar-ethics-system-report/

Pew Research Center, *A Portrait of Jewish Americans*, (2013)
https://www.pewforum.org/2013/10/01/chapter-1-population-estimates/.

Poling, Nancy Werking, *Victim to Survivor: Women Recovering from Clergy Sexual Abuse* (Wipf and Stoc, 2009).

Priebe, G. and C. G. Svedin, "Child sexual abuse is largely hidden from the adult society: An epidemiological study of adolescents' disclosures," *Child Abuse & Neglect 32 (2008), pp. 1095–1108.*

Puls, Darrel, *Let Us Prey: The Plague of Narcissist Pastors and What We Can Do About It* (Cascade Books, 2020).

Rabbinical Assembly, *A Code of Professional Conduct for Members of the Rabbinical Assembly*
https://www.rabbinicalassembly.org/sites/default/files/public/ethical_guid elines/code-of-conduct-2018-members.pdf

Rabbinical Assembly, "The Rabbinical Assembly to Review Its Code of Conduct and Ethics Procedures," *The Rabbinical Assembly*, April 22, 2021, https://www.rabbinicalassembly.org/resources-ideas/ethical-guidelines/code-conduct/press-release .

Radoff, Genendy, *The Price of Truth: A true story of child sexual abuse in the Orthodox Jewish world and one girl's courage to survive and heal* (Lioness Books, 2019).

RAINN, "Sexual assault: Grooming: Know the Warning Signs," *RAINN*, https://www.rainn.org/news/grooming-know-warning-signs.

RAINN, *The Criminal Justice System: Statistics*,
https://www.rainn.org/statistics/criminal-justice-system.

Ramachandran, Asha, "Opinion: NYU should sever all ties with Michael Steinhardt. The board of trustees must change the name of the Steinhardt School of Culture, Education, and Human Development given Steinhardt's proven record as a looter and sexual predator," *Washington Square News*, December 10, 2021, https://nyunews.com/opinion/2021/12/10/nyu-steinhardt-needs-a-name-change/.

Remski, Matthew, "Survivors of an International Buddhist Cult Share Their Stories. An investigation into decades of abuse at Shambhala International," *The Walrus*, November/December 2020, https://thewalrus.ca/survivors-of-an-international-buddhist-cult-share-their-stories/ .

Reuters, "French Catholic Church had an estimated 3,000 paedophiles since 1950s - commission head," Reuters, October 3, 2021, https://www.reuters.com/world/europe/french-catholic-church-had-estimated-3000-paedophiles-since-1950s-commission-2021-10-03/ .

Rezendes, Michael and Matt Carroll, "6 more priests removed on allegations of abuse," in *The Boston Globe Spotlight Investigation: Abuse in the Catholic Church: The Boston Globe* (2002), http://www.bostonglobe.com/arts/movies/spotlight-movie .

Ristaino, Christine, "When nice guys behave like monsters," *Washington Post*, April 11, 2014, https://www.washingtonpost.com/blogs/she-the-people/wp/2014/04/11/when-nice-guys-behave-like-monsters/.

Roberts, S. T., C. G. Watlington, S. D. Nett, S. V. Batten, "Sexual trauma disclosure in clinical settings: Addressing diversity," *Journal of Trauma Dissociation* 11, vol. 2 (2010), pp. 244–259, DOI:10.1080/15299730903502961.

Rosenbach, Naomi, Michael J Salamon & Leora Levine, "What impacts Jewish Orthodox womens' mikvah experience?," *Journal of Religion & Spirituality in Social Work: Social Thought* 40, no. 3 (2021), pp. 239-251, DOI: 10.1080/15426432.2021.1912687.

Rosenblatt, Gary, "A Rabbi's Accuser Wanted Me to Tell Her Story. Here's Why It Took 20 Years. When the Reform movement suspended Sheldon Zimmerman in 2000, a woman wanted the details known but feared retribution," *The Jewish Week,* May 26, 2021, https://jewishweek.timesofIsrael.com/a-rabbis-accuser-wanted-me-to-tell-her-story-heres-why-it-took-20-years/.

Rosenblatt, Gary, "Cohen's Fall Tests Border of Demography and Sexism: In wake of sexual harassment allegations against sociologist, throw out the baby with the bath water?" *The Jewish Week,* August 1, 2018, https://jewishweek.timesofIsrael.com/cohens-fall-tests-border-of-demography-and-sexism/ .

Rosenblatt, Gary, "Stolen Innocence: Rabbi Baruch Lanner, the charismatic magnet of NCSY, was revered in the Orthodox Union youth group, despite longtime reports of abuse of teens," *The Jewish Week,* June 23, 2000 https://www.bjpa.org/content/upload/bjpa/stol/Stolen%20Innocence%20-%20Gary%20Rosenblatt%20-%20Jewish%20Week%20-%20Sexual%20Abuse.pdf

Rosenfeld, Arno, "How a rabbi accused of sexual misconduct can stay in his pulpit," *Forward,* February 11, 2022, https://forward.com/news/482269/rabbi-suspension-sexual-misconduct-gerber-conservative-rabbincal-assembly/ .

Rosenfeld, Arno, "How a rabbi suspended for sexual abuse gets to keep his pulpit," *Forward,* February 9, 2022, https://forward.com/news/482269/rabbi-suspension-sexual-misconduct-gerber-conservative-rabbincal-assembly/ .

Rosmarin, David H., Steven Pirutinsky, Moses Appel, Talia Kaplan, David Pelcovitz, "Childhood sexual abuse, mental health, and religion across the Jewish community," *Child Abuse & Neglect* 81 (2018), pp. 21-28, ISSN 0145-2134, https://doi.org/10.1016/j.chiabu.2018.04.011 .

Ruttenberg, Danya, "Famous abusers seek easy forgiveness. Rosh Hashanah teaches us repentance is hard," *Washington Post,* September 6, 2018, https://www.washingtonpost.com/outlook/famous-abusers-seek-easy-forgiveness-rosh-hashanah-teaches-us-repentance-is-hard/2018/09/06/c2dc2cac-b0ab-11e8-9a6a-565d92a3585d_story.html .

Sales, Ben, "Conservative youth group cuts ties with ex-head accused of sexual misconduct. Jules Gutin denies allegations, which the CEO of the United Synagogue of Conservative Judaism says 'were wide ranging and all inappropriate,'" *Times of Israel,* December 18, 2017, https://www.timesofIsrael.com/conservative-youth-group-cuts-ties-with-ex-head-accused-of-sexual-misconduct .

Sales, Ben, "SAR Academy Officials Knew of Abuse By Administrator Who Molested 12 Students," *The Jewish Week,* October 6, 2018, https://jewishweek.timesofIsrael.com/sar-academy-officials-knew-of-abuse-by-administrator-who-molested-12-students/.

Sales, Ben, "'We feel like we failed': How one Jewish school is processing the arrest of a teacher who preyed on children," *JTA,* September 19, 2019, https://www.jta.org/2019/09/19/united-states/we-feel-like-we-failed-how-one-jewish-school-is-processing-the-arrest-of-a-teacher-who-preyed-on-children

Salamon, Michael J., *Abuse in the Jewish Community: Religious and communal factors that undermine the apprehension of offenders and the treatment of victims*, (Urim 2011).

Salamon, Michael J., "Walder Shamed Himself," *Times of Israel* blog, December 29, 2021, https://blogs.timesofIsrael.com/walder-shamed-himself/?fbclid=iwar0jhb-218xdbqoor817bxqfmpjyxtvn3ygjtclwey4wb4o9qxzclsn8x54 .

Sandalow-Ash, Rachel, "In Defense of Lashon Hara," *Lilith*, April 25, 2017, https://lilith.org/2017/04 /in-defense-of-lashon-hara/ .

Schaeffer, Rabbi Arthur Gross, "Rabbi sexual misconduct: crying out for a communal response," *The Reconstructionist* (1999), pp. 58-62, p. 58.

Schein, M., A. Biderman, M. Baras, L. Bennett, B. Bisharat, J. Borkan, Y. Fogelman, L. Gordon, D. Steinmetz, & E. Kitai, "The prevalence of a history of child sexual abuse among adults visiting family practitioners in Israel," *Child Abuse & Neglect* 24, no. 5 (2000), pp. 667–675, https://doi.org/10.1016/S0145-2134(00)00128-9 .

Secret, Mosi, "Brooklyn Rabbi Charged with Sexual Abuse of Boys," *New York Times*, January 31, 2013, https://www.nytimes.com/2013/02/01/nyregion/brooklyn-rabbi-charged-with-sexual-abuse-of-boys.html .

Seltzer, Sarah M., "Birthright Israel and #MeToo. Jewish Currents spoke with more than 50 Birthright Israel participants and staffers about their experiences with the often-fraught sexual and gender dynamics on the famous free trip to Israel. Here is what we found." *Jewish Currents*, April 18, 2018, https://jewishcurrents.org/birthright-Israel-and-metoo .

Sepler, Fran, "The Bullying We Don't Talk About: Women Bullying Women in the Academy," in Kirsti Cole, Holly Hassel, eds, *Surviving Sexism in Academia Strategies for Feminist Leadership*, (Routelage, 2017), pp 296-303

Shafran, Avi. "A Safer Space for Women in Orthodox Judaism's Rules for Sex: 'Do we really imagine that true respect for women can survive, let alone thrive, in a world where standard "entertainment" is saturated with their objectification and all too often actual abuse?'" *Tablet*, October 17, 2018 https://www.tabletmag.com/sections/news/articles/a-safer-space-for-women-in-orthodox-judaism

Shalev, Assaf, "Reform movement probing itself over history of bungling sex abuse allegations. Denomination's seminary, rabbinical association and synagogue network each hire different law firms to investigate cases of harassment and abuse to better ensure accountability," *Times of Israel*, August 12, 2021, https://www.timesofIsrael.com/reform-movement-probing-itself-over-history-of-bungling-sex-abuse-allegations/ .

Shalva Cares, "Profile of an Abuser," https://shalvacares.org/about-domestic-abuse/profile-of-an-abuser/ .

Shapiro, Joseph, "The Sexual Assault Epidemic No One Talks About," *NPR*, January 8, 2018, https://www.npr.org/2018/01/08/570224090/the-sexual-assault-epidemic-no-one-talks-about .

Shaviv, Paul J., *The Jewish High School: A complete management guide: Leadership, Policy and Operations for Principals, Administrators, and Lay Leaders* (CreateSpace, 2009)

Shupe, Anson D., *Spoils of the kingdom: Clergy misconduct and religious community*, (Urbana: University of Illinois Press, 2007).

Silberg, Joyanna and Stephanie Dallam, "Out of the Jewish closet: Facing the hidden secrets of child sexual abuse—and the damage done to victims," in Neustein's *Tempest in the Temple*, pp. 77-104.

Silverman, Gila, "In Judaism, Death, as Life, is with People," *HBI* blog, May 18, 2018. https://blogs.brandeis.edu/freshideasfromhbi/in-judaism-death-as-life-is-with-people/

Silverman, Rakhel, "The Harm of Tshuvah: A Letter from an Abuse Survivor," *Jewish Women's Archive*, September 12, 2018. https://jwa.org/blog/harm-of-tshuvah-letter-from-abuse-survivor

Sinai, Ruth, "When no one can hear you scream: After complaining that a senior rabbi harassed her, a settlement resident becomes an outcast," *Ha'aretz*. March 31, 2003, https://www.haaretz.com/1.4839853 .

Singer, Jenny, "Ari Shavit, Go Away and Don't Come Back," *Forward,* July 5, 2018, https://forward.com/opinion/404824/ari-shavit-go-away-and-dont-come-back/

Smith, Heather J. & Michael Hinman, "Jonathan Skolnick SAR Academy associate principal arrested, fired," *Riverdale Press*, September 16, 2019, https://riverdalepress.com/stories/sar-academy-associate-principal-arrested-fired,70003.

Sokol, Sam, "Child advocates blast systemic failures in Israel's handling of sex abuse cases. Political culture, stringent slander laws, inadequate sentencing and a taboo against reporting make it difficult to prosecute suspects, critics say," *Times of Israel*, July 3, 2019. https://www.timesofIsrael.com/child-advocates-blast-systemic-failures-in-Israels-handling-of-sex-abuse-cases/ .

Sommer, Allison Kaplan, "Not Just Weinstein: The Year #MeToo Rocked and Shocked the Jewish World," *Ha'aretz,* Sept 18, 2018, https://www.haaretz.com/israel-news/.premium-not-just-weinstein-the-year-metoo-rocked-and-shocked-the-jewish-world-1.6480994

Speights, Grace E., Sharon P. Masling, Martha B. Stolley, Jocelyn R. Cuttino, Ira G. Rosenstein. *Report of Investigation into Allegations of Misconduct at Hebrew Union College-Jewish Institute of Religion* (Morgan Lewis, November 3, 2021), http://huc.edu/sites/default/files/About/PDF/HUC%20REPORT%20OF%20INVESTIGATION%20--%2011.04.21.pdf   .

Spier, Devon, "Me Too: A Jewish Response to Abuse", Ritual *Well*, https://www.ritualwell.org/ritual/me-too-jewish-response-abuse .

Spraitz, Jason and Kendra Bowen. "Examination of a Nascent Taxonomy of Priest Sexual Grooming," *Sexual Abuse* 31, no. 6 (2019), pp. 707-728, DOI:10.1177/1079063218809095.

Spraitz, Jason, Kendra Bowen and Louisa Strange, "Proposing a Behavioral Taxonomy of Priest Sexual Grooming," *International Journal for Crime, Justice and Social Democracy*, 7, no. 30 (2018), 10.5204/ijcjsd.v7i 1.387.

Spröber, N., T. Schneider, M. Rassenhofer, A. Seitz, H. Liebhardt, L. König, J.M. Fegert, "Child sexual abuse in religiously affiliated and secular institutions: A retrospective descriptive analysis of data provided by victims in a government-sponsored reappraisal program in Germany," *BMC Public Health*, 14, no. 1 (2014), p. 282.

Sragovicz, Shayna, "Tell everyone," *Medium*, October 19, 2021, https://medium.com/@shayna99/tell-everyone-38e313990062.

Strutzenberg, C. C., Wiersma-Mosley, J. D., Jozkowski, K. N., & Becnel, J. N. (2017). "Love-bombing: A Narcissistic Approach to Relationship Formation," *Discovery, The Student Journal of Dale Bumpers College of Agricultural, Food and Life Sciences*, 18(1), 81-89. https://scholarworks.uark.edu/discoverymag/vol18/iss1/14

Supreme Court of the State of New York County of Nassau Daniel Weiss Plaintiff — Against — Nassau County Hebrew Academy of Long Beach School, John and Jane Doe 1-30, Members of the Defendants' Place of Board of Trustees of Hebrew Academy of Business, https://Iapps/Courts.State.Ny.Us/Nyscef/Viewdocument?Docindex=R3giqf2bxg97ib2qdmvhsg==.

Sztokman, Elana, "Don't use 'anti-Semitism' to protect sexual abusers: On the Steinhardt allegations: Why should the needs of the Jewish People come before the wellbeing of Jewish women?" *Times of Israel*, March 21, 2019, https://blogs.timesofIsrael.com/dont-use-anti-semitism-to-protect-sexual-abusers/ .

Sztokman, Elana, "Dynamics of the Patriarchy in Jewish Communal Life: An Infographic," *AJS Perspectives* (Spring 2019), http://perspectives.ajsnet.org/patriarchy-issue/dynamics-of-the-patriarchy-in-jewish-communal-life-an-infographic/ .

Sztokman, Elana, "If your board vice chair sends you a vibrator, your workplace is probably toxic" *The Roar*. https://elanasztokman.substack.com/p/if-your-board-vice-chair-randomly?s=w

Sztokman, Elana, "On Marc Gafni, the New York Times, and how sexual-predator rabbis get communal support", *Medium*, Jan 7, 2016 https://medium.com/@jewfem/on-marc-gafni-the-new-york-times-and-how-sexual-predator-rabbis-get-communal-support-ada9b97d5479

Sztokman, Elana, "Stop minimizing Freundel's actions by saying he is nonviolent." *Forward*, May 21, 2015, https://forward.com/life/308634/stop-minimizing-freundels-actions-by-saying-he-is-nonviolent/

Sztokman, Elana, *The Men's Section: Orthodox Jewish Men in an Egalitarian World* (Brandeis University Press, 2011).

Sztokman, Elana Maryles, "Gender, Ethnicity, and Class in State Religious Education for Girls in Israel: The Story of the Levy Junior High School, 1999-2002," Thesis for the degree of Doctor of Philosophy, submitted to the Senate of the Hebrew University of Jerusalem, February 2006.

Sztokman, Elana, "Why Are Women Dropping Out of Synagogue Life?," *Lilith*, October 10, 2017, https://lilith.org/2017/10/why-are-women-dropping-out-of-synagogue-life/ / .

Tener, D., A. Marmor, E. L. Weisrose, A. Almog-Zaken, T. M. Filtser, S. Turjeman, "Disclosing Sexual Abuse in Religious Communities in Israel: Lessons Learned by the Research Group on Child Sexual Abuse," in eds. D. Roer-Strier and Y. Nadan's *Context-Informed Perspectives of Child Risk and Protection in Israel. Child*

Maltreatment (Contemporary Issues in Research and Policy), vol. 10. (2020) Springer, Cham., https://doi.org/10.1007/978-3-030-44278-1_15.

Thoburn, John and D. Mitchell Whitman, "Clergy affairs: emotional investment, longevity of relationship and affair partners," *Pastoral Psychology* 52 (2004), pp. 491–506.

Thomas, Shannon, *Healing from Hidden Abuse* (Thomas 2016).

TOI Staff. "Convicted sex offender rabbi released to house arrest in ongoing fraud case. Court places severe restrictions on Eliezer Berland, including ban on contacting any of his followers, posting NIS 1.2 million bail, and having 2 wardens with him at all times," *Times of Israel*, February 15, 2021, https://www.timesofIsrael.com/convicted-sex-offender-rabbi-released-to-house-arrest-in-ongoing-fraud-case/ .

TOI Staff, "Ex-Labor MK says Shimon Peres sexually assaulted her in the 1980s: Colette Avital, a former senior diplomat, alleges the late statesman forcibly kissed her during a work meeting while he was PM, assaulted her at Paris hotel several years earlier." *Times of Israel*, October 7, 2021, https://www.timesofIsrael.com/ex-labor-mk-says-shimon-peres-sexually-assaulted-her-in-the-1980s/.

Valenti, Jessica, "Mike Pence doesn't eat alone with women. That speaks volumes. The vice-president's rule is insulting for men and limiting for women. But let's not let Pence's sexism distract us from his whole party's sexist agenda," *The Guardian*, March 31, 2017, https://www.theguardian.com/commentisfree/2017/mar/31/mike-pence-doesnt-eat-alone-women-speaks-volumes .

Valenti, Jessica "When you call a rape anything but rape, you are just making excuses for rapists," *The Guardian*, April 24, 2014, https://www.theguardian.com/commentisfree/2014/apr/24/rape-game-of-thrones .

Vieth, Victor I. and Basyle Tchividjian, "When the Child Abuser Has a Bible: Investigating Child Maltreatment Sanctioned or Condoned by a Religious Leader," *Centerpiece*, vol. 2, iss. 12 (2010), NCPTC, https://www.zeroabuseproject.org/wp-content/uploads/2019/02/e8299da4-centerpiece-vol-2-issue-12.pdf .

Walker, D. F., H. W. Reid, T. O'Neill and L. Brown, "Changes in personal religion/spirituality during and after childhood abuse: A review and synthesis," *Psychological Trauma: Theory, Research, Practice, and Policy* 1, no. 2 (2009), pp. 130–145, https://doi.org/10.1037/a0016211.

Wanis, Patrick,"The Profile: 25 traits of an abuser," https://www.patrickwanis.com/the-profile-25-traits-of-an-abuser/ .

Weitz, Gid, "Why She Didn't Report That Shimon Peres Sexually Assaulted Her: Colette Avital Tells All," *Haaretz*, October 14, 2021, https://www.haaretz.com/Israel-news/.premium.HIGHLIGHT.MAGAZINE-why-she-didn-t-report-that-peres-sexually-assaulted-her-colette-avital-tells-all-1.10295027 .

Welner, Dr. Michael, "Child Sexual Abuse: 6 Stages of Grooming," *Oprah*, October 18, 2010, https://www.oprah.com/oprahshow/child-sexual-abuse-6-stages-of-grooming/all#ixzz7BFxqWHgu .

Westervelt, Amy, *Forget Having It All: How America Messed Up Motherhood--and How to Fix It,* (Seal Press 2018).

Winer, Stuart, "Rabbi brothers suspected of sex abuse at their Jerusalem yeshiva. Rabbinical court rules students should no longer enroll in schools run by Yitzhak and Moshe Tufik, advises victims to file complaints with police," *Times of Israel,* August 30, 2021, https://www.timesofIsrael.com/rabbi-brothers-suspected-of-sex-abuse-at-their-jerusalem-yeshiva/.

Winston, Hella, "Trial Exposes Shadowy Chasidic 'Modesty Committees': Young woman's testimony reveals tactics of freelance 'purity' guardians in Satmar community," *The Jewish Week.* December 6, 2012, https://jewishweek.timesofIsrael.com/trial-exposes-shadowy-chasidic-modestycommittees/?fbclid=IwAR3EQXS1O4gyePcWpD0PvNKQfrur6UhnNUTyM1RmgKtQS-ATP4AlSjGu9rw .

Wolkenfeld, Shira, "Investigation: How Jewish Youth Groups Are Breeding a Toxic Sexual Culture For Teens," *New Voices,* July 13, 2021, https://newvoices.org/2021/07/13/investigation-how-jewish-youth-groups-are-breeding-a-toxic-sexual-culture-for-teens/?fbclid=IwAR1nKU0b_vZ1Wj96eaBla4_EE-VPlqVeYvbXogVDTlThlhqle2nl9RYKzo .

Yehuda, Rachel, Michelle Friedman, Talli Y. Rosenbaum, Ellen Labinsky, James Schmeidler. "History of Past Sexual Abuse in Married Observant Jewish Women," *American Journal of Psychiatry* 164, issue 11 (November 2007), pp. 1700-1706, https://doi.org/10.1176/appi.ajp.2007.06122030

Yonac, Lyn, "Sexual Assault Is About Power. How the #MeToo campaign is restoring power to victims," *Psychology Today,* November 14, 2017

Zaakah, "Child sexual abuse in the Orthodox Jewish community," https://www.zaakah.org/child-sexual-abuse-in-the-orthodox-jewish-community

Zalcberg, Sara, "The Place of Culture and Religion in Patterns of Disclosure and Reporting Sexual Abuse of Males: A Case Study of Ultra-Orthodox Male Victims," *Journal of Child Sexual Abuse* 26, no. 5 (2017), pp. 590-607, DOI:10.1080/10538712.2017.1316335.

Zarchin, Tomer, Yair Ettinger, "The Rabbi Elon Case: Sexual Abuse in the Zionist Orthodox Community. Allegations of abuse against Rabbi Moti Elon emerged more than five years ago via Takana—an organization that deals with sexual harassment in the Religious Zionist community," *Haaretz,* November 3, 2011, https://www.haaretz.com/jewish/1.5206161 .

Zauzmer, Julie, "'I not only envisioned it. I fought for it': The first female rabbi isn't done yet," *Washington Post,* May 24, 2016, https://www.washingtonpost.com/news/acts-of-faith/wp/2016/05/24/i-not-only-envisioned-it-i-fought-for-it-the-first-female-rabbi-isnt-done-yet/.

Zauzmer, Julie, "#MeToo goes to Jewish summer camp, a traditional place for teenage romance," *Washington Post,* July 14, 2018, https://www.washingtonpost.com/local/social-issues/metoo-goes-to-jewish-summer-camp-a-traditional-place-for-teenage-romance/2018/07/14/05c1fb28-86b8-11e8-8f6c-46cb43e3f306_story.html?utm_term=.9fe2b8c11aa6 .

Index

About the author

Dr. Elana Sztokman is a celebrated Jewish feminist activist, anthropologist, and educator, and two-time winner of the National Jewish Book Council Award. Her writings have appeared in *The Atlantic, Slate, The Independent, Everyday Feminism, Forward, Lilith, Jewish Week, Ha'aretz, Jerusalem Post, Jerusalem Report,* and more. Her work explores gender issues in Jewish culture, and she teaches, speaks, and consults around the world on these subjects. She is the founder of the Jewish Feminist Academy (www.jewishfeminism.org) that offers educational content and programs with Jewish feminist thought leaders. She blogs at A Jewish Feminist, (www.jewfem.com) and via her newsletter, *The Roar.* (elanasztokman.substack.com)
This is her sixth book

www.ingramcontent.com/pod-product-compliance
Lightning Source LLC
Chambersburg PA
CBHW022042020426
42335CB00012B/502